AF574618

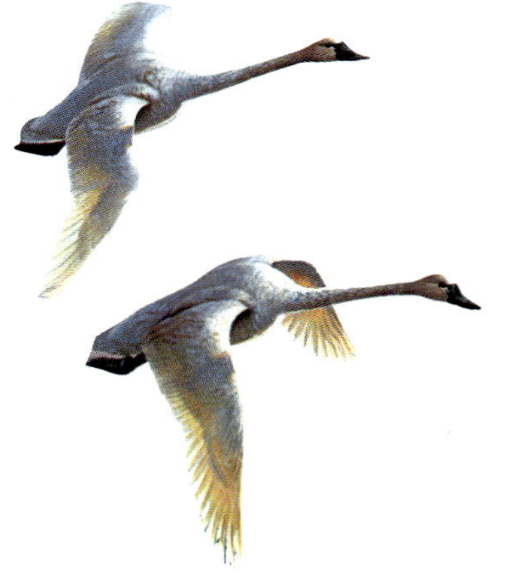

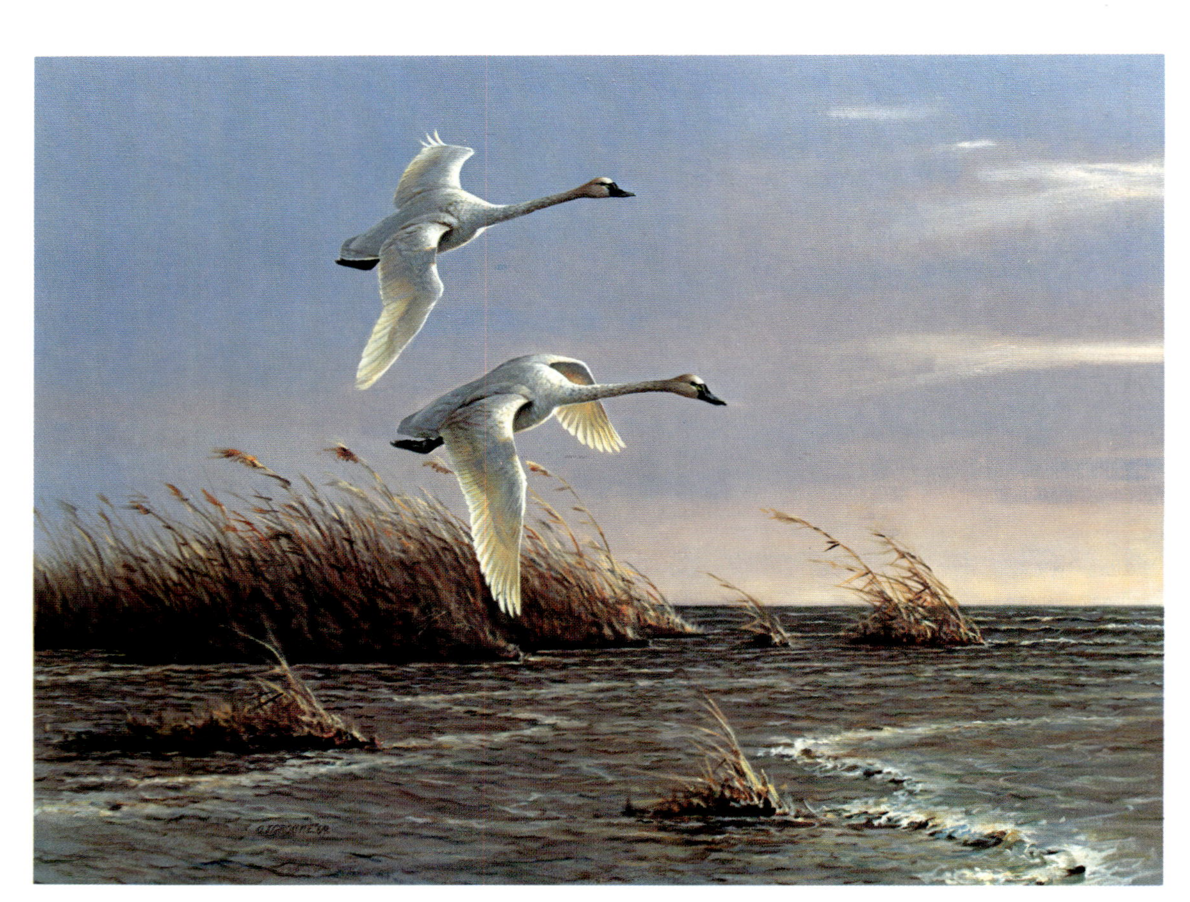

Whistling Swans

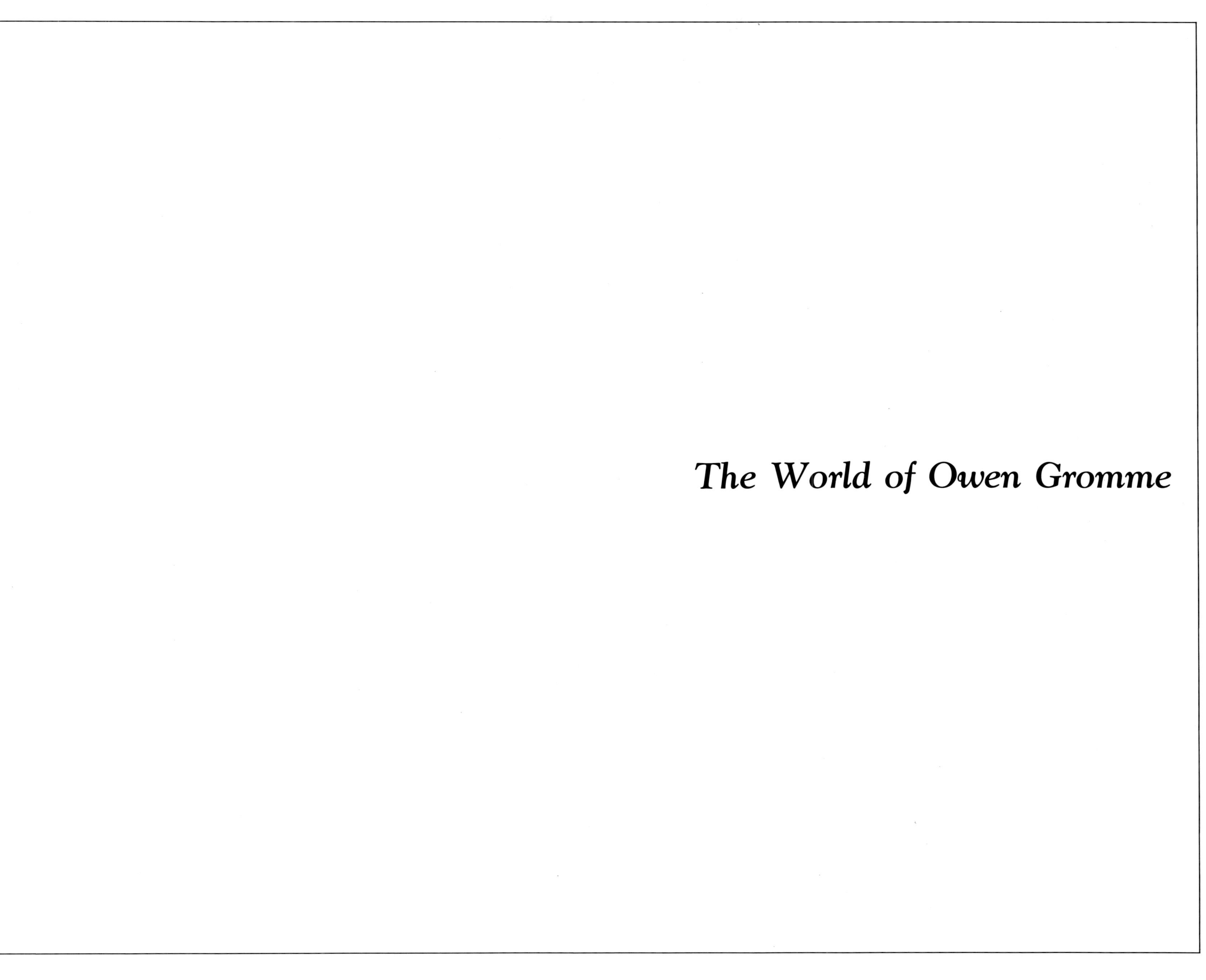

The World of Owen Gromme

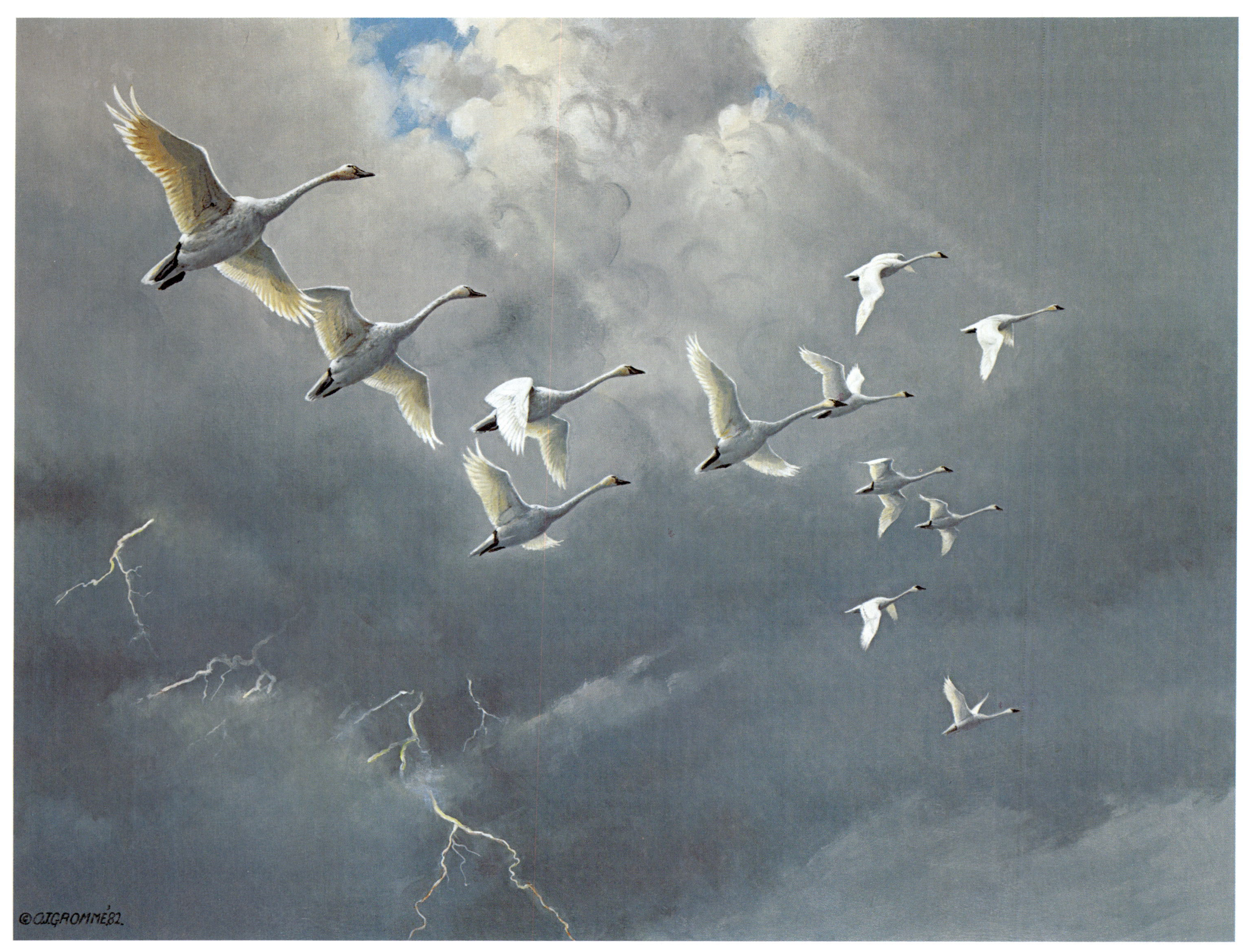

Beyond the Tempest

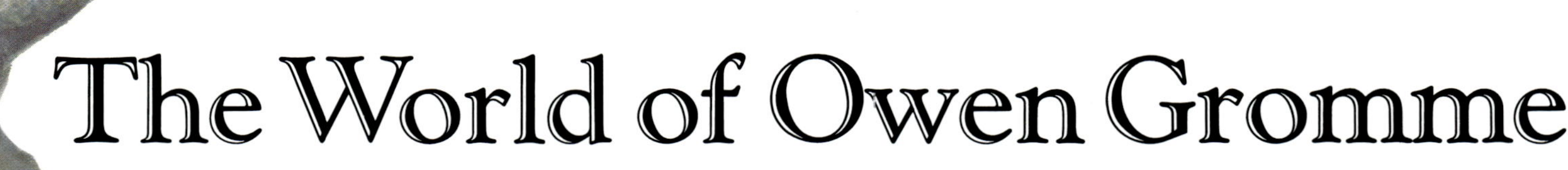

The World of Owen Gromme

Introduction by Roger Tory Peterson
Biography by Michael Mentzer
Commentaries by Judith Redline Coopey

Designed by Marian Lefebvre

NorthWord Press, Inc.

The World of Owen Gromme was first published in 1983 by Stanton & Lee.

This softcover edition is published by NorthWord Press, Inc.

Printed in Singapore.

NorthWord Press, Inc.
Box 1360
Minocqua, Wisconsin 54548

For a free catalog describing NorthWord's line of nature books and gifts, call 1-800-336-5666.

For information on Owen Gromme's limited edition prints, call Stanton & Lee 1-800-356-4600 or write Stanton & Lee, 2 East Mifflin Street, Madison, Wisconsin 53703.

The publisher would like to express deep appreciation to the M&I Marshall & Ilsley Bank for the right to reproduce the paintings in its collection and to bank Chairman J. A. Puelicher for his belief, encouragement and support. The publisher would also like to thank William B. Webster, President of Wild Wings, for his cooperation, Frederick L. Ott of Leslie Paper Company for his able assistance and counsel; Dexter Haney for his photographic work; and Daniel Duerst of Straus Printing and Publishing Company for his attention to detail. In addition to all of the private collectors who kindly granted permission to reproduce their paintings, the publisher would like to thank Ducks Unlimited, Inc. for permission to reproduce *Fall Kaleidoscope—Wood Ducks*; the Sand County Foundation for *Marshland Elegy—Aldo Leopold*; the Citizen's Natural Resources Association for *Requiem Horicon Marsh*; and Holiday House for *Egrets Below the Bridge*.

While many of the photographs appearing in the biography are from the artist's private collection, the publisher would like to acknowledge the following sources:

Dexter Haney for the photographs on pages 18, 20, 21, 23, 35, 39, 61, 65 (left), 70, 71, and 73; The Milwaukee Public Museum: 40, 41, 49, 50, 51, 52, 54, 57, and 66; C. P. Fox: 56, 62, 63 and 65 (right); Lou Coopey: 79; George Archibald: 24 (right); *The Milwaukee Journal:* 68; *The Fond du Lac Reporter:* 75; and *The Wisconsin Conservation Department:* 33.

The World of Owen Gromme was edited by Doug Bradley; Mark E. Lefebvre was editor-in-chief.

Library of Congress Cataloging-in-Publication Data

Gromme, Owen J.
The world of Owen Gromme / introduction by Roger Tory Peterson;
biography by Michael Mentzer; commentaries by Judith Redline Coopey.
— 2nd ed.
p. cm.
Includes index.
ISBN 1-55971-130-2: $29.95
1. Gromme, Owen J. 2. Painter—United States—Biography.
3. Birds in art. 4. Animals in art. I. Mentzer, Michael. II. Coopey,
Judith Redline. III. Title.
ND237.G665A2 1991
759.13—dc20
[B] 91-3764
CIP

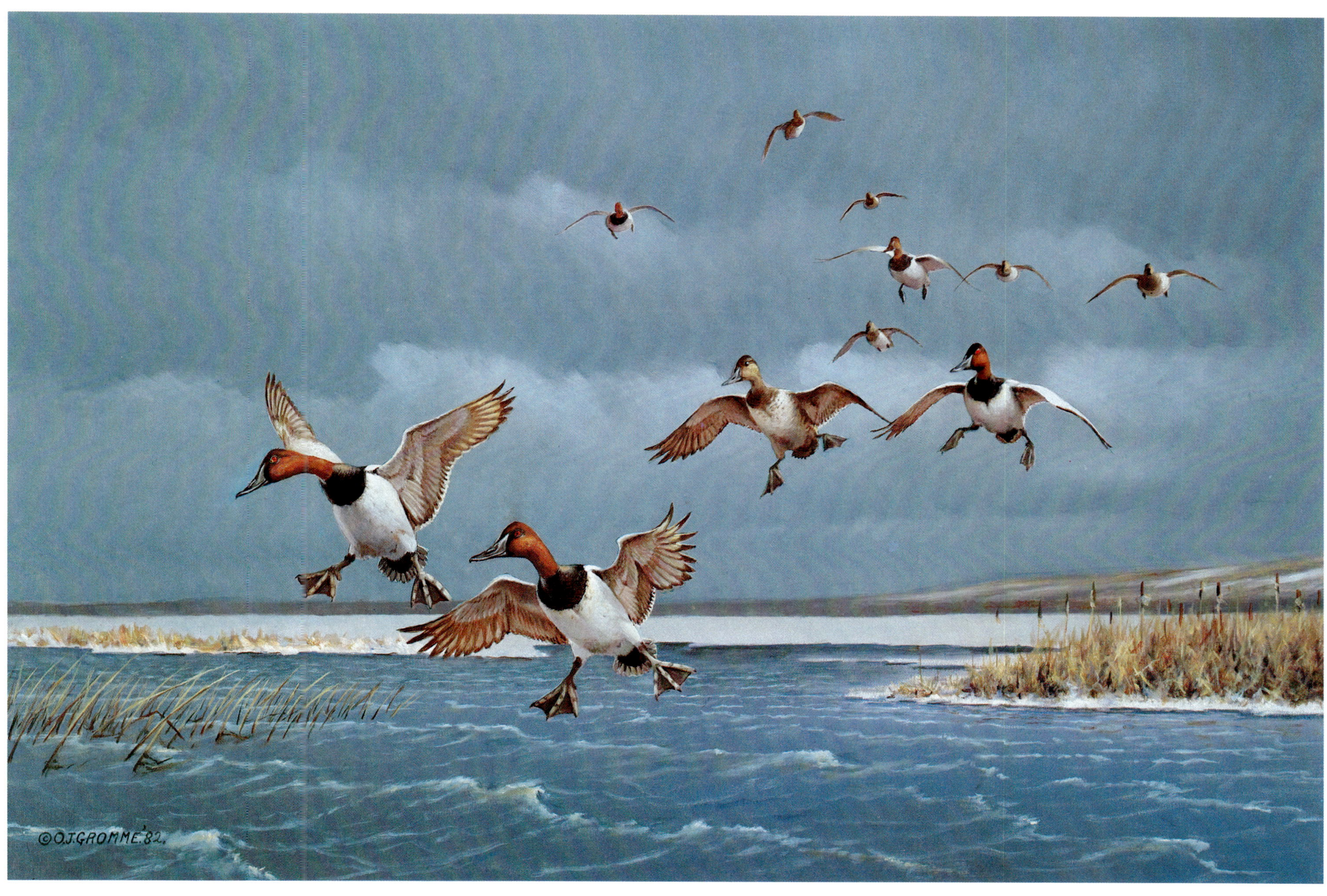

Canvasbacks

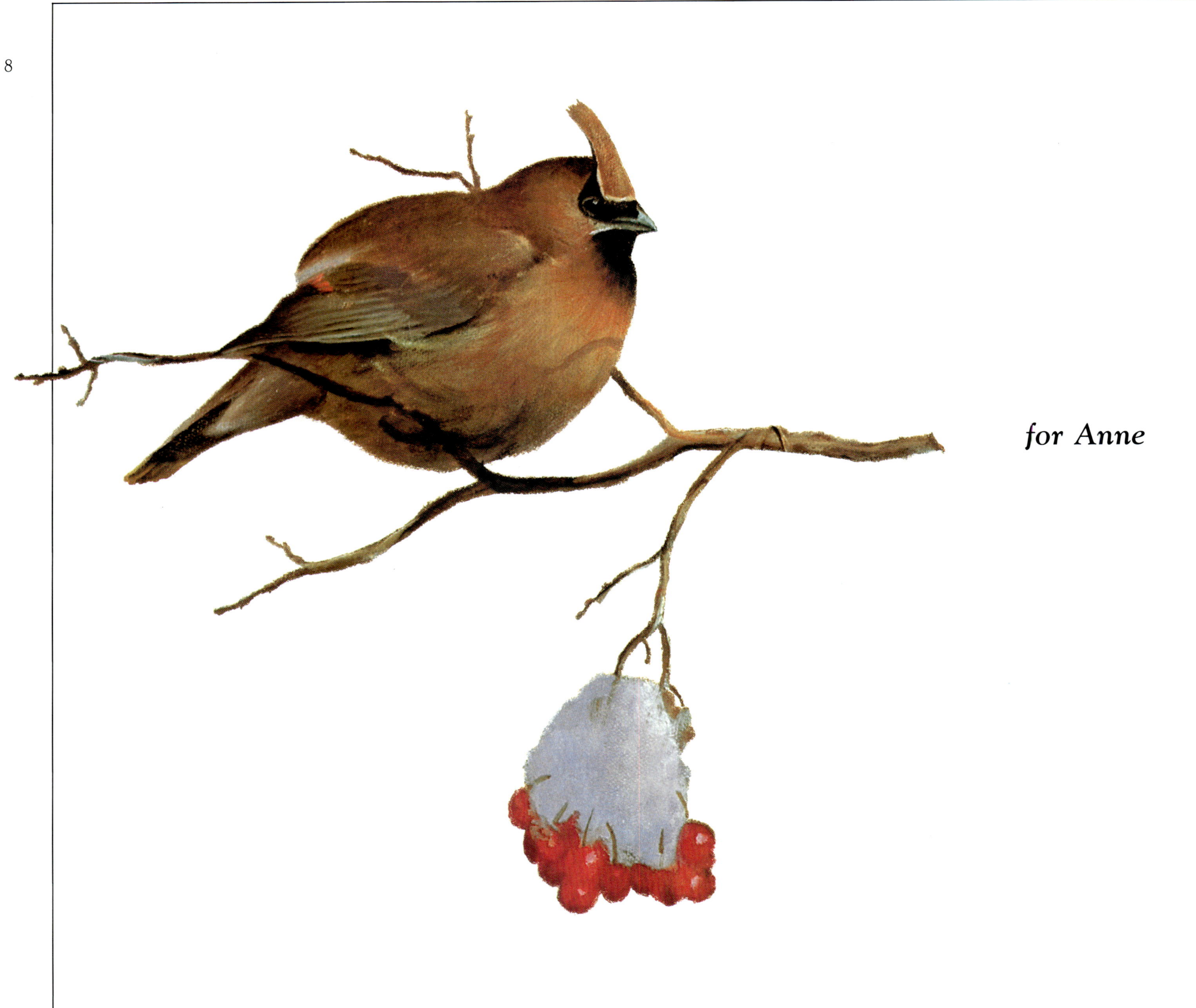

for Anne

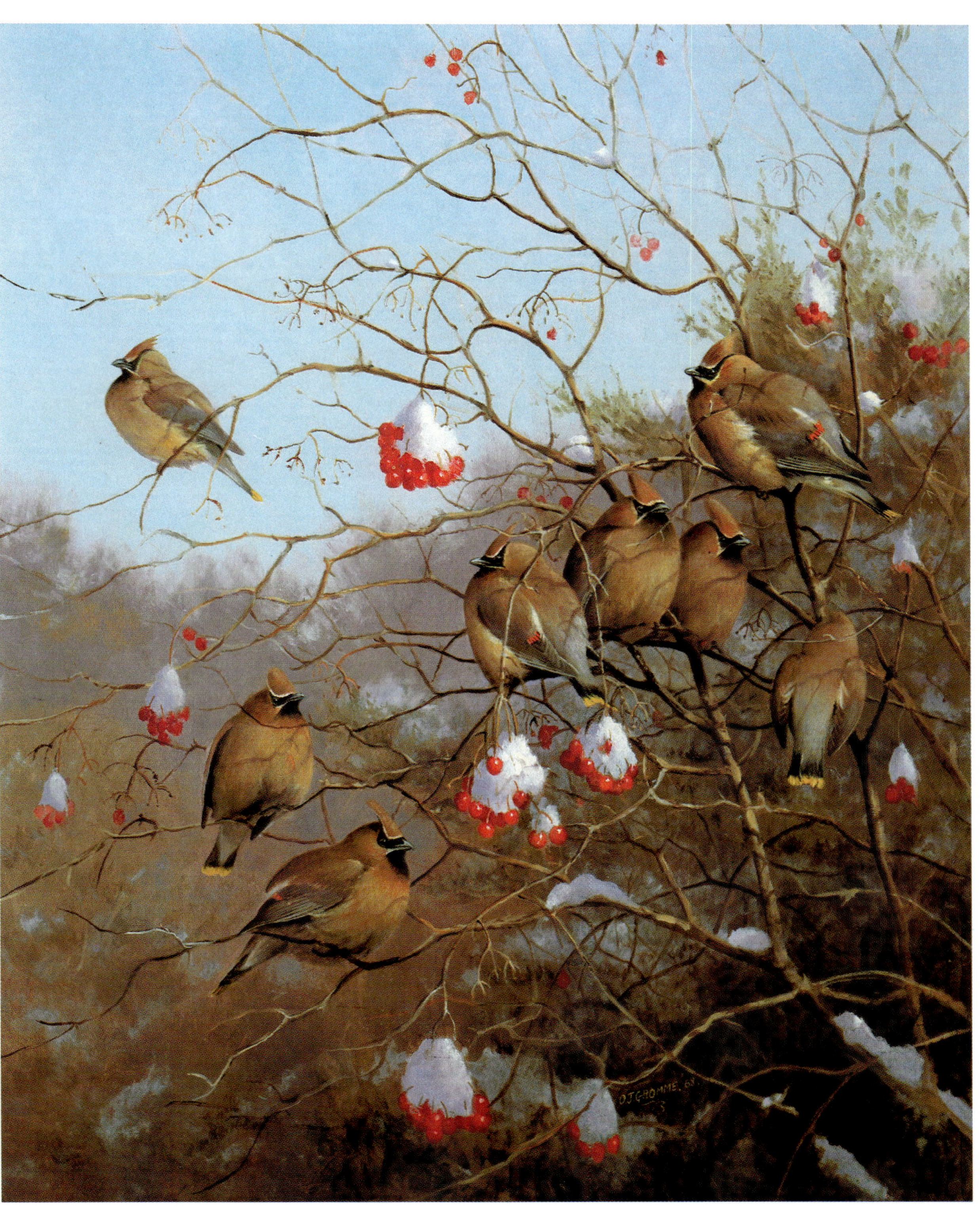

Cedar Waxwings

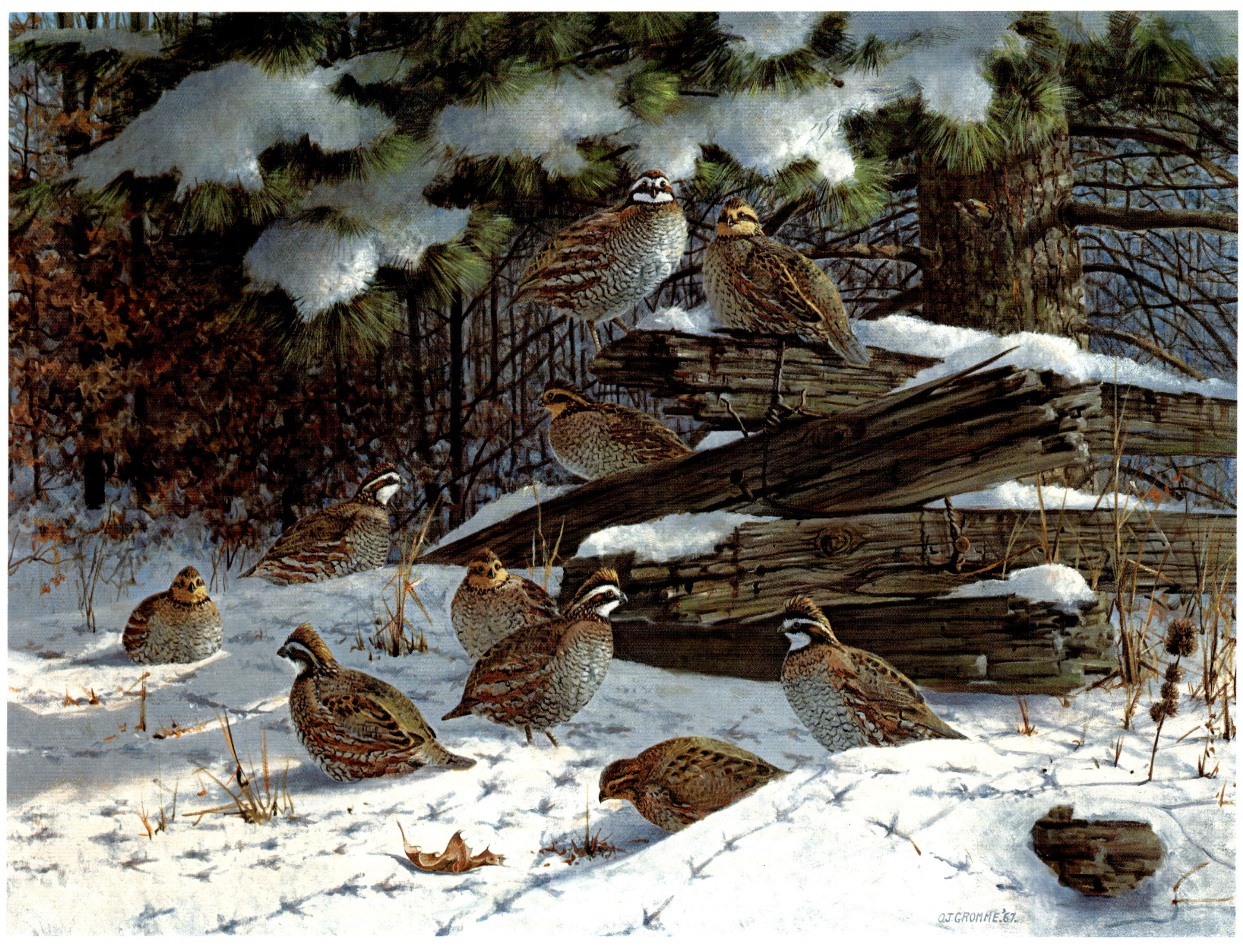

Bobwhites

Contents

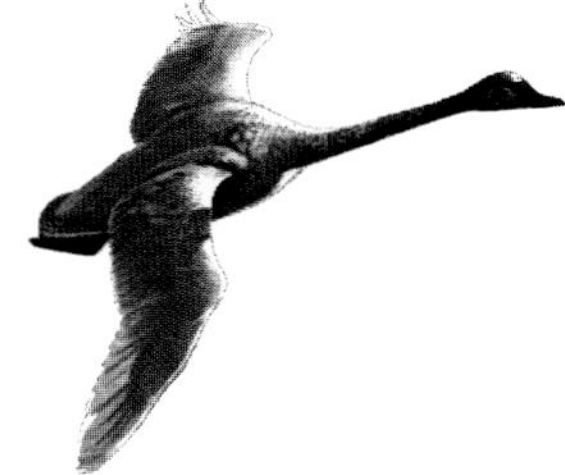

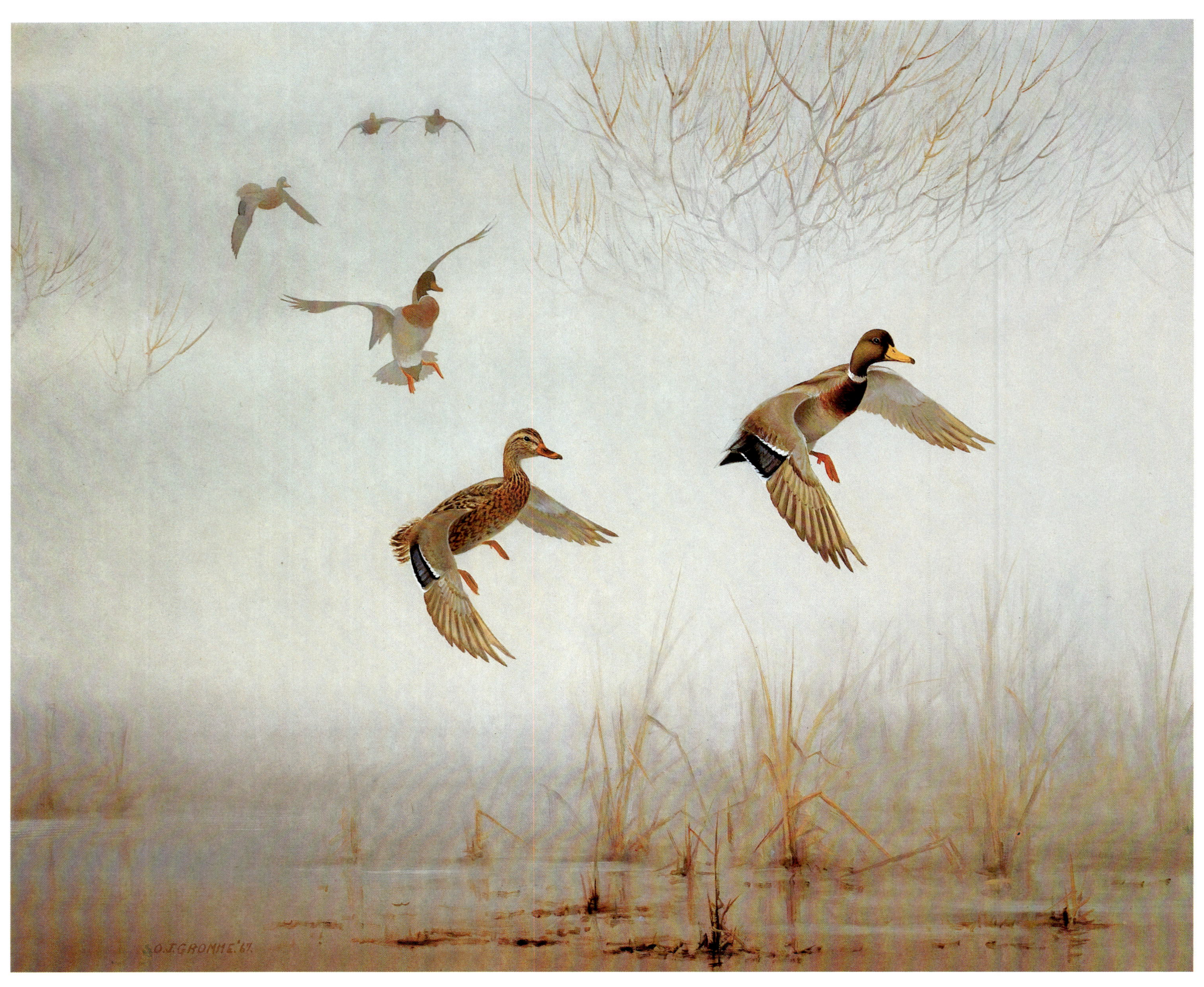

Mallards in Morning Mist

Introduction

Owen Gromme did not start out as an artist. This illustrious career was literally thrust upon him as he prepared exhibits for the public museum in Milwaukee in the 1920s and 1930s. Owen had already established himself as a jack-of-all-trades, not only collecting and skinning specimens but also taking photographs, filming and editing movies, handling finances (and many of the museum's administrative chores as well). Thus, it did not faze him when the museum's director asked him to paint some of the backgrounds for the exhibits.

However, Gromme was not completely unprepared for this new responsibility. Several years earlier, at the age of 21, the young Owen had taken a job as a taxidermist at the Field Museum of Natural History in Chicago. There, Herbert Stoddard, who was later to distinguish himself as the father of game management as we know it today, gave Gromme his first lessons in the mixing of paints. Color notes made in the field are very important in taxidermy, because colors of the eyes, beaks, and legs are transitory.

After his service with the 33rd Division in World War I, Gromme rejoined Stoddard — this time at the Milwaukee Public Museum where he progressed from taxidermist to curator of birds and mammals, and eventually head of the department. He retired in 1965 as Curator Emeritus.

"A museum naturalist-preparator," Gromme points out, "cannot be a specialist; he has to learn half a dozen professions." Perhaps more. As a taxidermist he must know musculature and anatomy; a wildlife artist who ignores this discipline does so at his risk since the undertaking inevitably involves modeling and sculpture. But he must also be a botanist and a geologist in order to prepare the habitat exhibits or dioramas. In effect he must be an environmentalist. And he must even be a carpenter and an engineer of sorts before he puts brush or paint to canvas in the process of creating the eye-deceiving backgrounds.

Although Owen Gromme had been painting for years at the Milwaukee Public Museum, his canvases were not known widely until the publication of his *Birds of Wisconsin,* a tour de force which featured a galaxy of 600 bird portraits depicting 328 species. Started in 1941, this masterwork took twenty years to bring to completion, finally gaining publication in 1963.

This handsome book falls into two parts: the first is a systematic collection of portraits of all birds known to have occurred in Wisconsin, with the exception of a few accidental and hypothetical species. More than one plumage is shown when the sexes differ. These illustrations were executed in transparent watercolor using a limited palette which was restricted mainly to alizarin crimson, pale cadmium yellow, and ultramarine blue, the primary colors from which most other colors can be mixed. A purist when handling watercolors, Gromme seldom resorted to gouache or opaque designer's colors.

The second section of *Birds of Wisconsin* is a gallery of ecological and behavioral compositions in which he drew on his skills as a museum preparator. Many of these illustrations are, in a sense, miniature dioramas. Gromme executed them all in oil on canvas, a medium that he handles with utmost confidence and dexterity. His waterfowl and other game birds are particularly outstanding, because he came into his profession by way of the fowling piece. As a boy in Fond du Lac he had often accompanied his father on hunting trips; he knew the marshes and woodlands of Wisconsin intimately, as well as the ducks, geese, grouse, and all the other denizens of the wild that lived there.

No one else has painted the various grouse as well as Owen Gromme. The prairie chicken, I suspect, is his favorite. He holds the title of "Old Pro" in the society of *Tympanuchus cupido pinnatus,* the organization dedicated to preserving the prairie chicken in Wisconsin. As a conservationist, he has also taken an active part in the affairs of a number of other wildlife and environmental organizations. He does not hesitate to speak his mind and has worked effectively in the legislative field toward improving laws governing our natural resources. He has been active in the Citizen's Natural Resources Association of Wisconsin and was elected president of Wetlands for Wildlife. On the scientific side, he helped to found the Wisconsin Society for Ornithology.

The environmental paintings in the second part of *Birds of Wisconsin* signalled the direction that Owen would take when he retired in 1965. At that turning point in his life, the Marshall and Ilsley Bank of Milwaukee commissioned him at the age of 70 to paint exactly what he pleased for three years. In fulfilling this artist's dream he produced 43 canvases which were put on permanent display (many of them are included in this book). An entire floor of the bank was turned into a wildlife art gallery. Each painting was illuminated by a carefully engineered lighting system. No cost was spared.

When the National Audubon Society held its annual convention in Milwaukee in 1970, the Gromme exhibit at the bank was the big attraction. Inasmuch as I had not yet seen any of his original canvases, I was unprepared for what I found. As I stood before each canvas I was dumbfounded. Here was an artist, twelve years older than I, doing his very best work at a time in life when so many other painters were putting their brushes aside. It was a moving experience; an extraordinary affirmation of life and vitality. An example to follow.

Owen Gromme demonstrates as convincingly as any man I know that creative growth can continue, and need not taper off or atrophy, when a person reaches the traditional age of retirement. Quite the contrary. It was then that his art — painting birds — soared to new heights. His output was prodigious, and it became almost a status symbol to own a Gromme original, many of which were reproduced as limited edition prints by Wild Wings, Inc. But the over forty years at the museum gave him the training and discipline that made his formidable skills possible.

Like many another successful artist, Owen has a strong competitive streak, but he is always competing with himself, striving to make each canvas his best, surpassing the preceding one. Those who do not draw often think of painting as a passive occupation requiring only that mysterious gift that artists seem to have. Contrary to popular belief creative work of any sort is draining, demanding not only a healthy attitude but also sturdy physical health as well. Gromme attributes his own vigor to an active outdoor life as a hunter and fisherman. His hand is rock-steady when handling a brush and his eyes, even in his 80's, are comparable to those of a much younger person. Although he has the confident air of a man who knows who he is — he can even be feisty at times — he has an underlying compassion for younger artists whom he unselfishly helps. He only asks that they do the same, thereby giving continuity to their mutual commitment to wildlife and its conservation.

In recent years there has been a burgeoning, almost explosive, interest in wildlife, especially birds, resulting in a breakthrough in environmental awareness on the part of the public. This has led to a greater understanding and acceptance of what the wildlife artist has been trying to say. And Gromme, whose lifetime of interpretive painting is celebrated in this book, takes the view that birds and other animals should be painted by those who know their subject and feel deeply about it.

Until recently, however, wildlife painting had seldom been considered "Art" (with a capital A) by the galleries and curators who dominate the art scene. But, I submit, those of us who paint wildlife, because of our fascination with the other creatures that share our planet, are just as true to ourselves as those who interpret the New York or Los Angeles scene as they see it in their abstract way. To us the "real" world is the natural world, and we cannot be other than realists in our interpretation of it.

But even in the old days, prior to the turn of the century, when artists painted in the academic tradition, animals were not considered worthy of canvas and paint unless they had some anthropomorphic connection with man. Anything else was considered illustration rather than art. There were, however, a few notable exceptions, Albrecht Duhrer was one, John James Audubon another, who painted mammals and birds in their own right, not as members of the human community in fur and feathers.

Wisconsin, Owen Gromme's home state, has long been a focal point of wildlife art and wildlife research. It was the first state to have its own museum devoted specifically to bird painting and sculpture — the Leigh Yawkey Woodson Art Museum at Wausau. Each year, in September, the top bird artists of the United States and Canada gather at Wausau to exhibit their most recent works and to honor one of their number with the "Master Wildlife Artist" medal. In 1976, Owen Gromme was the first to receive this prestigious award. This says a great deal about the esteem he enjoys in the fraternity of wildlife artists. "Fraternity" is perhaps the wrong word, because more and more women are now competing successfully in this specialized category of painting.

Owen Gromme is a fulfilled man. His habitat groups will continue to be seen by thousands for years to come — as long as the Milwaukee Public Museum itself stands. His awards and honors have been numerous. He has exhibited in many cities, and innumerable collectors now own his prints and originals. But it seems to me that the greatest satisfaction that any artist can aspire to is to have his work presented in a handsome retrospective book such as this.

Roger Tory Peterson
Old Lyme, Connecticut

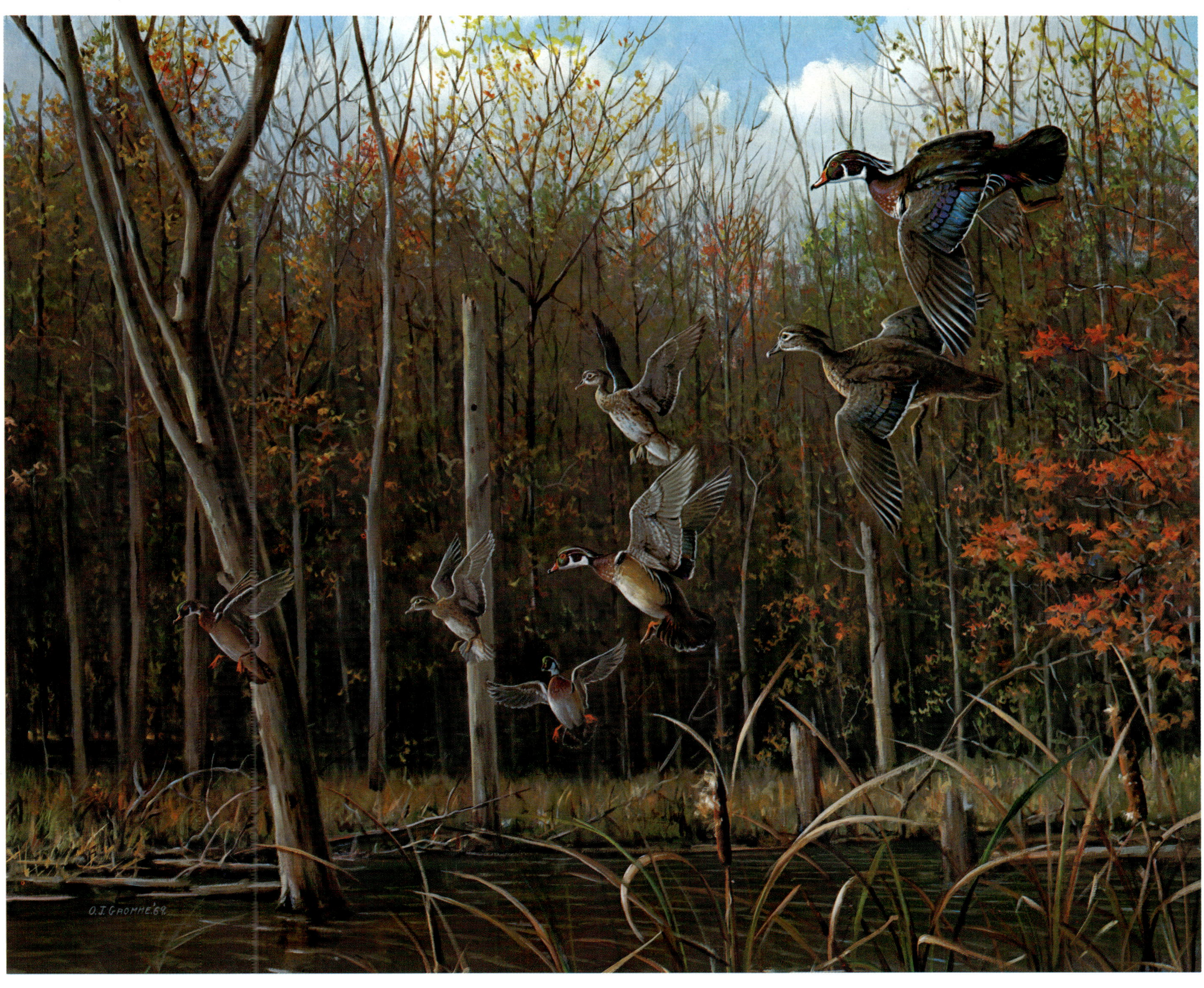

Secluded Pond — Wood Ducks

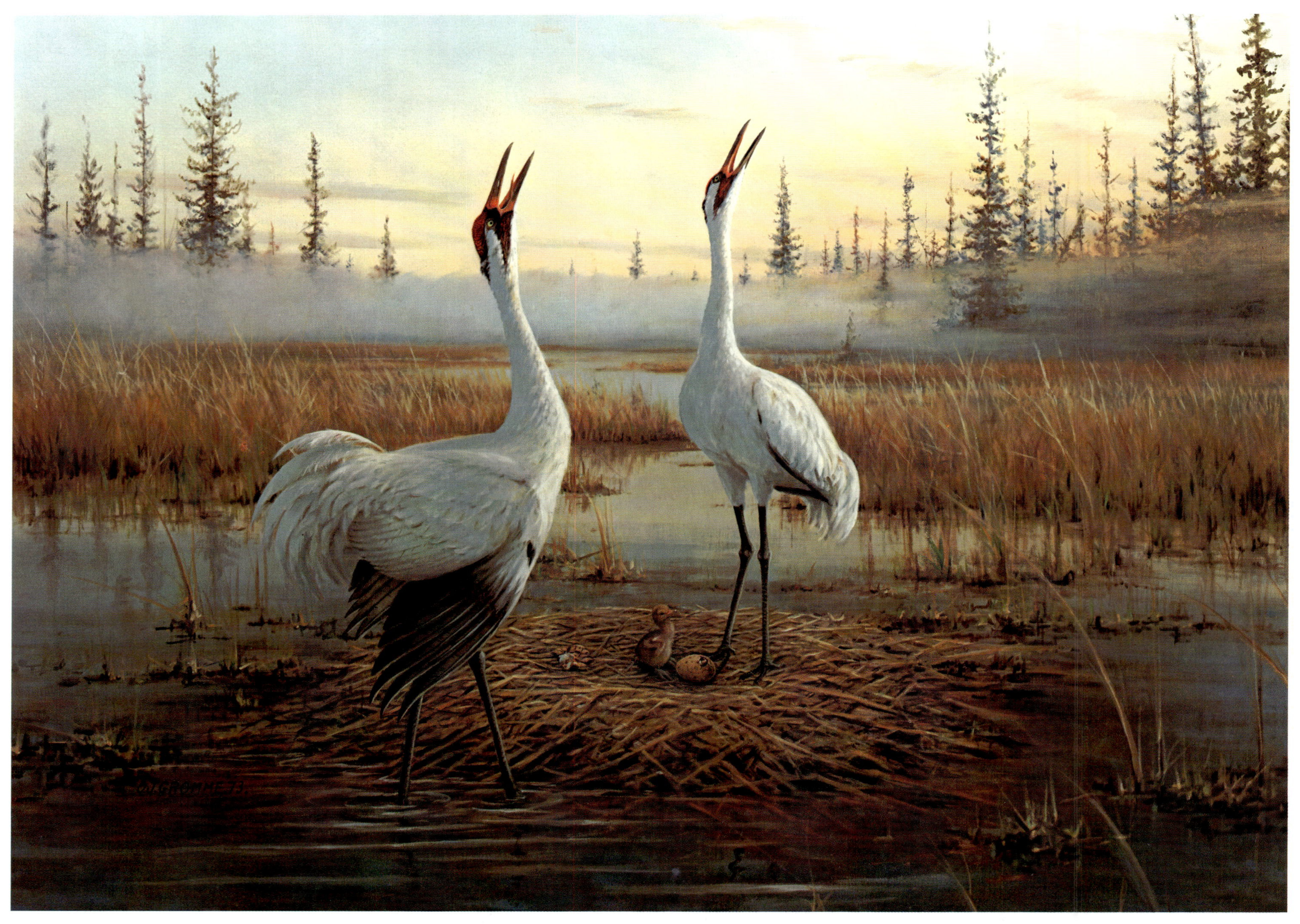

Salute to the Dawn — Whooping Cranes

Biography

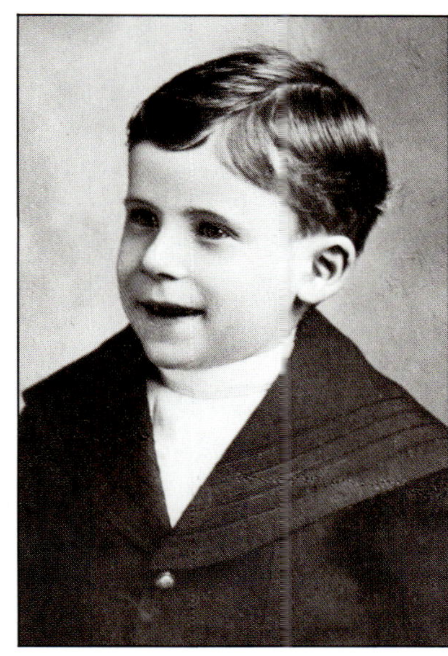
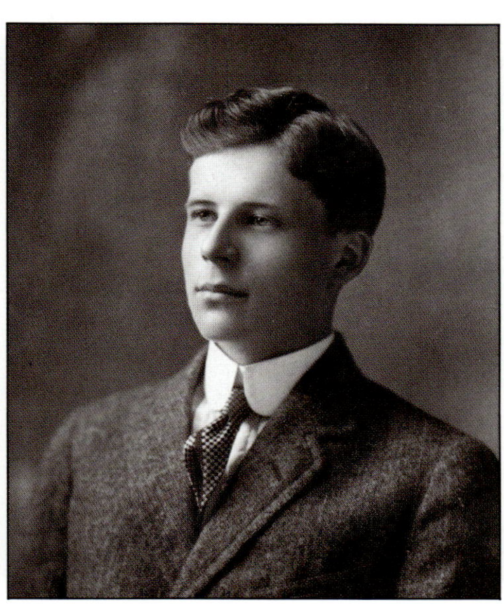
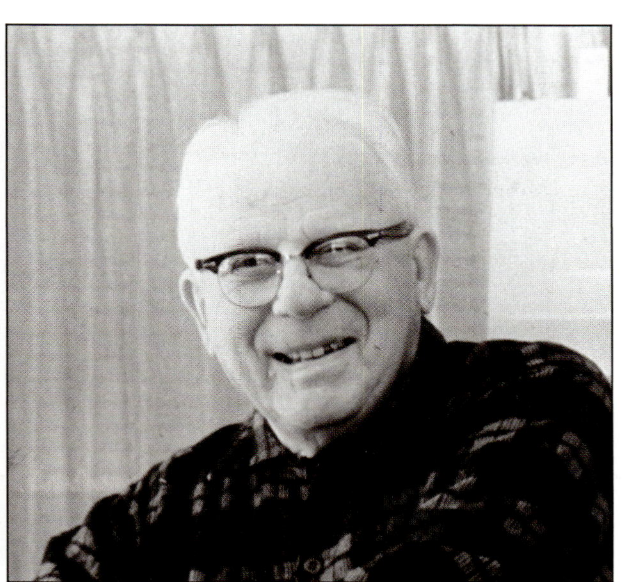

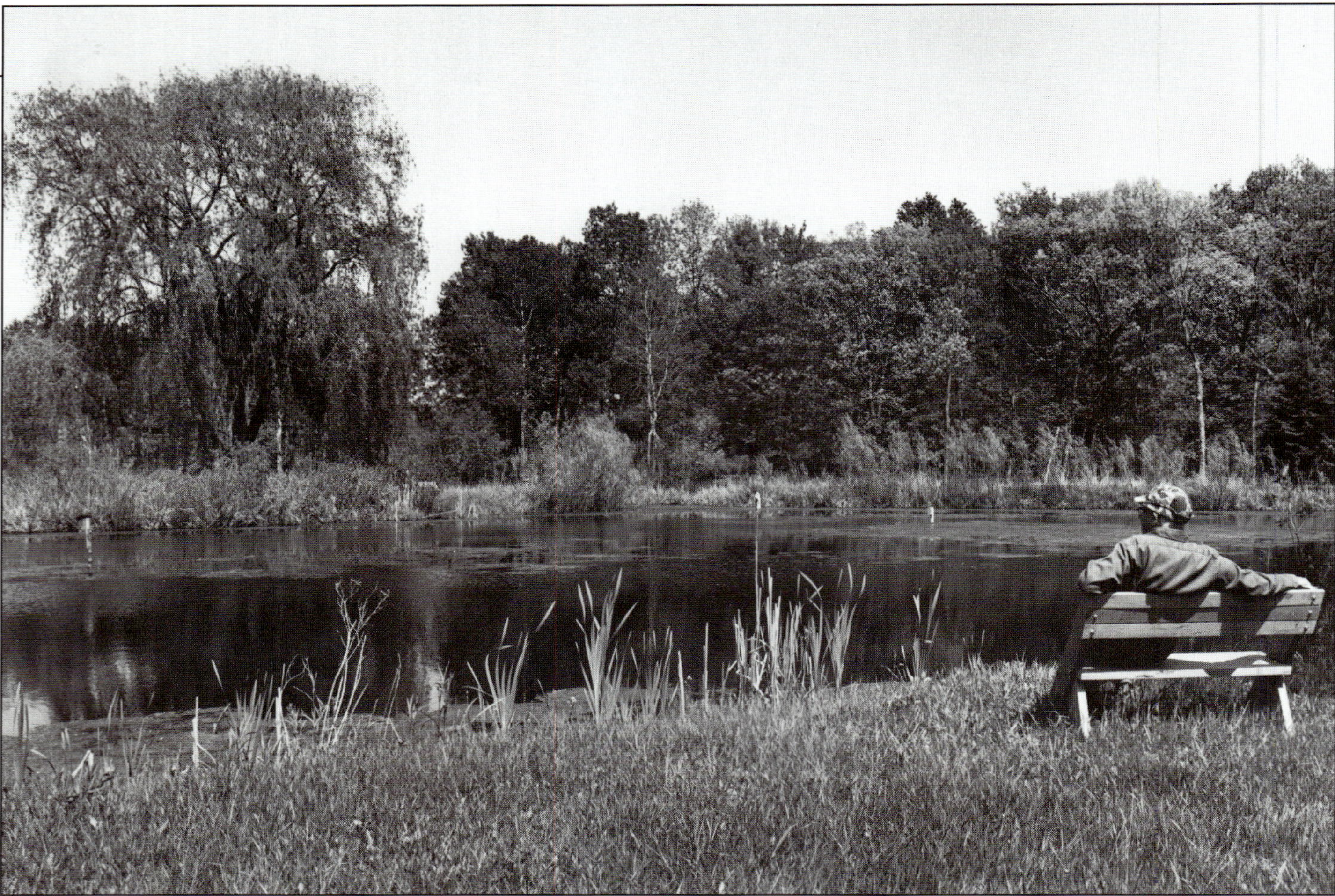

I

The Indians called it "Wanikamiu." The French used the term "fond du lac." But for a young man growing up at the turn of the century, the woodlots, wetlands, and waterways of this portion of east-central Wisconsin would combine to make the ideal environment for a wildlife artist to prosper.

Owen J. Gromme, regarded by many as the "dean" of wildlife painters, was born among the marshes of Horicon and Eldorado, the hardwoods and pines of the Kettle Moraine Forest, and the abundant wildlife that inhabited the regions along Lake Winnebago and the Fox River. The southern tip of Lake Winnebago may have been the terminal point or "end (foot) of the lake" for the French and the Indians, but it was only the beginning, and a very good one at that, for Owen Gromme.

Today, at the age of 87, Gromme and Anne Nielsen Gromme, his wife of 56 years, derive both strength and satisfaction from the natural environment they have fostered at their son Roy's farm on the outskirts of Briggsville in Wisconsin's renowned sand country. Their world is a 160-acre panorama of marsh, rolling farmland, ponds, thickets, and pines. Wildlife abounds, attracted to the security of the private refuge.

Owen Gromme remains hardy and vigorous. He relishes a brisk walk in the woods and the challenge of a duck blind under a slate gray November sky. Despite his age, he is dynamic. Ruddy-faced, white-haired and clear-eyed, he paints daily and strolls the well-maintained paths on the Gromme farm as the mood moves him.

He is still good with a shotgun and better than ever with brush, paint, and canvas. His art is in full bloom, and his paintings are more in demand than at any time in his life.

"Owen Gromme the artist" is easily the most acknowledged and acclaimed dimension of this man's character, but there are other facets of his personality that carry equal weight. There is the fiery-tempered crusader for environmental causes; the calm, dedicated, frugal public employee; the loving husband and father; the big game hunter; the author of more than 50 published articles and a major reference book; the photographer and movie maker; the carver and sculptor; the meticulous keeper of records; the man of a myriad of skills needed to run one of the top-ranked museum departments in the United States; the taxidermist and tanner; the door-to-door salesman and purveyor of "underground novelties"; and the World War I stretcher bearer.

The "real" Owen Gromme emerges as the synthesis of all these. And the roots of his varied careers and responsibilities can be traced to his boyhood and apprenticeship among the forests, waterways, and wildlife of his east-central Wisconsin hometown. It is the environment and Gromme's connection to it that have maintained him over the years.

Standing atop the ledge which encompasses the nature area bearing his name, Owen Gromme scans the valley of his boyhood below and describes how the Green Bay lobe of the Wisconsin glacier carved out the topography of the Wisconsin landscape where he was raised.

"I had a great life here when I was a kid," he says, motioning with a sweep of his arm toward Fond du Lac, the small midwestern town which wraps neatly around the foot of Lake Winnebago. "I've got great, great memories."

It was there in his hometown, following in the footsteps of his outdoorsman father John Justus ("Gus") Gromme, that Owen developed his powers of observation, sense of detail, and love of the outdoors. And it was there that he inherited from his Gromme and MacGregor ancestors a kinship with the natural world around him. Hunting was a way of life, and the characters of his youth were outdoorsmen — tough and hard, skilled with guns, and knowledgeable about wild game and the customs of the woods and waterways. They braved the elements, defied storms, told stories both full of truth and full of lies, and treated their hunting dogs with a brand of special reverence.

Gromme has cultivated the memories of his boyhood. He has made it a point to remember everything.

"Fond du Lac was a great town," he recalls. "Quite a place...tough town sometimes...lumber mills, loggers, lumberjacks, and railroads," he added in the characteristic Gromme style — the memories racing miles ahead of the words.

Out of his memory Gromme conjures a Lake Winnebago horizon where steamers plowed the waters, belching great, black plumes of soft-coal smoke overhead as they hauled rafts of logs toward Fond du Lac to be cut into lumber and shipped overland by railroad.

Lumber was a booming Wisconsin enterprise during Gromme's boyhood, but it was already doomed by the greed of timber barons bent on removing every tree in sight from the landscape. The lessons of turn-of-the-century logging were not wasted on Owen Gromme. Today, he describes such examples of greed and waste as "dividend dementia." And he is the first to admit the debt we all owe to the land we inhabit.

"Hell, we really don't own any of this," he says, gesturing with a wave of his hand to the rustic landscape surrounding his home. "We only use it for the short time we're here. We hold it in escrow for those who come after us."

For the many who have "come after" Gromme, the legacy of this environmentalist, taxidermist, ornithologist, and artist provides a vital link between the nineteenth and twenty-first centuries. It was a legacy bequeathed to him by the Indians, the pioneers, the hunters, and his own ancestors who strode the paths of the upper Midwest. Owen J. Gromme sees himself simply passing this legacy on to subsequent generations in the best way that he can.

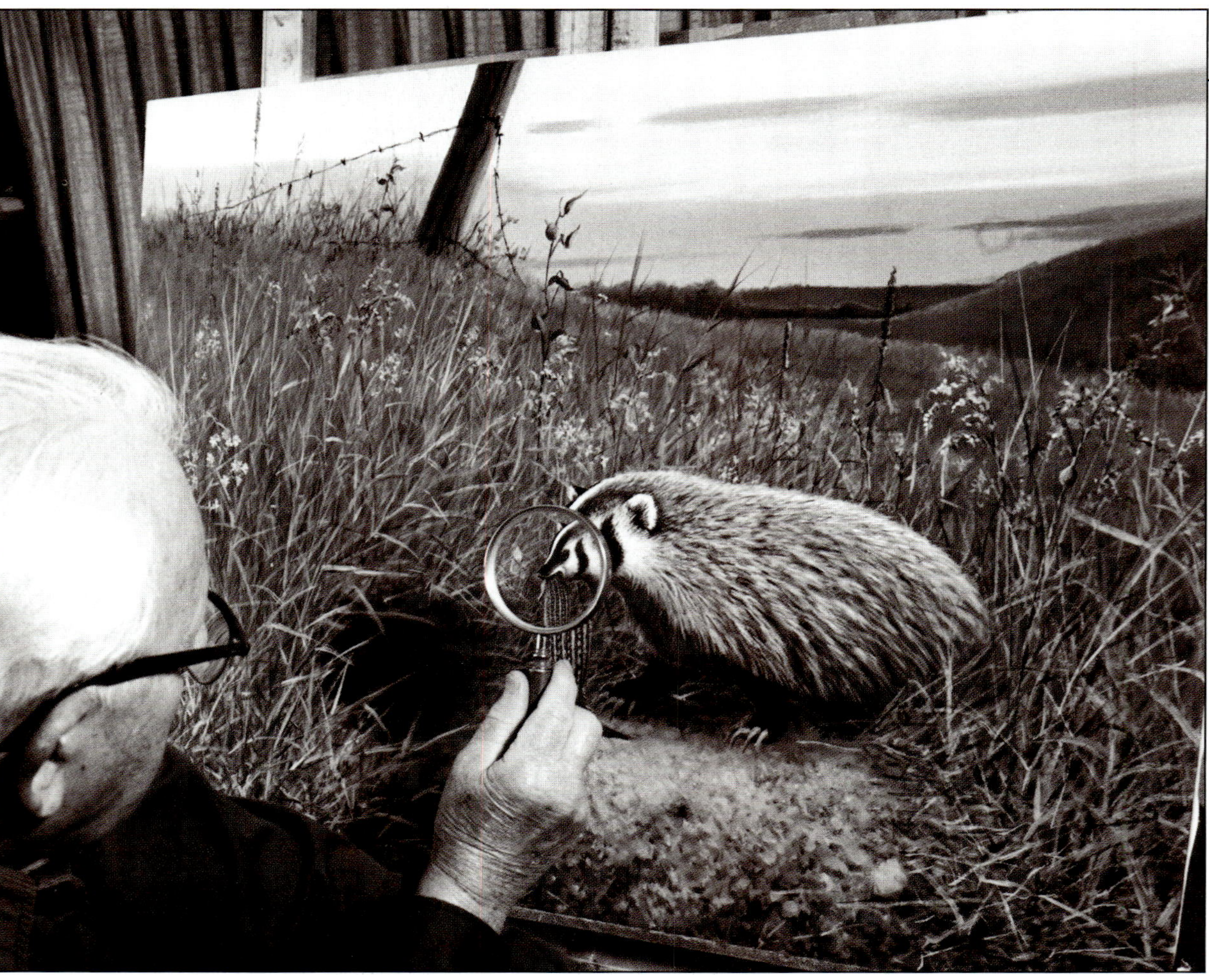

II

At the core of this multidimensional personality lies Owen Gromme the naturalist. For more than sixty years, conservation of natural resources and preservation of the environment have been the driving forces in his life. At times he has worked quietly and without recognition simply because it was his job. But at other times he has fought and struggled in the spotlight of controversy because it was his passion.

"It has never been easy," admits Gromme. "I've never enjoyed the fights or the controversy. But if I'm backed into a corner and someone has to speak up, then I won't shy away from it."

Over the years Gromme has stood toe-to-toe with hunting organizations, the Wisconsin Conservation Commission, the Wisconsin Department of Natural Resources, the U.S. Fish and Wildlife Service, the U.S. Department of the Interior, federal, state, and local politicians, and a host of others.

And now, more than at any other time in his life, he is frustrated and angered by the policies of the current federal administration. Gromme believes that the progress wrought by a generation of environmentalists like himself is now on the auction block. He cautions that while "we may in time change the government, there is not much we can do to replenish our natural resources."

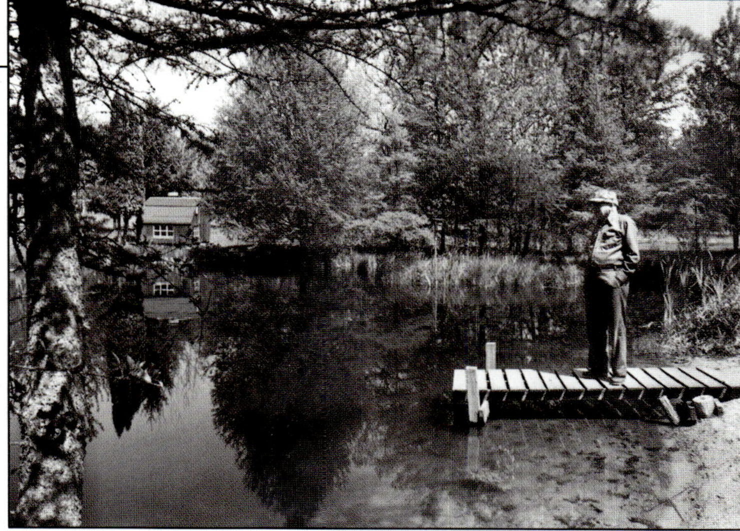

Owen and his son Roy have tried to make the Briggsville farm a showcase of proper environmental planning.

"Once the resources are gone, they're gone," Gromme argues. "We'll never have them back again. Current policies are turning our natural resources into fat bank accounts, and that is what really disturbs me."

Gromme laments what he calls a "change in emphasis" at the Department of the Interior in particular. "I want my grandchildren to have fresh air to breathe and clean water to drink. I don't think that's too much for any of us to ask."

Even though he has suffered more than his share of disappointment in environmental battles over the years, Gromme has also savored the taste of victory in a number of causes. Honor after honor has been bestowed upon him in recent years, acclaiming not only his artistic talent and ability, but also acknowledging his lifelong concern and regard for wildlife, his expert knowledge of the subject, and his message of stewardship. Gromme expounded on this environmental ethic in detail during a commencement address at Fond du Lac's Marian College in June of 1978: "We owe a great deal to those who came before us, and it is our duty to pass on to posterity a world morally and physically as good or better than the one we live in. . . By every legal means, it is our duty to oppose those who, out of greed and avarice, or for selfish or other reasons, would pollute, defile, or destroy that which means life itself to every living being."

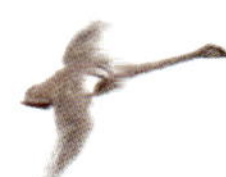

These words take on depth and dimension in the form of the Gromme home and farm at the edge of a tiny farming community in a part of Wisconsin more widely known for pine trees and sand. Owned by the Gromme's son Roy, this 160-acre tract of marshland, hardwoods, and pine seems an apt setting for a man and woman who have devoted their lives to the sometimes lonely, oftentimes frustrating, demands of conservation and environmental causes.

Home for Owen and Anne since 1972 when they moved somewhat reluctantly from Milwaukee, the Gromme farm also serves as a haven and a retreat for their children — Roy of Lincolnshire, Illinois and Anne Marie Ross of Minneapolis — and their five grandchildren.

"No one could live in the same house for very long with Owen Gromme and not be interested in the outdoors," says Anne Gromme. "It has been a way of life for all of us."

Long before outdoor education and recreation came into vogue in this country, the Gromme children were well versed in environmental concepts and concerns.

"Sunday was family day," remembers Anne Marie. "Dad put his painting aside, and most every Sunday we went out to hike in the woods, or to see the geese, or to explore the Cedarburg swamp. We almost always went with a group of people or another family, and it was as natural as going to church on Sunday."

As a youngster growing up in Milwaukee, Anne Marie became a nature consultant for the city's recreation department, following the example set by her father and her mother, one of the volunteer nature consultants for the Milwaukee Area Girl Scout Council, Inc. An avid angler, Anne Marie still ties flies and poppers for her father just as she did as a girl accompanying him and her brother Roy on fishing outings.

Roy recalls that his mother was the one who first nurtured their outdoor interests in wildlife when they were young.

"Mother took care of all those birds and animals we were always bringing home," he remembers.

Yet it was his father who expanded his interest in wildlife by introducing him to the outdoor world, to hunting, and to a close-knit circle of friends and acquaintances who, in turn, exerted their subtle influence.

"My father's art and his work at the museum attracted the kind of people who were interested in the outdoors and outdoor issues," Roy explains. "There's no doubt in my mind that they had an effect on me."

The "effect" manifested itself for young Roy in his 1959 purchase of a parcel of land from his aunt. Situated at the edge of Briggsville, Wisconsin and bought as a tree-farming enterprise, the land has developed over the years into an award-winning nature area under both his watchful guidance and that of his parents.

"There's a lot of me in it," Roy admits as he speaks of the farm he and his father manage.

There, at the farm, Owen Gromme, observing nature from a second-floor studio flooded with natural light from all directions, oversees a panorama of rolling farmland punctuated by the natural setting he and his family have fostered.

"It's all I need," Gromme remarks as he surveys the landscape. "Many of the backgrounds and settings for my paintings come largely from what you see right here."

With a discernible degree of pride, Gromme details his conservation efforts and those of his son.

"We've tried to make this a showplace, more or less. We hope that when we leave, this place will, in some way, be used as a demonstration area."

A lifelong student of the environment, Gromme would be the first to admit that his idea of preservation and conservation is not a new one. But it is a demanding one, for it follows in the traditions of the Indians who treasured the land, as well as other giants of the environmental movement in Wisconsin, among them John Muir and Aldo Leopold, both of whom had ties to land not far from Gromme's central Wisconsin home.

Former Wisconsin Congressman Henry Reuss, a highly regarded environmentalist in his own right, places Gromme on the same plane with the nation's premier outdoorsmen. Author of *On the Trail of the Ice Age* and a driving force in the preservation of the Ice Age Reserve Trail, Reuss describes Gromme "as a true American — a salty, peppery individualist in the mold of Muir and Leopold." He added: "Real outdoorsmen like those men are a vanishing breed."

John Muir, a self-taught naturalist who left his native Wisconsin and became a western explorer, is regarded as the father of the national park system. A student at the University of Wisconsin in the 1860s, Muir's devotion to the study of natural history led him to the Sierra Mountains of California where he discovered sixty-five active glaciers. And his first published accounts of these findings in the *New York Tribune* (December 1871) marked the beginning of a new era in American natural history — the age of the preservationist.

In his writings, Muir urged the federal government to reserve land for public use as national parks. His crusade helped transform California's Yosemite Valley into a national park, and

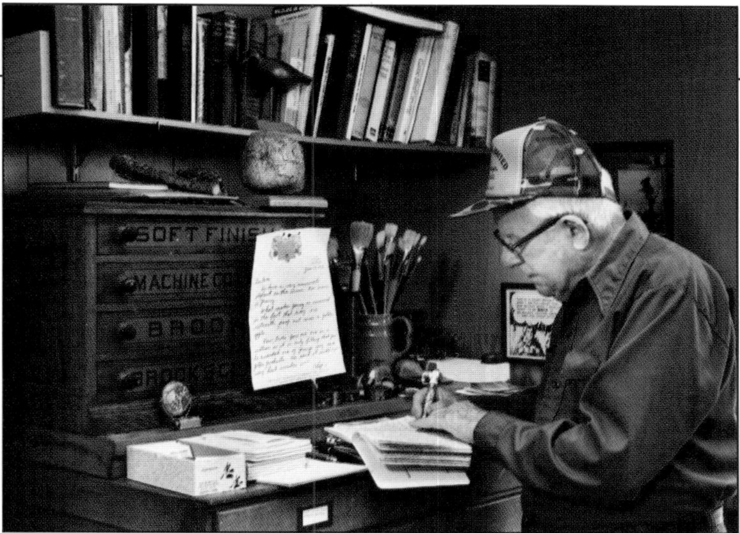
Gromme continues to observe and note environmental changes and alterations in bird populations in his Field Notes.

his persistence blazed the trail for the founding of the National Park Service. Muir was successful in opening the eyes of the nation to the concept that land was worth saving just because it was scenic, wild, or unique.

In the void left by Muir's passing came another exceptional naturalist to the fertile intellectual soil of Wisconsin's "sand country." Aldo Leopold, a legend in the conservation movement, breathed life into the concept of "land ethic" in a series of essays entitled *A Sand County Almanac.* A University of Wisconsin professor and one of the world's greatest naturalists, Leopold's writings evolved as the gospel of the environmental movement. In his essay, "Land Ethic," Leopold stated: "A thing is right when it tends to preserve the integrity, stability, and beauty of the biotic community. It is wrong when it tends otherwise."

The paths of Gromme and Leopold crossed often in their professional lives — Gromme as curator of birds and mammals at the Milwaukee Public Museum and Leopold as professor of wildlife management at the University of Wisconsin. Moreover, the Gromme home at the outskirts of Briggsville, Wisconsin lies in the heart of Leopold's beloved "sand country," home to the poetic musings and shack sketches rendered in his writings. Gromme describes Leopold's *A Sand County Almanac* as his bible.

"Leopold had a great mind," Gromme says with reverence. "A great analytical mind. He was one of the deepest thinkers I have ever known. He was an artist with words, and he applied his science beautifully."

If Leopold applied his science beautifully, then it should also be noted that Gromme applied his art in a similar manner. Speaking of his painting entitled *Marshland Elegy,* a title he selected in honor of his favorite Leopold essay, Gromme remarks: "I simply tried to put in paint what Al Leopold put in words."

Gromme created the painting as a financial benefit for the Head Foundation, now known as the Sand County Foundation, which maintains the Leopold Memorial Reserve. Gromme donated the publication rights of the original painting as a means of providing funding for environmental education at the Leopold Reserve.

According to Frank Terbilcox, manager of the Leopold Reserve along the Wisconsin River, "That painting is an important part of our fund-raising efforts. It is a tie between Aldo and Owen; and it is helping us carry on the work Aldo Leopold started many years ago."

Gromme's painting depicts sandhill cranes whiffling and sideslipping to the safety of the marsh. Far in the distance stands the "shack" made famous by Leopold in his writings. It was there in that renovated chicken coop that Leopold drafted "Marshland Elegy," in which he wrote: "Our ability to perceive quality in nature begins, as in art, with the pretty. It expands through successive stages of the beautiful to values as yet uncaptured in language. The quality of cranes lies, I think, in this higher gamut, as yet beyond the reach of words."

Cranes have held a particular fascination for Gromme throughout his career. In fact, among the many paintings he has created for the benefit of conservation groups and environmental organizations over the years, *Salute to the Dawn* and *Sacred Cranes over Hokkaido* stand out. Both paintings serve not only as symbols of Gromme's interest in these rare and mysterious birds but also

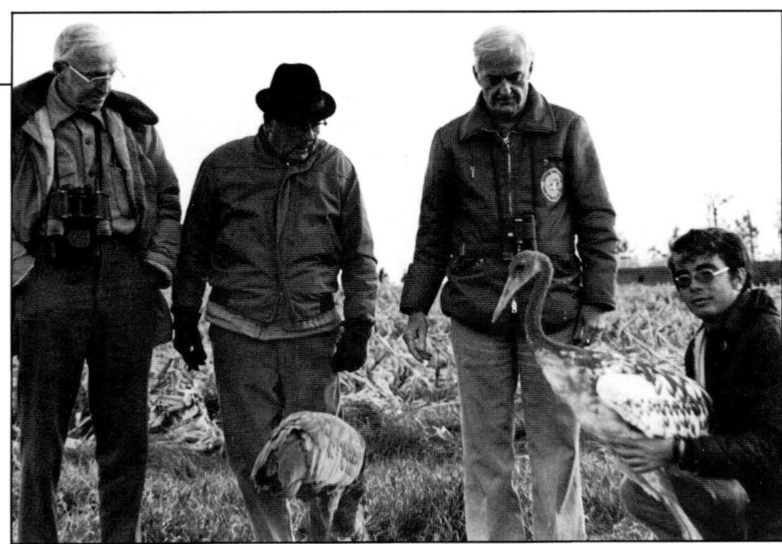

Gromme's dedication to the preservation of cranes has involved his friends and colleagues. Here he is seen with (left to right) Professor Joseph Hickey, Gromme, noted ornithologist Roger Tory Peterson, and (sitting) ICF Director George Archibald.

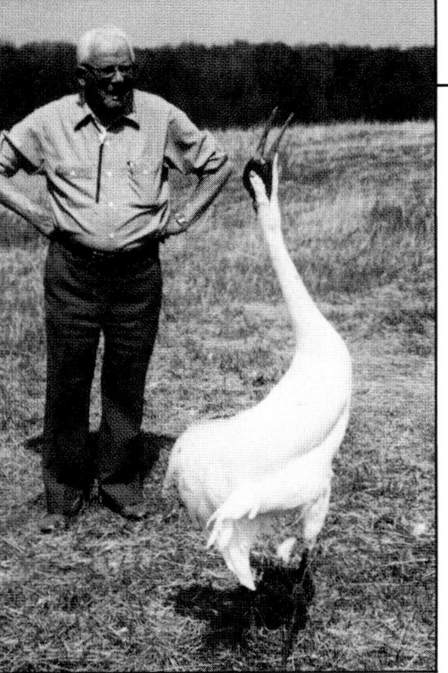

Gromme is pictured here with "Tex," one of ICF's most famous residents. Before she was killed by raccoons in the summer of 1982, Tex mothered a crane who was later named "Gee Whiz."

as indicators of his dedication to preserving this species for coming generations. Such devotion has prompted Gromme's placement on the Board of Directors of the International Crane Foundation, Inc. (ICF) located in Baraboo, Wisconsin.

"I've always been interested in cranes," Gromme asserts. "Maybe it's just because they are one of the largest and most spectacular of our birds in Wisconsin. I can still remember the first time I ever heard the call of a crane — it just about made my hair stand on end."

Gromme's first "close encounter" with cranes occurred in 1929 ("there were hardly any left at the time" he recalls), and since then he has had many occasions to observe these endangered birds. In fact, Gromme has made a record of most of his observations in his *Field Notes*, a personal compilation of facts, anecdotes, and information which spans more than *seven* decades of environmental awareness.

For example, in October of 1954 at Sandhill Farm near Babcock, Wisconsin with his friend Wallace Grange, another of Wisconsin's vigorous environmentalists, Gromme crouched in the marsh grass and witnessed one of the largest gatherings he had seen to that point in his life. He wrote in his *Field Notes*: "Soon after we got set, I heard the wild clarion clamor of sandhill cranes off in the mist and about three-quarters of a mile away. Once heard, the sound of over a hundred sandhill, all calling at once, is an unforgettable experience. The misty atmospheric condition in the gray dawn seemed to magnify and blend the sound into a hair-raising ringing bedlam which echoed and reverberated over the marsh."

Fifteen years later, Gromme was amazed to find hundreds of cranes resting in an area near the farm at Briggsville. This happened on October 9, 1969, not far from the twisting Neenah Creek. When he and Anne returned home that night, Gromme added this "evening to remember" to his *Field Notes*:

"We advanced a few paces and there they were, all over the small pond, almost entirely surrounded by brush and fairly heavy oak woods. The strong wind made such a noise that the birds could not hear us, and it was just dark enough so they could not make us out. We got a good look at them through the glasses as their gray forms loomed up well in dusk. They uttered their whole repertoire of calls, from the peeping of the immature to the contented grunts and rattles of others."

He added: "It is hard to describe the feeling of one like myself who suddenly finds himself close enough to be one of them, and who understands the difficulty of survival of these noble birds, let alone their mastery of storms and the vast areas of the northland this gathering (of sandhill cranes) represented."

Calling on his mastery of ornithology and artistry several years later, Gromme created a stunning painting of a pair of whooping cranes trumpeting in unison above their newly-hatched offspring. In the background, dawn breaks on a fog-shrouded marsh — the symbol of a new beginning. The painting is entitled *Salute to the Dawn*, and prints from the original generated much-needed funds for the non-profit International Crane Foundation.

"That painting was a great shot in the arm," says ICF Director George Archibald. "Back then, ICF was just an idea, but Owen believed in it from the start."

The Crane Foundation, which now exerts global impact on the fight to save cranes from extinction, was founded in 1971 by

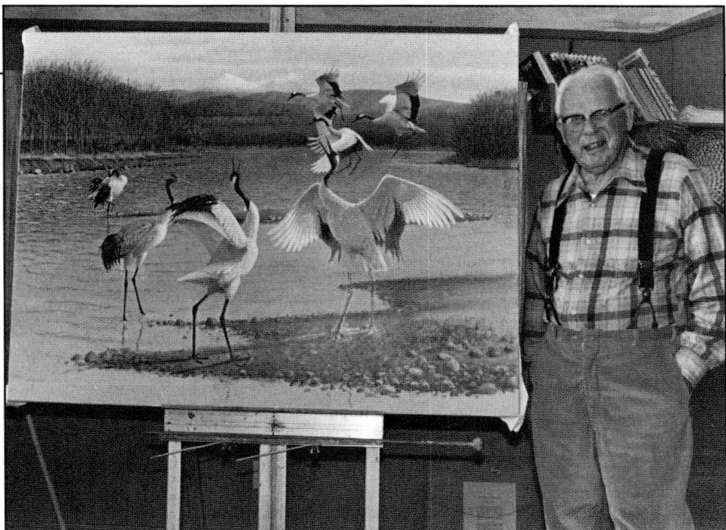

Gromme stands alongside another of his crane paintings, *Tancho*, which he completed in 1980.

Archibald and Ron Sauey, a native of central Wisconsin. Both men, but especially young Sauey, had more than just a passing interest in the wildlife artist who was living at nearby Briggsville.

"I was interested in Owen Gromme's paintings when I was in high school, and a friend of my parents took me to meet him," Sauey remembers.

When Sauey wanted to attend Cornell University and needed a letter of recommendation, he renewed his association with Gromme. Sauey and Archibald met at Cornell where Archibald was engaged in crane research, trying to develop a technique for propagating the birds while in captivity.

"We decided that we wanted to start the Crane Foundation, and it is still a reality a decade later," notes Archibald.

The horse ranch owned by Ron Sauey's parents became a home for a passel of endangered crane species and the foundation of a dream to stave off extinction. Over the years the dream has evolved into substance through the dedicated service of Archibald and Sauey. Crane music that would have been snuffed out long ago echoes today off the hillsides of central Wisconsin.

"When George and I first started ICF, we knew one of our biggest problems was money," says Sauey. "That's how Owen's painting came about."

Sauey commissioned Gromme to paint whooping cranes sounding their unison call; and when it was completed, Gromme donated the reproduction rights to the infant organization. Every individual who bought a print of the original painting was helping to finance the International Crane Foundation.

Gromme was influential in other areas as well. Aware of ICF's need for legal expertise and leadership abilities, he sought out the assistance of two close friends, John and Mary Wickhem of Janesville.

"Anne and Owen invited us over and we were sitting around the table," John Wickhem recalls. "They were both really enthused with what Sauey and Archibald were trying to do, and they wanted us to get involved."

Mary Wickhem remembers: "Owen and Anne intrigued us so much, we couldn't say no." She became the first president of the Crane Foundation's Board of Directors, and she continues to serve in that capacity today.

The birth of the Crane Foundation also enabled Gromme to display the selling abilities he had acquired in his youth. Whenever the opportunity would present itself, Gromme pressed for donations.

"He would bring somebody over to see the cranes," says Sauey, "and then he'd say to them, 'You've got plenty of money. Here's something worth giving to, so give them something.' "

But if anyone ever made the mistake of uttering an uncomplimentary word about the International Crane Foundation, they would most likely find the white-haired, red-faced Gromme in their path.

"Thomas Huxley was Darwin's bulldog, and Owen Gromme is our bulldog," notes Sauey. "He has always been willing to help and defend us any way he can. He is a wonderful person to have on your side. I wouldn't want to go up against him."

For the first five years of its existence, the Crane Foundation operated on a shoestring budget and volunteer labor, but in 1978 the Board of Directors expanded to a force of fifteen, including Gromme. In the same year, Anne and Owen donated the initial funds for the purchase of 165 acres not far from the present site to be used for expansion of ICF.

"He is a very caring, very gentle person," confides Archibald, playing down the bluster Gromme often exhibits. "He is outspoken and outgoing — that is apparent whenever you see him. But underneath, he is a gentle person who really cares about other people and the world around him."

There are officials at the Wisconsin Department of Natural Resources (DNR) and the U.S. Fish and Wildlife Service who might have difficulty envisioning Gromme as anything but outspoken, single-minded, and tough. Since the 1930s, he has been a vocal — some might say vociferous — critic of policies governing the water level at Horicon Marsh in central Wisconsin. In a 1976 confrontation with the Wisconsin DNR and the U.S. Fish and Wildlife Service, he expressed his outrage against the drawdown of the water level at Horicon in a painting entitled *Requiem: Horicon Marsh, 1916-1976*. Featuring the colors of mourning and death, the painting depicts thirteen tired and hungry geese preparing to land on "a stinking, filthy, disease-ridden mudhole, that" continues Gromme, "was once a paradise for the migrating flocks."

"It is my only propaganda painting," laments Gromme, "but it said something that had to be said."

Throughout Gromme's life, Horicon Marsh has been a battleground, frequently pitting conservationists like himself against land speculators, fast-buck artists, and others who would use the marsh for profit or political convenience. And Owen J. Gromme has participated in more than his share of the battles in a personal "crusade" which spans more than six decades.

When he was a boy growing up less than thirty miles from the vast marsh, young Owen listened and learned from the Fond du Lac hunters about the ravages of drainage. During that era of widespread marsh drainage, wetlands everywhere bore the open wounds of the dredge claw, and though Gromme did not know the meaning of the word at the time, he was, in every sense of the term, a "naturalist." He was a true student of the outdoors, unsuited for the stuffy discipline of a turn-of-the-century classroom. The lessons that intrigued him were not to be found in books.

"I was a hunter," Gromme recalls. "That's what I was before I was anything else. At that point in my life, painting and art had absolutely no meaning for me. They never even entered my mind."

Young Owen Gromme was much more interested in the things that affected his outdoor way of life. He learned the lessons of wetland drainage as he watched the disappearance of streams, ponds, lakes, waterfowl, muskrats, and other wilderness animals. Where once there had been a wildlife paradise, afterward only cattails, thistles, and desolate mudflats flourished.

And then came the fires. "When the wind was right, the smoke from the peat fires would drift from the marsh all the way into Fond du Lac," Gromme remembers. "And at night you could stand at the edge of the marsh and see the fire winking and blinking in the darkness like charcoal." The sight of it branded itself on the young man's memory.

The drainage of those 40,000 acres of marsh was in direct defiance of a 1908 Wisconsin Supreme Court decision, yet speculators and promoters tried everything to convince a skeptical public that great benefits would follow in the wake of the drainage effort.

Gromme remembers: "They said Horicon would be the greatest farmland ever produced. They told the people they would be able to grow onions as big as pumpkins and beets as big as basketballs. And during the night they would sneak into the marsh with railway cars full of nitrate to fertilize the soil. Once they were through with it, the marsh lay there for years, little more than a biological desert. It was good for nothing."

Fire smoldered in the dried peat, burrowing deeper each year until the marsh was pocked with holes that reached into the sand layer of the prehistoric lake which had receded thousands of years ago. In Owen's second year as a Milwaukee Public Museum taxidermist — on October 19, 1923 to be exact — the Wisconsin Division of the Izaak Walton League of America adopted a resolution which stated that Horicon Marsh should be established as a refuge for wildlife. The same resolution was unanimously approved at the National Convention of the Izaak Walton League in Chicago a year later. The stage had been set for an epic struggle.

As the battle lines were drawn on both sides, Gromme's personal interest in environmental and conservation issues was growing day by day.

"When I look back, it seems to me that my concern for the environment came about as part of my job at the museum," Gromme recalls. "I was always interested in birds, animals, and the outdoors because I was a hunter and a taxidermist. But I could see how it all fit together once I started working at the museum."

Gromme was guided in those early museum years by Herbert L. Stoddard, an accomplished taxidermist and outdoorsman who later became a pioneer in wildlife management. And his emerging concern was further bolstered by the emphasis placed on environmental issues, especially those that affected Wisconsin, by Milwaukee Public Museum Director S.A. Barrett.

"I'll never forget it as long as I live," remarked Gromme. "Dr. Barrett said to me, 'Gromme, as long as you are an employee of this institution, conservation of natural resources is part of your job.' "

Gromme took Barrett's directive to heart, and the young museum employee made a lifelong commitment then and there to work for the restoration of Horicon Marsh as a wildlife preserve. As the marsh battle dragged on, exhausting members of both sides, Gromme persisted, along with a few other unswerving souls, among them the late Louis "Curly" Radke of Horicon.

"If it wasn't for Curly Radke, there would be no Horicon Marsh as we know it today," Gromme asserts. "He was the leader, and if anyone deserves credit for getting water back on Horicon, it's Curly Radke. I only helped."

That is a modest appraisal of his own diligent efforts, gauging by the hundreds of pages of correspondence, reports, and research that he developed during the crusade to reclaim the marsh as a wildlife area.

Gromme was *there* on April 20, 1935 — Duck Liberation Day — to celebrate "the dawn of a new day for wildlife on Horicon Marsh." Members of the Izaak Walton League, Wisconsin's women's clubs, state and federal conservation officials, and conservationists from Wisconsin and several other states converged on the marsh to liberate wild ducks and geese in the hope of restoring wildlife to the marsh areas.

Judging by his *Field Notes*, it was a day of optimism for Gromme: "The famous Horicon Marsh battle has been won thanks to Mr. Louis Radke of Horicon, and it is now a vast wildlife refuge. People were there from all over the state, and mallard ducks were sent from practically every state in the union. About 1,200 ducks were liberated, and the enthusiastic crowd of conservationists numbered somewhere in the neighborhood of 3,000. In my opinion this is the largest number of conservationists ever to gather in one body at any time in our fair land, and I feel that these conservationists really made history at Horicon this day."

Gromme was *there* after the "war" was apparently over to guarantee that the "peace" would not be violated, arguing with both the U.S. Biological Survey and the Wisconsin Conservation Commission (later the DNR) that drainage was still occurring and waterfowl were being destroyed. In the years since then, the Rock River has slowly and inexorably covered the marsh, reaching into every low spot, dousing the seemingly unquenchable peat fires, filling the potholes and sloughs, and restoring the vast area to a semblance of its glory in the days before dredges and drainage engineers. And for almost four decades Owen Gromme has returned in the spring and fall, stirred by the seasons of change, to witness the miracle of Horicon.

He was *there* as well in the late 1930s when drought in the Dakotas, coupled with heavy rains in southern Wisconsin, filled Horicon not only with water but also with a literal storm of ducks from the drought-stricken areas of the West. Gromme and hunters of his vintage still remember the incomparable duck hunting in 1938 "out in the willows."

He was *there* in 1949 with his son Roy to behold the ever-expanding flocks of geese on their way to Hudson Bay and to watch a thousand or more birds pour into the dredge channel as his son looked on in amazement from a hiding place along the bank.

He was *there* in the 1950s to remind state and federal government officials that the intent of marsh restoration was to establish adequate water levels and resultant management to serve all species of waterfowl. He warned game managers that they were allowing the burgeoning flocks of geese to become a public relations tool of the Fish and Wildlife Service.

He was *there* in May of 1960 to decry the growing number of "skybusters" and other violators who practiced deplorable goose-hunting practices that had evolved along with the influx of vast numbers of Canada geese. Some referred to this practice as the "managed hunt" or "harvest." But Gromme had another word for it — "shameful." Because of the public outcry, the practice no longer exists.

Although he retired in 1965 from the Milwaukee Public Museum, Gromme's job as a protector of the state's natural resources continued in full force. He maintained his ties to Horicon Marsh, watching with interest the men who managed the refuge and the policies they employed.

Then came the "bolt from out of the blue" in 1976. Even though the decision by federal and state agencies to lower the water level and haze the geese at Horicon Marsh was particularly painful for Gromme and other conservationists, it did not catch

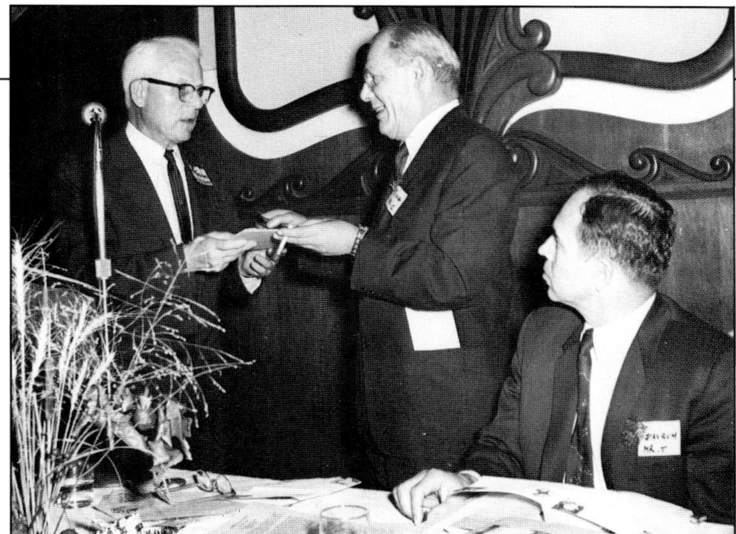

Not all of Gromme's conservation efforts went unnoticed — here he receives a Silver Acorn Award from the Citizen's Natural Resources Association (CNRA) in recognition of his outstanding conservation work. Presenting the award is the Association's then president, Clarence Jung (1961).

bird alive — the wildlife lovers. We hunters must bear in mind that numerically this class of people has a much greater stake in our wildlife than the comparatively small number of us who buy a hunting license and duck stamp and who consider that all wildlife is ours alone."

Some years later, Owen designed a stamp similar to the Wildlife Federation stamps in order to focus public attention on the need for "inviolate wildlife refuges," hoping that a specially-designed stamp would arouse "the non-hunting but nature-loving public." In the spring of 1954, Gromme presented his proposal to the Board of Directors of the Citizens Natural Resources Association and the organization's president, Wallace Grange. He designed a watercolor painting of a pair of Canada geese, donated it to the CNRA, and arranged for the engraving at cost. By the end of April 1954, more than 30,000 Wisconsin Wildlife Refuge stamps had been distributed to conservation clubs and organizations. And, in turn, the stamps were being affixed to letters and other mailings to promote the slogan, "Keep Our Wildlife Refuges Inviolate."

Gromme's crusade, however, was not confined to designing wildlife refuge stamps. By 1955 he was completely frustrated with the lack of response from state and federal officials regarding his complaints about the scarcity of waterfowl, except in the Horicon Marsh area where the birds could find refuge. To this end, Gromme pressed Wisconsin administrators for a closed season on ducks. In November 1955, he urged the Wisconsin Conservation Commission in particular "to change this situation if you are willing to buck the tide and the politicians."

To demonstrate his frustration and disgust, Gromme refrained from duck and goose hunting in the fall of 1960 for the *first* time since he was a boy too young to join his elders. Noting the decline of ducks and other waterfowl and the lack of hunting ethics displayed by many hunters, especially in the Horicon area, Gromme declared, "I'm abstaining out of principle."

In May of 1961, he took his case to Washington and newly-appointed Secretary of the Interior Stewart L. Udall. Arrangements for the conference were handled by Rep. Henry Reuss of Milwaukee, an avowed outdoorsman and Udall's fellow Democrat.

"To be effective, I knew we needed the help of people who could get things done," Gromme explains. "And Henry Reuss was a man who was interested in the environment, and he was a man who knew how to get things done. If I accomplished anything important, it was because I was able to convince some key people in government that something had to be done."

For Reuss and Gromme, their association was a beneficial blend of business and pleasure. At times they shared a Horicon Marsh blind and tested their skills with goose calls while their conversation regularly focused on environmental issues. It seemed only natural that Reuss would provide the opportunity for Gromme to "make his pitch."

Gromme took full advantage. "We made it clear to Secretary Udall that we were expressing the sentiments of the multitudinous, non-hunting, unorganized public who have a greater stake in our refuges than the proportionately few hunters whose wishes up to then had been given greater consideration."

Gromme, reflecting the concerns of thousands of Wisconsin environmentalists, urged Udall to remove all hunting blinds within federal refuges and to prohibit hunting of any kind inside the boundaries of refuges. He asked that grain surpluses be used on federal refuges as a means of reducing crop depredation on surrounding farms and also as a means of insuring that migrating waterfowl would have adequate food in addition to cover. He pressed for a seasonal bag limit on geese on a flyway basis and pointed out to Udall what he viewed as a deterioration of sportsmanship as a result of federal policies in Wisconsin.

Today, some of Gromme's proposals are in force thanks to his efforts and those of many others. Hunting is no longer allowed in the federal portion of Horicon Marsh, and a seasonal bag limit based on flyways now exists, even though it is often unpopular with hunters. Feed for the migrating flocks remains a controversial subject, and the hunting ethics of some "sportsmen" still detract from the spectacle of the waterfowl migration. But there have been many improvements.

Still, game hogs, "sky busters," wetland drainage practices, and overshooting of waterfowl and other game animals are as anathema to Gromme today as they were in 1935 or 1957 or 1961. But now, his paintings do the talking. His wildlife art not only touches the spirit of the outdoor-loving public, but it also generates hundreds of thousands of dollars to support the environmental causes of organizations such as the International Crane Foundation and Ducks Unlimited.

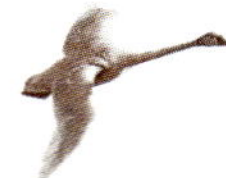

While Horicon Marsh and waterfowl issues have consumed vast amounts of Gromme's time and energy over the years, they are, by no means, perceived as more important or more significant than other environmental concerns such as the preservation of birds of prey. In fact, at a time when most hunters and the public in general were viewing hawks and owls and other birds of prey as nothing short of a menace, Gromme was doing all he could to explain their role in the natural order.

In March of 1935, for example, Gromme led a fight to stop what had been advertised in the state's largest daily newspaper, the *Milwaukee Journal,* as a "varmint hunt." The hunt was proposed and sponsored by the Milwaukee Gun Club, an organization which Gromme had vigorously chastised for its plan of indiscriminately killing creatures such as hawks, owls, and crows which they categorically described as "varmints." He enlisted the aid of Wilhelmina LaBudde, President of the Conservation Division of the Wisconsin Federation of Women's Clubs, as well as the Izaak Walton League, which had been instrumental in the Horicon Marsh restoration project. During the next few days the *Milwaukee Journal* devoted several columns to the pros and cons of the controversy. Gromme was especially buoyed by the comments of fellow conservationists, remarking in his *Field Notes* (March 1935) that "by bringing the matter before the public the Gun Club did more to perpetuate the 'so-called' varmints than to exterminate them."

He added: "The public mind is slowly grasping the fact that birds of prey possess virtues along with a propensity for destruction. I expect that as a result of being responsible for the cancellation of this statewide hunt, I shall be called a 'sentimental

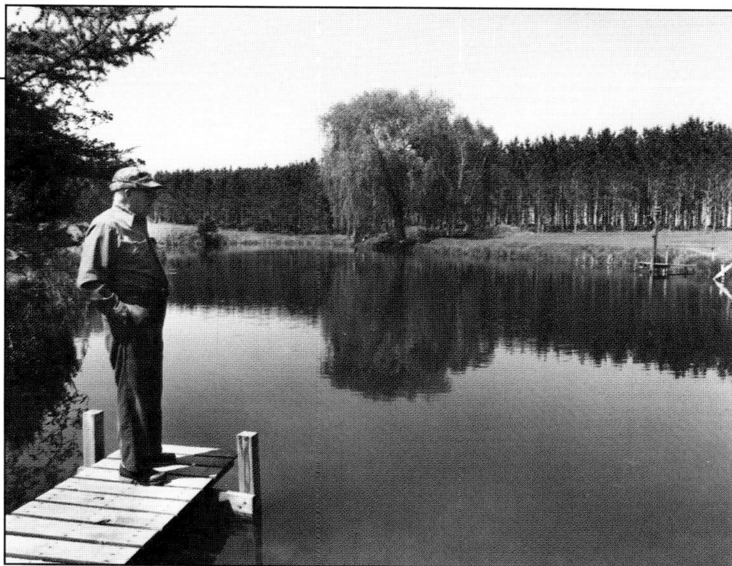

"At the core of this multi-dimensional personality lies Owen Gromme the naturalist . . ."

crank.' " Within a few days the misguided hunt was cancelled, thwarted by the public outcry against it.

Gromme attributes his concern about hawks and other predators to the knowledge of the species he acquired as a museum curator.

"I guess you could call it applied science," explains Gromme. "I learned about the environment because it was expected of me. It was part of my job. The more I learned about the environment, the more it became evident to me that we are all dependent on one another and that everything in nature is dependent on something else. I'm part of everything, and everything is part of me."

He can recall a time when even great blue herons were threatened by an army of angry hunters who felt they were detrimental to Wisconsin's fish population. Reports from the 1920s and 1930s tell of entire rookeries exterminated by shotgun wielding "protectors" of Wisconsin's fisheries. In this instance, Gromme sought documented research from specialists to learn whether or not herons did indeed pose a threat to fish because of a parasite which they allegedly carried. He learned that a variety of water birds, not only herons, could be carriers, and that the relationship among the birds, parasites, and fish was virtually unknown. Gromme concluded: "It is our conviction that the persecution of any water bird as a carrier of fish parasites is absolutely unjustifiable when so little is known of these complex relationships." He added that "any move to control a parasite by eliminating one of its hosts is obviously a step in the dark which might have far-reaching consequences. Must a large section of the vertebrate fauna of a region be sacrificed in order to free a few fish from parasites?"

Carried in the Milwaukee press, Gromme's comments attracted the attention of Aldo Leopold in Madison. In March, 1933, Gromme and Leopold met at the University of Wisconsin in Madison to discuss the need for an amendment to the Wisconsin State Statutes which would prohibit any shooting within 1,000 yards of bittern and heron nests or rookeries. Their proposal later became law, making Wisconsin one of the country's leaders in providing protection for herons in their nesting areas. Walter Pelzer, a colleague of Gromme's for more than thirty years at the Milwaukee Public Museum, credits Gromme for pioneer legislation which protected not only herons and bitterns but hawks and owls as well.

"Owen was fighting for those kinds of laws long before most people even thought about it," says Pelzer.

An inveterate bird bander, ornithologist and outdoorsman, Gromme studied his environment without fail on a daily basis. Little, if anything, about birds and their surroundings escaped his trained eye. It is not surprising, then, to learn that he was among the first in Wisconsin to notice a startling decline in the numbers of raptors, songbirds, and other birds. In the mid-1950s, Gromme's *Field Notes* indicated his concern that bird populations among various species were declining. He observed on several occasions that hawks, birds of prey, and warblers were especially scarce, and he wasted little time in discovering why this was the case. However, he was distressed to learn that the widespread spraying of chemicals to control insects, especially those carrying Dutch Elm disease, was at the heart of the problem.

Later, in July of 1957, Gromme, Anne, and Milwaukee Public Museum colleague Lester Diedrich were members of a group which surveyed a popular Milwaukee park to determine the effects of insecticides and chemical fogging upon birds. Owen observed that "by comparison with one to two years ago, the birds are gone. I am noting this because our national craze for the irrational and widespread use of poison is creating an alarming and dangerous situation over the whole country."

A year later, in the midst of what should have been the warbler migration through Wisconsin, Gromme entered this report in his *Field Notes:* "Weather hot and bright — an ideal day at what should have been the peak of the warbler migration. Like yesterday the general warbler list was 90 percent below par and the birds concentrated in a few places. As noted by omissions on the bird list, many birds which should have been numerous were entirely missing. In some of the states to the south, aerial spraying has been entirely stopped. Some of the chemical companies are boasting a 90 percent kill of insects, and the resulting loss among some birds must be appalling."

Moreover, in his position as curator of birds and mammals at the Milwaukee Public Museum, Gromme was the recipient of a flood of letters and telephone calls from Milwaukee residents wanting to know why so many birds were becoming scarce. In typical fashion he went straight to his favorite means of communication, the daily newspaper, to publicly protest what he termed "the wholesale slaughter of our birds."

"The greatest enemy of insect life is other predatory insects, birds, and some small mammals," Gromme explained, "but DDT kills indiscriminately, including nature's own safeguards or policemen. In the name of progress are we to become victims of our own diabolical means of insect control to provide temporary comfort, only to lose out to destroying insects later on? By what means will we control new pests which will attack remaining tree species after the elms are gone, when nature's safeguards (the birds) have been wiped out by poison?"

Alarmed by such large numbers of dead and dying birds, Gromme campaigned vigorously against widespread use of insecticides. And the comments he first made in Milwaukee were eventually carried to millions through Rachel Carson's nationally acclaimed book, *Silent Spring* (1962). In it, Gromme again speaks to the dangers of indiscriminate spraying and a "chemical-drenched world where spraying destroys not only the insects but their principal enemy, the birds."

Research undertaken in Wisconsin (between 1959 and 1964) by UW Professor of Wildlife Ecology Joseph J. Hickey indicated that the spraying of insecticides not only killed large numbers of birds but also rendered segments of the bird population incapable of reproduction. Hickey also discovered that DDT deposits in Lake Michigan were contaminating lake fish which, in turn, were being eaten by birds, thereby spreading the DDT contamination. By 1964 Hickey and his associates had determined that an entire bird species had been wiped out along the eastern seaboard as a result of DDT spraying.

Public outcry against the use of dangerous chemicals in the environment led to an eventual ban on DDT and restrictions on other types of insecticides. It was a painful lesson, but one that

Owen Gromme cautions must not be forgotten.

"It was a frightening thing at the time," recalls Gromme as he contemplates the nearly "silent springs" of the late 1950s. "Just think what it would mean if suddenly certain species were wiped out, gone forever."

As he spoke, Gromme was remembering the eulogy of the passenger pigeon, an extinct species memorialized by a monument in Wisconsin's Wyalusing State Park near the confluence of the Mississippi and Wisconsin Rivers. Among those present in May of 1947 to witness the dedication of the memorial were two of the committee members who had made arrangements for the marker, namely Aldo Leopold and Owen Gromme. Leopold had composed a stirring essay in conjunction with the dedication.

"We have erected a monument to commemorate the funeral of a species," wrote Leopold. "It symbolizes our sorrow. We grieve because no living man will see again the onrushing phalanx of victorious birds, sweeping a path for spring across the March skies, chasing the defeated winter from all the woods and prairies of Wisconsin.

"For one species to mourn the death of another is a new thing under the sun. The sportsman who shot the last passenger pigeon thought only of his prowess. . . But we, who have lost our pigeons, mourn the loss."

Long before Leopold penned those words, Gromme grieved for the species he never knew, "the biological storm" that disappeared forever into thin air on the fading echo of a shotgun blast.

"My Dad told me about passenger pigeons back in 1932," explained Gromme, noting that his father was recalling a time in the 1880s. "He told me how his brother, Conrad, and he had discovered a small colony of nesting passenger pigeons on the east shore of Lake Winnebago at a place named Deadwood Point. When he was a boy, the sun would be obscured for minutes at a time by passenger pigeons going overhead. He used to shoot into the immense flocks with his arrow, but he doesn't remember killing any.

"They were good eating and good sport," Gromme continues, "fun to shoot at. So the hunters shot them for the hell of it, fed 'em to the pigs, sold 'em for a nickel, shipped 'em by the barrelful until they were gone."

The last passenger pigeon ever seen in Fond du Lac County tumbled to its death on Deadwood Point in the early 1890s, a few years before Owen Gromme was born. There is no monument to a passenger pigeon there, but Gromme retains one of his own — the old muzzle loader which his uncle used that day while hunting pigeons along the lake. It serves as a reminder.

In his essay on the passenger pigeon, Leopold concluded: "To love what *was* is a new thing under the sun, unknown to most people and to all pigeons. To see America as history, to conceive of destiny as a becoming, to smell a hickory tree through the still lapse of ages — all these things are possible for us, and to achieve them takes only the free sky, and the will to ply our wings."

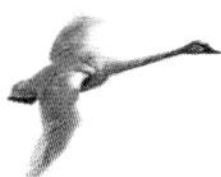

"An inveterate bird bander, ornithologist, and outdoorsman, Gromme studies the environment on a daily basis."

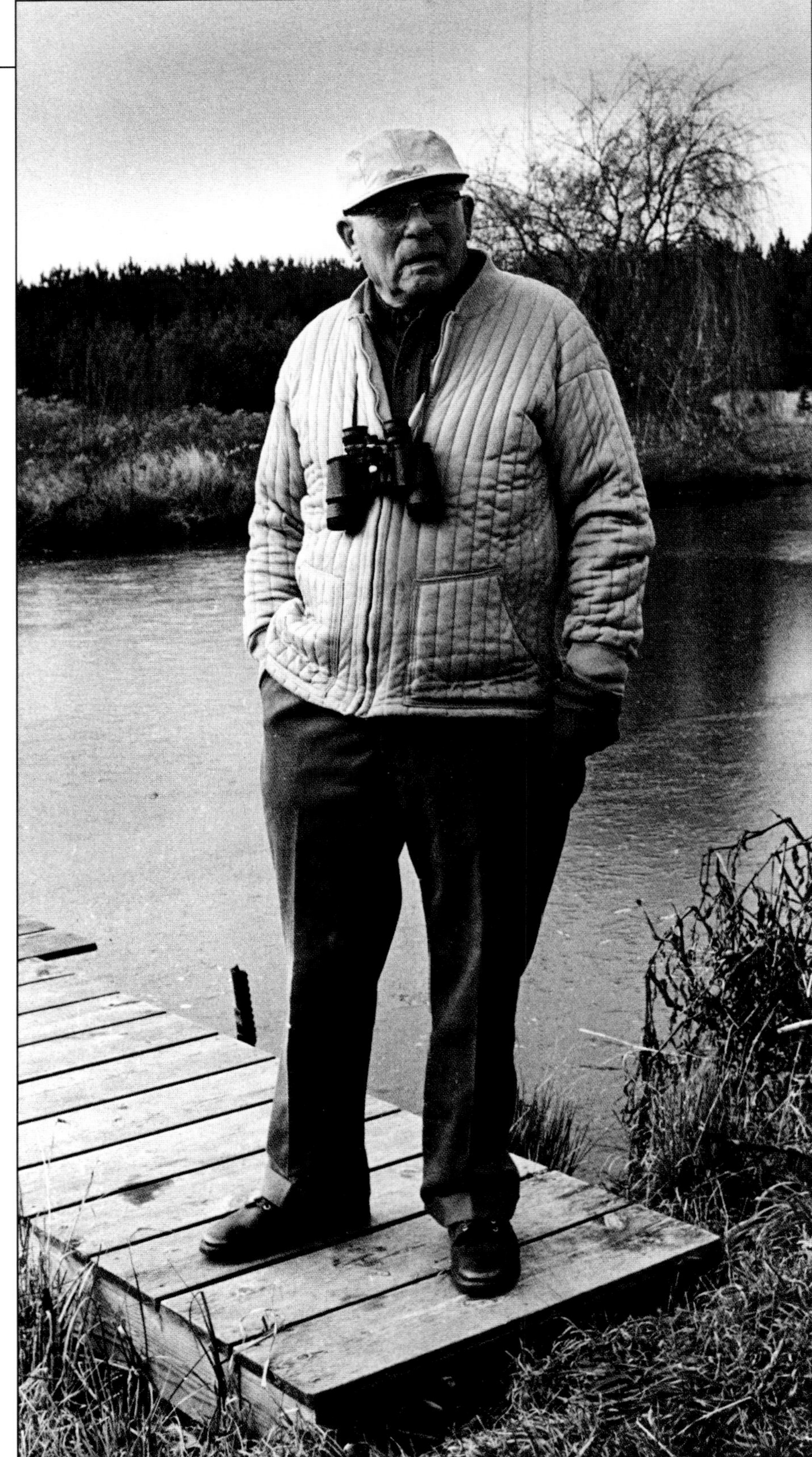

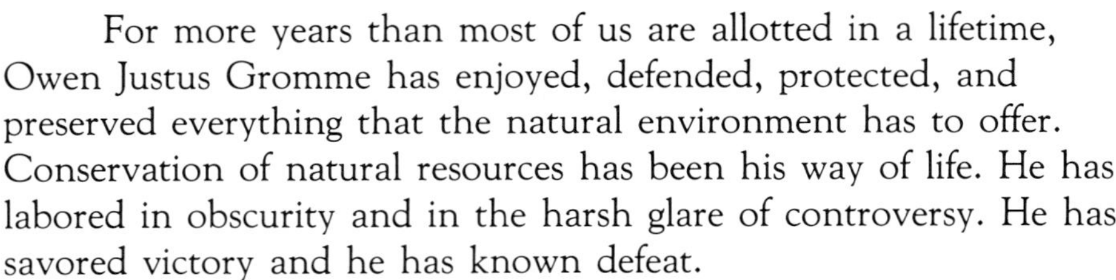

For more years than most of us are allotted in a lifetime, Owen Justus Gromme has enjoyed, defended, protected, and preserved everything that the natural environment has to offer. Conservation of natural resources has been his way of life. He has labored in obscurity and in the harsh glare of controversy. He has savored victory and he has known defeat.

Despite the setbacks, the frightening prospect of acid rain, the continued erosion of some of our nation's most precious topsoil, the threats to pure water, and the expanding list of endangered species, Gromme remains hopeful. He is convinced, much as he was in 1935, that education of the nation's young people will insure the preservation of our country's natural resources.

"If we are to save this fair land of ours," he contends, "conservation must be taught to the school children."

Pausing for a moment, he adds, "I like to reduce things to a few sentences, something easy to understand. If you think about it for a minute, it's all very simple. The next generation needs pure water and clean air. It's our job to make sure they have it."

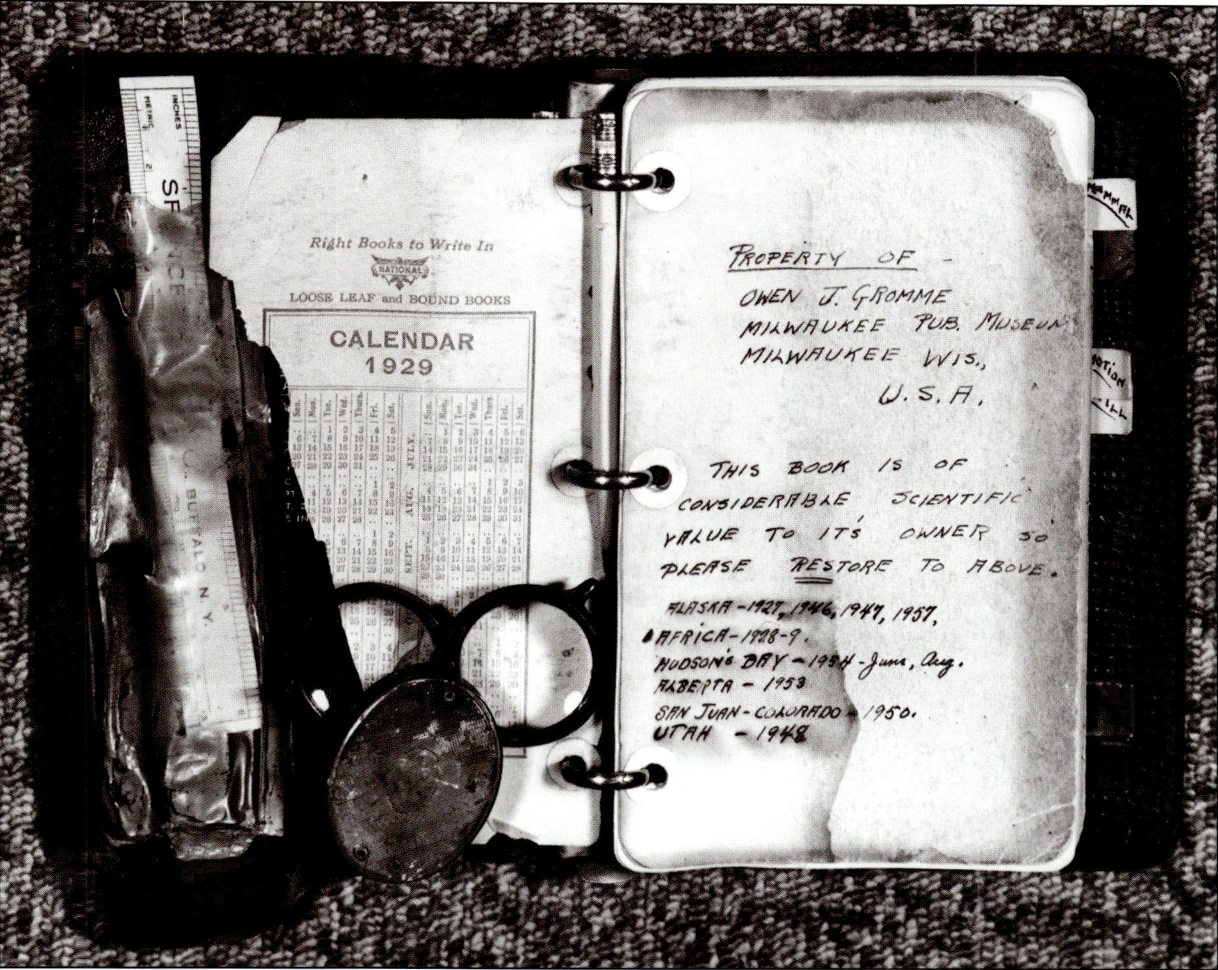

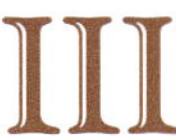

III

Pursued methodically and relentlessly over several miles of volcanic slag and grassy plain, the black rhino confounded its trackers by disappearing, unexpectedly, into the tangle of brush and the angle of the African landscape. Owen Gromme and his fellow Milwaukee Public Museum taxidermist I.J. Perkins followed as closely as they dared until they found themselves in a perilous situation — their visibility was suddenly restricted to no more than fifty feet by the sweep of a giant thorn tree; and somewhere in the rocky ravine beyond the trees and brush lurked an enraged rhino, a creature as unpredictable and dangerous as any on the African continent.

Silence closed in around them almost as thick as the impenetrable brush. Gromme could feel his heart pounding in his chest and hear his pulse thudding in his ears. Beads of perspiration on his face and back soon became trickles under the glare of the blistering Tanganyikan sun as he strained to detect any hint of movement in the tangle around them.

The breeze shifted slightly, and Gromme and Perkins noticed a thrashing in the brush to their left. Their rifles' safeties were off like a reflex action. In the next second, the cornered rhino, with the scent of its tormentors in its nostrils, charged the two men with its head down, looking like a runaway steamroller.

"We knew it couldn't see us," observed Gromme, "but it barreled down on us, leaving no doubt just what it had in mind."

In his *Field Notes* of October 20, 1928, Gromme chronicled the incident this way: "We were standing so that I was the only

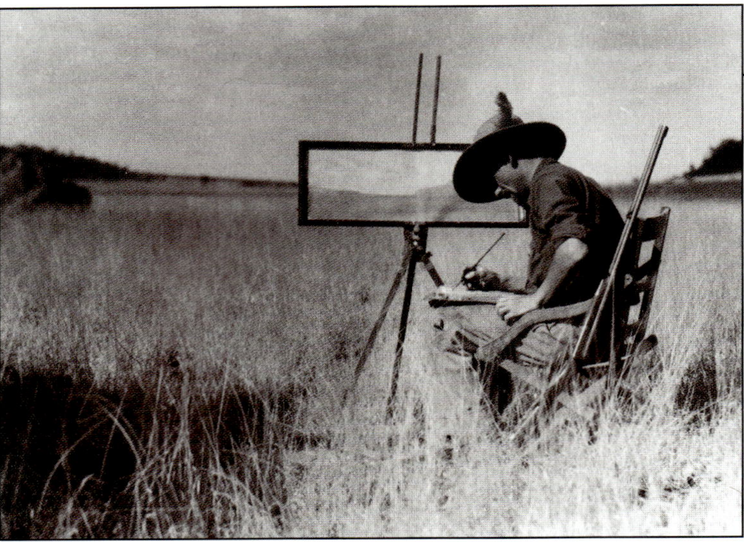

Gromme painting rhino background study — Serengeti Plain, Africa (1928).

one who could see the beast. With his head straight out, he came on. And when I realized he was only about fifty feet away, I tried to find a fatal spot to shoot, but the massive horn covered the vitals of the head. The next instant the rhino turned for Perk, who stood ready, but who could only see the animal's feet. I blasted the first barrel of the .470 into its shoulder. It spun like a top. Instantly I fired the second barrel into the right shoulder, knocking the rhino clear off its feet and sending it rolling like a barrel down the hill where it lodged against a six-inch thorn tree after rolling thirty feet."

Gromme, Perkins, their gunbearers, and guide breathed a collective sigh of relief, then commenced the arduous task of erecting a tarpaulin over the carcass, skinning, skeletonizing, salting the skin, making the necessary measurements of the animal, formulating color notes, and transporting it all back to camp for eventual shipment to Milwaukee where it would be re-assembled by the museum staff in a grouping.

Milwaukee Public Museum Director S.A. Barrett and taxidermists Gromme and Perkins spent eight months collecting specimens such as this and other data in Africa. In addition to the rhino, the East Africa expedition produced enough material for 44 mammal, 37 bird, and 10 ethnological groups. Long after Gromme, Perkins, and Barrett were back on the job in Milwaukee, the packing crates they had so carefully assembled in Nairobi, Kenya continued to arrive at the museum. In all, they collected 312 mammals, 1,390 birds, and thousands of artifacts from African tribes for use in museum displays.

Financed by contributions from staunch Milwaukee Public Museum boosters, along with funds raised by museum officials and staff members, the African expedition of 1928-29 was one of the most successful ever undertaken by museum employees anywhere.

"We were told by the Prince of Wales (later to become King Edward VIII of England until he abdicated the throne in 1936), who was in Africa at the same time we were, that we had obtained some of the best specimens ever taken out of that country," notes Gromme. "It was a tremendous undertaking for us."

And for the young taxidermist from Fond du Lac, Wisconsin, the eight months in Africa represented one of the most significant turning points in his life as well. Before the expedition was completed, Gromme would encounter a veritable menagerie of Africa's wildlife, hunt big game, develop the broad outlines of an art career, define more clearly his beliefs in conservation of natural resources, and survive an illness which was virtually incurable during that era.

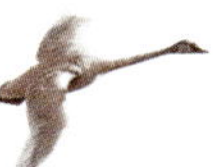

For Owen Gromme, the African trip marked the logical extension of a lifelong interest in nature and a devotion to his career as a museum taxidermist. He takes pride in the African trip in particular and his museum career in general, and refers to his former colleagues as a rare and talented breed entrusted with the mission of preserving the past.

Indeed, Gromme is a man of myriad skills, many of which he developed and refined during a career spanning more than four decades at the Milwaukee Public Museum. Some of his closest

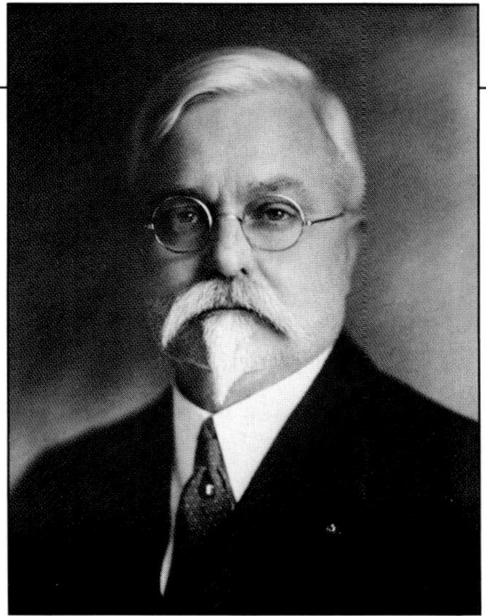

Milwaukee Public Museum Director S.A. Barrett, the motivating force behind the museum's African expedition in 1928-1929.

associates contend that his career as a museum taxidermist served as the foundation on which his fame as a wildlife artist was built.

"I have some very strong feelings about what a museum — especially a museum such as the Milwaukee Public Museum — should be," says Gromme. "Many of those feelings can be traced right back to the men who influenced me when I was first starting out."

The emphasis in Gromme's formative years focused on natural history, and early in his career he learned that a museum serves a powerful function as a bridge to the past and to the future.

"We have to preserve the past to create the future," says Gromme. "A museum, in my opinion, should serve as a storehouse of references to the past. It should link the past to the present."

Gromme never lost sight of that fact during his forty-three years as a public employee at the Milwaukee Public Museum. He demanded perfection from himself and those with whom he worked. "I knew the public was paying the freight, and I wanted to make sure they got their money's worth" is the way Gromme sums up his years of service.

The public got more than its money's worth out of Gromme. In the course of his career, he was shot by a fellow hunter, charged by a rhino, scarred by a goshawk, barely survived a bout with "black water fever" in Africa, overturned in his car twice on icy roads, weathered a hair-raising ride through Alaskan passes in a disabled plane, and endured the indignity of saddle sores.

Yet Gromme answers without hesitation that he "loved every minute of it."

Throughout his museum career, Gromme devoted himself to accuracy and a sense of exacting detail. As he worked to develop a museum group or to assemble a set of data for future reference, he was conscious of the fact that he was preserving a record for those who would follow.

"I can remember Dr. Barrett telling us that our notes and records were as important as the specimen itself," Gromme recalls, adding that "the specimens I collected and the mounts and groups I was responsible for are there forever for people to study and enjoy."

According to Gromme, he operated on two sets of principles during his long museum career. "I wanted to be able to show people the beauty of a bird or a mammal in an ecological setting, but I also wanted them to learn something about what they were enjoying. And from that I hoped they would gain a greater appreciation of that particular bird or animal's place in the scheme of things."

Those same principles manifest themselves in his wildlife paintings. He strives to present beauty, but there is more. "I want it to do some good," he insists.

"Above all else, Owen is a museum man," explains Frederick L. Ott, a close friend and associate. "His craft stems from his years there, and he got involved in all of those environmental causes because he was a museum man. His whole life centered around his years at the museum."

In retrospect, Ott's assessment seems accurate. For while

Owen and his esteemed colleague and friend Herbert L. Stoddard (foreground) as they observed bird life at St. Mark's refuge (Georgia) in 1958.

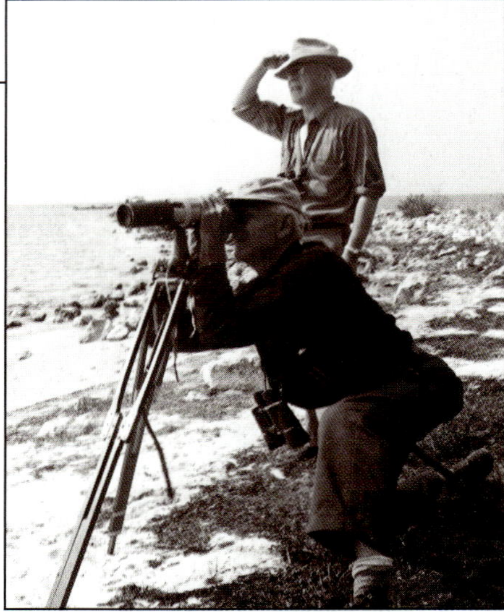

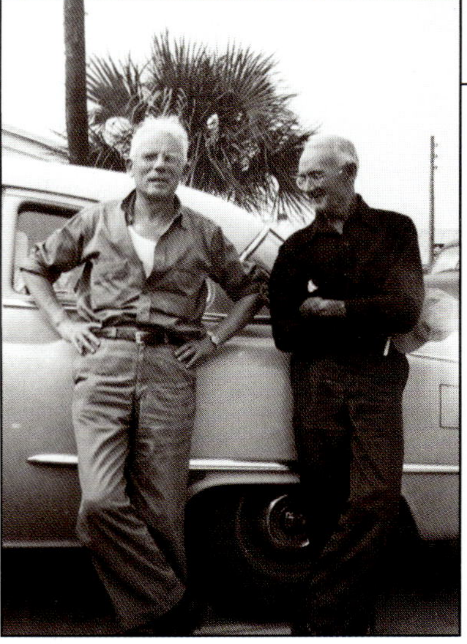

Gromme (left) and Stoddard at St. Mark's (1958).

Gromme's job demanded proficiency with a shotgun and skill as a taxidermist, it was the talented and devoted environmentalists with whom he was associated who channeled those pursuits in the proper direction. Milwaukee Public Museum Director Dr. S.A. Barrett was a prime example, stressing to his employees that conservation of natural resources was an integral part of their job. To be guardians of the state's resources, they had no recourse but to get involved. "I suppose you could say I became an environmentalist as part of my on-the-job training," contends Gromme.

Before Barrett, it was Herbert L. Stoddard Sr., a noted taxidermist and pioneer ecologist, who provided Gromme's training. Stoddard introduced the young Gromme to concepts of conservation, wildlife management, forestry management and preservation. And it was Stoddard who made him conscious of dwindling natural resources and encouraged him to learn the tools of the museum man's trade.

"To do the kind of work we did back then," Gromme recalls, "you'd have to be a jack-of-all-trades and damn near a master of them all. A good museum man must have a solid background as an all-around scientist, artist, carver, sculptor, lecturer, writer, photographer, cinematographer, bookkeeper, taxidermist, and hunter."

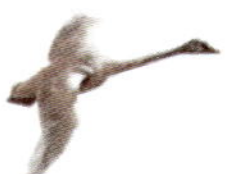

For Gromme, life as a museum man began in the summer of 1917 when he was hired as an assistant taxidermist at the N. W. Harris Public School Extension of the Field Museum of Natural History in Chicago. Ironically, five years later, while on his way to take a job as a candy salesman in Milwaukee, he detoured long enough to visit an old friend and instead of selling candy for a living, launched a museum career spanning more than forty years. On both occasions, it was Herbert Stoddard who played the pivotal role.

"There were three men who had the most influence on my life," explains Gromme. "First of all, there was my father. Then there was Dr. Barrett. And, of course, there was Herb Stoddard. They were great moral men in my life, all possessing a great force of character, mental stimulation, and massive integrity."

To know something of Herbert Stoddard is to know more about Owen Gromme as well. A former apprentice of famed Wisconsin River fur buyer, taxidermist, and outdoorsman Ed Ochsner, Stoddard was in charge, in 1917, of preparing small life-history groups of birds, mammals, reptiles, and amphibians at the Field Museum's Harris Extension. Seven years Gromme's senior, Stoddard was already an accomplished outdoorsman, ornithologist, natural scientist, and taxidermist when he and Gromme began working together.

Stoddard had received his training at the "school of hard knocks" under Ochsner's careful supervision, toiling as a hired man on a Prairie du Sac farm during the growing season and studying the art of taxidermy during the winter. Through Ochsner, Stoddard met Alfred Ringling and other members of the

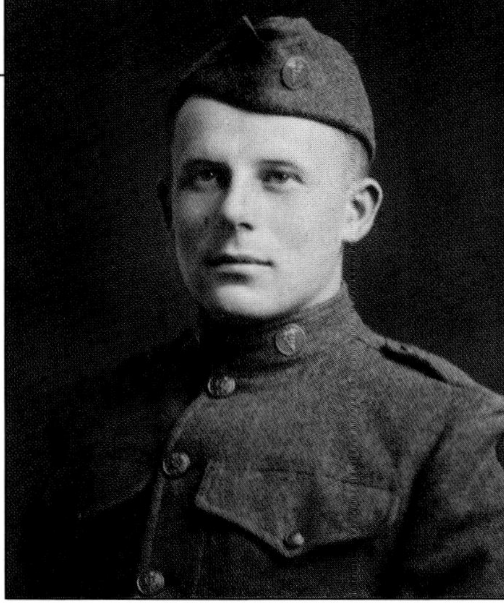

Owen Gromme, the soldier, pictured here prior to the World War I armistice (1919).

Ringling Brothers Circus which maintained its winter quarters at nearby Baraboo along the Wisconsin River. And it was through Ochsner and the Ringlings that Stoddard was introduced to George Shrosbree, chief taxidermist of the Milwaukee Public Museum.

Shrosbree was influential in the museum's hiring of Stoddard, and in March of 1910 the young farmhand became a Milwaukee Public Museum employee. After three years under the tutelage of Shrosbree, Stoddard left to take a position at the Field Museum in Chicago.

In the meantime, Gromme was learning the art of taxidermy in his spare time in the basement of his Fond du Lac home. Following his mother's unexpected death in 1911, Owen, at the age of 15, decided to quit school and work on developing his skills as an outdoorsman and taxidermist. It soon became apparent to the hunters of his hometown that the young Gromme possessed a special talent for taxidermy. His reputation began to grow in and around Fond du Lac.

Yet it was the arrival in town of Ed Ochsner, the living legend of the Wisconsin River Territory, that truly changed Gromme's standing as a fledgling taxidermist. A business acquaintance of Owen's father, Ochsner accepted an invitation to hunt and visit with the Grommes in the winter of 1914.

For Ochsner, it must have seemed like a classic case of *déjà vu*. In many ways, Gromme was the mirror image of Stoddard. Beyond the obvious fact that they shared an intense interest in the outdoors and wildlife, they were also alike in more subtle ways. Neither had finished high school — in fact, Stoddard had never begun — but they were dedicated, self-taught, and well-educated in the disciplines of natural science and the environment. They were curious, persistent, hard-driving, and analytical. And both seemed to thrive on hard work.

Not only was Ochsner impressed with young Gromme's abilities as a taxidermist, he was also amazed by the young man's proficiency with a shotgun. "We were hunting together on the flats outside of town when we suddenly jumped a couple of prairie chickens," Gromme remembers. Owen downed the birds with two cracks from his .20 gauge. Ochsner, recognized as one of the best rifle and pistol shooters in the Midwest, was flabbergasted by such shooting from a mere youth. As a result, a feeling of mutual admiration grew, cementing the association between the two. And just as he had encouraged Herb Stoddard to seek his fortune at a big-city museum, Ochsner convinced Owen Gromme to pursue a career as a "museum man."

Ochsner pointed out to Owen that Stoddard's old position as an assistant taxidermist at the Milwaukee Public Museum was still vacant and urged his young friend to apply for the job. But Gromme misunderstood him and ended up in the "wrong" place at the "right" time.

"Ochsner did a lot of talking about Stoddard and what he was doing down at the Field Museum," Gromme chuckles. "He was trying to tell me that I should go to Milwaukee and ask for Stoddard's old job, but I was all mixed-up. So I ended up going to the Field Museum in Chicago and meeting Stoddard in person. He hired me on the spot."

Stoddard and Gromme spent only a few months together at the Field Museum before the United States entered World War I, and each went his separate way into military service. Yet a bond had been established that would not be broken.

Years later, in his book, *Memoirs of a Naturalist*, Herb Stoddard himself would attest to this when he wrote: "Gromme and I were destined to become as close as brothers and to work as colleagues for many years."

Following the war years, Stoddard returned to his old job at the Field Museum, but Gromme, who had been wounded shortly after the Armistice while deactivating a mine, was not as fortunate. The small salary which the Field Museum was willing to pay him was simply not enough to cover the added responsibilities of caring for his father who had become an arthritic cripple while Owen was overseas. So, Gromme returned to Fond du Lac and took a job at the Fred Rueping Leather Co. It was dirty, grueling, back-breaking labor, but it paid more than the museum job. For a short time, he even sold Fuller brushes door-to-door and was employed by the Northern Casket Co. as a salesman of what he now calls "underground novelties."

Despite his day-to-day jobs, Gromme continued to hone his skills as a taxidermist, working in his basement workshop whenever he could find time. His career as a taxidermist would have ended there in the basement if it were not for Owen's lifelong friend, Fred Rueping, the son of the local tannery owner.

"I was working in the basement, pickling deer heads, and there was salt water on the floor which I had been using for my taxidermy work," Gromme recalls. "I reached above my head to turn on a light and when I touched the damn fixture I made one of the nicest electrical conductors you ever saw in your life."

Gromme slumped to the floor, pulling the fixture and the cord down with him. A few moments later Fred Rueping arrived, and, seeing no light in the basement, he immediately turned the light switch at the head of the stairs. Rueping believed that he was actually turning the basement light *on*, but in reality he was turning the light (and electrical current) *off*, thereby saving his friend's life. "If it hadn't been for Fred Rueping, I would have died right where he found me, right there on the basement floor," Gromme asserts.

It was the first of many times Gromme would brush with death in his years as a hunter and museum man. And while it was less spectacular than a charging rhino or a grizzly bear, it was no less frightening.

Late in 1921, Gromme received a call from Harry Johnston of the Robert A. Johnston Candy Co. offering him a job as a salesman. On his way to Johnston's, Gromme stopped at the Milwaukee Public Museum to visit his old friend Stoddard who had left the Field Museum in Chicago to take charge of the ornithology branch of the taxidermy department in Milwaukee.

Stoddard was stunned when he saw Gromme walk in the door. "Owen, how did you get here so fast? I just mailed the letter yesterday!" exclaimed Stoddard. An equally-surprised Gromme replied, "What do you mean? I'm in town about a sales job with Johnston's."

But the candy sales job was over before it began, and Gromme gladly took a position as an assistant taxidermist once again under Herb Stoddard's direction.

As a museum taxidermist and later as head of the department, Gromme participated in a variety of expeditions around the globe — Wisconsin, the western United States, Canada, Alaska, and Africa. But one of his most memorable field

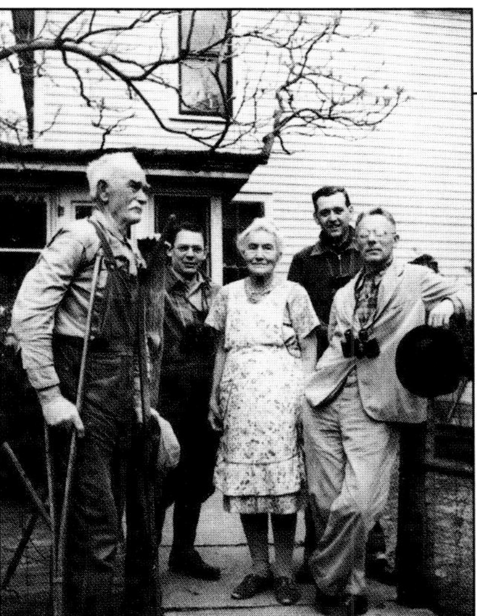

Gromme (far right with hat in left hand) paying one of his many visits to the home of Bert Laws (left). The group also includes (left to right) Clarence Jung, Mrs. Laws, and Phil Sander (1923).

trips occurred only a few months after he was hired.

In the early spring of 1922, he and Stoddard had decided to collect a "flying wedge" of Canada geese for display at the museum. At the time it was an ambitious undertaking because geese in Wisconsin were not in abundance then such as they are today at Horicon Marsh. In addition, the equipment necessary for such an undertaking was woefully inadequate by modern standards. Nevertheless, Gromme and Stoddard decided to try their luck at Lake Wisconsin near Prairie du Sac where Stoddard had learned taxidermy as an apprentice to Ed Ochsner.

"That goose-collecting trip was one of the roughest, most strenuous, and most frustrating trips I ever undertook," Herb Stoddard wrote in 1969. "Owen and I took all sorts of chances in old boats in dangerous waters made doubly treacherous by floating ice. It seemed that Mother Nature was on the side of the geese from the outset."

The geese, attuned to the movements of Stoddard and Gromme, foiled the hunters at every turn. They eventually enlisted the help of their mutual friend, Ochsner, and began working the sandbars of the Wisconsin River in the hope of collecting enough geese to complete the wedge group.

After scouting a couple sandbars frequented by large groups of geese, Gromme stationed himself in a long-abandoned goose blind constructed of railroad ties and driftwood. Ochsner chose to hunt in the heavy bottomland timber along the river not far from Gromme's sandbar blind; Stoddard headed downriver by boat. The plan, according to Gromme, was for Stoddard to position himself in the tall grass downriver and retrieve any of the Canada geese Gromme was able to shoot. The day wore on, but unknown to the hunting party, the flood gates at the hydroelectric dam ten miles upriver had been opened, and the treacherous Wisconsin River was rising fast. By the time Stoddard realized the seriousness of the situation, Gromme was clinging to the goose blind for dear life while Ed Ochsner, watching the river rise higher and higher, was torn with anxiety. He felt certain that Gromme would be swept to his death unless he attempted to swim for shore.

"I wedged an old bamboo pole into the blind and hung my binoculars and shotgun from it," Gromme recalls. "I was going to try to swim for it."

In the meantime, Stoddard was frantically trying to reach his friend, but the stalling outboard motor and raging current hindered his progress. He finally reached Gromme, snatched him from the submerged blind, and transported him across the river to Ochsner. The leaking boat was deemed unsafe for three passengers, so a soaking Gromme, clad only in his underwear and shoes, and Ochsner were forced to trudge along the prickly ash back to a nearby farm along the river.

All three were exhausted and irritable when they finally arrived at the home of Bert Laws overlooking the river. But to Gromme's amazement, the day wasn't over. After dinner, Stoddard motioned to his assistant, "Well, Owen, let's get these geese cleaned up before we call it a day."

Gromme remembers, "At first I couldn't believe my ears. After all we had been through, we still had to sit up half the night and skin those geese." He learned that night that it was a violation of the fieldman's code of ethics to leave any of the day's collecting until the next day.

Stoddard was an exacting taskmaster, but he provided "the

finest and most thorough training that a young field naturalist could have had," Gromme asserts. He shared his knowledge and his contacts with Gromme, taking his young assistant with him almost everywhere he went.

In fact, Stoddard introduced Gromme to the outstanding outdoorsmen of the day — men such as Albert Gastrow and Bert Laws — whom he regarded as "a rare and vanishing breed." Stoddard was convinced that men of their caliber were indispensable to the success of investigations of wary birds and animals. "Outstanding woodsmen are becoming extremely rare in the United States," he remarked, "and there can be no doubt that upon woodsmanship depends success or failure in such professions."

Through Stoddard, Gromme also was introduced to the techniques of some of the greatest taxidermists and naturalists of the era, including Carl Akeley, a onetime Milwaukee Public Museum taxidermist; Charles B. Cory of the Department of Zoology at the Field Museum in Chicago; Leon L. Waters and Leon L. Pray, Field Museum taxidermists; Charles Corwin, a master painter of museum backgrounds; and George Shrosbee, the man Stoddard described as his "incomparable teacher."

Long before he had been hired as a museum taxidermist in Milwaukee, Gromme had become familiar with the mastery of Shrosbee, spending hours admiring the man's contribution to the museum's collection.

"When I was just a kid," explains Gromme, "a friend of mine from Fond du Lac — Adelbert Bray — told me about the beautiful mounts he had seen at the Milwaukee Public Museum. So one day I decided I had to see them for myself. I was awestruck. The work was amazing to me, and I wanted to meet the man who had set up all those fine mounts."

Although Gromme did not know it at the time, the man he wanted to meet was George Shrosbree. But word was sent down to Gromme that the taxidermist was too busy to meet with him.

"I was crestfallen, and I never forgot it. And when I eventually became department head, I let everyone know that if they ever turned away a kid, they were through then and there, no questions asked. As far as I know we never turned away a kid while I was head of the department." In fact some of the "kids" whom Gromme refused to send away — C.P. ("Chappy") Fox and Frederick Ott — eventually played a key role in Gromme's later success as a wildlife artist.

In his first years at the Milwaukee Public Museum, Gromme was not only introduced to the rigors of expeditions and the art of taxidermy "Shrosbree-style," he also was put in touch with the science of bird banding. He joined Stoddard and Clarence Jung, an amateur Milwaukee ornithologist, in bird-banding missions in Milwaukee parks and along the Lake Michigan shore. Together they witnessed some of the largest hawk migrations in the state's recorded history.

During the early 1920s Stoddard became convinced that his newly-devised, bird-banding project would disclose some of the mysteries of migration routes and life histories of birds. And to his credit he was instrumental in convincing the others of the project's value. It was through this activity that Stoddard became associated with the embryonic bird-banding program of the U.S. Biological Survey. In 1924 he concluded his fourteen-year museum career and joined the Biological Survey in Georgia.

His new career in Georgia, however, did not mark an end to his acquaintance with Gromme. They remained lifelong friends, and Stoddard continued to exert his influence. Over the years, Gromme traveled several times to Thomasville, Georgia to visit him.

In 1940, for example, Gromme led an expedition to Stoddard's Sherwood Plantation in the hope of collecting a wild turkey group for display at the Milwaukee Public Museum. As a guest of Stoddard, Gromme and his fellow museum personnel were able to collect two toms, two hens, a southern pileated woodpecker, a hooded warbler and a cardinal. Today the specimens make up part of the museum's vast collection. And as an added benefit, Gromme was able to complete a detailed study of the wild turkey for future artistic reference. Two wild turkey paintings were among the Gromme works that were displayed in 1980 during the dedication of the Owen J. Gromme Special Exhibits Hall at the Milwaukee Public Museum.

In 1964 it was Stoddard's turn to visit his friend Gromme in Wisconsin. The two men returned to the Prairie du Sac area along the Wisconsin River where Stoddard had learned his trade and had spent years collecting specimens for display at the Milwaukee Public Museum.

It was the final year of Gromme's museum career, and the visit by Stoddard sparked fond memories of how it all had begun. In his *Field Notes* of May 21, 1964, Gromme wrote: "In 1922 I spent my first month as an employee of the Milwaukee Public Museum with Stoddard in the Prairie du Sac area. In retrospect those were golden days for both of us, and we reminisced about all those things and events that only an old-time taxidermist knows — the old workshop with its familiar smells, the companionship of simple folk who were wise in nature lore and tales, and the rainy afternoons we spent cracking butternuts and in conversation."

Today, Gromme refers to Herb Stoddard as the foremost ornithologist of Wisconsin in his day and one of America's most distinguished naturalists. Stoddard's book, *The Bobwhite Quail: Its Habits, Preservation and Increase*, once regarded as controversial, is recognized today as a classic in the field of wildlife management. Gromme ranks his mentor alongside Aldo Leopold as a giant in the annals of modern game management. "Stoddard's and Leopold's ecological ideas were very similar, and this close kinship of ideas shows up in the writings of both," wrote Gromme in his memorial to H.L. Stoddard in a 1977 edition of *The Passenger Pigeon*, the publication of the Wisconsin Society for Ornithology.

It was obvious to Gromme — and it became even more apparent to him as the years passed — that Herb Stoddard's influence upon him during those early years at the Milwaukee Public Museum helped to establish the course Gromme would follow throughout his forty-three-year museum career.

"To me the job of a civil servant involves complete and thorough dedication," Gromme points out. "I believe the people we elect or appoint to public office or who achieve prominence in a public job should set the example for other people. I tried to set a good example during my years at the museum."

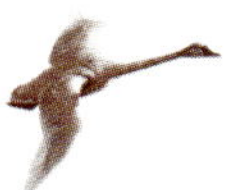

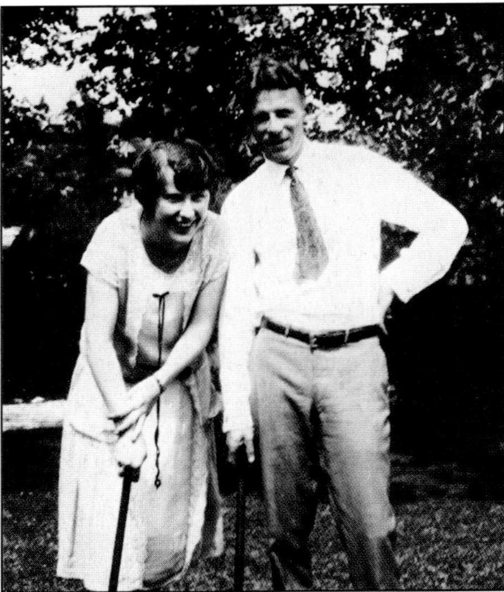

Anne Nielsen (left) and Owen Gromme during their courtship in 1925.

Owen Gromme on his honeymoon — photographed by Anne on Mamie Lake, Vilas County, Wisconsin (1927).

Long hours of work were a Gromme trademark in his early years at the Milwaukee Public Museum. He regularly studied textbooks on taxidermy and scrutinized the work of his colleagues in order to learn their techniques. And as the work day drew to a close for his fellow employees, Gromme was invariably engrossed in a project which would detain him for several more hours.

"In those days, they turned off the musem's electric lights at 10 o'clock, but they still had the old-fashioned gas lights, and there were plenty of nights when I worked by the light from the gas lamps," said Gromme. "So did Dr. Barrett. He often came back after everyone was gone so he could finish his work for the day without interruption."

Barrett was impressed by the energetic, ambitious young man from the taxidermy department, and he watched Gromme's progress with a sort of paternal interest.

"I really didn't have anything else to do or anyplace special to go," Gromme admits. "I wasn't married, and I liked the job, and I liked being around the museum."

In October of 1924 Gromme discovered yet another reason for spending as much time as possible at the museum. Her name was Anne Nielsen, a bright new employee in the Visual Education Division of the museum's Department of Education. A 1924 graduate of Milwaukee Normal School, a college for teachers, Anne's plans for a teaching career in high school biology changed abruptly before graduation when she was recommended by one of her professors for a position at the museum.

"I prepared material for slide programs for the Milwaukee schools," Anne recalls. "We wrote the narrative to match the slides which we selected as sets for a number of different topics. I learned more in that job at the museum than I did in my three years at Normal School."

Gromme was on a photographic expedition with Barrett at Isle Royal in Michigan's Upper Peninsula when Anne was hired, but he wasted no time in meeting her once he returned.

"All of a sudden this cocky guy appeared on the scene," Anne remembers with a chuckle. "Our slide department was in a little bitty place at the end of the fourth floor at the old museum, and there was a water fountain about halfway down the hall. At the other end of the hall was the Taxidermy Department, and before I knew it, Owen was floating down the hall to the fountain quite often, always managing to find his way down to our department."

To Anne Nielsen it was apparent her future husband was a persistent individual, and she was flattered by his obvious interest and his flair with the written word. "Owen's letters were really something," she said. "And he was so persistent!"

She added: "Owen was at that fountain so often and down at our end of the floor so much that Dr. Barrett finally reminded him that his department was down at the other end of the hall."

Slowly but surely Anne and Owen's relationship developed, and they began traveling with mutual friends on field trips to some of the popular locations in the Milwaukee area.

"I had always been interested in the outdoors, even as a young girl," she said. "I hunted and trapped with my older brother, and I was always more interested in what he was doing than what was going on in the kitchen."

Their mutual interest in the outdoors and environmental issues contributed to their interest in each other, and Gromme

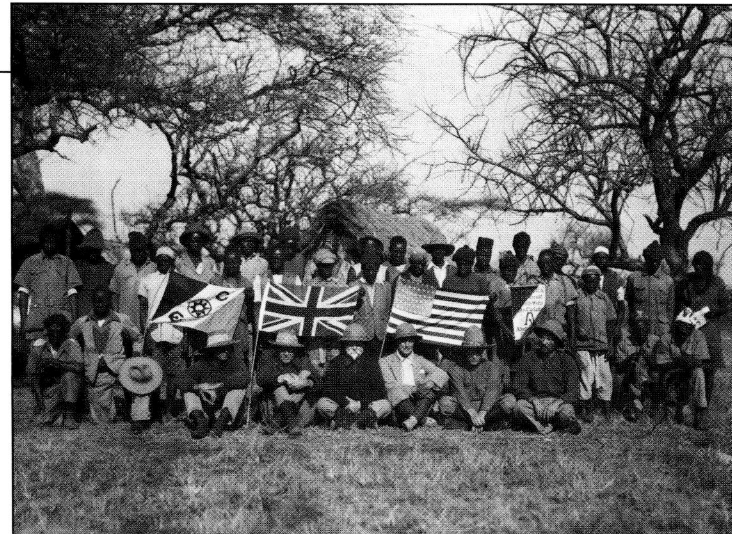

The expedition participants and their native assistants. This photo was taken by Gromme and includes the flags of (left to right) the Explorers Club, the Union Jack, and the U.S.A.

remembers that his long nights at the museum became less frequent. He soon introduced her to his family and friends in Fond du Lac, and she did the same in her hometown area of Briggsville in the "sand country" region of central Wisconsin. The setting captivated Gromme, and after they were married, her father's Briggsville farm became a frequent haven for resting, visiting, hunting, and testing the skills he would employ as a wildlife painter. In those early years, Anne and Owen had no way of knowing that they would someday own a home on the outskirts of Briggsville and spend their retirement years there creating a natural preserve on land once farmed by Anne's sister, Bertha Nielsen Hickethier, and her husband.

On September 5, 1927, Anne Nielsen and Owen Gromme exchanged their wedding vows in an outdoor ceremony beneath towering aged oaks just a mile and a half from their present-day home. It seems appropriate now fifty-six years after the event, that these two staunch environmentalists would pledge their love and respect for one another in an outdoor setting.

The wedding followed an especially active year for Gromme, Dr. Barrett, and the other natural history specialists at the museum. From May 1 to June 23, 1927, Gromme had devoted his energy to the John Cudahy-Osborne Goodrich-Milwaukee Public Museum Expedition to Port Moller and surrounding areas on the Alaskan Peninsula, the first of four treks by Gromme into the Alaskan wilderness. The journey yielded six brown bears, three emperor geese, ptarmigan, and valuable photography of bears and wildlife on the nation's last frontier.

On June 27, only four days after returning from the trip to Alaska, Gromme repacked his gear and departed with Barrett and fellow taxidermist I.J. Perkins to Pyramid Lake, Nevada to photograph and collect specimens of pelicans for the ever-expanding North American natural history groups at the museum. Described by Gromme as a "gem in the desert," Pyramid Lake introduced him to the rigors of photographing rookeries and other birdlife on rock ledges, an experience which would prove invaluable later.

It was during this expedition that Gromme and Perkins first learned that they would be members of the museum's massive African expedition. "We were camped out under the stars one night, just staring up into the sky, when Dr. Barrett told me I'd be going," Gromme recalls. "I didn't know what to say."

The Africa trip was Barrett's dream, his bedrock for future expansion and development of the Milwaukee Public Museum as one of the premier natural history institutions in the United States. Despite contributions and fund-raising efforts, financing for the expedition was extremely tight. Barrett was compelled to devise ways of attaining all the things he hoped to accomplish with the limited resources he had at his disposal. And from his colleagues, he was counting on skills in a number of diverse fields.

One of Barrett's most efficient and far-reaching decisions was to designate the dumbfounded Gromme as the museum artist for the expedition. Barrett knew he had a first-rate hunter, ornithologist, taxidermist, and photographer in Gromme, and he was confident that his young subordinate could do an adequate job with the sketches. What he had no way of knowing was that Gromme possessed an untested talent which would eventually establish him as one of the nation's greatest wildlife artists.

The expedition officially began in June of 1928, the

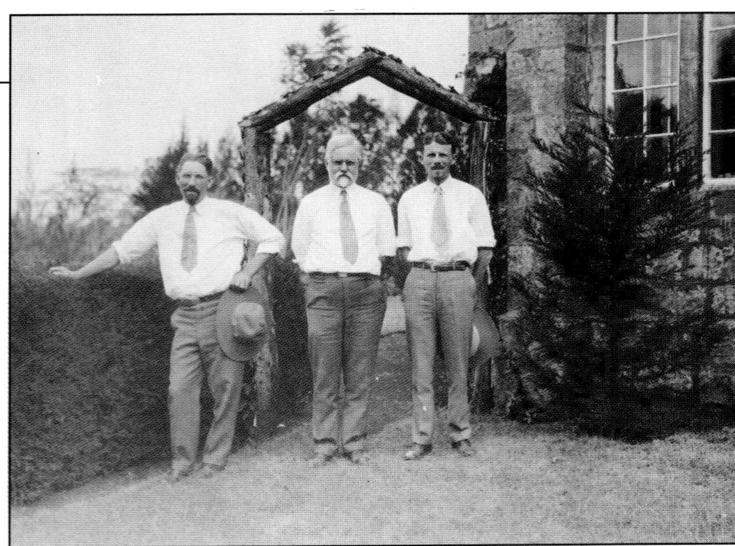

I.J. Perkins (left), S.A. Barrett and Owen Gromme at the home of Martin and Osa Johnson in Nairobi (1928).

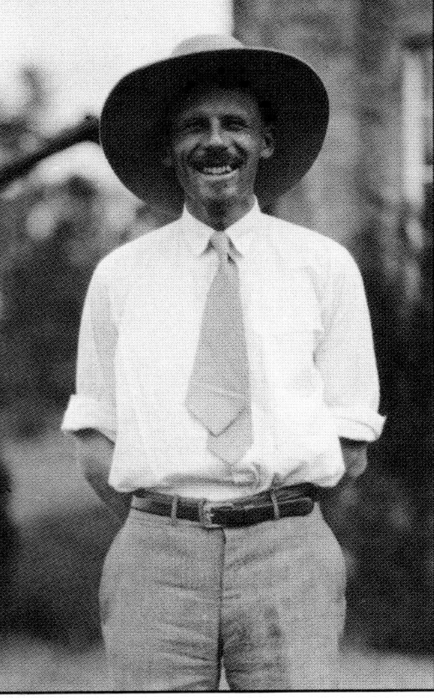

Owen Gromme at the home of Martin and Osa Johnson — Nairobi (1928).

culmination of years of planning and dreaming by Dr. Barrett. In several meetings with Carl Akeley, the "dean" of African collectors, Barrett had discussed the possibilities of someday acquiring a series of African environmental groups for display at the Milwaukee Public Museum. Akeley, the museum's first taxidermist, had encouraged Barrett in his dream for an African expedition.

On June 21, 1928, Owen Gromme became a key figure in Barrett's dream as they sailed from England to the Kenyan seaport of Mombasa on the Indian Ocean. It marked the beginning of a journey which spanned more than 35,000 miles in eight months and included 10,000 miles of bone-rattling travel in the wilds of Africa.

At Mombasa, the eager group boarded a train for Nairobi, headquarters for the expedition's African operations. There they became friends with Martin and Osa Johnson, an American couple famous for their work in photographing African lions. Gromme in particular developed a close friendship with the Johnsons. Their assistance proved to be "absolutely priceless," according to Gromme, as the Johnsons shared their knowledge and expertise with Gromme and Perkins, thus helping to save thousands of dollars in photographic expenses. And when they were not providing advice on photography, the Johnsons were busy fascinating the Fond du Lac native with tales of the massive herds they had seen migrating across the vast African plains.

Once the expedition's camp was established, it soon became apparent to Gromme and the others that the months in Africa would be busy and challenging. Not only was Gromme expected to take still and motion pictures, maintain detailed records, track, hunt, and kill lions, buffalo, zebra, antelope, and waterfowl; he also was obligated to make color notes of all the specimens and create background sketches and oil paintings of their habitat for reference in developing backgrounds for museum groupings. Once skinning and color notes were completed, Gromme was then responsible for providing comparative, anatomical-outline drawings of the physical structure of the bird or animal. Needless to say, the demands on him as the expedition's artist contributed a great deal to his growing knowledge about wildlife and natural history, not to mention his burgeoning talent for painting.

The accumulation of detailed records comprised only a small part of the overall job that consumed about sixteen hours or more of every working day. Gromme and Perkins spent countless hours searching for excellent specimens, singling them out of the herd or flock and hunting with rifle and photographic lens until they bagged or captured on film the birds and mammals that would constitute a representative sample of African fauna.

And for Gromme, the end of an exhausting day afield in searing equatorial heat would find him perched on a folding chair, brush in hand and a Ridgway color index at his side trying to capture the fleeting tones and colors of the African landscape before they faded into darkness.

Then, after many of his colleagues "turned in" for the night, Gromme would huddle in the glow of a tent lamp and record his observations for the day in his *Field Notes*.

Amid the velvet blackness of an August 1928 evening, Gromme recorded the setting of the safari camp this way: "In the bright reflected light of a car, all the animals appear to have brilliant electric lights on their faces. The bare spaces at the edge

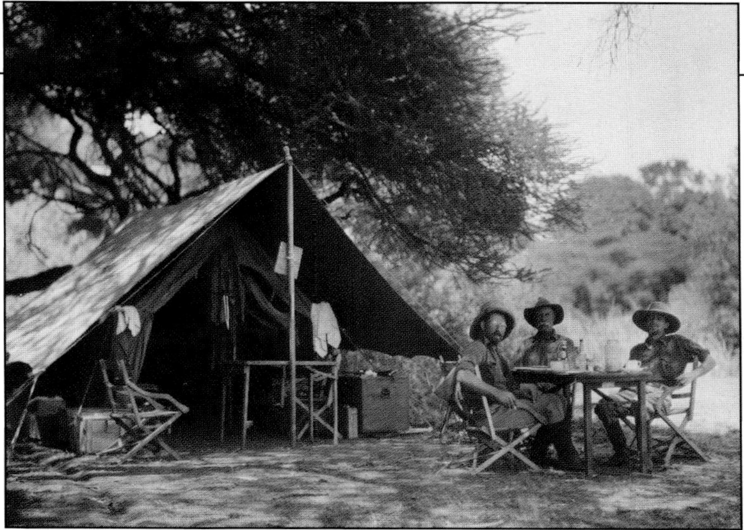

One of two Milwaukee Public Museum camps at Lake Manyara. Pictured left to right are: I.J. Perkins, Rudolph Dnaudee, a Boer guide, and Gromme.

of the donga fairly sparkle like so many fireflies."

The camp, which had taken shape in Nairobi through months of effort on behalf of the outfitter and Dr. Barrett, resembled a miniature city in itself. In addition to the 6,000 pounds of equipment transported from Milwaukee to Nairobi, the expedition consisted of forty native porters, skinners, truck drivers, and gun bearers, as well as tons of other paraphernalia needed to sustain a safari in the wilderness including eight still cameras, three movie cameras, five motion picture hand cameras, 60,000 feet of motion picture film, thousands of plates and film rolls for the still cameras, cooking utensils, fuel and oil, food, two distilleries for manufacturing pure water, tents, cots, mattresses, salt, plaster, formaldehyde, carbon bisulphide, and a myriad of other items necessary for preserving and packing specimens. And, of course, fine-mesh netting was an absolute necessity to ward off the attacks of mosquitoes, chiggers, and tsetse flies.

The expedition actually included four safaris during the eight months in Tanganyika (now Tanzania) and Kenya. The first safari pushed south 226 miles from Nairobi into the Saronia District of Tanganyika and the world famous Serengeti Plain. Collecting was carried on at a feverish pace, with Gromme and Perkins achieving an incredible rate of success.

"It was a lot of damn hard work," notes Gromme. "We were out at the crack of dawn hunting and photographing. We worked hard, and we were proud of the work we were doing."

But oftentimes it was a bone-wearying, lonely existence. Gromme pointed out in his *Field Notes* (August 20, 1928) the joy derived from letters he had received that day from his wife and his father. He wrote: "Unless one has been out in the blue, hundreds of miles from civilization, he can in no measure realize how cheering and eagerly sought are notes from the dear ones at home."

The safari to the Saronia District produced more than a host of bird and mammal specimens. While Gromme and Perkins were hunting, Barrett focused on the cultures of the African tribes. With the cooperation of tribal leaders, he was able to develop detailed exhibits of life in East Africa. For Gromme, the Massai tribe proved especially interesting. In retrospect it is easy to understand the wide-eyed amazement of a young man from a small midwestern town as he dined with Massai warriors on the veldt of Africa. His *Field Notes* reflect this:

"They were smeared with paint from head to foot with curious designs on their legs and bodies. Some wore headdresses of ostrich feathers and others of babboon fur. Soon the dance was on; it was the war dance. It started with all the men in a squatting position on their haunches. A faint murmur arose which grew in intensity to a weird chant. No drums were used, but the men rose one after the other and started moving slowly forward. The leader went through the motions of chopping down the enemy with a hand axe. Finally, all were doing a dance of menacing motions. . . .

"Suddenly, the sun came out brilliantly. Words could not describe the splendor of the spectacle. Women and children were shimmying, and as the sunlight played on the dangling array of fancy headdresses of the men, it almost made me dizzy to look at it — all of this in the most beautiful setting of euphorbia trees and grass huts."

Prodded by the rains of late September, the caravan

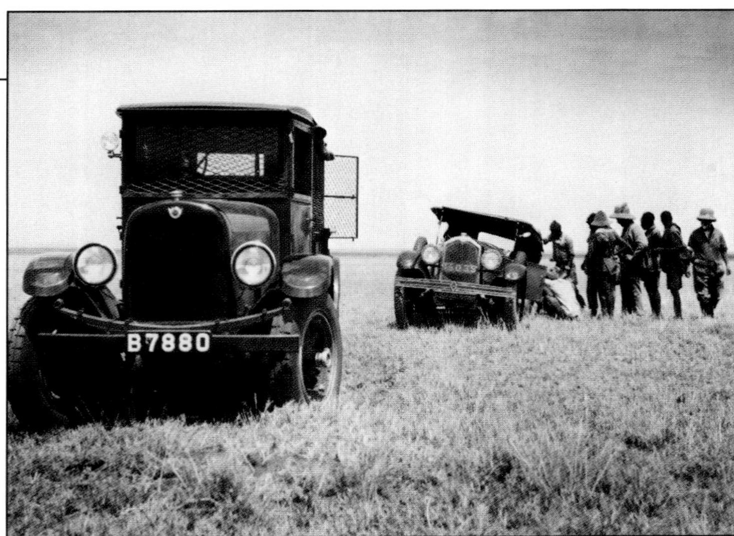

Problems were ever-present during the expedition — here one of the safari cars breaks down on the Serengeti Plain.

returned to its headquarters in Nairobi to pack skins and to prepare for the second safari of the expedition. In mid-October of 1928, the caravan again headed south, this time into the land of snow-capped Mount Kilimanjaro, the vast alkali flats of Lake Manyara, and the world of the rhino and the flamingo.

For Gromme the six weeks in the land 600 miles south of Nairobi produced adventures that few ever experience. The journey itself served as a foreshadowing of the excitement ahead. With Kilimanjaro to the east, the safari plunged into the volcanic ash at the base of Mount Meru. Creeping along at a snail's pace with visibility at near zero, the eight engines of the caravan whined in the night as they labored in second gear.

"We couldn't see anything," said Gromme. "We could hardly breathe, as a matter of fact." Then, through the billowing dust, Gromme spied the unmistakable glow of a veldt fire, one of the most terrorizing phenomena of the African plains.

"We knew we couldn't go back. Our only hope was to try and outrun it," Gromme remembers. Drivers pushed their vehicles to the limit as they searched for an escape from the onrushing flames. But shouts from the lead car sent hearts racing as the caravan ground to a halt with the fire only a little more than a hundred yards away. The gasoline supply truck was disabled against an embankment, and the safari's only hope was to load the supplies onto the remaining vehicles and push ahead. Delay would mean disaster.

Yet the African landscape allowed escape as quickly as it had produced danger. Beyond the embankment that had snared the gasoline truck lay an expanse of grassless donga which afforded an island of safety in a sea of flames.

Once camp was established in the Lake Manyara region of northern Tanganyika, attention was focused on cape buffalo and rhino. On October 28, 1928, after tracking a rhino over three miles of grassland, gravel and rock, Gromme and Perkins pursued the beast into a ravine camouflaged by thorn trees. There, Gromme completed the rhino group with two perfect shots.

With the rhino group finished, Gromme turned to the massive flocks of flamingoes that inhabited the alkaline waters of Lake Manyara. He was determined to photograph the birds at close range and take a number of the species for a detailed museum exhibit. With time slipping away, Gromme decided he would approach the flock on foot by way of the shallows which extended miles into the lake.

Several attempts proved fruitless, and during the final effort, Gromme and his associates were forced by high winds and a driving rain to flee for their lives. Hampered by the suction of the mud and the weight of his boots, Gromme pulled them off and plodded on in his stockinged feet, never thinking what effect the alkaline water might have on his skin. The exhausted band eventually made it to shore, but already Gromme was in great pain. When he examined his feet and legs, he noticed that they were "a mass of open round sores which made my legs appear as though they were peppered by buckshot." Yet despite such miserable conditions, Gromme and Perkins had been able to collect four excellent flamingo specimens, shoot 500 feet of movie footage, and take a dozen photos.

In the days following the Lake Manyara adventure, Gromme nursed the blistered sores and concentrated his efforts on background sketches. Ever watchful of the weather and his companions, Barrett decided in late November to take no chances on the rainy season. He ordered a return to Nairobi where specimens could be packed and Gromme could obtain medical attention. Here he was confined to the Kenya Nursing Home for a week before being sent to Mombasa on the Indian Ocean to recuperate. He remained there until January 8, 1929 while his colleagues journeyed into the Cherengani Hills of northwestern Kenya. It was a trying time for him not only because he was anxious to resume his work in the field, but also because he was far from home at a time of the year when families and friends are closest.

On January 8, Gromme hurried to meet Barrett and Perkins at Lake Nakuru northwest of Nairobi, never dreaming that he was about to begin a life and death struggle with one of Africa's tiniest but most deadly creatures the Anopheles mosquito. After only seventeen days in the field following his recovery from the alkali infection, he began exhibiting the classic symptoms of malaria. Barrett and Perkins had departed camp to finish work in another locality at the time Gromme was stricken. When he had left, Barrett had instructed Gromme to meet him in Nairobi at the end of the month.

"I knew something was wrong with me, but I didn't think it was serious enough to pack up," said Gromme. Indigestion and nausea persisted, and when his temperature plunged far below normal, he knew he was in trouble. Then Chombo, one of the men in charge among the natives, told Gromme that he looked just the way Mr. Akeley (Carl Akeley of the Milwaukee Public Museum) did the night before he died in 1926.

"When I heard that, I ordered them to get everything packed, and quick," said Gromme. "My only thoughts at the time were that the specimens and equipment should get to Nairobi and that I should find someone who could help me."

Within eight hours of his arrival at the hospital in Nairobi, Gromme's urine was the color of iodine, the tell-tale symptom of black water fever, a complication of malaria. At the time, black water fever was virtually incurable, so the hospital staff prepared him for the worst. "They told me my chances were slim, and I told them I had a bride and an invalid father back home and I'd be damned if they were going to bury me there," recalls Gromme. "I was determined to survive, no matter what they said."

In his *Field Notes*, he wrote: "I was not allowed to move. My skin had turned yellow with jaundice, and I was little more than a skeleton."

Gromme attributes his miraculous recovery to a chance meeting with the late Dr. George Crile, a renowned surgeon of the 1920s from Cleveland, Ohio, whom he met on the first leg of the African voyage from New York to London. Dr. Crile instructed Gromme and his colleagues to refrain from taking quinine *until* they had first contracted malaria.

"It used to be customary for people entering Africa to stuff themselves with quinine," Gromme explains. "But this brings about a condition where the ever-present malaria germs in the system are brought to a quiescent state until the general health of the victim is lowered by residence in the tropics. Finally, once the first real attack of malaria comes, additional quinine doses have no effect, and the disease becomes chronic. The latest way, as proven, is to take no quinine until after the malaria is first contracted. Crile had convinced us to try his method, and if I

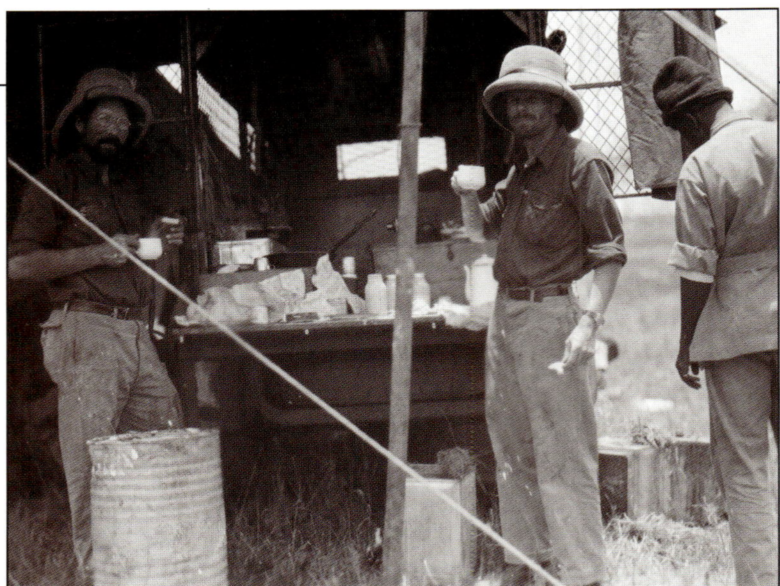

I.J. Perkins (left) and Gromme (right) at the back of a safari wagon in Africa during the Milwaukee Public Museum's 1928-1929 expedition.

hadn't, I would have been dead more than fifty years ago."

Dr. Barrett managed to get fresh milk for the recovering Gromme every day and took him out daily in order to acclimate him for the 1,000-mile return voyage to the headwaters of the Nile. Meanwhile, oblivious of the struggle her husband was going through, his wife Anne, who was working at the museum at the time, anxiously awaited word from the expedition. "Dr. Barrett never notified any of us," she said, "and I believe that was for the best because it might have caused us more worry."

Anne met her husband in New York, and quickly realized that he had endured a trying ordeal. "Owen had an attack while we were coming back through Chicago," she remembers. "We wasted no time getting him home."

Owen Gromme had undergone a transformation during his eight months in the wilds of Africa. His skill as a hunter and taxidermist had always been acknowledged, but now his talent with a brush and his eye for recreating a setting also demanded recognition. As a member of the highly successful museum expedition, he had gained an incalculable measure of confidence in his own ability, not to mention the wealth of knowledge about birdlife and animals and their interrelationship with the forces of civilization.

And even beyond those discoveries, Owen Gromme must have been happy and thankful just to be alive, considering his most recent scrapes with the grim reaper.

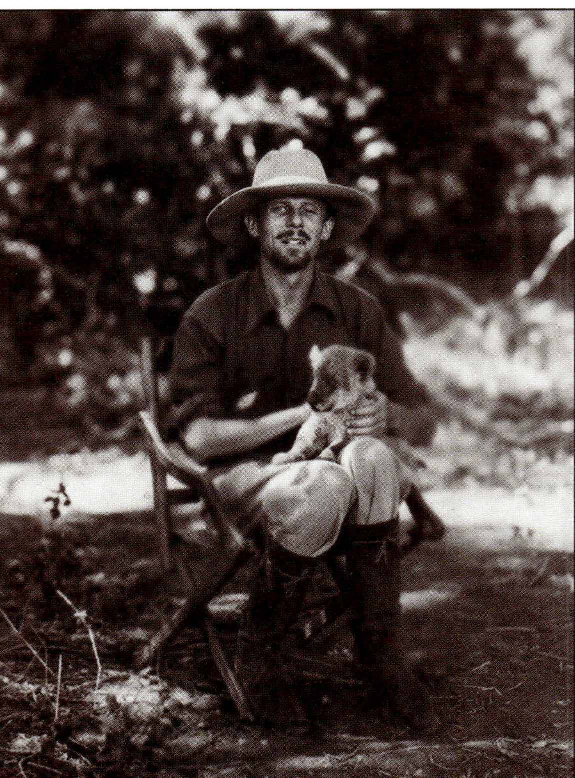

Gromme and safari's pet lion "Simba" near Tanzania (1929). Gromme's drooping visage is due to the fact that he had just contracted malaria.

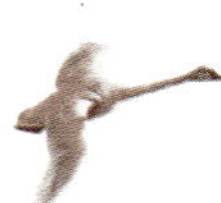

The stock market crash of October 1929 and the Great Depression marked the end of an era in America, and the Milwaukee Public Museum and institutions like it were forced to absorb the shockwaves of change. The money that had been available for expeditions only a few years earlier disappeared. It was not until 1946 that Milwaukee Public Museum employees would again embark on journeys to the world's great frontiers.

As a result, Gromme and his colleagues confined their efforts to the more familiar territories of central and northern Wisconsin. His favorite collecting grounds included the Bar Creek area north of Milwaukee along Lake Michigan, the boyhood hunting grounds around Lake Winnebago and Eldorado Marsh, Lake Mason near Anne's hometown of Briggsville, the Wisconsin River region near Baraboo and Prairie du Sac, and, of course, Horicon Marsh, the scene of some of Wisconsin's most stirring environmental battles.

But being "confined" to Wisconsin had its positive side too. In May of 1934, for example, Gromme and taxidermist Walter Pelzer were able to photograph the first recorded nesting of the northern goshawk in Wisconsin. Notified of the event by Frank Zirrer of Rusk County, Gromme and Pelzer loaded all the necessary photo equipment into a car and wasted no time traveling to the northwoods. They spent several days building a blind high in an adjacent tree and photographing the nestful of young hawks. Yet before their work was complete, both Pelzer and Gromme were forced to don turbans and helmets to withstand the fierce attacks of the adult goshawk. Years later, Gromme would recreate the scene in a striking painting of goshawks and their young nestled high on a northwoods perch.

Throughout the 1930s Gromme's efforts alternated from taxidermy and natural history groupings to environmental concerns at Horicon Marsh and training of potential museum employees in the Milwaukee Public Museum's WPA Project, one of the many programs of the "New Deal" designed to create jobs for the jobless.

"It took a hell of a lot of our time," says Gromme, "but it gave those people gainful employment and put food on their tables. And, in turn, we learned from them and they learned from us."

At one point there were as many as 300 people involved in the museum project, including unemployed artists, artisans and craftsmen who provided a wealth of talent and experience at a time when their gifts easily could have been wasted.

"Our department, in particular, made good use of those talented people because we were in the process of building all those large bird and mammal groups at the time," Gromme observes. He worked with several bird artists to develop murals and backgrounds for many of the groups which were collected in Africa and Wisconsin. "In the process, we developed some fine museum artists," said Gromme.

In addition to the artists and craftsmen who found their way to the museum in the 1930s, there were also several young men who arrived on the scene simply because they were interested in the marvels of the museum — just as Gromme had been as a "kid." Three of the most influential of these young men were Walter Pelzer, who later became a friend, an "in-law," and a museum colleague for thirty-three years; Frederick L. Ott, who was among those who were instrumental in having Gromme's

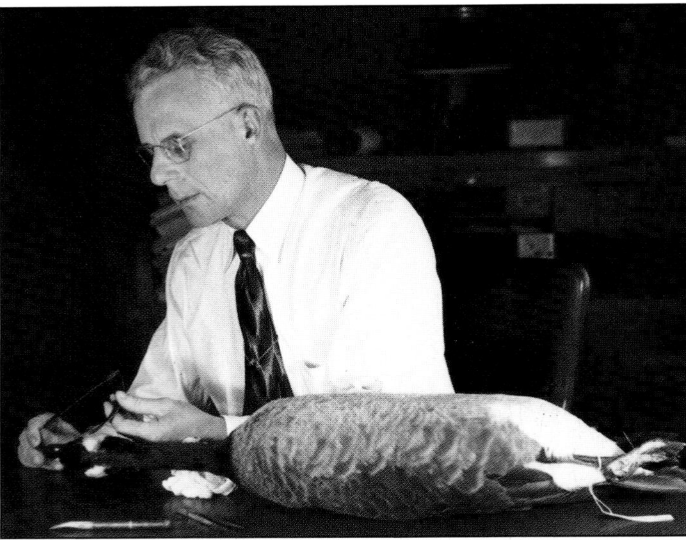

Gromme at work in the Milwaukee Public Museum (1945), measuring the skin of a Canada goose.

Birds of Wisconsin published in 1963; and "Chappy" Fox, who became the first director of the Circus World Museum at Baraboo, Wisconsin and who made it widely known that O.J. Gromme was not only a talented museum man, but also a first-rate wildlife painter.

Walter Pelzer came to the museum in 1932 after working in his Fort Atkinson, Wisconsin, hometown as a sculptor, taxidermist, and naturalist. Dr. Barrett, who had once detected the raw, natural ability of a museum man in Gromme, also sensed in Pelzer a "real diamond in the rough." "I can't hire you," Barrett told Pelzer, "but I can put you to work."

Pelzer could not afford the $1.50 a week for a downtown room, so he lived in a walled-off corner of the taxidermy studio, washing dishes in Wisconsin Avenue restaurants to pay for his meals. All the while, he watched and learned. When an opening became available, he stepped in to become a permanent Milwaukee Public Museum employee.

"Anne and Owen were really good to me," says Pelzer of his first months at the museum. "They invited me to their home quite often, and when they had to go out of town, they always asked me to stay and watch the house. I guess you could say they treated me like family."

And it wasn't long before Pelzer was a full-fledged member of the family. "They played Cupid," Pelzer chuckles. "They made sure Florence and I met and got to know each other . . . and the rest is history."

Florence Bush became Mrs. Walter Pelzer and a ready source of information about the exploits of Owen Gromme, her Fond du Lac cousin.

"Florence's mother practically raised Owen," notes Anne Gromme. Owen's mother died while he was in high school, and Meta Bush and her husband, Leslie, moved into the Gromme home to help take care of Owen, age 15, and his sister Mary, age 7. They stayed on as the years passed to care for Owen's father "Gus" when he became crippled by arthritis.

Pelzer and Gromme worked together for thirty-three years, accompanying each other on a number of major expeditions and leaving an indelible mark on their place of employment. He credits Gromme as being a "first-rate bird taxidermist, a person with great natural ability." Gromme returns the compliment by attesting that "Walter Pelzer is one of the best, maybe he is the best, mammal taxidermist in the world."

Gromme was not a difficult person to work for or with, according to Pelzer. "He gave me free reign. But that doesn't mean we didn't have disagreements from time to time," Pelzer adds. "He was always very loyal to his people, but he would chew the hell out of you if he felt there was cause for it."

One of Gromme's greatest talents, in Pelzer's estimation, was his ability "to get the ball rolling and then keep it going." He points to Wisconsin's legislation to protect herons and birds of prey and the Milwaukee Public Museum's numerous collecting trips as examples of Gromme's unique abilities.

"He was a master at it," Pelzer recalls. "We made several trips, and it seemed like we always needed a sponsor or a donation to get it going. Owen would always go out and get what we needed!"

For Pelzer, the post-World War II expeditions to Alaska and the Southwest rank among his fondest memories in his forty-year

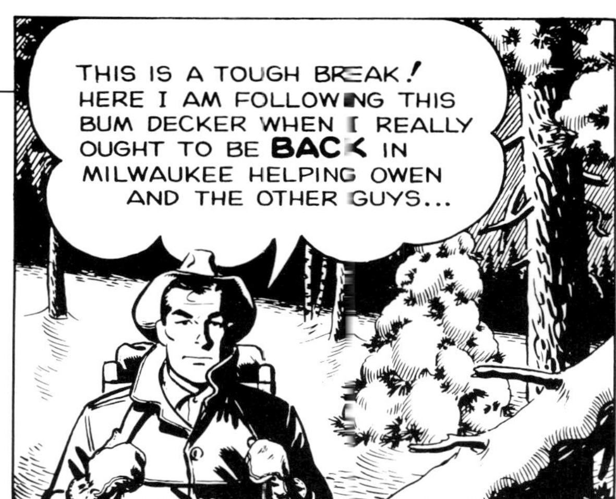

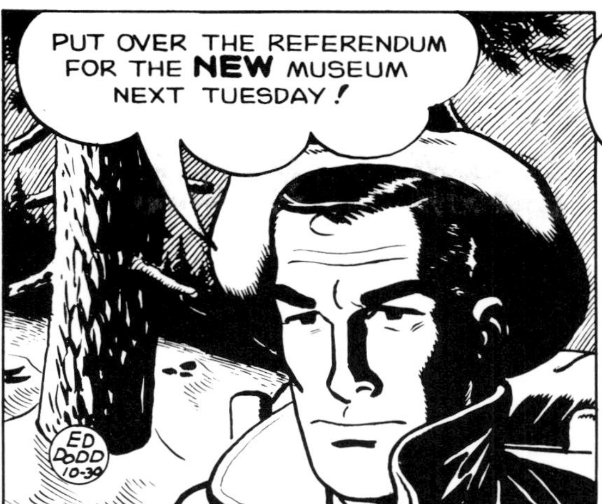

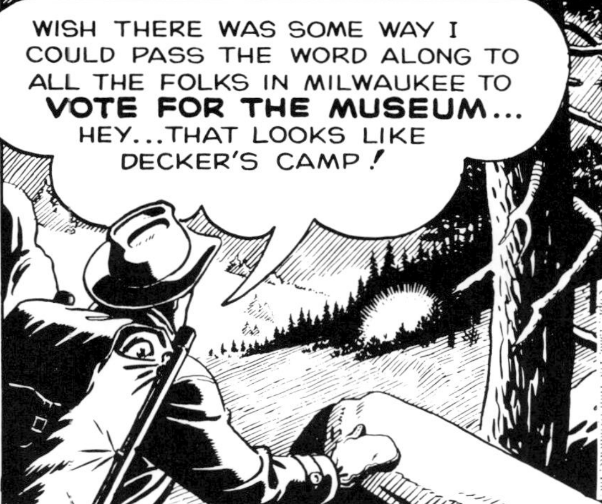

Ed Dodd's famous "Mark Trail" comic strip of October 30, 1956 depicting his hero's concern for the Owen Gunn (Gromme) supported referendum for the new Milwaukee Public Museum.

Round Mountain and traveled several miles up a broad valley through which runs Canyon Creek. From a willow-grown hill overlooking Canyon Creek they saw what they were after — a herd of moose far up the valley.

"The stalk began. The wind was in their favor most of the way, though one can never be sure of the shifting winds in the mountain country. When they were within 150 yards of the scattered herd they saw what was going on. One big bull moose had appropriated four cows for a harem and six other bulls were hanging around, afraid to come close.

"Gromme, weary and breathing hard from exertion, had planned to remove his pack frame and shoot deliberately but forgot the pack was on his back. When within range, he had Branham size up the bulls carefully and agreed the harem boss was the one they wanted.

"The distance was 150 yards or better and it was an uphill shot. Gromme's first shot from the .30-'06 struck the bull perfectly on the shoulder. Low down, it pierced the heart. Another shot landed higher up on the shoulder. The big fellow sagged and trembled. Two more shots went through the dewlap and through an antler, but the big fellow's time was up when that first one hit him."

It was at that point that the real work began. Gromme and Pelzer skinned and butchered the moose and prepared for the exhausting trek back to camp. They took turns carrying the massive antlers and equipment in addition to the packs of meat as they lumbered back to camp.

As usual, the expedition was marked by another of Gromme's close calls. On a side trip from Anchorage to Port Heiden on the Alaska Peninsula, Gromme, MacQuarrie, and Diedrich experienced a foreshadowing of the treacherous Alaskan weather that makes air travel there so dangerous and unpredictable. Piloted by Bud Branham, the plane was forced to fly at an extremely low altitude to avoid icing. On the return trip to Anchorage, Branham encountered some of the worst flying conditions of his career.

"We all just hung on," recalls Gromme. "To go up meant fatal ice. To go down, a crash. To go ahead, a deep gray pall."

Branham, who had been through the Lake Clark Mountain Pass hundreds of times, peered into the blur hoping to locate some landmark. After a prolonged silence, he was finally able to pick up the faint signal of the Anchorage airport. Once on the ground, two mechanics from the amphibian operations hangar ran out to the group and the first thing one of them said to Gromme was, "Brother, how would you like to kiss the ground." A cursory examination of the plane revealed that the antenna was frozen and the air speed indicator was full of ice. The group had been flying at full throttle all the time and did not know it!

In his final expedition to Alaska, and his last as an employee of the Milwaukee Public Museum, Gromme arranged a trip to gather Dall sheep for another of the North American groups. In all, the expedition netted five rams, two ewes, and a lamb.

But not all Gromme's expeditions were successful. One in particular — the spring 1948 mountain lion hunt in southwestern Utah — was especially frustrating. There, Gromme and Pelzer tracked and hunted mountain lions without success amid the scorching Utah heat. Each day was like the one before, and the two men — so accustomed to success in the field — were forced to admit defeat.

On a later trip — the June 1950 photographic expedition on the San Juan and Colorado Rivers — Gromme's artistic perceptions were evident. Armed with cameras, Gromme and Walter Pelzer, his longtime colleague and traveling companion, and Robert Uihlein Sr., the sponsor of the expedition, joined a group for a rafting adventure on the river. The region represented a true wilderness area in every sense of the word, and Gromme's artistic senses were dazzled by the extraordinary landscape.

As he approached Monument Valley near Mexican Hat, Utah on the San Juan River, Gromme recorded this observation in his *Field Notes:* "Toward evening, as we suddenly topped a rise, there arose before us the incomparable panorama of Monument Valley. From there on into Mexican Hat the great rock spires of grotesque shapes, buttes, and mesas appeared and unfolded one of the most stupendous and awe-inspiring views on the North American continent. I can understand now the terrific inspiration that motivated our great western painters to do their masterpieces. The beauty at sunset, with the natural red of the rocky formations being enhanced and intensified by the last fiery glow of the setting sun, is overwhelming."

Yet for Gromme, the inspiration that stimulated his desire to recreate the environment of his midwestern homeland took root not in the fiery glow of a sunset, but in the more subtle tones of his career as a natural scientist devoted to the causes of the environment.

"I was a museum man, first and foremost," says Gromme. "I was a curator of birds and mammals, and it was my responsibility to supervise that department. I didn't let my other interests interfere with that."

In one instance, though, Gromme did allow his interest in art to "interfere" with his career as a museum man. During the years that he served as director of the *Milwaukee Sentinel's* Wildlife Art Exhibition, he became acquainted with Ed Dodd, a nationally syndicated cartoonist who produced the "Mark Trail" comic strip. Impressed with Gromme's credentials and his abilities as an outdoorsman, Dodd decided to add a new character to his strip who would accentuate environmental themes. That character was Owen Gunn, a museum taxidermist with a heady knowledge of the outdoors. Any similarity to Owen Gromme was expressly intended.

Owen Gunn became a frequent character in the "Mark Trail" series from August 30, 1956 to February 17, 1957. In one of the episodes Dodd urged Milwaukee voters to approve the referendum for a new Milwaukee Public Museum building. Even though the comic strip was not presented in the Milwaukee papers that day, local voters supported the referendum, and a new museum was completed in 1963, about a year before Gromme retired.

The appeal of a full-time art career and his persistence in the museum-sponsored *Birds of Wisconsin* project intensified as the sunset of his museum career loomed on the horizon. More and more, Gromme's spare time was being devoted to painting and the development of his artistic skills.

"I had been working on *Birds of Wisconsin* for over twenty years," said Gromme. "The museum backed me, especially Mr. McKern (Museum Director William McKern). And people like 'Chappy' Fox and Fred Ott did everything in their power to make sure it got published."

Birds of Wisconsin was published in 1963, coinciding nicely with Gromme's 67th birthday in July and changing his life. The retirement for which he and Anne had been preparing was destined to become a new career, replete with recognition and acclaim beyond his wildest dreams. *Birds of Wisconsin* would establish him as a force in the world of wildlife art, and the best was yet to come.

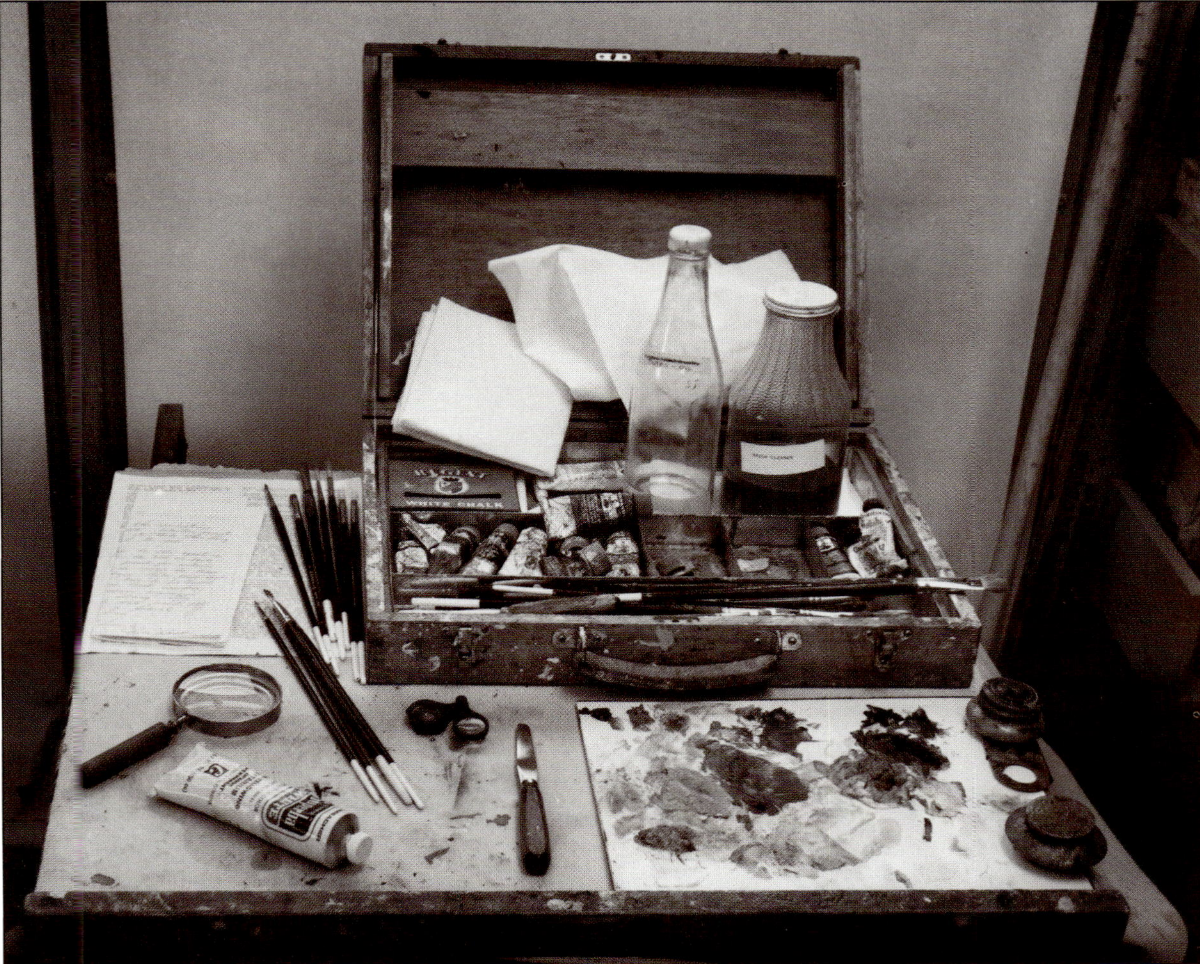

IV

The pungent aroma of turpentine and linseed oil permeates the room, while a flood of natural light focuses on two contrasting paintings, each in a different stage of development. Field notes and the recorded data of a lifetime line the bookshelves. Vintage paintings of decades past — some that were never finished — lie stacked on the floor. Off to one side on a nearby card table stands a pile of newly-published fine art prints that await the artist's final touch — his signature. A leopard skin drapes an old traveling trunk, and the head of a Grant's gazelle oversees the quiet studio. Outside, a numbing January wind tears at ragged oak leaves near the house, whistles through the blue spruce along the back hedge, and rolls off along the corn stubble into the marshland.

Seated in an old stuffed chair that faces his paintings is 87-year-old master wildlife artist Owen J. Gromme, a silent silhouette against the wall of windows along the northern end of his studio, his white hair virtually translucent in the harsh winter light, his pet dachshund Rusty dozing in a splash of sunlight at his feet. Obviously lost in thought, his attention is focused on his paintings, and over the next few hours he will rise from time to time, approach his easel, add touches of green to the background of a new deer painting, redefine the foreground and redirect the focus of the water line. Earlier in the day he had changed the horizon line of this particular piece, thus solving a major problem of perspective that had bothered him from the very beginning of the painting.

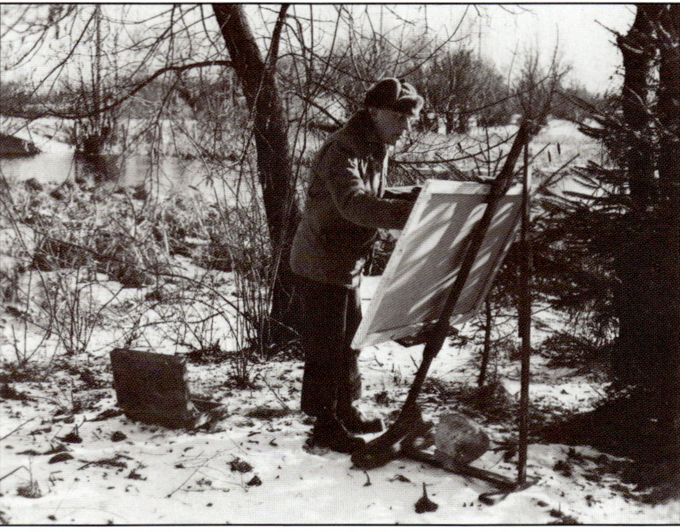

Gromme at work in the outdoors, capturing the vitality of the natural environment (1950).

"I have to make my changes now," Gromme explains. "After today, I can't touch that background for two weeks. It will take that long for the paint to dry sufficiently." Since he works strictly with oils, Gromme maintains a detailed record of each day's progress in order to prevent any drying problems with portions of a painting in various stages of development.

Gromme's brush strokes are sure and deliberate, and he works quickly, in this instance roughing in a portion of his painting of a doe and her fawns approaching the water. For the most part, he prefers to paint in silence. But if someone is with him, he thinks out loud, talking non-stop because that is his nature. As he paints or when he sits down to study what he has done, Gromme explains his motives and weighs his ideas, rejecting some and accepting others.

Pointing to an almost-completed winter grouse painting, he observes, "I think that might be the best background I ever painted." He may be right. A male ruffed grouse struts in the foreground while another grouse stretches to pluck a crimson nightshade berry from a bush. Behind them, a snow-covered pathway beckons, drawing the viewer's attention into the wooded background.

Yet Gromme remains dissatisfied, wondering aloud if he has captured the proper effect of the light. Holding a fanned-out tail of a ruffed grouse up to the light, he notes that "you have to be careful, especially with the shadows on snow. They have to be right, or people will sense that something is wrong. They might not know exactly why it is wrong, but they will know."

As an artist, Owen Gromme spends hours of his "painting time" in his chair along the north bank of windows — evaluating, studying, planning, and deciding his next step.

"I never know exactly how a painting will look once I begin," he admits. "I have a fairly good idea because I make a pencil sketch and draw in my reference points, but a lot of things can change between the time I start and the time the painting is completed."

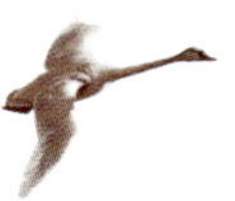

In each of his paintings, Owen Gromme draws on years of experience and knowledge of his subject. "When I paint today, I call on the experiences of a lifetime," he explains. His paintings strike a responsive chord in virtually everyone who sees them. As an outdoorsman and conservationist, he knows instinctively the qualities that will appeal to his audience.

Gromme competes with himself and time for further excellence and defines his latest creation as his best effort. The untouched canvas which awaits the Gromme touch is referred to by the artist as yet another challenge and "perhaps my finest hour."

Interestingly, the multi-talented Gromme, one of the world's most knowledgeable and technically accurate wildlife artists, has had little in the way of "formal" artistic training. Gromme's classroom was the outdoors and the day-to-day demands of his museum career.

"His knowledge of ornithology and the outdoors has allowed Owen to paint with great breadth," observes William Webster, president of Wild Wings, Inc. of Lake City, Minn., a wildlife print

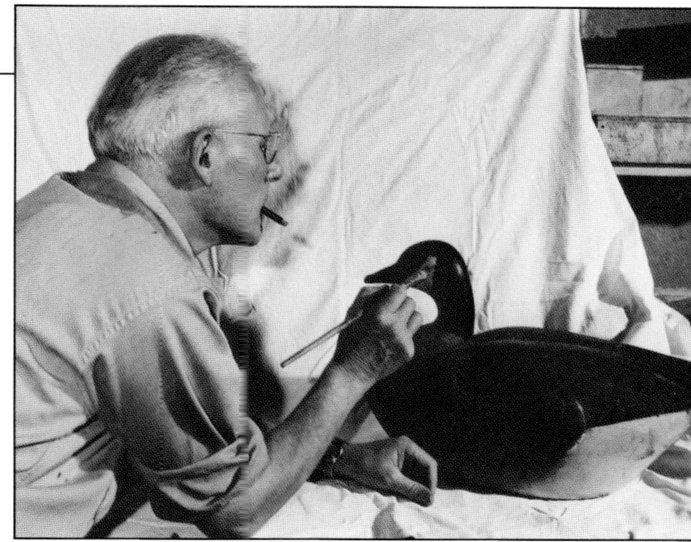

Gromme painting one of the decoys at the Milwaukee Public Museum (1945).

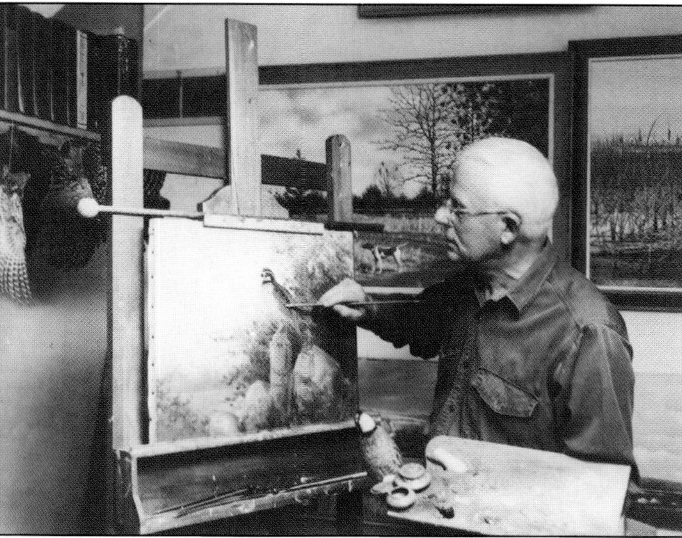

Gromme at work on a quail picture in his studio at his home in Milwaukee (1950).

company which features a number of Gromme's most popular works. "There are no more than ten artists I can think of who can, without photos or other means, draw and paint birds in flight really well. The ability to do it comes with years and years of experience and knowledge of the various species. It takes a truly talented individual such as Owen Gromme to paint the way he does."

According to Webster, Gromme's accuracy and his vast knowledge of birds, animals, and the outdoors are traits that set him apart.

"I'm a hell of a lot different than most other artists," Gromme admits. "I'm not motivated by what other artists have done before me. I think one main reason that I am different is the simple fact that I didn't have formal art lessons and all that sort of thing. I paint because I love it. It's as simple as that. And I figure my paintings speak for themselves."

Gromme's fierce independence does not necessarily mean that he is without his own favorite wildlife artists. John James Audubon, Louis Agassiz Fuertes and the Swedish painter, Bruno Liljefors, rank as the greats of wildlife painting in Gromme's estimation. As for bird artists, Audubon and Fuertes remain his personal favorites. And if any one wildlife artist has exerted a profound impact on Gromme, it was Fuertes, a fellow member of the American Ornithologists' Union (AOU), who was a lecturer at Cornell University in the mid-1920s when Gromme knew him.

Drawn to each other by their mutual interests in ornithology, taxidermy, illustration, and painting, Gromme and Fuertes met and corresponded often until Fuertes' death in 1927.

"I met him a number of times when we were attending AOU meetings," remembers Gromme. "And when he was in Milwaukee on business he usually visited us at the museum. He looked at some of my early paintings and told me that I was a pretty good prospect. He offered to get me into Cornell, but I had a good thing going at the museum, so I had to say no."

Since most of Gromme's art education consisted of on-the-job experience, the artists who left their mark on him were the ones who openly shared their own knowledge and discoveries. One such artist was a German immigrant by the name of H.L. Stoltenberg.

"He painted the best clouds I had ever seen, and I had always had trouble with that sort of thing," remarked Gromme. "One day I told him how much I admired his clouds and asked if he would show me how he did them."

Stoltenberg slapped a glob of titanium white onto a canvas and then brushed burnt sienna through it. "It produced the most beautiful pink and just the right tone," continues Gromme. "Anytime that I want pink in a cloud, that's the way I do it."

Speaking of the artists, artisans and craftsmen who sought refuge at the Milwaukee Public Museum during the economic storm of the 1930s, Gromme states, "We learned a lot from them, and they learned a lot from us. They shared techniques and knowledge and made the museum a better place because of it."

Gromme adds, "I believe that all artists should do the same thing. There are a lot of artists today who don't want anyone to know how they do certain things. They want to keep it all to themselves. I like to share what I know with today's young artists.

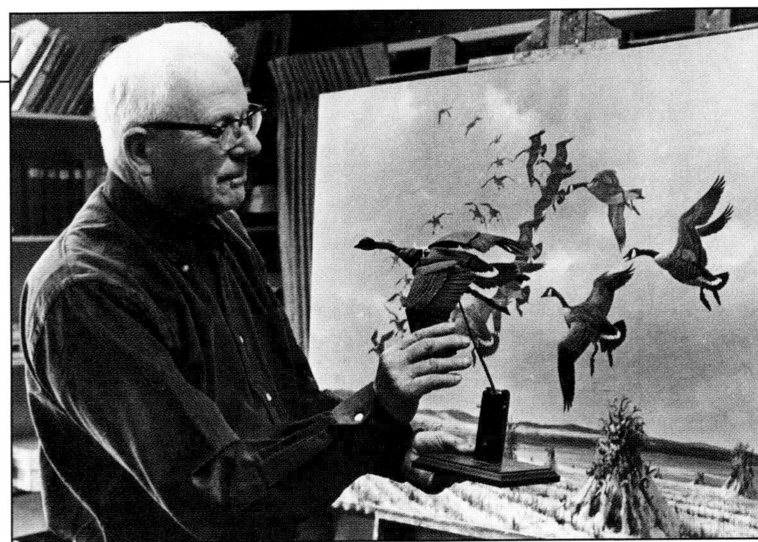

Gromme holding his goose model up to another of his geese paintings.

I happen to believe that you can't give your brain to someone or will your talent or anything like that. Why not share the knowledge?"

He concludes: "That's how we make progress. It's the same in every field of endeavor. We are standing on the shoulders of the giants who have come before us."

The philosophy and depth of thought which steer the Gromme course today seem light years removed from the dark-haired youngster who developed an interest in drawing by watching his cousin pen cartoons for the fun of it.

"When I was a kid, I had a cousin — Royal McLain — who was quite a cartoonist," recalls Gromme. "He drew pictures of everything. He really enjoyed it."

By the time Owen Gromme was ten years old, he was entertaining his friends with cartoons and caricatures of his own design. It was a talent which set him apart. He learned in short order, however, about critics.

"I was drawing cartoons of one of my teachers one day, and unknown to me she was standing right behind me while I was doing it," Gromme remembers. "Well, she didn't like that cartoon at all, and she really boxed my ears. That was the end of my sketching for a while."

It was not, however, the end of his special regard for cartoons and caricatures. "A lot of people turn up their noses at cartoons," he says. "But I have a lot of respect for them. The cartoonist can say a lot with those few lines he uses. It's art in its own way."

Along with the advent of his museum career in Chicago in the summer of 1917 came the reawakening of Gromme's skill with a sketching pencil. Encouraged by H.L. Stoddard, who was in charge of the school loan exhibition at Chicago's Field Museum, Gromme soon began detailed sketching of feet, bills and eyes for scientific reference. Stoddard convinced Gromme to expand his skills further.

"I could draw and do the sketches without any trouble," explains Gromme, "but Herb wanted me to be able to do the color notes. He had learned much of what he knew about color notes from the museum artists, and he taught me all he could teach me." Not only was Gromme responsible for color notes of birds and mammals, he also was expected to record the necessary notes for wildflowers and foliage. "We had to know how to mix our colors with great accuracy," he adds.

When Stoddard and Gromme rejoined forces at the Milwaukee Public Museum in 1922, Gromme picked up where he had left off. Under Stoddard's direction, he collected the birds and animals, mounted them for display, assembled the school loan displays and painted the backgrounds. But sandwiched between his brief stay at the Field Museum and his forty-three-year career at the Milwaukee Public Museum was one of the most trying periods of Gromme's life, years which undoubtedly influenced his later commitment to strive to create something uplifting.

Eager to answer his country's call to arms, Gromme enlisted in the U.S. Army in February of 1918, serving in France as a stretcher bearer for the 108th Engineers of the 33rd Division. From that vantage point he witnessed all the horrors of war.

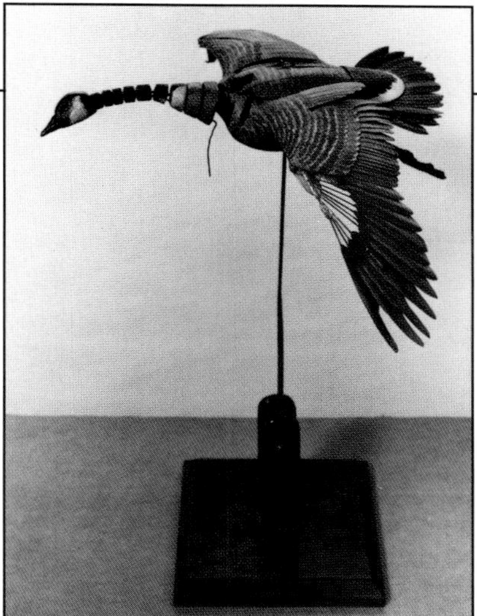

Close up of Gromme's Canada goose model.

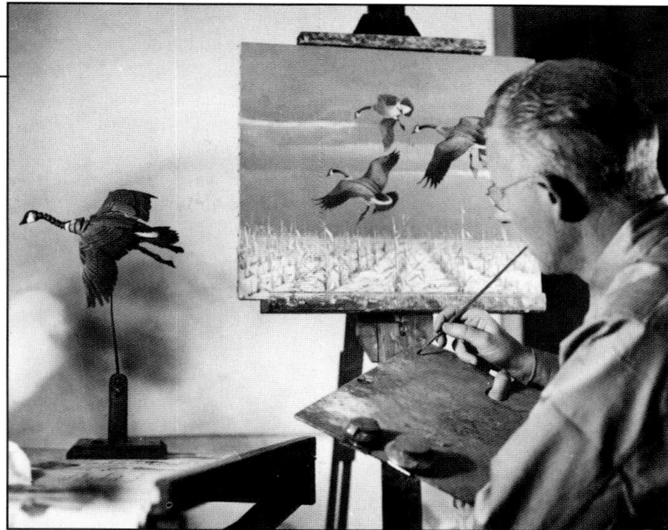

Gromme's model lends itself to the execution of a painting of Canada geese (1945).

Eager to discuss almost any topic imaginable, Owen Gromme has nothing to say about the "Great War." His eyes betray the impact of those memories.

Gromme luckily survived the battles unscathed, but he suffered a serious injury while deactivating a mine field following the Armistice. "I really don't know what happened," recollects Gromme. "All I know is that someone threw me across a mule and got me out of there." He points to a deep scar perpendicular to his lower lip and says, "The accident ruined my bird whistling. I was pretty good at it when I was a kid."

When Gromme returned to Fond du Lac after the war, he found that his once dynamic father had become an arthritic cripple, and his hope of returning to the Field Museum became a victim of simple economics. "I had to earn enough money to help my dad out of debt," explains Gromme. "They couldn't pay me enough at the Field Museum."

Nine years later "simple economics" again played a pivotal role in a decision that changed Gromme's life forever. There was not enough money to hire an artist for the East Africa trip in 1928, so the artistic responsibilities fell on the shoulders of Gromme, seemingly by default.

This marked an obvious turning point in his life, and Gromme never lost sight of the debt of gratitude he owed to the man who selected him — Museum Director S.A. Barrett. From the outset of the journey, Gromme sketched constantly, recording the views of each of the port cities they encountered along the way. In his *Field Notes* of June 30, 1928, he wrote: "As we pull away from Genoa, the hills are a mass of twinkling lights. . .Straight ahead is the moon, and as the blinking lights of Genoa fade into the blue of the night, I think back to the day Christopher Columbus pulled away from his home port."

In a way, Gromme must have felt a kinship with the fifteenth century explorer. But instead of a new world, Gromme was destined to discover a hidden talent.

It was a grueling, sometimes exhausting, assignment because of the mental and physical challenges. Gromme was compelled to devote time and energy not only to hunting and taxidermy but also to sketching and painting. Yet the experience captivated and disciplined him. From that point on he was an artist — and more specifically, a wildlife artist.

His first painting to be published as a print can be traced to the African trip. He created a small oil painting of a black rhino and its calf in a typical East Africa setting for the frontispiece of the 1928-29 Milwaukee Public Museum Yearbook. A small number of prints were then reproduced from the frontispiece plate. "Not many people know it," says Gromme, "but technically that was my first painting ever to be published as a print."

The frontispiece painting signaled a new beginning, and throughout the 1930s — an era when his time and energy were consumed by environmental battles at Horicon — Gromme began the process of refining and enlarging his talent. His work was well-respected among friends and colleagues, but it was virtually a secret among buyers of realist art.

"It was obvious that he possessed great talent even back then," claims "Chappy" Fox. "I have a little painting of cedar waxwings which Owen did in 1935, and it's absolutely exquisite.

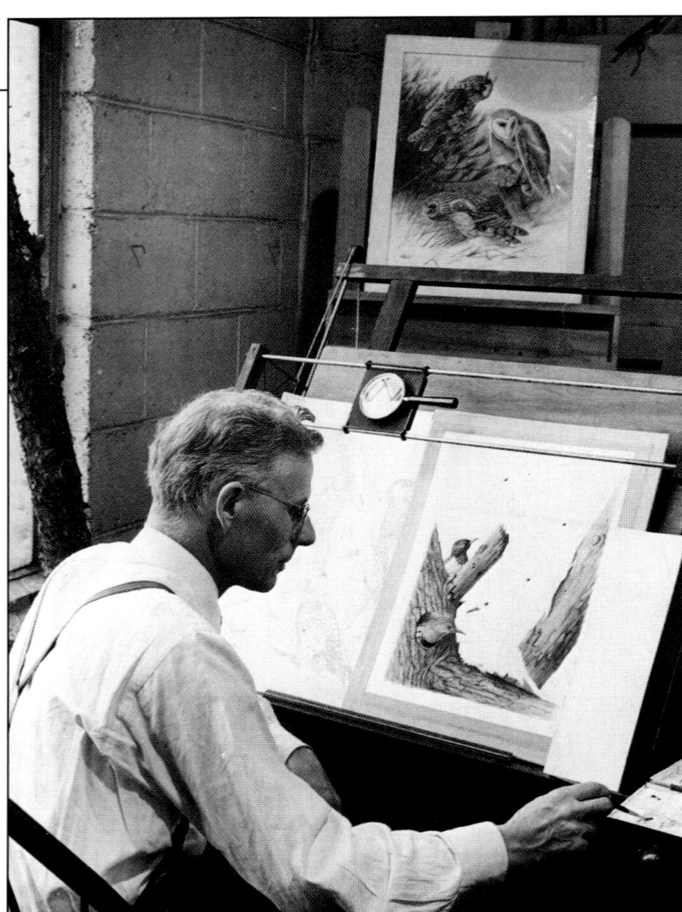

Gromme at work on pictures for *Birds of Wisconsin*.

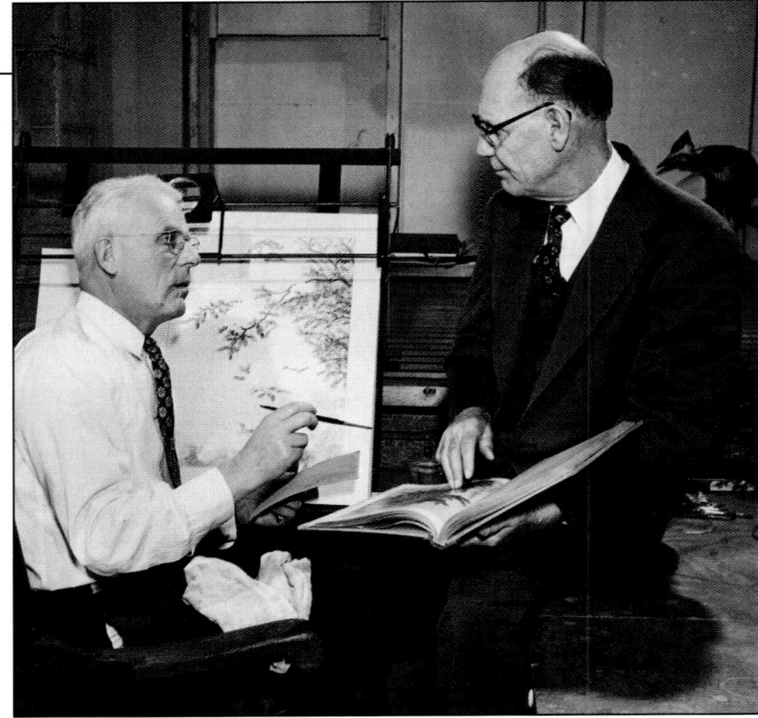

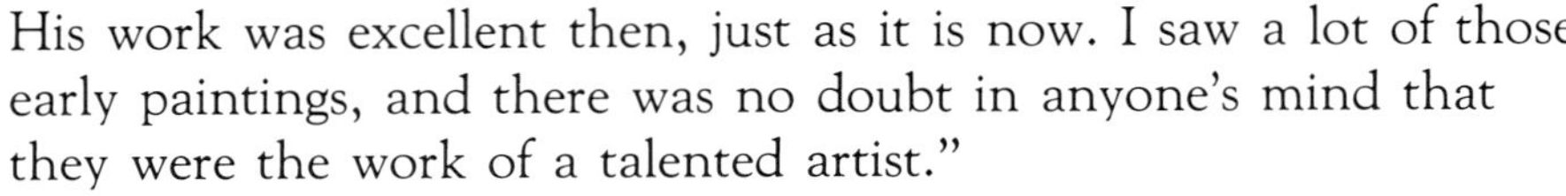

His work was excellent then, just as it is now. I saw a lot of those early paintings, and there was no doubt in anyone's mind that they were the work of a talented artist."

Fox points out that Gromme painted as often as possible but adds that in those early years of Gromme's career art was secondary. "He was holding down a job in the taxidermy department and doing all those other things he was involved in. He only painted when he had the time."

But before long word of Gromme's outdoor paintings filtered through the museum walls and out into the community. A sample of his work was available for all to see one Sunday morning in May of 1934 as the *Milwaukee Journal* published a full-color, eight-column reproduction of an original Gromme painting of snow geese winging their way north along the Lake Winnebago shoreline at Fond du Lac. Gromme still has the painting, but he claims that he will never sell it. "A guy was up here not long ago and wanted to buy it," Gromme says, "but I just told him flat out that no one could buy it, and that's final. Some things just aren't for sale."

In the fall of 1936, Gromme reached another artistic milestone — the sale of his first paintings. The first buyer of a Gromme original was George Weinhagen Jr., an executive with the A. George Schulz Paper Box Company of Milwaukee. Anne remembers: "Owen and Junior talked for a long time, and then Junior asked if he could see some of Owen's paintings. He looked at quite a few and by midnight he had put three of them aside. It was all pretty exciting at the time."

Then, without any further hesitation, Weinhagen said, "Well, Owen, how much?"

"I didn't know what to say," admits Gromme. "I thought about it for a minute and told him $300 for the three of them. He just looked me straight in the eye and said, 'Gromme, I'm going to tell you something I want you to remember all your life. The world accepts a man at the value he places on his own face. You're selling yours pretty cheap.' "

While sharing that piece of advice, Weinhagen wrote a check for double the asking price.

"That was an important day for me," says Gromme. "It

proved to me that my work had some value. It made me want to sell more."

Weinhagen played another important role in Gromme's career a short time after purchasing the paintings. He made the first donation for the proposed reference book, *Birds of Wisconsin,* the volume which would make Gromme a household name among ornithologists and showcase his abilities as a wildlife artist.

Gromme worked for more than twenty years to produce the gallery of 600 portraits depicting the 326 bird species contained in *Birds of Wisconsin.* Yet there were times along the way when he became so discouraged that he almost ended the project.

"If it hadn't been for Museum Director William McKern I don't think I would have made it," explains Gromme. "He encouraged me to keep on trying, to stick with it. When people kept asking him why the book wasn't finished, Mr. McKern defended me at every point. He understood the difficulties and he told them to be patient. He'd always say, 'Give him time; give him time. He'll make it!'"

McKern, who served as director for fourteen years, affirms that he never doubted Gromme's ability to complete the book.

"He was a good man, and he had great talent," notes McKern. "But he was busy with a lot of other things. He had a lot of responsibilities. I told people that all he needed was time and he'd get the job done."

Gromme's son Roy remembers the final years of the book project when his father's time at the museum was virtually consumed by the bird paintings. According to him, "there were a lot of days when Dad set aside his lunch hours just so he could work on the *Birds of Wisconsin* paintings."

Birds of Wisconsin began in 1940 with the support of the Milwaukee Public Museum's Board of Trustees, a decision reached by board members after Gromme had presented them with a painting of a ruby-throated hummingbird as an example of his work.

"They took a look at it and said, 'You'll do,'" Gromme remembers with a wry smile.

With the unqualified backing of Milwaukee Public Museum Director Ira Edwards, Gromme formally announced in 1940 that the museum would provide the necessary resources for a new *Birds of Wisconsin* to update the original done by Kumlien and Hollister in 1903-05. In July of 1940, Gromme stated in the *Milwaukee Journal* that the "task is so huge that it will be at least five years before the book is actually published." In fact, the project consumed twenty-three years from the date of Gromme's announcement until actual publication. Gromme also noted in the 1940 announcement that *Birds of Wisconsin* "must be accurate and scientific to answer the demands of ornithologists; it must also be a field guide for the general public; and it must be simple enough for classroom use."

His main goal in producing the illustrations was simplicity and accuracy. "My main emphasis was the individual bird," explains Gromme. "That was the only thing that mattered. I wanted to show each bird in a familiar pose so the average person could identify a particular species and learn more about it." Each of the portraits was executed in transparent water color.

In addition to the bird illustrations, *Birds of Wisconsin* contains a frontispiece and sixteen reproductions of Gromme paintings that showcase his talents as a wildlife artist. "Those

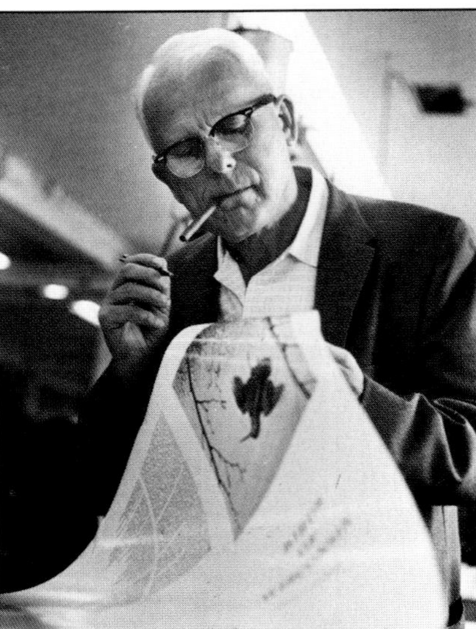

Gromme proofing a galley sheet from Birds of Wisconsin *(1957).*

paintings in the back of the book were Chappy Fox's idea," notes Gromme. "That's why I always say that he had so much to do with my career as an artist."

Fox suggested that the book be enlarged to contain a few of Gromme's creations. A fan of Owen's art for many years, Fox was anxious to move the artist's work out of the shadows and into the spotlight.

"I happened to attend one of the meetings with all the people who were involved with the book," Fox recalls. "I listened for a while and then — because it seemed so obvious to me — I suggested that they try something with the book that had not been done with any other book of its kind." The result was a "personalized" Gromme section entitled "Birds in Action and Habitat." The paintings transcended illustration and served as an example of Owen Gromme's art.

"Those paintings in the back of *Birds of Wisconsin* really set Owen apart," claims Fox. "They showed what he could really do, and I'm convinced they contributed a great deal to his popularity as a wildlife artist."

For Roger Tory Peterson, this country's most widely known ornithologist and one of its premier bird artists, the frontispiece depicting two bald eagles and an osprey also demanded a lion's share of acclaim. In the Foreword to the later editions of *Birds of Wisconsin*, Peterson stated: "The bald eagle has long been a favorite subject of ornithological illustration from Audubon to this day, but I can state unequivocally that Gromme's canvas is the finest bald eagle composition ever painted."

Still, Gromme endured more than his share of anxious moments about the book over the years. For example, in 1954 a fire at the Mueller Engraving Plant in Milwaukee destroyed and damaged a number of color plates that he had designed for the book. And from the very beginning, the lack of adequate financing had haunted the project.

"Fred Ott did more to get *Birds of Wisconsin* published than anyone," affirms Gromme. "He ran all over Milwaukee getting money wherever he could." Ott and Will McKern founded the Friends of the Milwaukee Public Museum in 1959 and dedicated the organization to the publication of the book as its first order of business.

First released in the fall of 1963, *Birds of Wisconsin* is currently in its fifth printing, making it one of the largest selling books ever produced by the University of Wisconsin Press at Madison.

Data and paintings for *Birds of Wisconsin* were not, however, the only concerns that Gromme encountered in the years between 1940 and 1963. In fact, they represented only a fraction.

In 1945, for instance, his painting of shoveler ducks became the Federal Duck Stamp design, insuring for him a place among the legendary wildlife artists of the twentieth century.

"I received a letter from the Secretary of the Treasury inviting me to submit a design. Well, I was thrilled that they wanted me to try, but I never expected to win it. When I was selected, I was flabbergasted. It was a great honor. It still is."

Art Molstad of Fond du Lac, Wisconsin is the man who convinced federal officials to invite Gromme to participate in the design contest. A friend of Gromme's since the 1930s in Milwaukee, Molstad was a dedicated environmentalist and a fellow member of many conservation organizations.

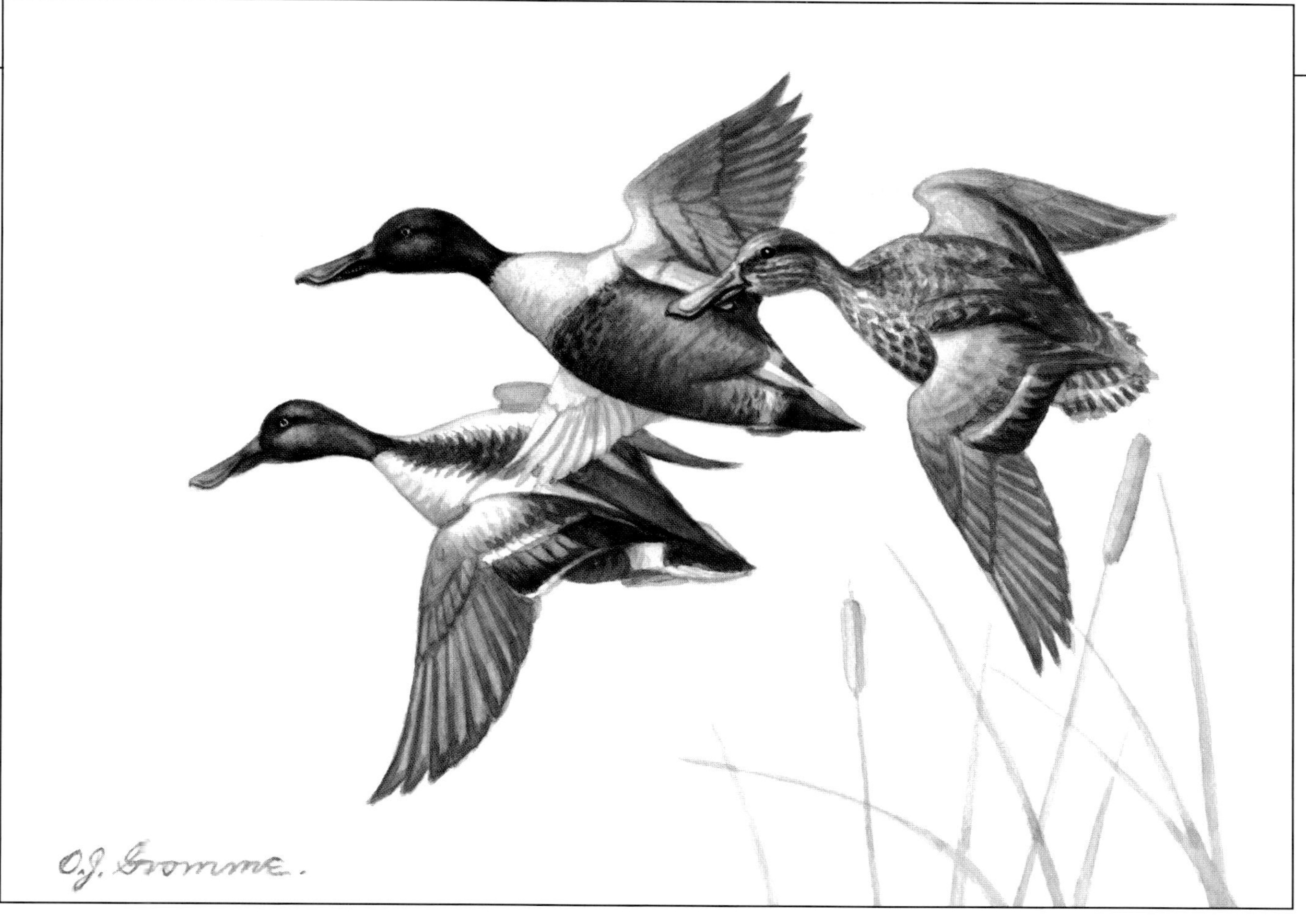

1945 Federal Duck Stamp.

"I urged Owen to get involved in the Federal Duck Stamp contest lots of times," recalls Molstad. "But he felt he wasn't good enough. I knew he was good enough and so did a lot of others. It so happened that I knew some people in the Fish and Wildlife Service, and I told them they should invite Owen to take a crack at it. He did, and the rest is history."

Currently, a print of Gromme's 1945 design is valued in excess of $6,000, the highest amount among living artists. Only 250 prints of the original, which sold for $15 each, were published. By contrast, today's Federal Duck Stamp, selected in the government-sponsored Migratory Bird Hunting and Conservation Stamp Contest, is considered the richest art competition in the world, according to *National Geographic* magazine. Prints of the winning design are privately produced and sold for well over $100 each.

In April of 1950, Gromme the wildlife artist was the focus of a *Look* magazine feature article, providing national exposure of his talents as a painter.

"I think that was the first real national publicity Owen ever received. It showed people all over the country what he could do," observes "Chappy" Fox, who was instrumental in convincing *Look* to learn more about Gromme.

"Chappy had all kinds of contacts," recalls Gromme. "I was thrilled when I first learned that my paintings were going to be in a national magazine. At that time *Look* and *Life* were the two biggest magazines in the country."

The two-page spread featured five paintings in full color along with an inset of the lean, white-haired artist grinning broadly for the camera. In a brief article accompanying the photos, Gromme pointed out that he had been painting for many years, but added, "I have never painted a bird yet that satisfied me." That same comment applies today, thirty-three years later. Every painting he completes represents his "best effort," but the empty canvas remains his next biggest challenge.

Gromme's national exposure coincided with one of the most heated controversies during his career as an artist. In the early

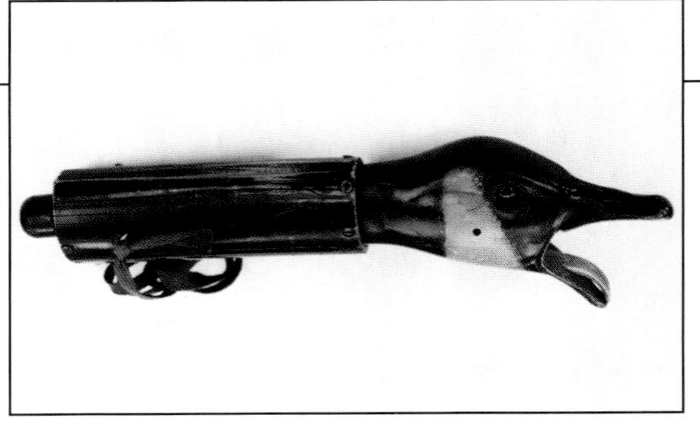

Another tool of the artist/hunter's trade — a handmade goose call.

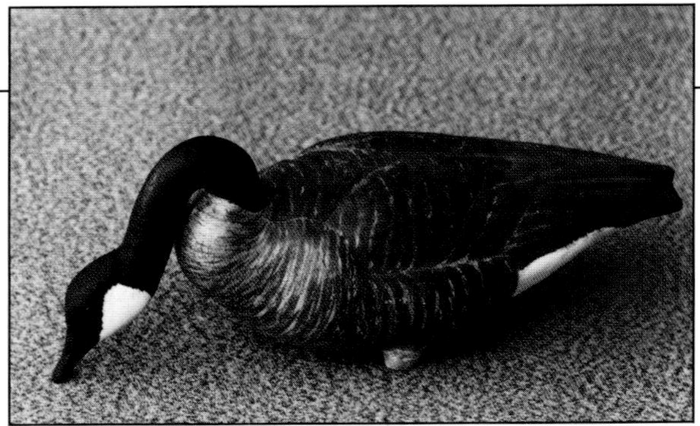

A handmade Canada goose decoy.

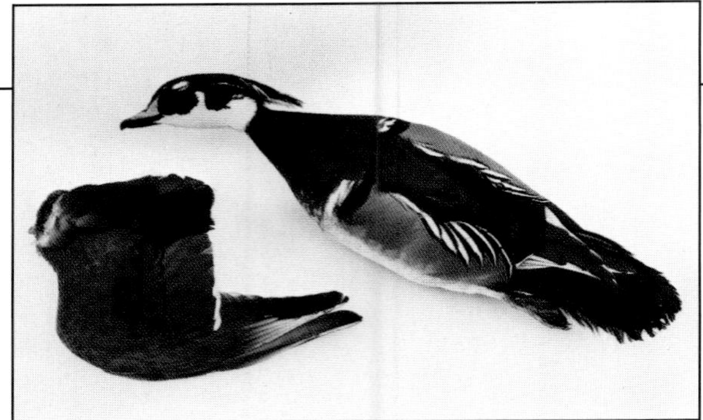

A male wood duck study skin.

1950s, he leveled both barrels on "modern art" and triggered a controversy which rumbled in the Milwaukee press for days. Even today, the mere mention of "modern art" is enough to put Gromme in a fighting frame of mind.

In a blistering letter to the mayor of Milwaukee in May 1952, Gromme declared that he was dismayed to learn that public funds were being earmarked for the purchase of modern art to be displayed in schools and other public buildings. He told the mayor, "I was prone to laugh off the present-day trend in art as a passing fad, but I have suddenly awakened to the fact that it is being presented to our school children as the ultimate of excellence."

He added: "The good, old art — you can call it 'realistic' if you want to — is being piped down. I feel I have a right to ask that something be done about it."

The response to Gromme's criticism was anything but abstract — from both sides of the issue. He was applauded and vilified, glorified and denounced. Both the president of the Public Museum Board and chairman of the City Art Commission described Gromme as being "all wet." Letter writers referred to him as that "character" or that "crank" and advised him to stop meddling in the affairs of art. Others praised him for speaking out and defying the critics.

As the controversy cooled, Gromme conceded that "much of the modern art is good," but added quickly that "much of it is bad." His main concern, he said, had stemmed from the lack of recognition for realistic art. "We must fight for democracy in art which will give realistic and conservative art an equal showing and recognition alongside the so-called 'modern' art."

His daughter, Anne Marie (Gromme) Ross of Minneapolis, was 16 years old at the height of the controversy and can remember her father venting his anger at the breakfast table or during dinner.

"I really believe that he was more frustrated and angry at that time in his life than he has ever been," she recalls. "He was doing very good work, but it seemed like no one cared. The emphasis at that time was on modern art."

Throughout the 1950s and into the '60s, Gromme did his utmost to promote wildlife art and "realist" artists in his position as director of the *Milwaukee Sentinel* Sport Show's National Wildlife Art Exhibition. Each year he invited artists from across the country to display their works in the show. And on a number of occasions he and other museum artists added their paintings to the popular assembly.

By the time Gromme retired on January 1, 1965, the popularity of wildlife art was skyrocketing nationwide. And while the reasons for the widespread popularity remain open to conjecture, there is no doubt about the effect it had upon Owen Gromme — it changed his life radically. In fact, within three years after his retirement Gromme had created forty-three paintings for permanent display at the new Marshall & Ilsley Bank in Milwaukee. The display of original Gromme paintings was the brainchild of M&I Bank President (now Chairman) Jack Puelicher, an outdoorsman who had been influenced by the teachings of Professor Aldo Leopold while a University of Wisconsin student in the 1940s.

As a native Milwaukeean with an intense interest in the environment, Puelicher was well aware of Gromme's involvement

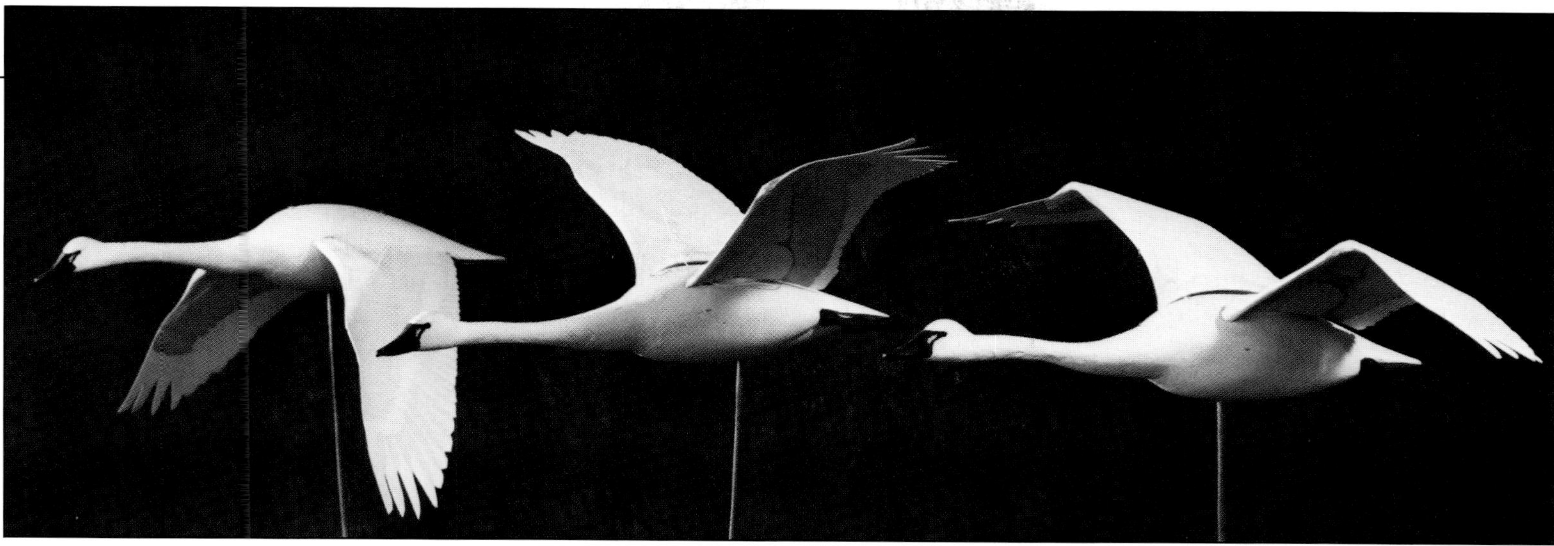

Gromme's whistling swans study models.

in environmental issues and his eloquence as a wildlife artist:

"We were in the process of building a new bank building and I had been thinking for a long time about ways to make the new building special and attractive. I wanted something of beauty that was of particular interest to people of Wisconsin. The more I thought about it, the clearer it became."

Puelicher made his decision and then approached Gromme with his proposal. He presented the deal to Gromme high above the central Wisconsin countryside while piloting a Twin Beech airplane. The two men and their wives were bound for Puelicher's northwoods retreat at Lake Julia not far from Crandon, Wisconsin.

"I turned to Owen and said, 'How would you like to work for the bank painting all the kinds of pictures you've ever wanted to do and never had the time for?' He didn't say anything at first. I'm sure he thought I was joking. Then he just laughed and said he'd think about it."

Gromme wasted little time making a decision. "I didn't know if Jack was serious or not," recalls Gromme. "The whole thing came as a total surprise to me. He told me that he wanted a city block of Gromme paintings on the sixth floor. When I heard that, I told him to get the airplane down on the ground and we'd talk about it."

The deal was straightforward, according to Puelicher. "I told Owen he could paint for two years, anything he wanted." Puelicher stressed that because the M&I Bank was a Wisconsin institution the emphasis in the paintings had to focus on Wisconsin environment and wildlife. The proposal was tailor-made for a man of Gromme's background. And each month for two years he produced one striking painting after another. He had never before enjoyed the luxury of devoting time exclusively to painting, and he was determined to make the best of it.

"I was delighted with each new painting as it appeared," Puelicher recalls. "They were absolutely fantastic. There's no other way I can describe them."

In the Foreword to *Birds of Wisconsin*, Roger Tory Peterson describes the collection of paintings in the M&I Wildlife Gallery as "an extraordinary affirmation of life and vitality." Gromme explains that they represent "some of the best work I've ever done."

At the end of the two-year contract with the M&I Bank, Gromme was reluctant to put aside his brushes and his ideas.

Puelicher remembers: "Owen came to me and said he hadn't had so much fun in all his life. He wondered if the bank would consider extending his commission for another year. We didn't hesitate a minute, and that's how Owen's extra year came about."

At the end of three years, Gromme's output of forty-three paintings lined the walls of the entire sixth floor and portions of the fourth. For Puelicher, the assemblage represents a "tour de force" of wildlife art that ranks among the best on display anywhere.

One of his personal favorites is the quail painting which was selected as the cover for *The World of Owen Gromme*.

"I have a special feeling for that painting," laughs Puelicher. "That split rail fence in the foreground is a piece I swiped from the Milwaukee Country Club. Owen was doing his research for the painting, and he told me he wanted to use a split rail cedar fence because it was common to see quail huddled around a fence like that. Well, I figured if Owen needed a prop, then I was going to make sure he got it."

Puelicher points out that he later compensated the Milwaukee Country Club quite fairly for the borrowed piece of fence by making arrangements for cedar fence to be shipped from the northern part of the state to the country club.

For a man who has observed Gromme's wildlife art with a special interest since the 1950s, Puelicher is intrigued by Gromme's ability to create mood in a painting. "I have a little quail painting of my own that Owen painted in 1943," Puelicher points out. "That painting, as far as I'm concerned, captures the mood of a winter snowstorm like no other that I know. To me, that is what's special about Gromme's paintings. They create a feeling within you."

In retrospect, *Birds of Wisconsin* and the M&I exhibition serve as critical points in Gromme's rise to fame as a wildlife artist. But sandwiched between those milestones was the welding of two very different personalities into a friendship that produced a flourishing business in the world of sporting art and even greater recognition for Gromme the artist.

It all began in 1964 when a Minnesota businessman by the name of William Webster knocked on the door of Gromme's Milwaukee home in the hope of acquiring one of the artist's Federal Duck Stamp prints. A longtime collector of such prints and stamps, Webster was familiar not only with Gromme's 1945 design but also with a number of Gromme paintings that he had seen in various publications.

"I knocked on the door and Owen invited me in to the house," Webster remembers. "He was working on a painting, but we talked as he worked, and I ended up staying much longer than I had planned."

Each time Webster had business in Milwaukee, he made it a point to visit Owen and Anne. "It was perfectly obvious to me and to anyone else who saw his work that he was a great talent," he says. Consumed by his avid interest in art — wildlife art in particular — Webster focused his energy on one of the biggest gambles of his life in 1967. He decided to form his own company to handle the wildlife art of a handful of talented painters, including Owen Gromme.

Webster dubbed his fledgling corporation "Wild Wings, Inc." and quietly went about building it into the largest publishing and catalog house in sporting art in the United States. Wild Wings published and distributed 1.5 million catalogs in 1982, a far cry from the 6,000 which were printed in 1970, the first year their catalogs were available.

The first original painting to be published as a limited edition fine art print was one from Webster's personal collection. Produced by Gromme in the late 1960s and entitled *Wintering Quail*, the painting became the acid test of the lucrative market that now exists in this country for wildlife art.

Since *Wintering Quail* in 1970, more than 115 additional Gromme paintings and hundreds of others by fellow artists have been distributed all over the country by Wild Wings.

"Owen was the key person in our development," attests Webster. "And he was the major factor in the acceptance of wildlife art. In my opinion, one of the greatest things Owen Gromme did for art in this country was the limited edition print. Through fine art prints — prints that will last for more than a

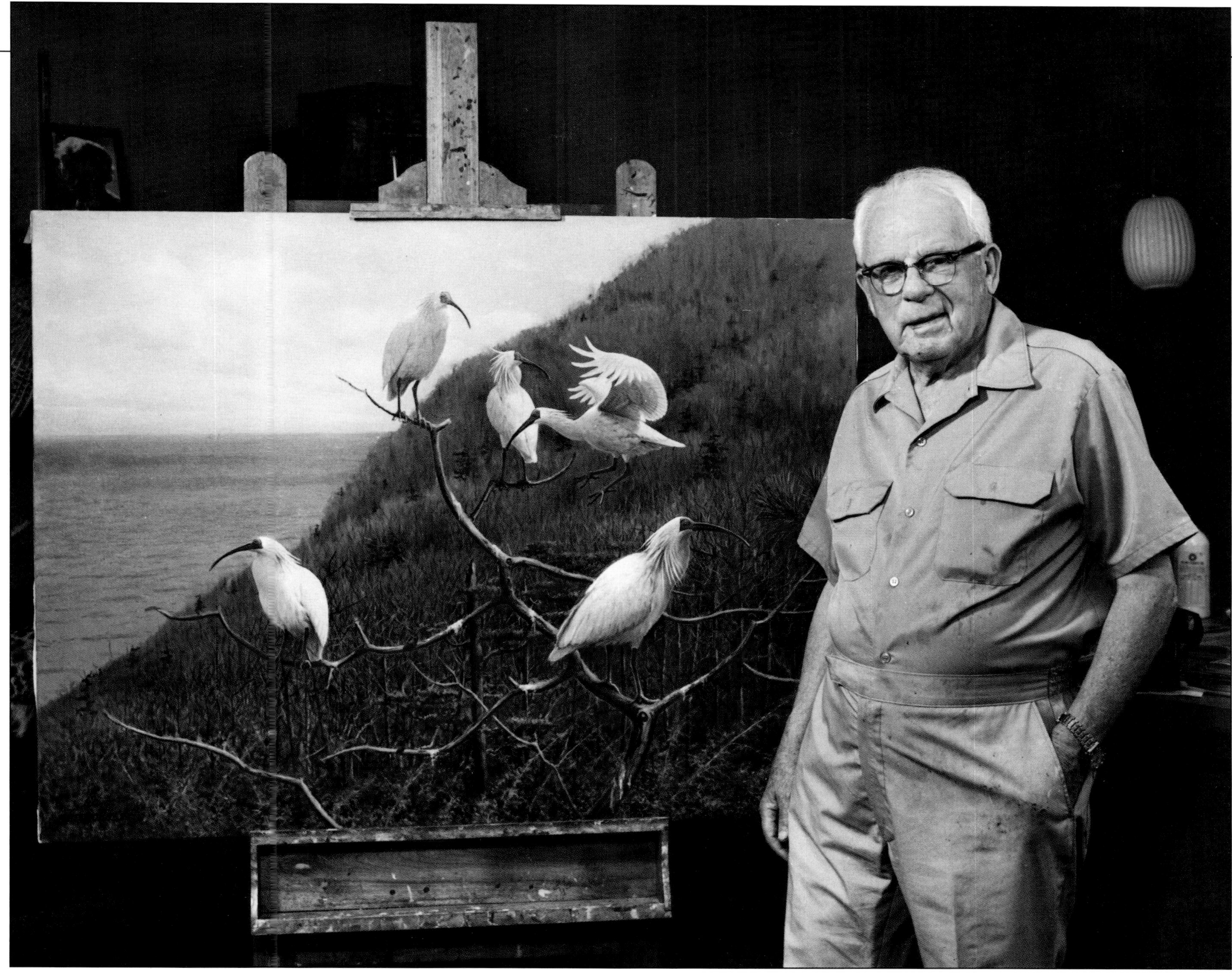

Gromme is pictured here alongside his 411th painting, completed in the summer of 1983 — The Last Toki.

rapid wing motion, as in the case of a hummingbird or members of the grouse family when in flight."

He paints with uncommon speed, concentrating his efforts on one aspect of a single painting at a time. His day in front of the easel usually lasts no longer than three to four hours. Extended periods of painting are counterproductive, he believes. "I don't work to the point of tiredness. Painting demands constant mental exercise. It's not good to push it too far."

When he is painting, Gromme always stands. "You lose perspective sitting down," he argues. And in order to cut back on the light that floods into his studio, Gromme usually wears a billed cap to reduce the overhead glare.

"You have to be careful when you're working hard on a painting that it doesn't take control," he explains. "A lot of people don't believe this, but I know it's true — a painting can hypnotize an artist. You have to get back from a painting once in a while and look it over."

Gromme uses a mirror to break this "hypnotic" effect. Standing several feet from his painting, he turns his back and holds a small mirror at the proper angle to study the reflection. "Some of the European artists who worked at the museum during the Depression taught me that," Gromme adds. "It helps you to see things you don't normally see."

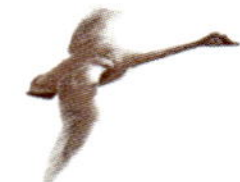

Owen Gromme has had many honors bestowed on him during his 87 years. One of the greatest, because it entailed acclaim for his service to the Milwaukee Public Museum as well as his artistic ability, occurred in June of 1980 when the Milwaukee Public Museum dedicated a special exhibits hall in his honor.

"These things usually happen after a man is dead," remarked an elated Gromme on the evening of the dedication ceremonies. "I'm just glad to be around to see it."

On display from one end of the exhibit hall to the other were Gromme originals. Some were on loan from the M&I Bank, others were there through the courtesy of friends, and still others were obtained through the special efforts of museum staff members.

Looking around the room, Gromme commented: "Having these paintings here in one place is almost like having a reunion of old friends. I haven't seen some of them since the day they were sold."

In 1982 Owen Gromme became the first artist to be enshrined in the American Museum of Wildlife Art in Minnesota. A painting of a loon, derived from field notes he had written in 1927, became the first painting to be included in the new museum. According to William Webster, the founder of both Wild Wings and the new museum, the facility "is dedicated to the preservation and perpetuation of this country's wildlife and sporting art heritage.

"The wildlife artists of today, unlike those of the past, are achieving greater recognition and monetary rewards. But there has been a reluctance to perceive their works as fine art," Webster adds.

On display at the museum are original paintings, signed prints, decoys, books, and journals of the world's foremost wildlife artists and writers. And in this "world" of wildlife art, Owen Gromme is unequaled in terms of tenure and accomplishment.

"There is no one, absolutely no one, who can paint ruffed grouse the way Owen can," claims Fred Ott. And to that, William Webster adds: "When it comes to painting swans and grouse, he simply has no equal." Finally, Roger Tory Peterson affirms in his "Introduction" to this volume that "Owen Gromme demonstrates as convincingly as any man I know that creative growth can continue, and need not taper off or atrophy when a person reaches the traditional age of retirement."

At 87 Owen Gromme remains as constant, consistent and unshakeable as ever. And Anne Nielsen Gromme, his partner and confidante, remains a factor in her husband's art career.

"Anne does everything for me," admits Gromme, "and she's my most important critic — always has been. Whenever I think I have a picture just about ready, I ask Anne to take a look. If it meets with her approval, then I know I'm on the right track."

On one occasion, Anne stood before one of Owen's paintings, scrutinizing its skyline in particular. She promptly told him: "Your clouds look like a bunch of biscuits."

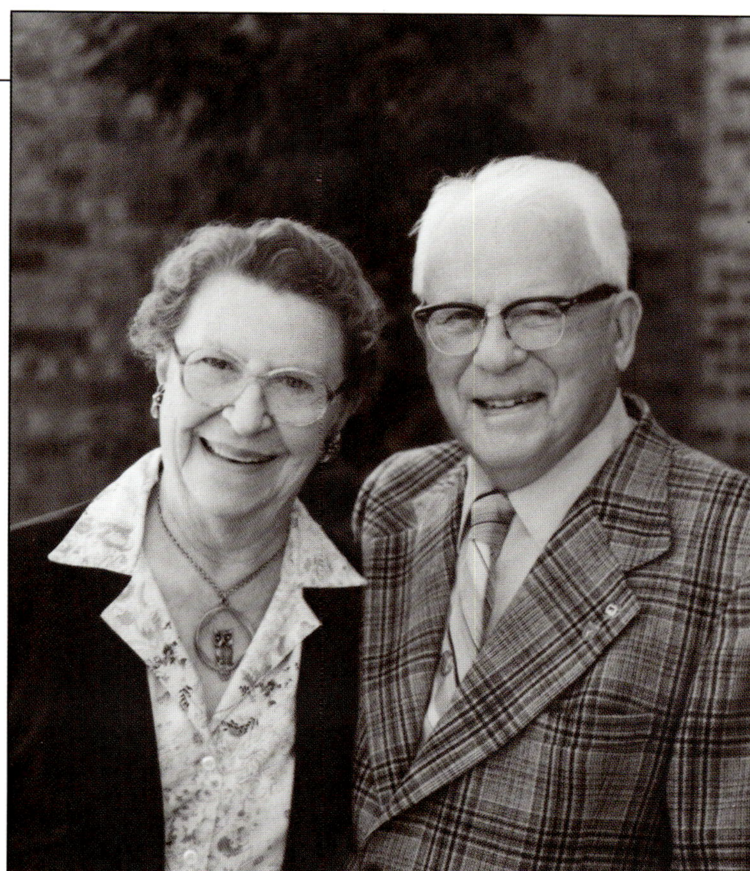

A long-lasting friendship and a shared commitment to the environment have been the hallmarks of 56 years of marriage for Anne and Owen Gromme.

Recalls Gromme: "I knew there was something wrong, but I couldn't put my finger on it. Anne saw it right away."

Intensely protective of Owen's time, Anne screens his calls, politely refuses many of the requests for special appearances, and intercepts those who knock at their door seeking an autograph or a "few minutes" with the artist.

"I have to be tough sometimes," she says. "But that's the way it must be if Owen is going to get everything done."

"We've had a great life," insists Gromme. "I don't think there is a more contented artist than I am. I don't think Anne and I would change anything."

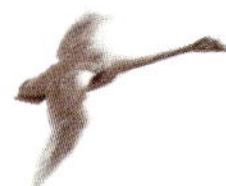

Owen Gromme will be back at his easel again tomorrow, continuing his painting and his support of environmental causes. And if you ask how long it takes for him to do a painting, he'll answer without hesitation, "All my life."

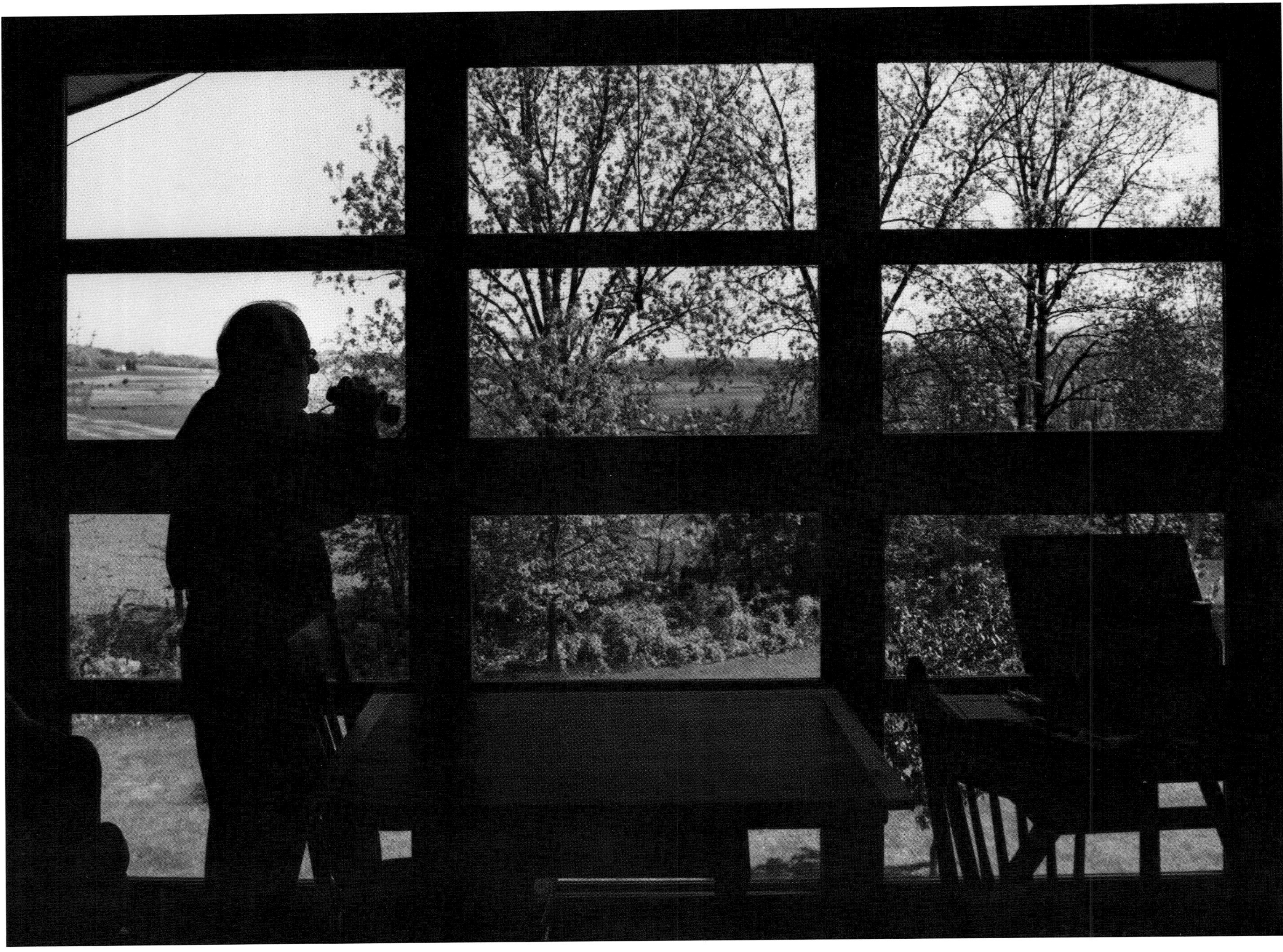

The ever-vigilant Gromme is always prepared for a new idea, a new image, or a new background. Most of these are available to him right out his studio window.

Color Plates and Commentaries

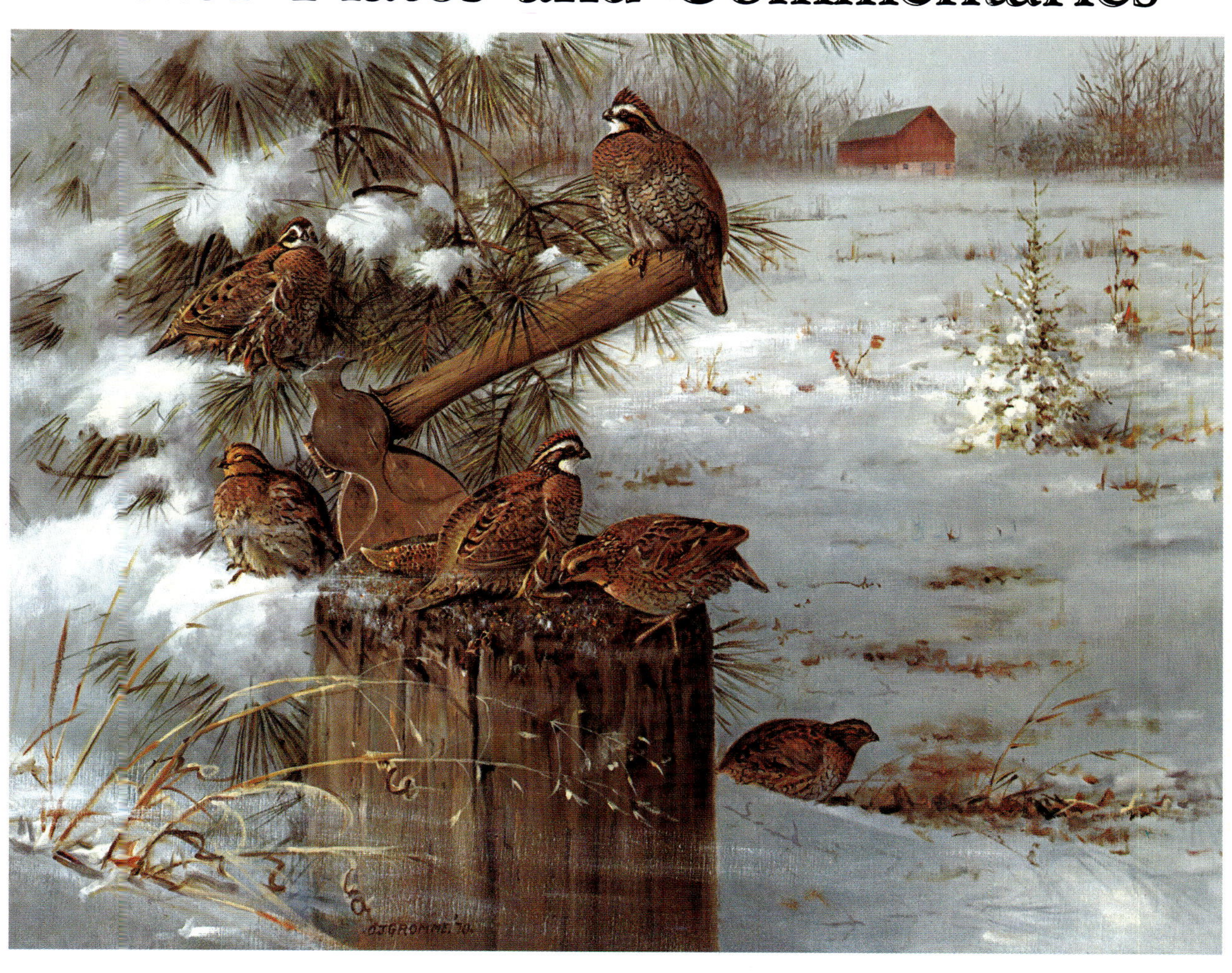

Wintering Quail

My work as most people know it, through the medium of the limited edition print, began with this painting of northern bobwhite quail feeding on a chopping block on a wintery day. This was my first painting ever reproduced as a limited edition, and in fact, it was the very first print released by Wild Wings, Inc. of Lake City, Minnesota.

One day in the late 1960s a man by the name of William Webster called me at my Milwaukee home. A collector of duck stamps and duck stamp prints, Bill was trying to find a print of my 1945 Federal Duck Stamp. After we spoke briefly on the telephone, I invited him to my house to discuss the possibilities of locating such a print.

Bill Webster's first visit lasted all day, including his being invited to stay for dinner. Our talk was of hunting, wildlife, and art, and at some point, he asked me if I had any of my work on hand. At that time I had this picture, *Wintering Quail*, and to my surprise Bill Webster bought the painting on the spot.

He then broached an idea of his that had been forming for some time — why not try to have a painting like this reproduced in fine lithography, in a small number, to sell to other collectors who would appreciate and enjoy it as much as he did. I liked the suggestion, and we worked out an agreement whereby we would share the cost of producing a limited edition of *Wintering Quail*, and share in the profit or loss as the case might be. We made up a list of potential customers, sent out a single-sheet mailing, and sold out an edition of 550 in a relatively short time! And so was born Wild Wings, Inc.

In retrospect, it is easy to see what made this such a strong beginning print — six engaging little quail, huddled in the lee of a white pine, out of the wind, filling their crops with cracked corn, comfortable and unconcerned.

Like so many of my paintings, this scene has its origins in the immediate surroundings of my Briggsville, Wisconsin home — the stump was one my sister-in-law used to chop kindling on; the hatchet, a family relic left by a deceased relative; and the barn, moved a bit to improve composition, still stands on my son's farm.

1970, oil, 32" x 24"

Ruffed Grouse Budding

Ruffed grouse usually feed on the ground, eating berries, fallen fruit or tender leaves from shrubs. But in the winter when everything is covered with snow, they sometimes turn to budding — eating the buds off trees — to keep themselves alive.

If startled while budding, the grouse will freeze in one position, clamping down their feathers tightly so they appear to be about half as thick as they actually are, hoping to resemble the broken-off stub of a branch. Jack Puelicher, Chairman of the Marshall and Ilsley Bank, saw this scene and described it to me, right down to the detail of the one grouse losing its balance and frantically trying to right itself.

1967, oil, 32" x 40"

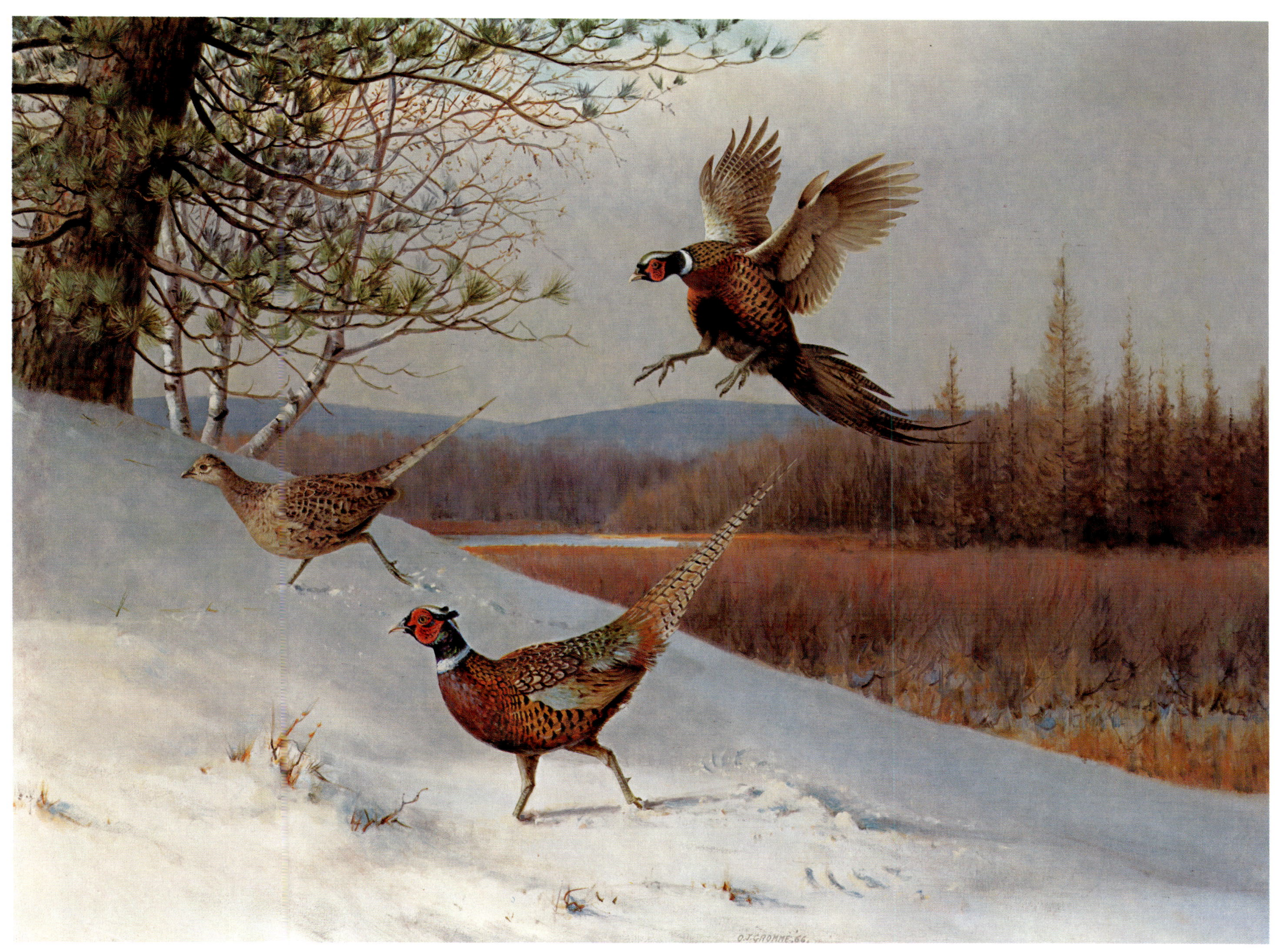
O.J. GROMME. 66.

Winter Afternoon — Pheasants

This painting shows three ring-necked pheasants flying over a corn field on my son Roy's farm. The corn was left standing for wintertime forage. It is late afternoon, and the birds are heading for a nearby marsh where they will roost for the night.

The ring-necked pheasant is not native to North America, but rather was introduced from Asia. Brought into Wisconsin by the Pabst family, the pheasant took hold quite readily. They are now fairly plentiful in the Dakotas and the Central Plains, but their numbers seem to be declining in our state.

Pheasants face the same problems of diminishing habitat as many other birds do today. They like to nest in alfalfa fields and fence rows, but given the modern methods of farming, there is less and less cover for them. In the fall, for instance, if a farmer plows his corn under, there is very little left for the birds to eat during the difficult winter months. It is important to realize that by putting every square inch of ground under tillage we are depriving our wildlife of food and habitat. This can eventually lead to eradication of many species.

All species cannot live in the woods. Some birds and animals are able to survive only in open country; others need marshes, but many of these are being drained in order to increase tillable land. As a result, wildlife loses. And as wildlife loses, so do we all in the long run, because we need one another. All life is dependent upon all other life. We have to remember this if we are to survive on this earth.

1962-63, oil, 36" x 24"

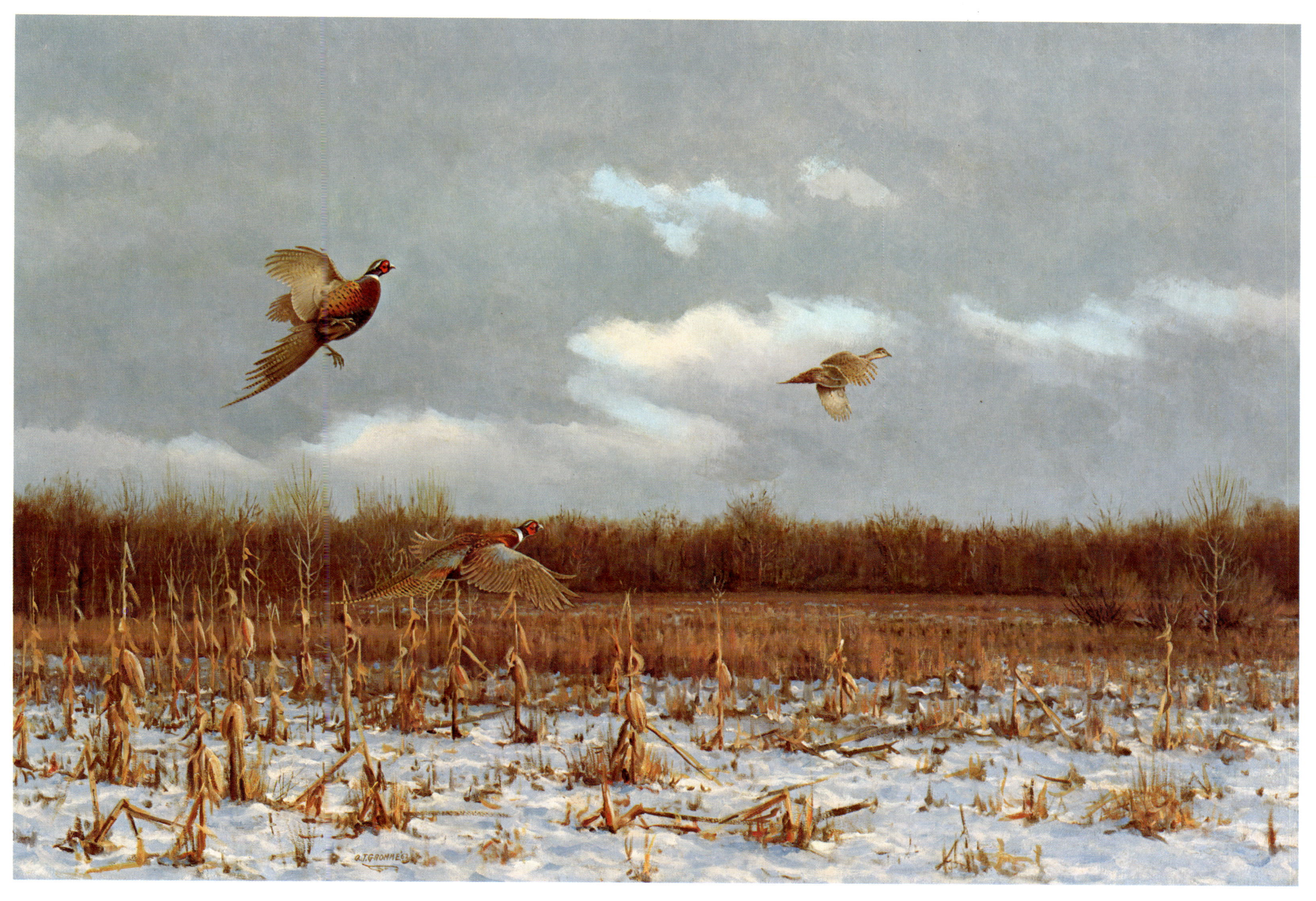

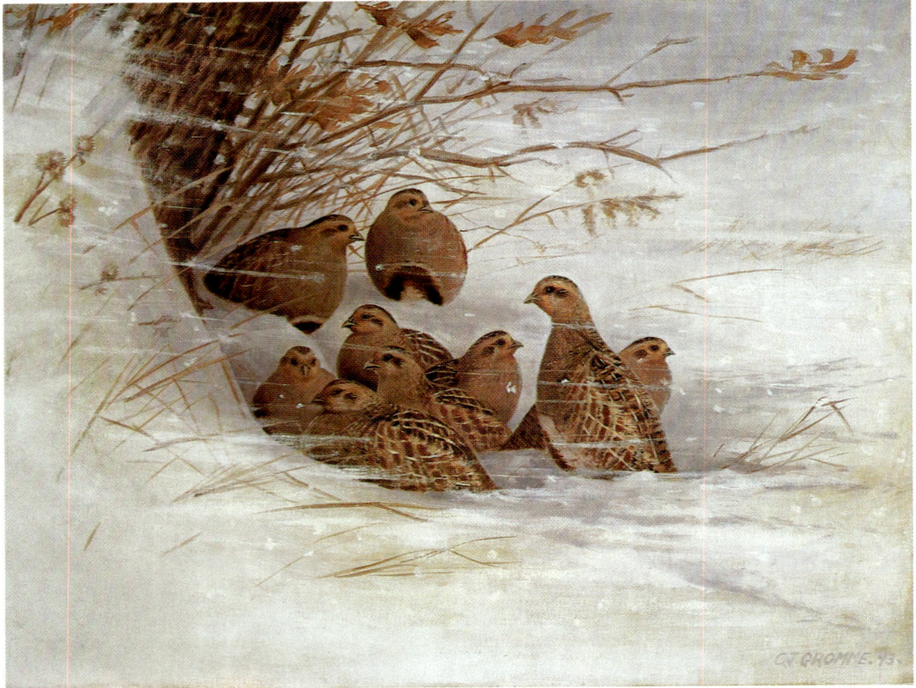

Hungarian Partridge

When we resided in Milwaukee, across the street from Mt. Mary College, we were practically living in the country. All around us were open fields where there were quite a few gray partridge, a species introduced into Wisconsin many years ago. We used to feed them, but it was always necessary to keep the several flocks separate because they would form cohesive groups and get into fights. So, we fed one covey on one side of the house, one on the other, and a third out back.

This painting recreates a scene I witnessed from our kitchen window during a severe blizzard. The snow was blowing wildly, forcing the gray partridge to take up their position in the lee of an old bush where they could gain shelter from the storm.

I did this painting during World War II when it was difficult to buy good paints and canvas, and I had to restore it later because of the inferior wartime materials that I was forced to use.

1943, oil, 24" x 18"

Among the Shocks — Prairie Chicken

Greater prairie-chickens are rapidly becoming a bird of the past as they fight a losing battle against the infringements of civilization. In Wisconsin's early years the pioneers practically lived on prairie chickens, because of their abundance and good eating. And whereas their close relatives, the sharp-tailed grouse, seem able to hold their own against man, the greater prairie-chicken is less able to adapt. They need more open country for their habitat, and in this day and age, most open country is cultivated.

In the winter prairie chickens assemble in large flocks, but they become so wild that it is almost impossible to get close to them. I have painted these birds as they were commonly seen among the corn shocks, either perched on a fence rail or huddled in the snow.

1975, oil, 36" x 24"

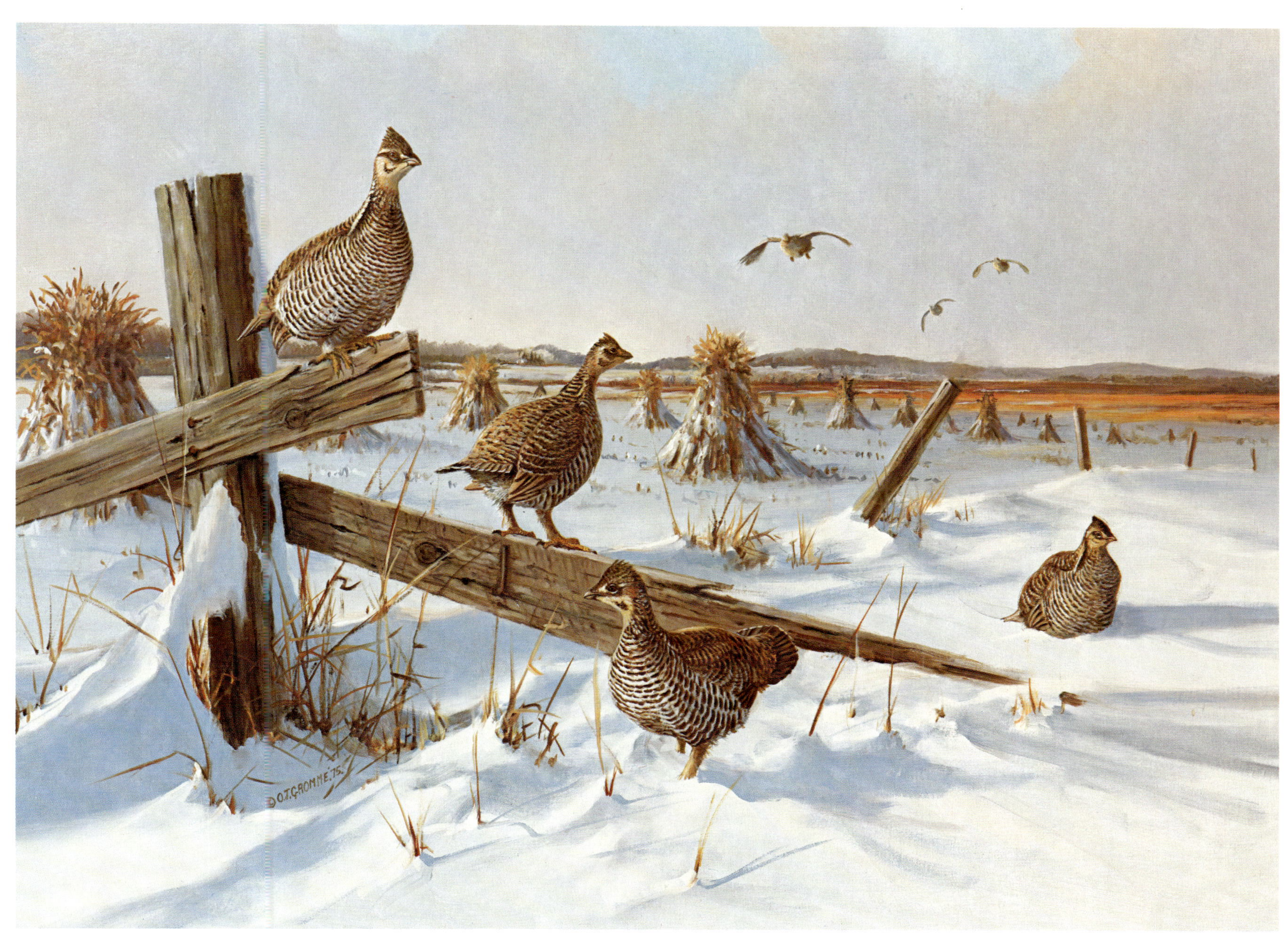
©O.J.GROMME.75.

Prairie Chickens

This picture is significant for me because it depicts an incident which helped to set my direction toward a career as a naturalist.

In 1914 I was a young taxidermist in Fond du Lac, Wisconsin, trying to learn all I could from a few outdated books. In my father's travels as a salesman, he had met Edward Ochsner of Prairie du Sac, a well-known taxidermist, fur buyer and champion rifle shot. Knowing how much it would mean to me to meet a man like Mr. Ochsner, my father invited him to look at my work when he was in Fond du Lac. I was delighted when he stopped by one winter day.

Examining my work, Mr. Ochsner suggested that he could give me some lessons if we had some birds to work on. Birds were scarce around Fond du Lac in mid-winter, but I was fairly certain that I could find some greater prairie-chickens out on the flats just east of town.

It had snowed a few days earlier, and I thought the prairie chickens would be perched on top of the snow banks and would see us coming. What I did not know then was that in times of severe winter weather, greater prairie-chickens bury themselves in the snow all the way up to their heads. When disturbed, they will literally "explode" into flight, sending up a cloud of snow several feet into the air.

So, when we arrived at the place where I used to put up birds, two cock prairie chickens suddenly burst out of a snow bank a few feet in front of us. Pulling up my gun, I got off two shots in rapid succession — both birds fell to the earth. I must admit that I was pleased with myself.

Back home that evening both Ed Ochsner and I took a bird, and he led me through the process of mounting step by step. Needless to say, I was a very happy young taxidermist that night.

That incident marked the beginning of a long friendship with Edward Ochsner, who eventually helped me to land my first taxidermy job at Chicago's Field Museum of Natural History and who always encouraged me in my life's work as a naturalist.

1967, oil, 40" x 32"

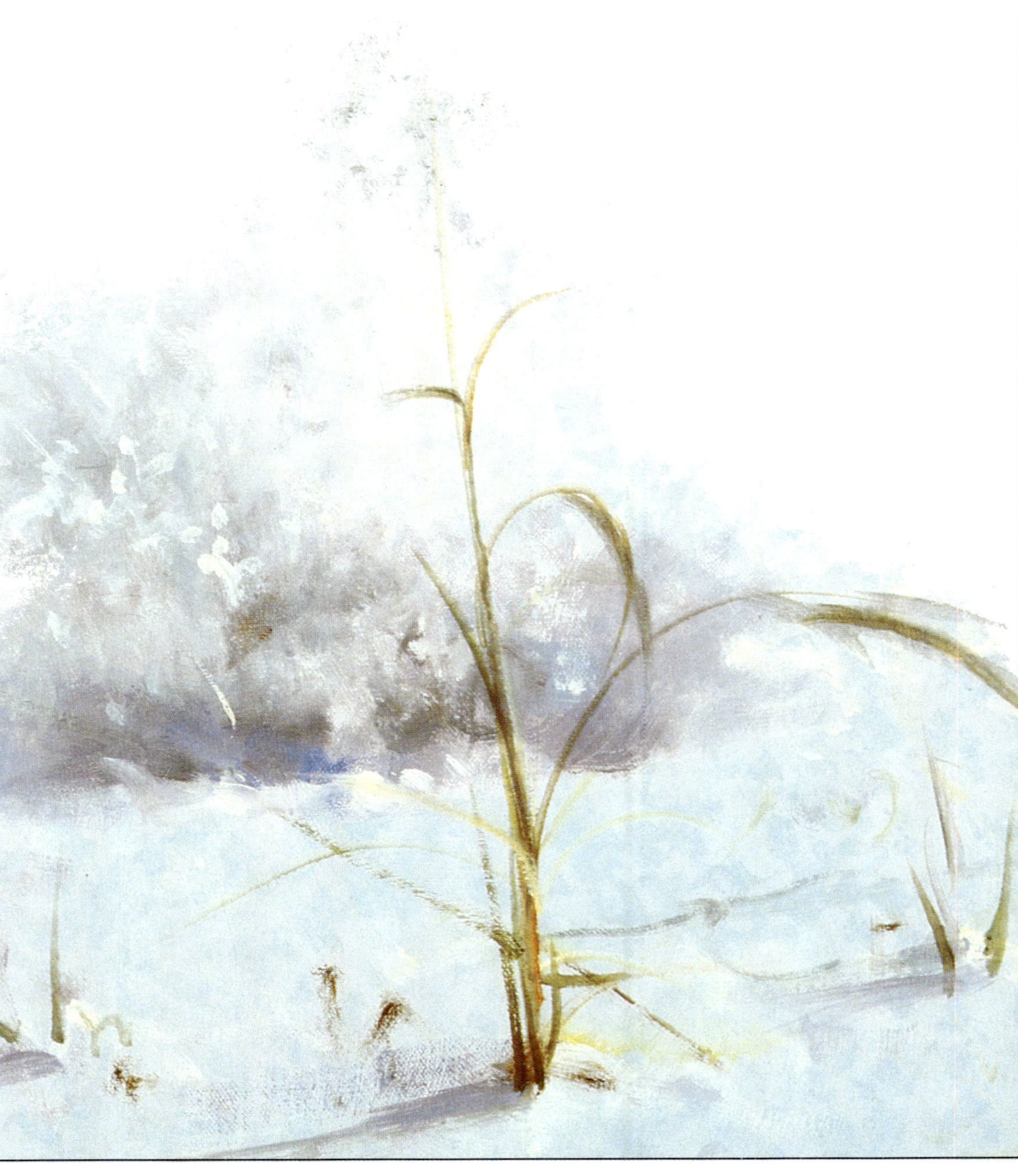

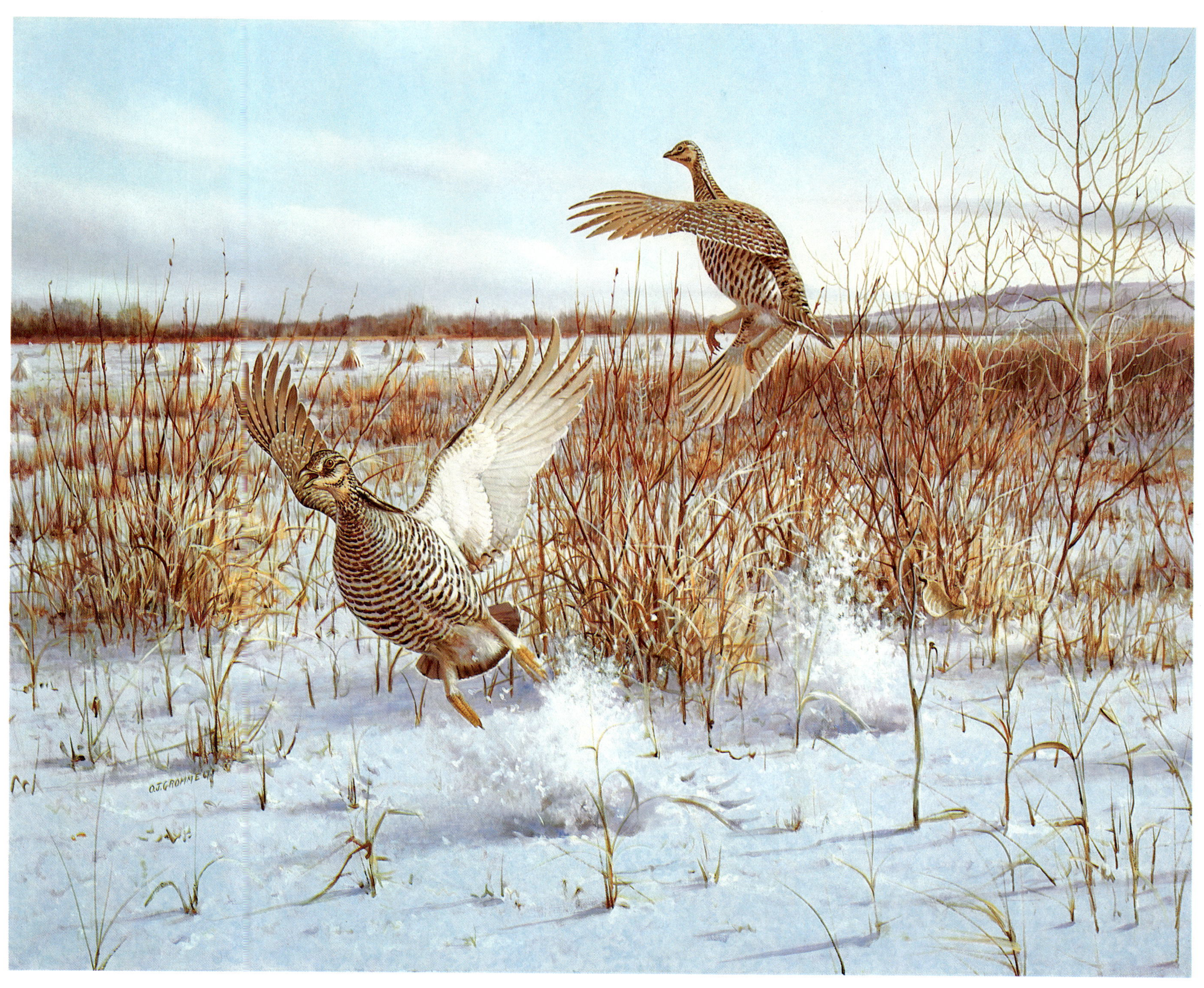
O.J.GROMME

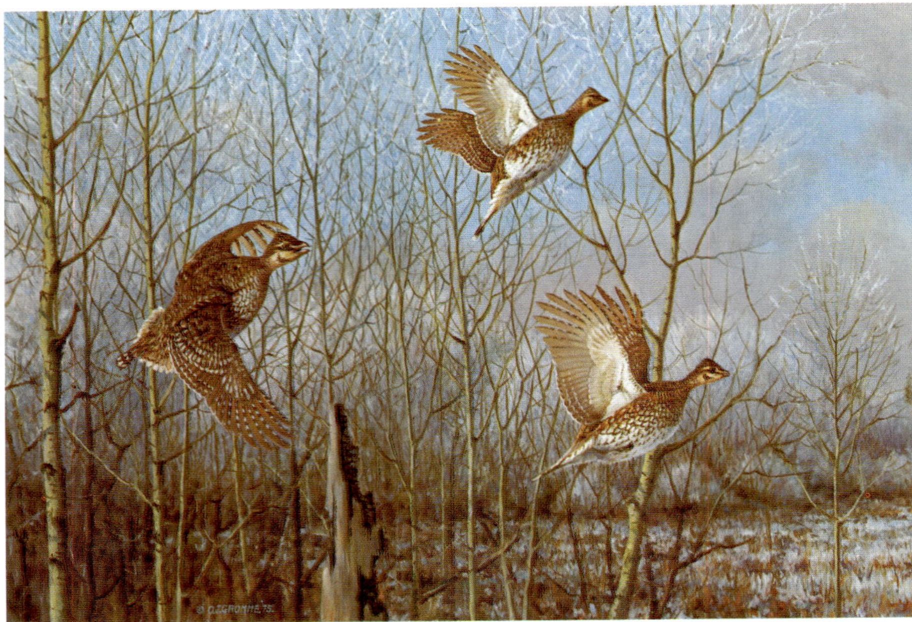

Sharp-tailed Grouse

I think of the sharp-tailed grouse as a bird which comes in after a forest fire. They prefer a habitat of open brush and small timber, usually young poplar and birch trees. In this picture I have depicted that type of growth, including the charred stump to show that the fire has been there.

Similar to the greater prairie-chicken in appearance and behavior, the sharp-tail is a powerful flyer and an excellent table bird. Their habit of getting up one-at-a-time (when flushed) works against them, because it is possible for a hunter with a good dog to wipe out an entire covey. For this reason the hunting of sharp-tails is closely monitored, and, in Wisconsin, the Department of Natural Resources is careful to see that they are not overshot.

While the onslaught of civilization has destroyed a great deal of the sharp-tail's habitat, they seem to adapt fairly well to agricultural areas. However, insecticides and herbicides are taking a heavy toll on the birds.

In addition to their problems with man, sharp-tails are prey to several other predators. But the fact that they have large broods of between eight and fourteen eggs enables them to keep their numbers fairly stable.

1975, oil, 26" x 24"

Sharp-tails, Prairie Chickens — Dancing

As a boy growing up in Fond du Lac, Wisconsin, I used to go out in the very early spring, hide in the ruins of an old barn, and watch the prairie chickens "boom" (dance and strut). This painting shows one instance when both sharp-tailed grouse and greater prairie-chickens (pinnate grouse) danced on the same dancing ground. Having witnessed this, I have recreated it here, using the Jackson County, Wisconsin, area as background. When these birds were more numerous, they shared a similar habitat, but the prairie chicken prefers more open country than the sharp-tail.

As the painting demonstrates, the birds go through intricate strutting, fluttering and inflating of their neck sacs. The tympanic membrane on the greater prairie-chicken is bright orange, while that of the sharp-tail grouse is a lavender or purple. Their coloration is different, too, with the stripes of the prairie chicken going straight across, like a Plymouth Rock chicken, while the stripes of the sharp-tail form a "v" pattern, like an arrow.

Both species have diminished greatly over my lifetime. The greater prairie-chicken appears to be in more trouble, though, since the sharp-tails always seem to be able to find enough scrub country to get along.

1967, oil, 40" x 30"

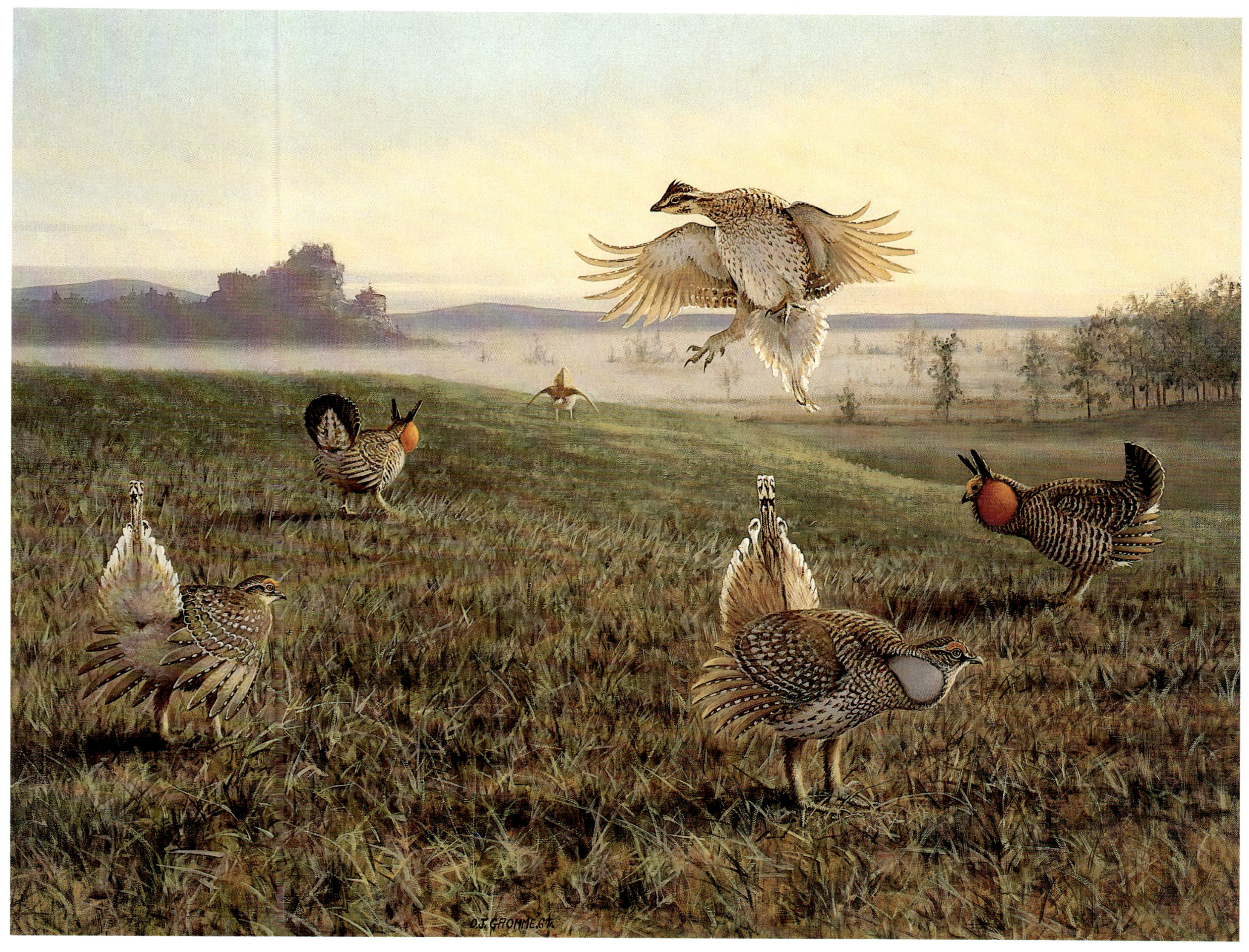
O.J. GROMME.'67

Midday Retreat — Bobwhite

Northern bobwhite quail are lovable little birds, known by their call, and are quite popular with lovers of wildlife art.

On cold winter days a bevy of quail often came up under this young pine tree, huddling together out of the winter and dozing in the warm sun. When bobwhite quail roost for the night, they form a tight little circle with their tails together and their heads facing outward. Then if a predator should strike, they can all fly out in different directions without bumping into one another. The quail shown here are not roosting for the night, so they are scattered around in varied positions.

The quail is a very vulnerable bird. Here in Wisconsin we are near the northern limit of their range, and they repeatedly have trouble during cold winters. For example, sometimes when quail roost for the night it snows and they are covered up. This is not a major problem as long as the snow does not form a crust, but once that happens the quail usually die. They are simply not strong enough to break through the crust as a grouse or a prairie chicken can. As a result, many a farmer will come along in the spring and find the remains of an entire bevy, huddled together with their heads pointing out, buried under the crust of snow.

1975, oil, 32" x 24"

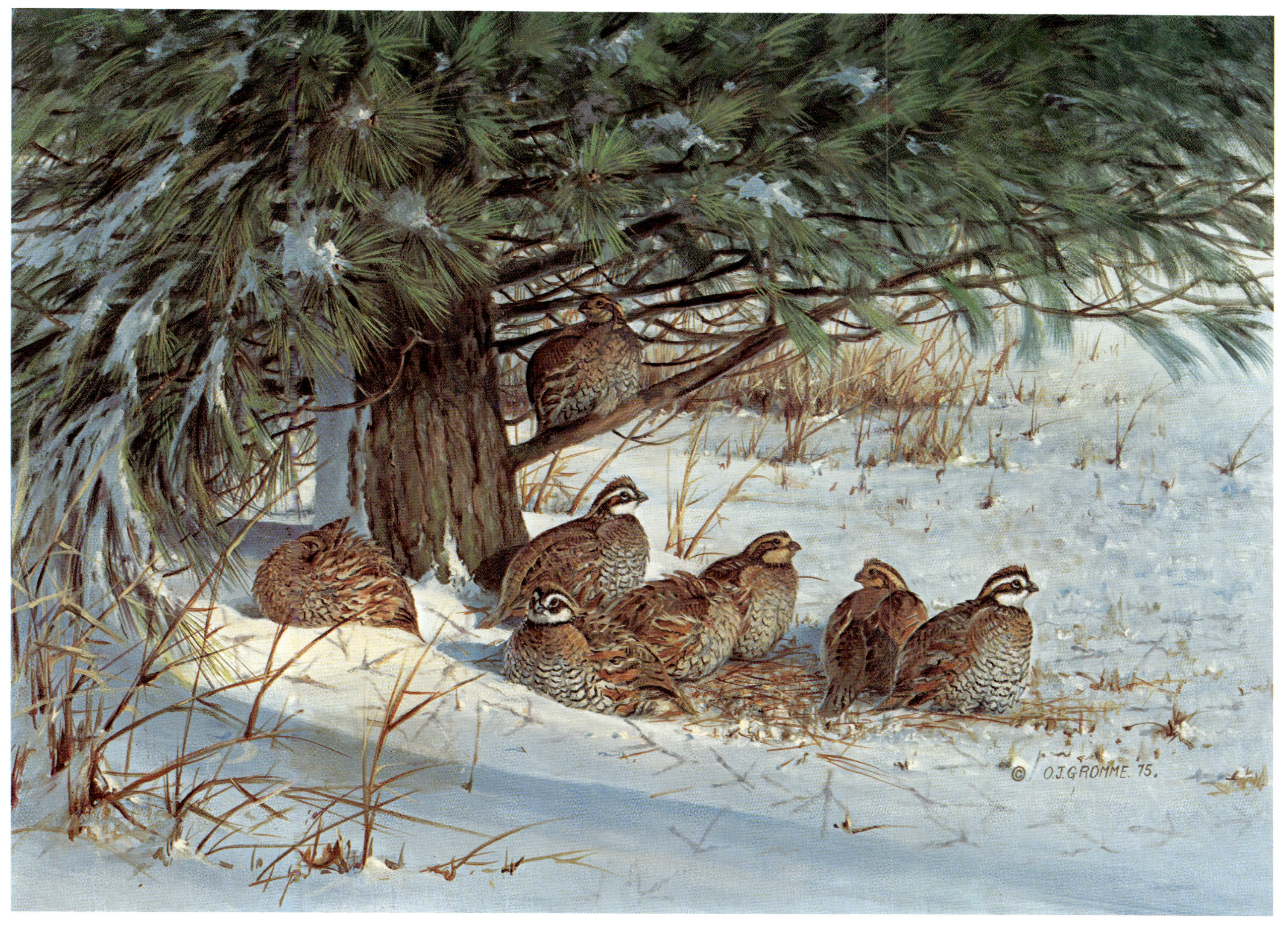
© O.J.GROMME. 75.

Bobwhite — Winter Day

I am quite critical of the damage being done to our environment be it by a farmer, an industry, or any individual who is careless and unthinking. I do not apologize for that, because I think not nearly enough can be done to draw public attention to the destruction of the interconnected chain of life.

However, at times I am gratified by the efforts of conservation groups that attempt to make life better for one species or another. The International Quail Foundation is just such a group, their sole purpose being to preserve habitat for the northern bobwhite and other sub-species of quail.

This painting, completed several years ago, was recently chosen as the 1983 International Quail Foundation print. It shows one of the brush piles on my son Roy's farm, mostly pine boughs from a recent trimming, with five quail huddled close for protection from the wind. In the background stands our machine shed, added here to reflect the quail's association with man.

Quail are friendly little birds, usually seen just this way. Plus, they survive as I have depicted — on the edge of man's domain. Yet they can certainly use all the help that we can give them, whether it is by providing cover or food.

We do our part around our Briggsville, Wisconsin, home to provide habitat for quail. We leave brush piles so that they can find cover, especially during the bitter winter, and we feed them cracked corn.

1970, oil, 32″ x 24″

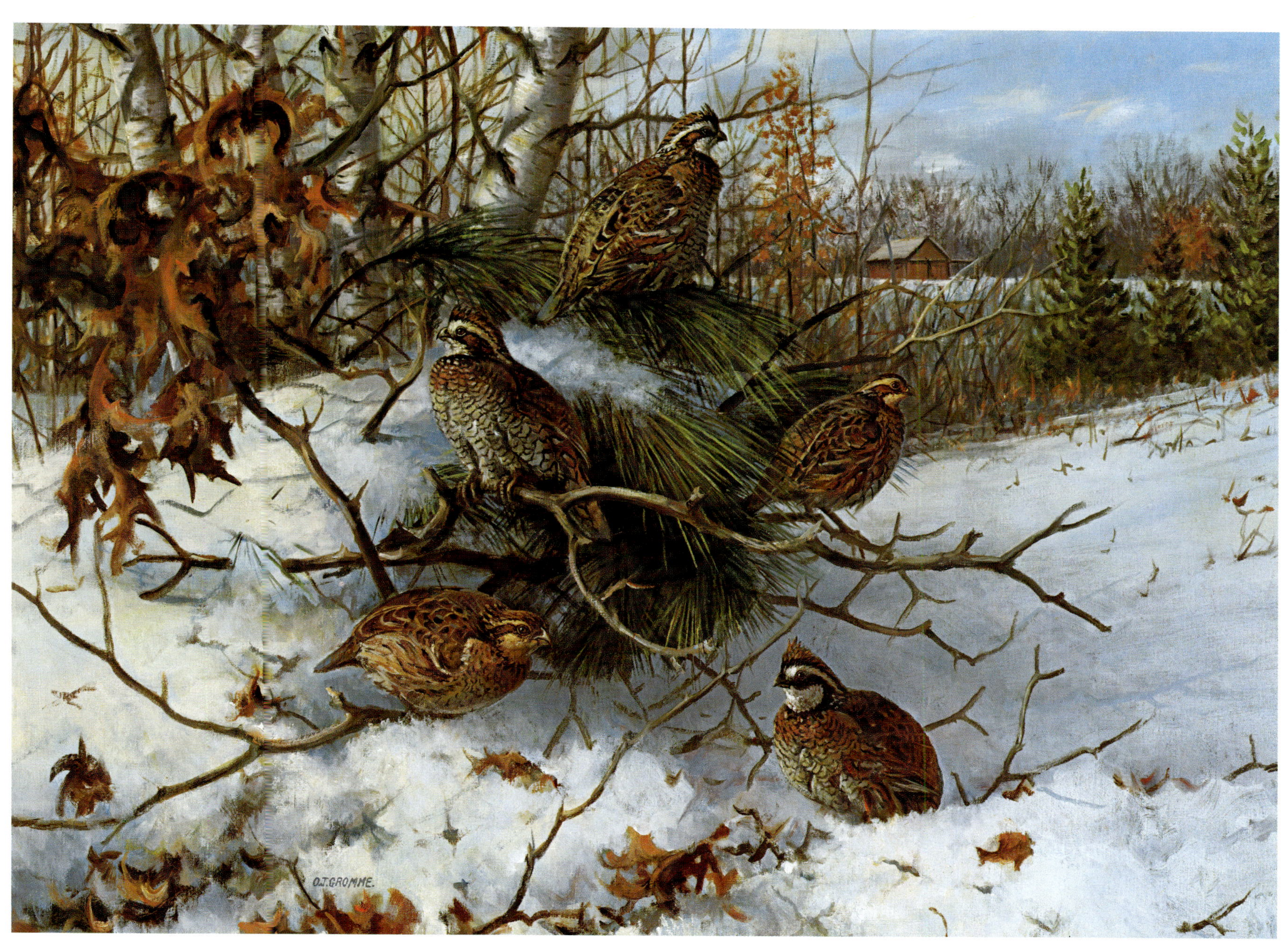
O.J.GROMME.

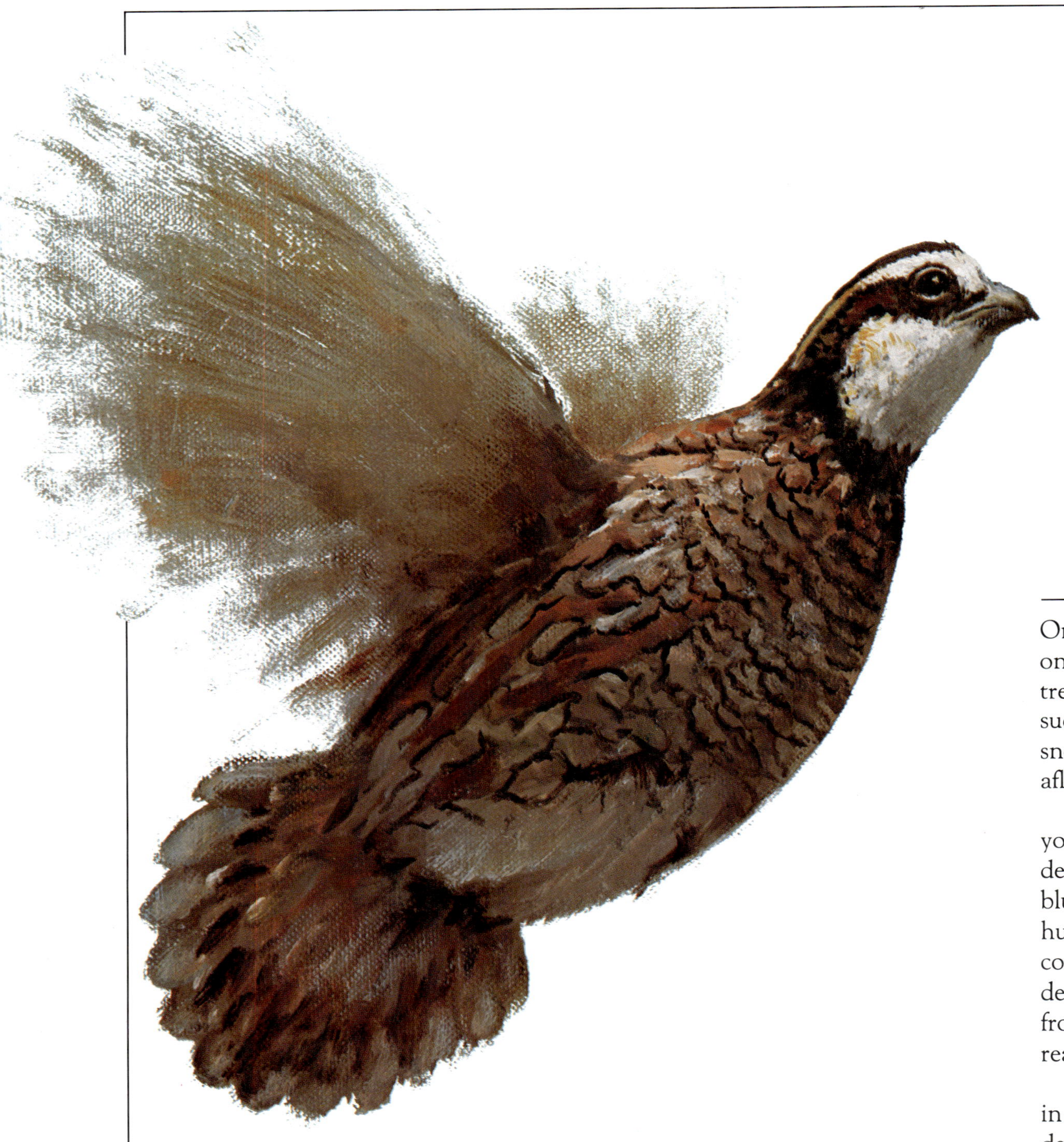

Trio of Bobwhites

One morning I was snowshoeing down the path to our pond after one of those light, fluffy snowfalls, when the snow sticks to the trees like a layer of soft cotton. Three northern bobwhite quail suddenly flushed out of a sumac bush in a flurry and a cloud of snow. This painting represents the exact way I saw them, wings aflutter and snow flying everywhere.

Quail have a very rapid wingbeat. They move so fast that you cannot see the individual wing feathers. You can see the detail of the body, including the eye, but the wings are completely blurred. I have tried to show this before in paintings of a hummingbird and a ruffed grouse drumming, and I have now come to the conclusion that a bird painting should show only the detail that is obvious to the normal eye when motion is rapid, from a distance of about six feet. Anything more detailed is not realistic.

I currently use this as my guiding principle in painting, but in my earlier days, I used to put in much more detail. This demonstrates to me that I continue to learn and alter my technique everyday. That's why I will often show these fast flyers with their wings blurred, because that is how they actually look when you see them.

1980, oil, 28″ x 24″

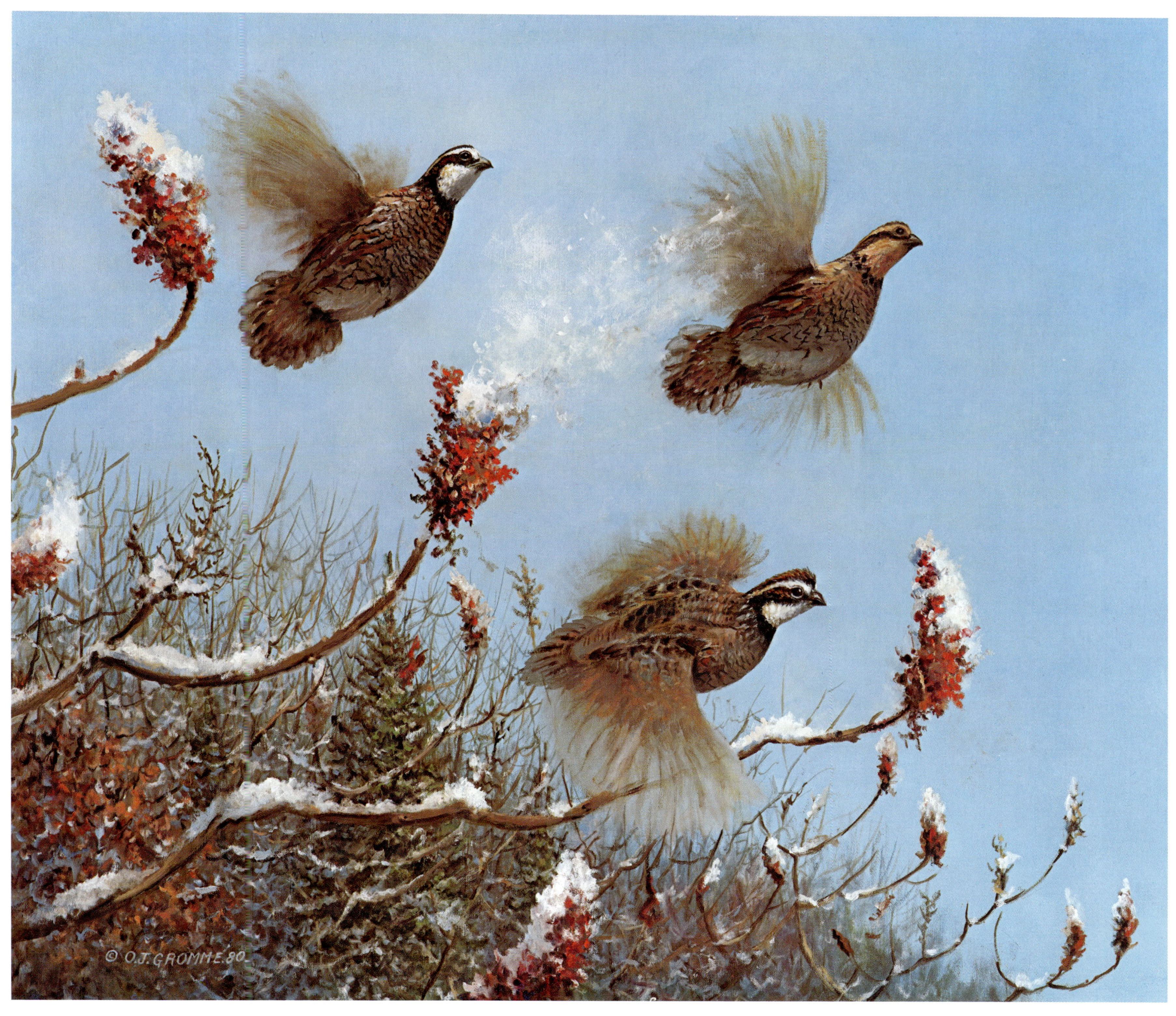
© O.J. GROMME 80

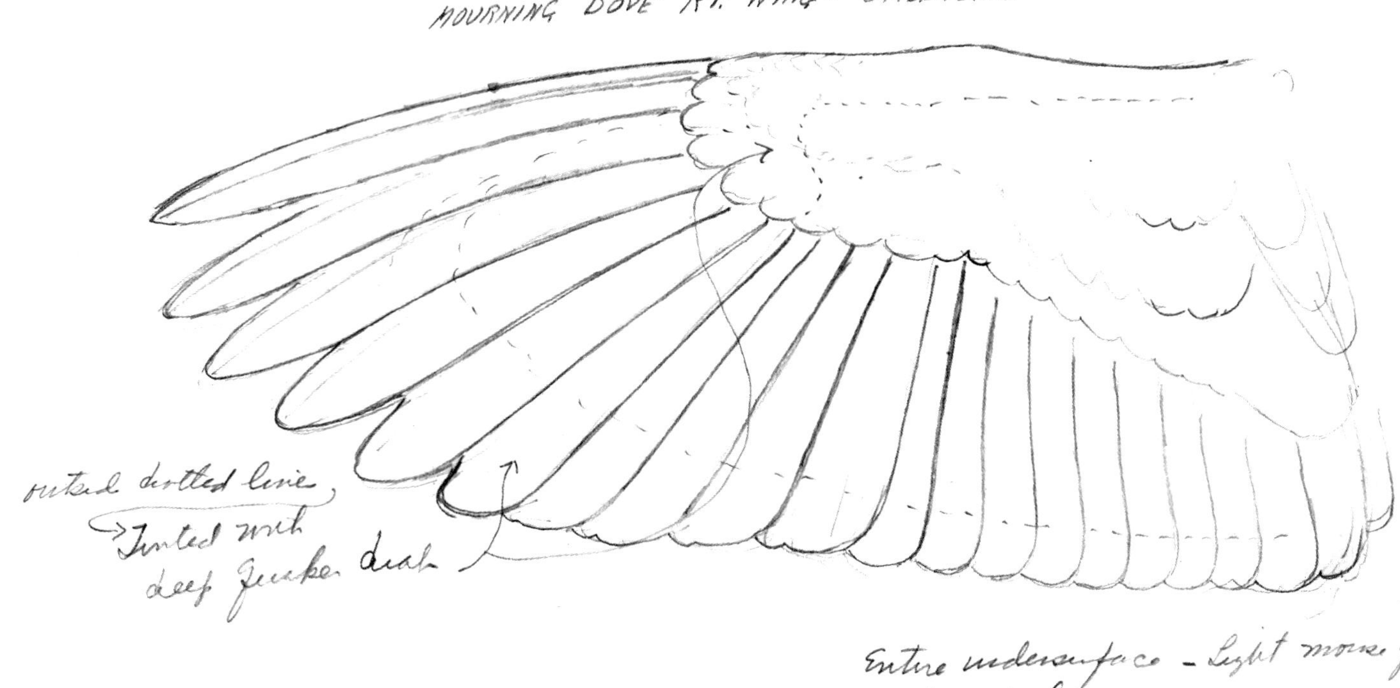

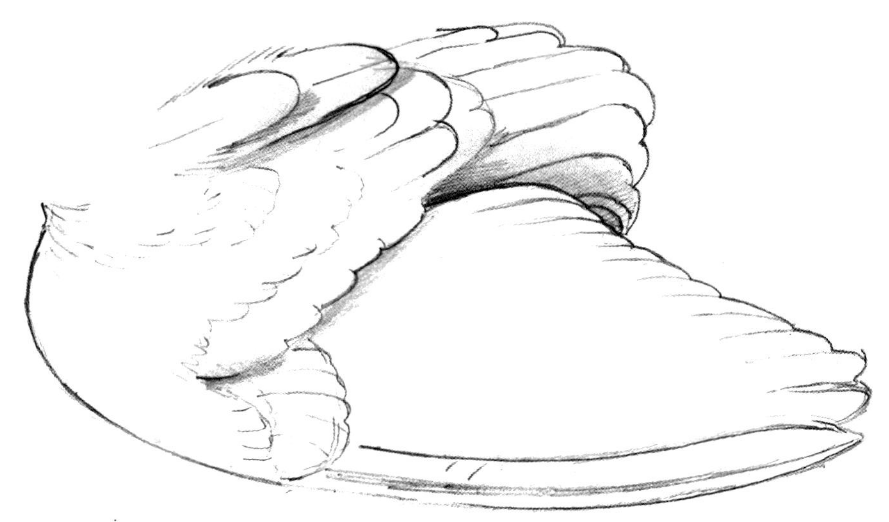

Dropping In — Mourning Doves

The mourning dove is thought of as a songbird in Wisconsin, but in the South and West it is considered a game bird and is hunted in great numbers. Personally, I wouldn't want to see them classified as a game bird in Wisconsin, and while I do not necessarily consider the dove a bird of peace, even though they are depicted that way all over the world, I do love to hear them cooing in the morning. I have shown them here dropping into a corn field against a background that could be found either in Wisconsin or in the South. The birds travel in large flocks down South, but in the Midwest they are usually seen alone or in small groups on telephone wires, fence posts, or nesting in dooryards.

The closest relative to the mourning dove that we have ever had in Wisconsin is the passenger pigeon. When I was at the Milwaukee Public Museum, people would often call us and say they had sighted a passenger pigeon. Although I was quite skeptical that the caller had indeed spotted a passenger pigeon, I would always follow up for fear that they might be right. But every time we went out to investigate, the alleged passenger pigeons turned out to be mourning doves.

1974, oil, 36" x 24"

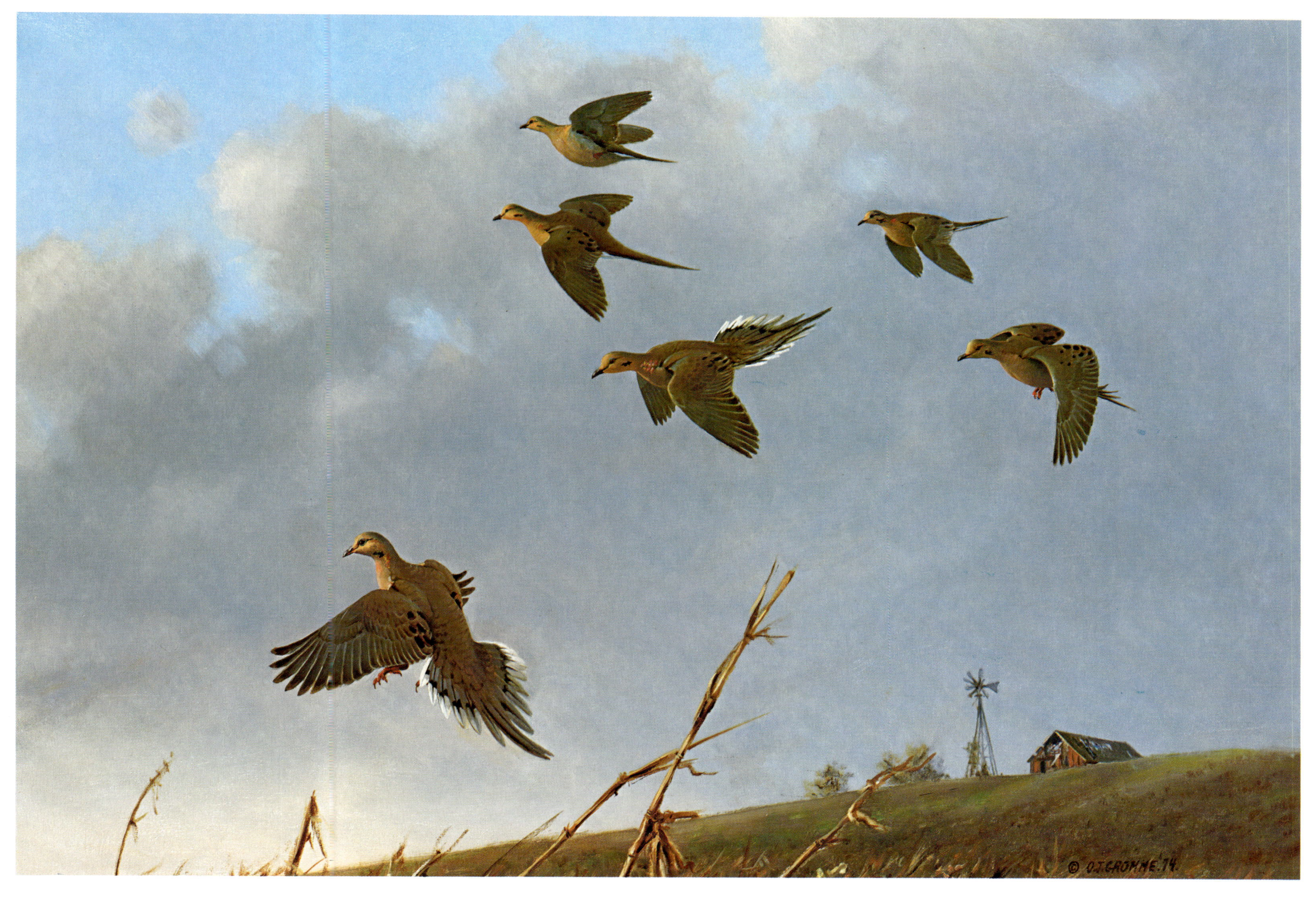
© O.J.GROMME.'74

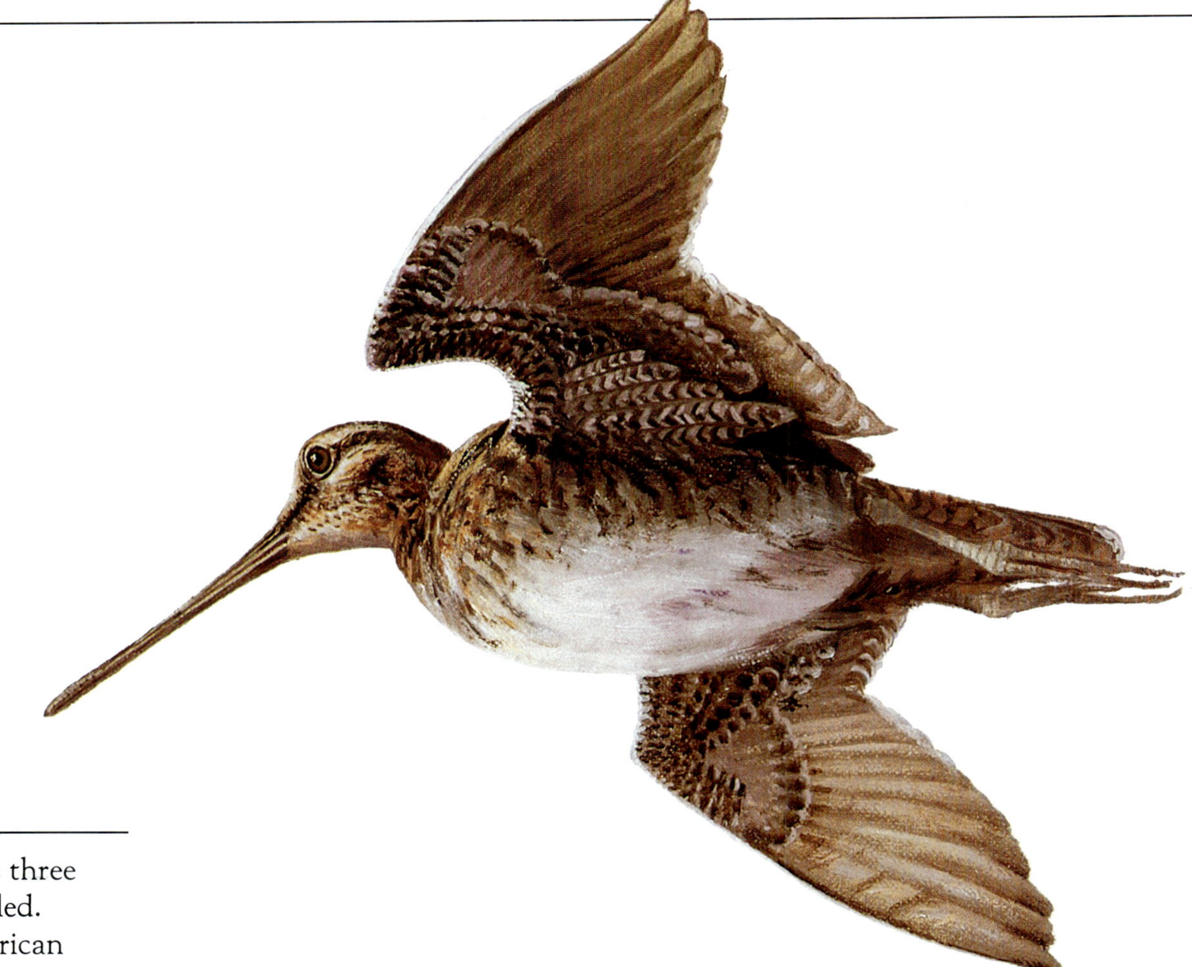

Wilson's Snipe

Pictured here flying past a nearly-naked stalk of wild rice are three Wilson's snipe, or jack snipe as they are more commonly called. Snipe are large shorebirds, similar in appearance to the American woodcock, and they likewise use their long, prehensile bills to probe in the marsh mud for worms.

Once the ground freezes to a point where they can no longer probe for worms, jack snipe will then flock and begin to migrate. From my years of observing them, I have surmised that they migrate mostly at night and spend their days resting and searching for food in the marsh.

The flight pattern of these birds is quick and erratic. Like quail and grouse, snipe get up to full speed the moment they leave the ground. For this reason they are very difficult to shoot in flight, and few hunters will ever try them.

The "jacks" perform an interesting mating ceremony in flight wherein they produce an eerie whistling sound, called "whiffling." If you have ever been out on a marsh in the spring, you have probably heard it, such a strange sound that it is, but you might not have known exactly what it was.

1967, oil, 18″ x 26″

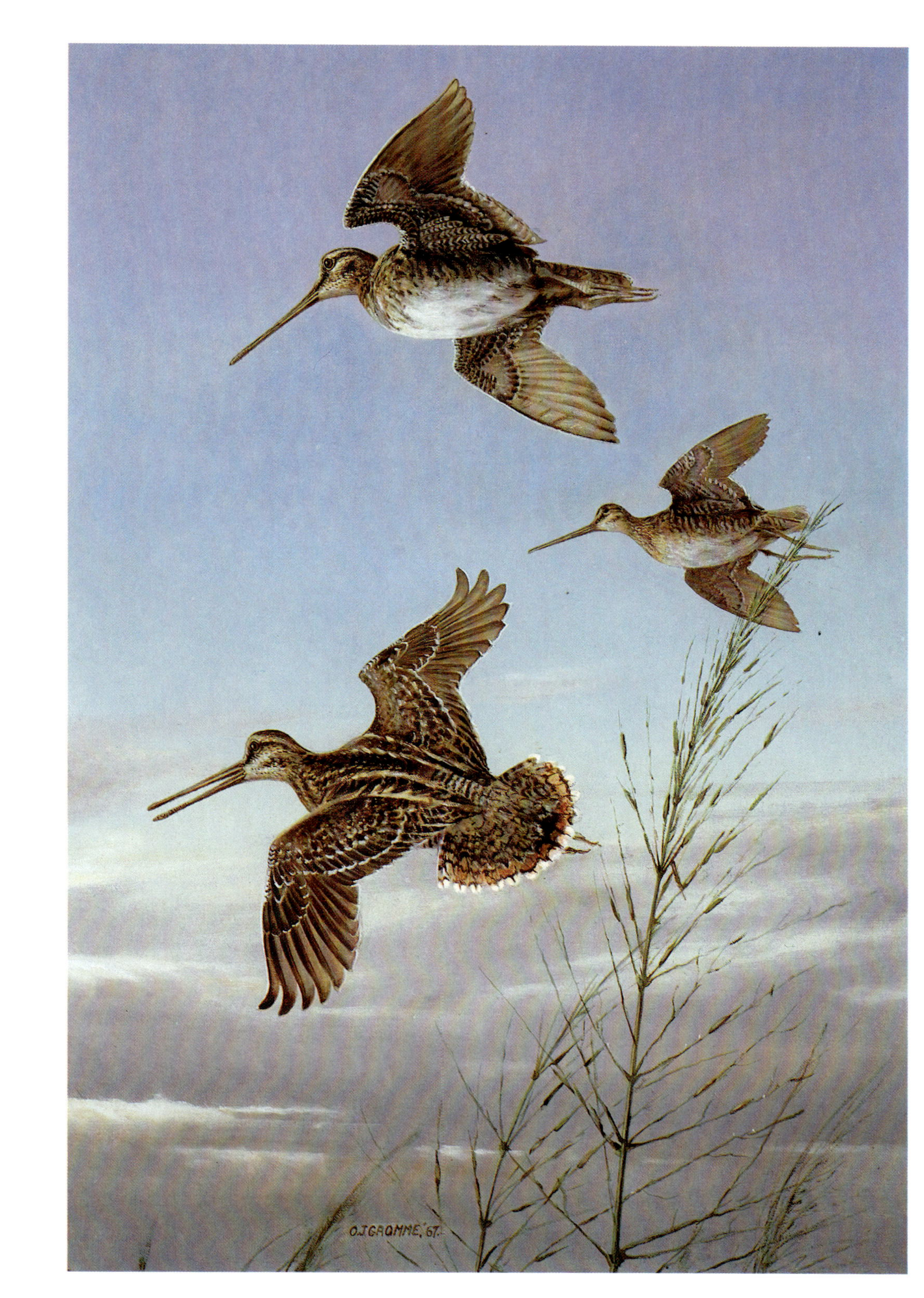
O.J.GROMME '67

Southern Pines — Wild Turkeys

Anne and I used to go down to Georgia practically every spring to visit my old friend Herb Stoddard. We stayed at his home on Sherwood plantation where he had retired to work on his book, *The Bobwhite Quail.*

Southern Pines — Wild Turkeys depicts a couple of turkey gobblers as we so often saw them flying down there. In most paintings turkeys are shown either strutting or grouped on the ground. But in flight they are quite a streamlined bird in appearance, especially when you realize that they weigh up to twenty or more pounds.

There is another important element involved in this painting. Each year in March or April, fires are deliberately set throughout the South's turkey country. Since southern pines seem to be more fire-resistant than our northern pines, the Southerners, taking a cue from the Indians, use fire to control the underbrush in their area.

Thus, through the use of controlled burning every spring, three results are achieved: 1) combustibility is reduced — if a fire starts accidentally there is not enough undergrowth to feed it; 2) the ground is "opened" for the growth of feed for turkeys and quail; 3) the population of wood ticks, a major nuisance in that area, is greatly reduced.

So when we visit Georgia at that time of year, the air always carries the acrid smell of burning pine which I like. Some of the pine trunks are charred ten feet up but it doesn't seem to harm them. And while fire burns over the smaller pines, many of them will come right up again.

Recently, a man from the South commented about this painting, saying, "I can almost smell the smoke." I was pleased by his observation because the bluish haze in this painting is there to show the ecological use of controlled burning.

1966, oil, 33" x 25"

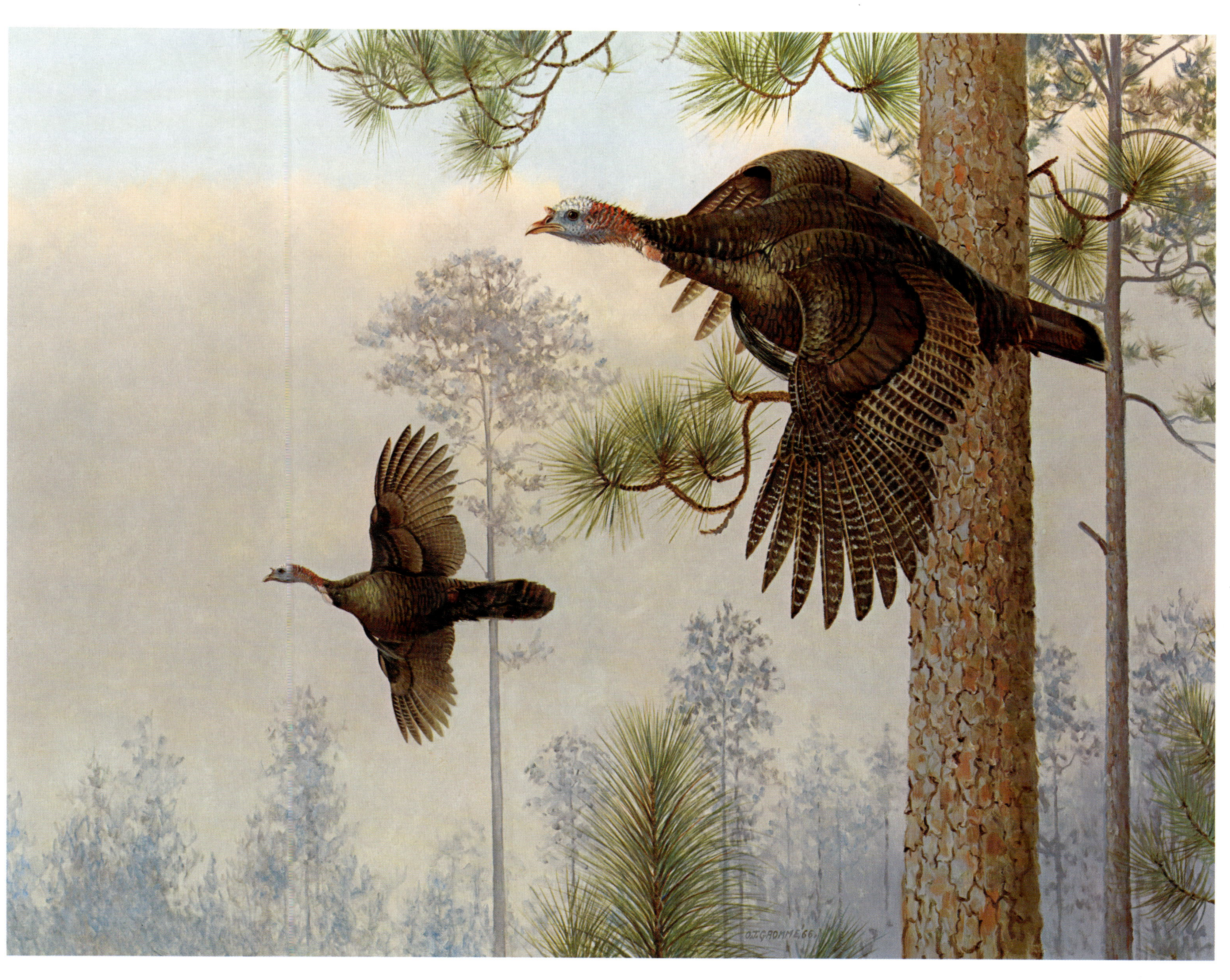
O.J.GROMME '66

Evening Stillness — Barred Owl

There is an old maple tree in our yard which has a large rotted-out cavity in it. I often thought that I would like to include that maple in a painting, but I needed just the right place for it. Finally, the barred owl gave me my excuse, for they regularly nest in cavities such as this.

The barred owl is both a daylight and nocturnal owl, and it is a beautiful bird to paint because of the barred markings on its breast. While most owls have yellow eyes, the barred owl's eyes are brown, with an inky-blue cast to them. In fact, their eyes are so dark that they appear to be enormous.

Like other owls, the barred owl is a silent flyer, a result of a series of small hooks on the forward part of the leading feathers of each wing. These owls do not migrate, preferring to remain the year round and subsisting on a diet of small birds and mammals.

One of the most distinctive characteristics of the barred owl is its call: "Who cooks for you? Whooo? Whooo? Who cooks for you?" The call is easy to imitate, and it is not uncommon for a barred owl to answer a person calling in the woods. You can hear these owls on the coldest winter nights or on the warmest summer evenings. When the young are out of the nest, you can hear the whole family calling. They have quite a repertoire.

1976, oil, 24" x 30"

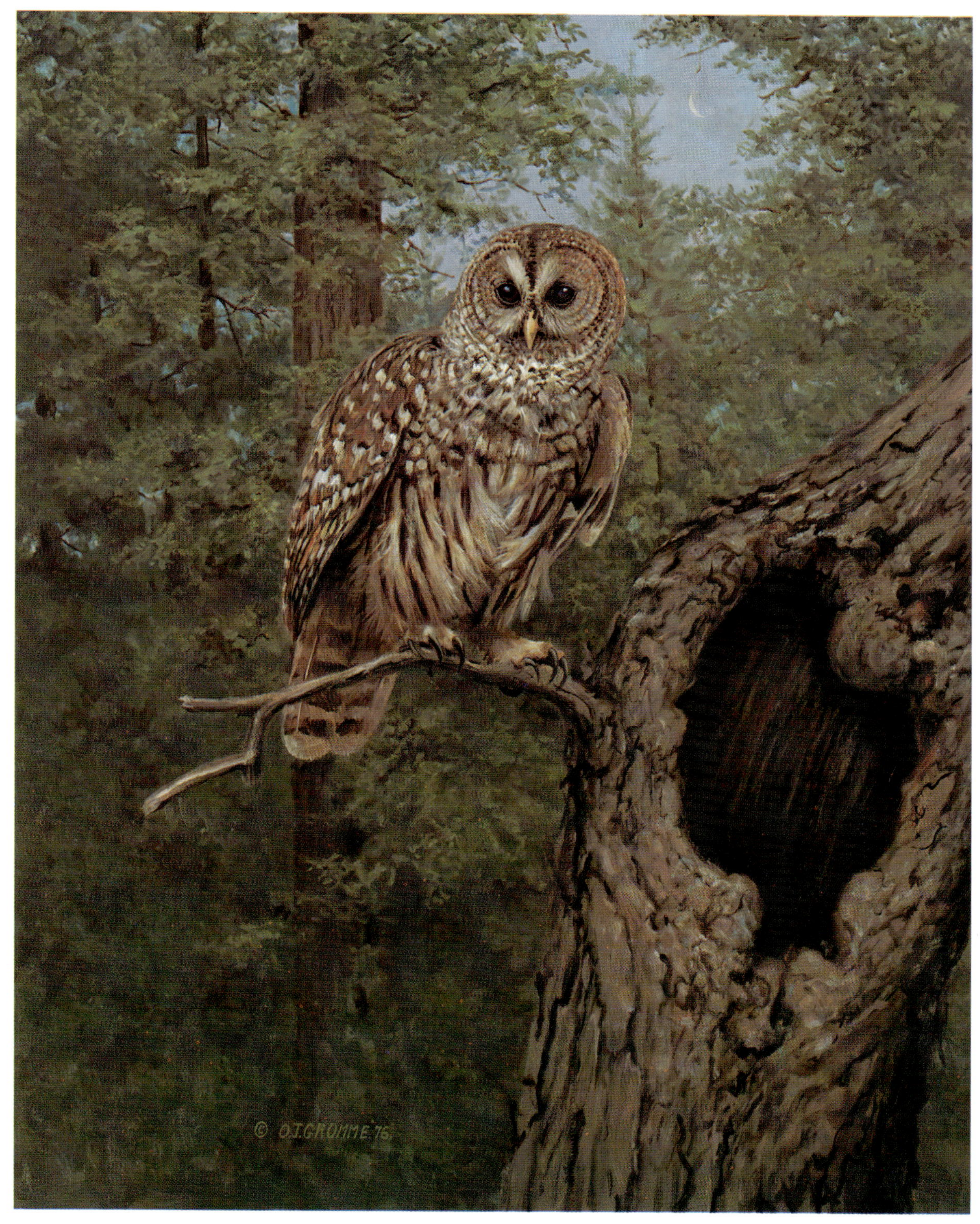
© O.J.GROMME 76

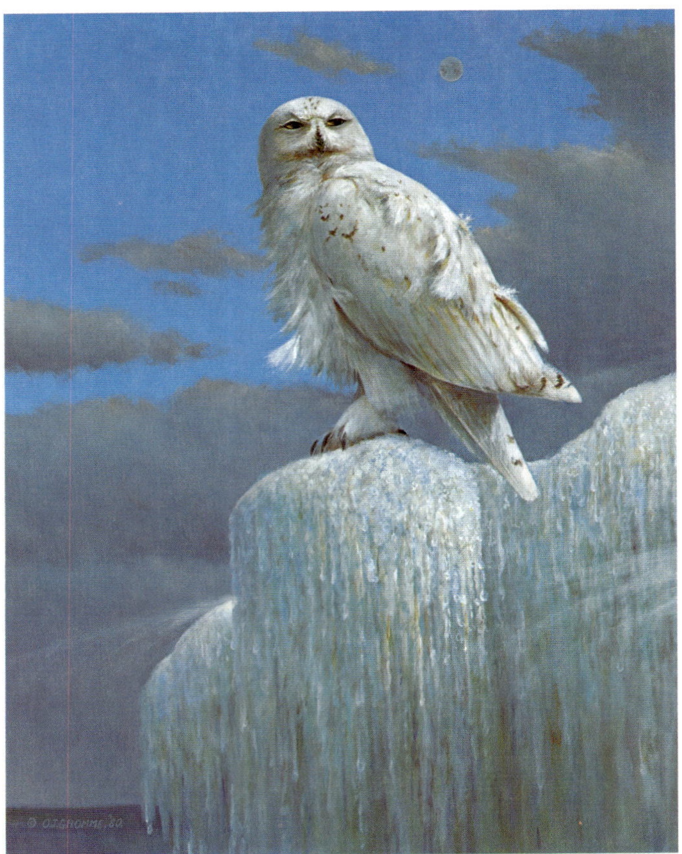

Snowy Owl

I saw this snowy owl one day perched atop an ice-covered piling on the Lake Michigan shore near Port Washington, Wisconsin. The spray from the lake freezes on those pilings, adding layer upon layer of ice until they are more than twice as thick as normal.

This is another case where a natural phenomenon creates a scene so subtle in its variation of color and texture that I as an artist feel compelled to try and recreate it in all of its cold beauty. Ice and the owl are a challenge to the artist because they are primarily white, and yet they show a wide range of shades and colors which define their form. The blue sky contributes to the cold intensity of the scene, as does the solitary bird, his feathers fluttering in the wind.

1980, oil, 28" x 36"

Snowy Owl, Bufflehead, Crow — Lakeshore

During a hard Arctic winter when food, especially the lemming, is scarce, snowy owls will venture south in search of easier sustenance. They eat rodents, fish, birds or whatever they can catch. This snowy owl is perched on top of a sand dune on the shore of Lake Michigan with the ice piled high along the beach. He would be quietly devouring that bufflehead he just caught or found dead if it were not for his old nemesis, the crow.

Crows and owls seem to have an affinity for each other. The American crow depicted here has no designs on stealing the duck; he just can't resist bothering the owl. He flits closer and closer, hoping for a chance to dig the owl with his claws. The owl might trick him into coming close enough, then jump up and grab him, so the crow is playing a dangerous game.

Snowy owls find the living much easier along the Lake Michigan shores than in the Arctic. Life is especially good for them around ice fishing shanties because they can sit on the shanty roofs and wait for the fishermen to throw out any undesirable fish.

1967, oil, 40" x 32"

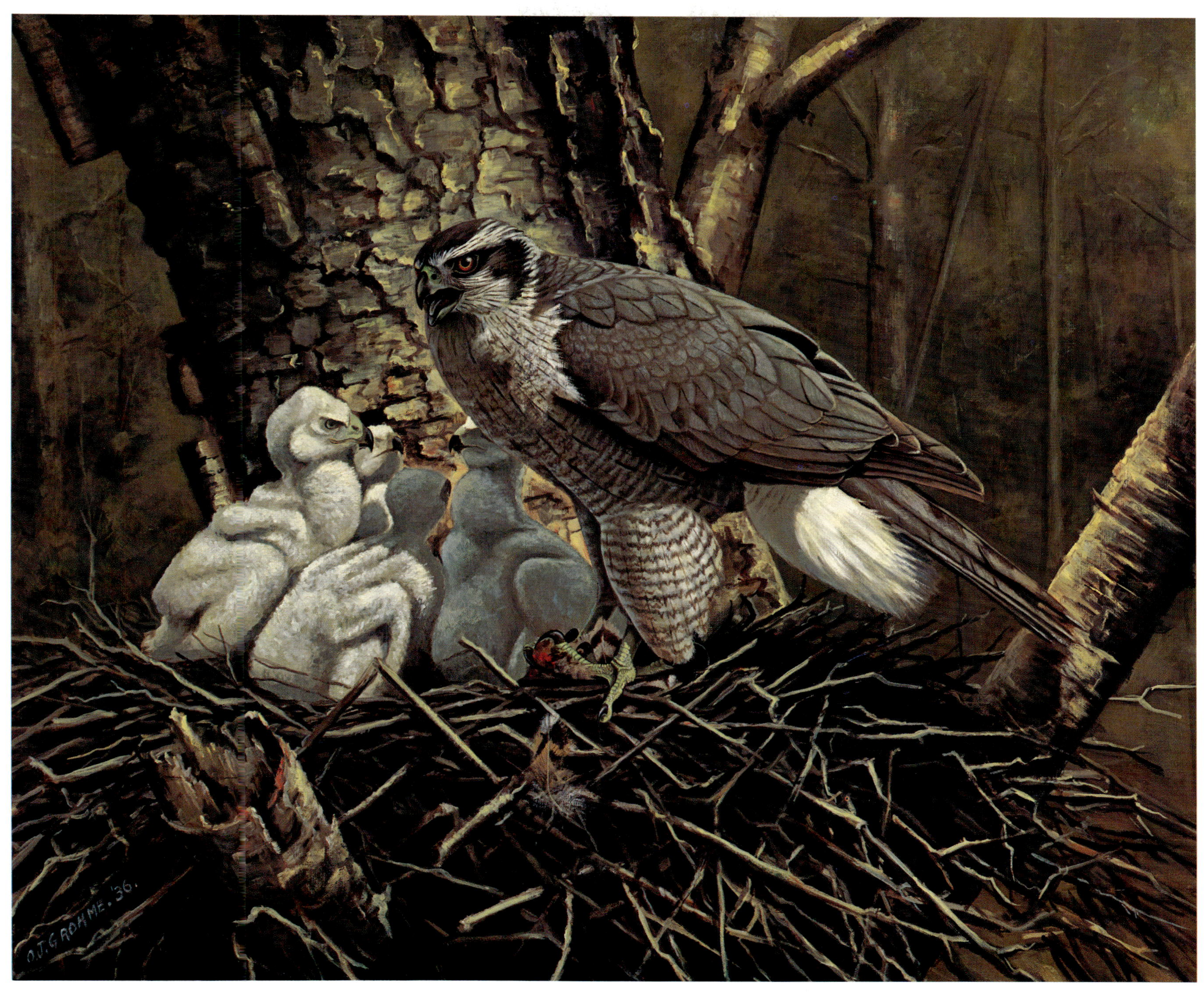
O.J. GROMME. '36.

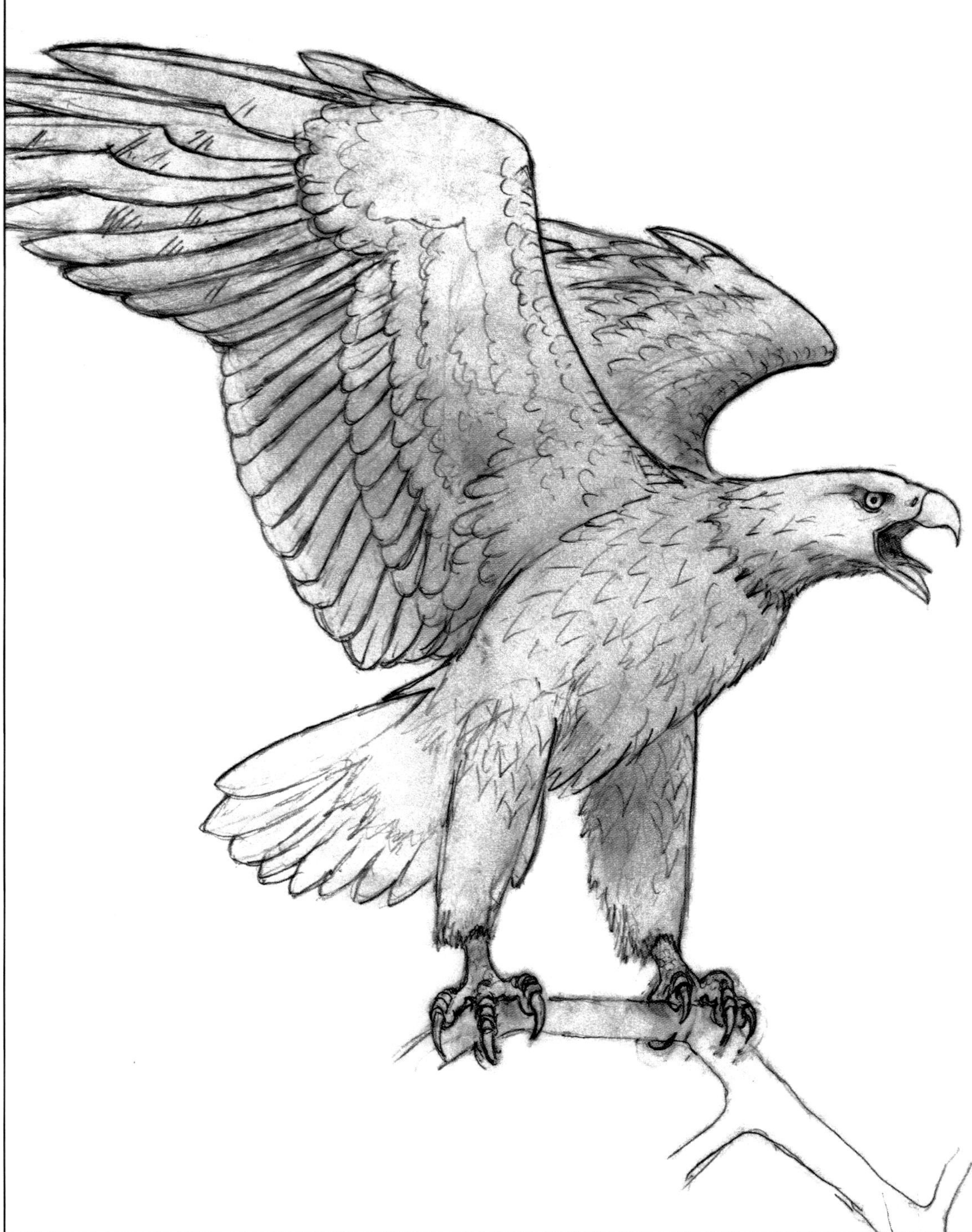

Eagles at the Dells

I have had a number of adventures trying to do photographic studies of bald eagles. In 1926, for example, I was in northern Wisconsin building a blind from which I was to photograph an eagle's nest. Climbing up to the blind, I grabbed a rope which I thought was being held by someone on the ground. It was not. I fell through the air, trying desperately to keep my thoughts clear, did at least one somersault, and landed *on my feet* in a deep bed of sphagnum moss. I was still holding onto the rope, which had caught in the last ten or so feet of my fall, and it had burned the skin off both my palms. In all, I had fallen 77 feet and didn't break a bone!

I never went back to get those pictures, but when I journeyed down to the Wisconsin Dells to do photographic studies for this painting of the Dells eagles, I again almost fell off a cliff! I finally decided that maybe I had better give up trying to photograph bald eagles and stick with painting them instead.

These glorious birds are familiar to the people of Wisconsin Dells because they fly over the town every day in the winter in their journey to and from open water. Bald eagles often winter near dams and electric power plants because there they can find open water and easy fishing.

1979, oil, 48″ x 36″

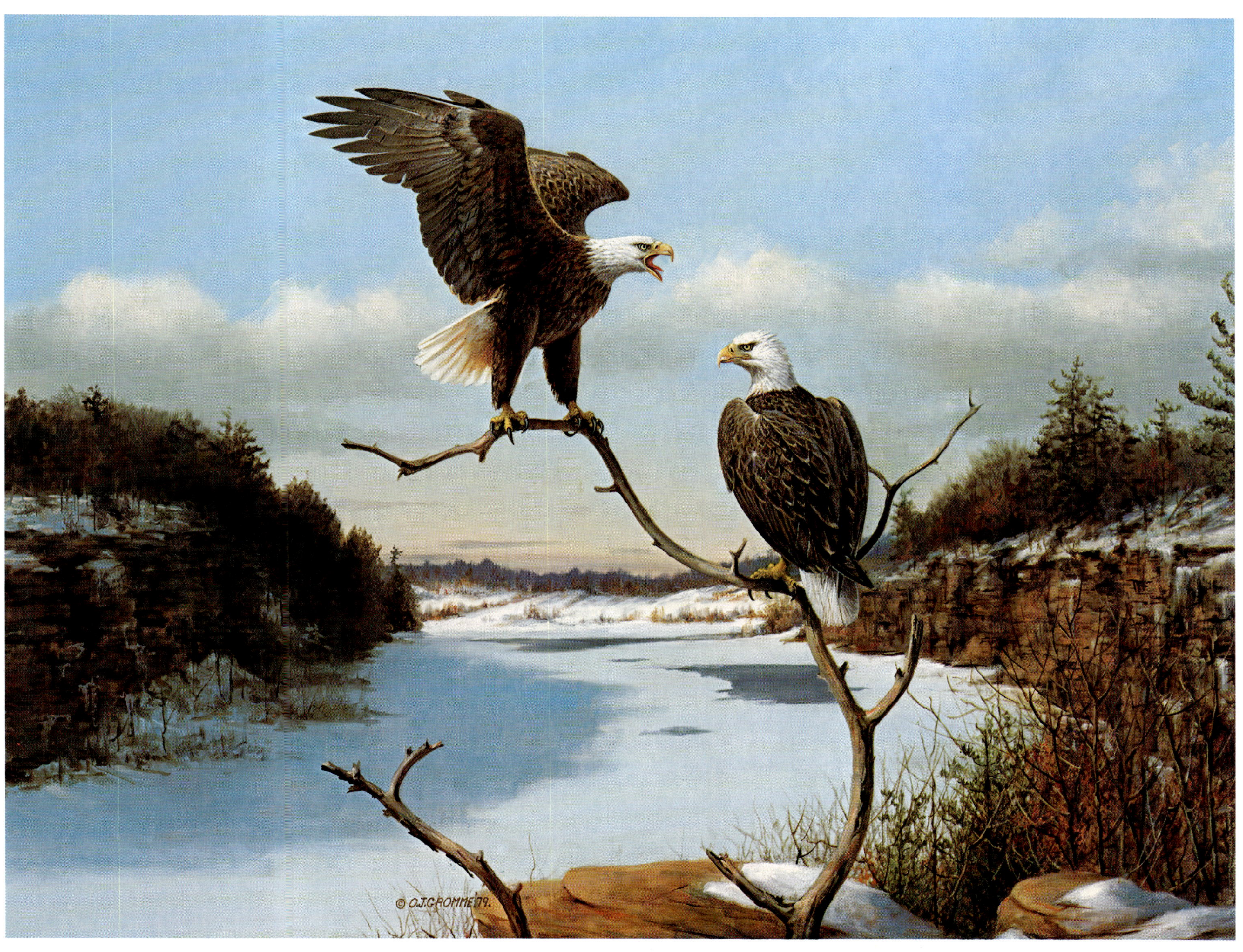
© O.J.GROMME '79.

Marsh Hawks in Spring — Food Transfer

On one of those crisp, windy March days during my boyhood in Fond du Lac, Wisconsin, I walked out to the flats east of town and observed a pair of northern harriers (marsh hawks) going through their spring mating antics.

One of the mated pair had captured a gopher or a field mouse and had flown high up in the air. The other northern harrier followed, and the two floated around for some time, soaring, banking and climbing the thermals. Then suddenly, the one hawk dropped the prey, and the other caught it! The birds continued the ritual, passing the prey back and forth for a long time.

As I have shown it here, the male is flying on his back in mid-air, catching the gopher dropped by the female.

1968, oil, 30" x 40"

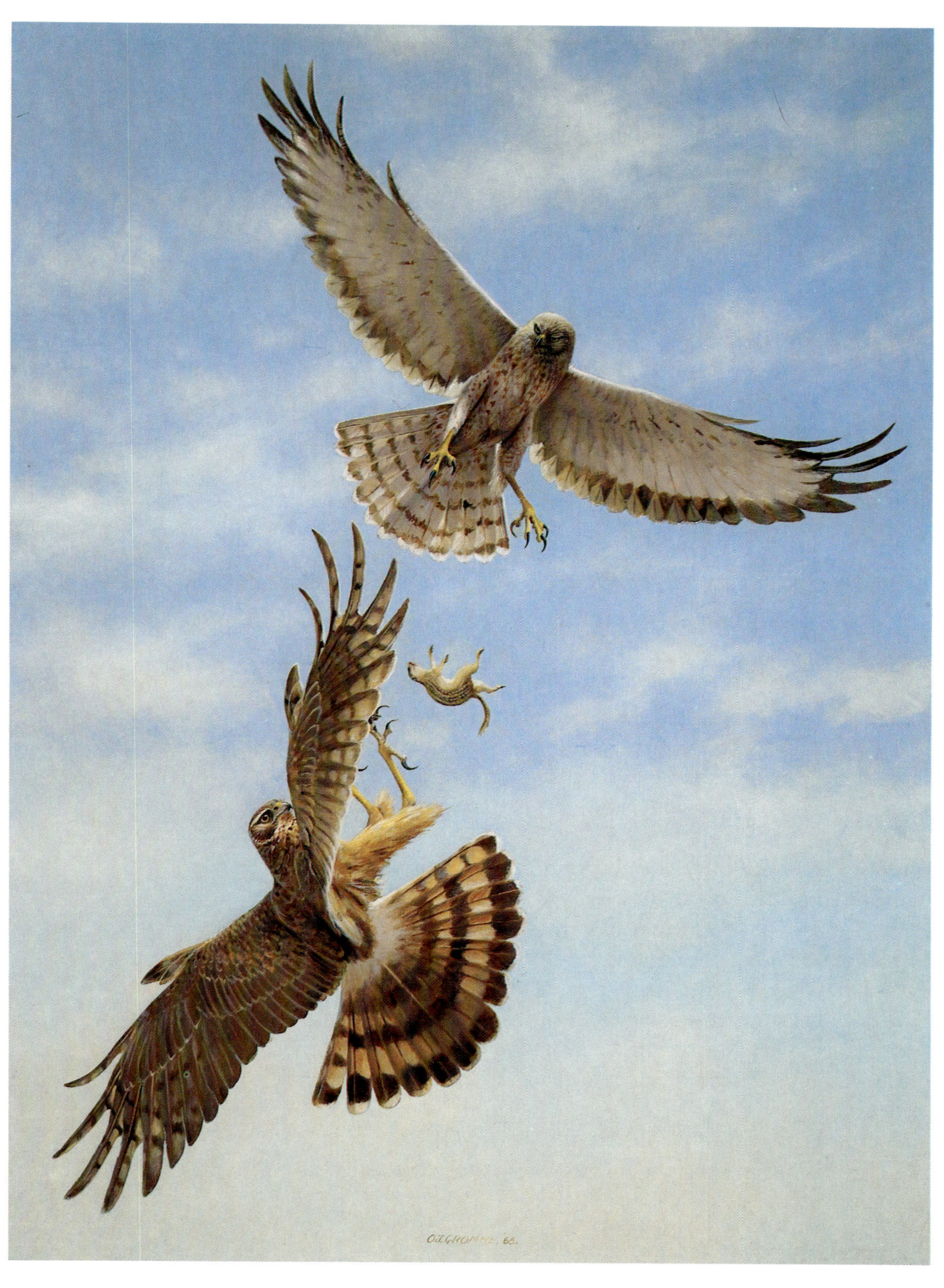

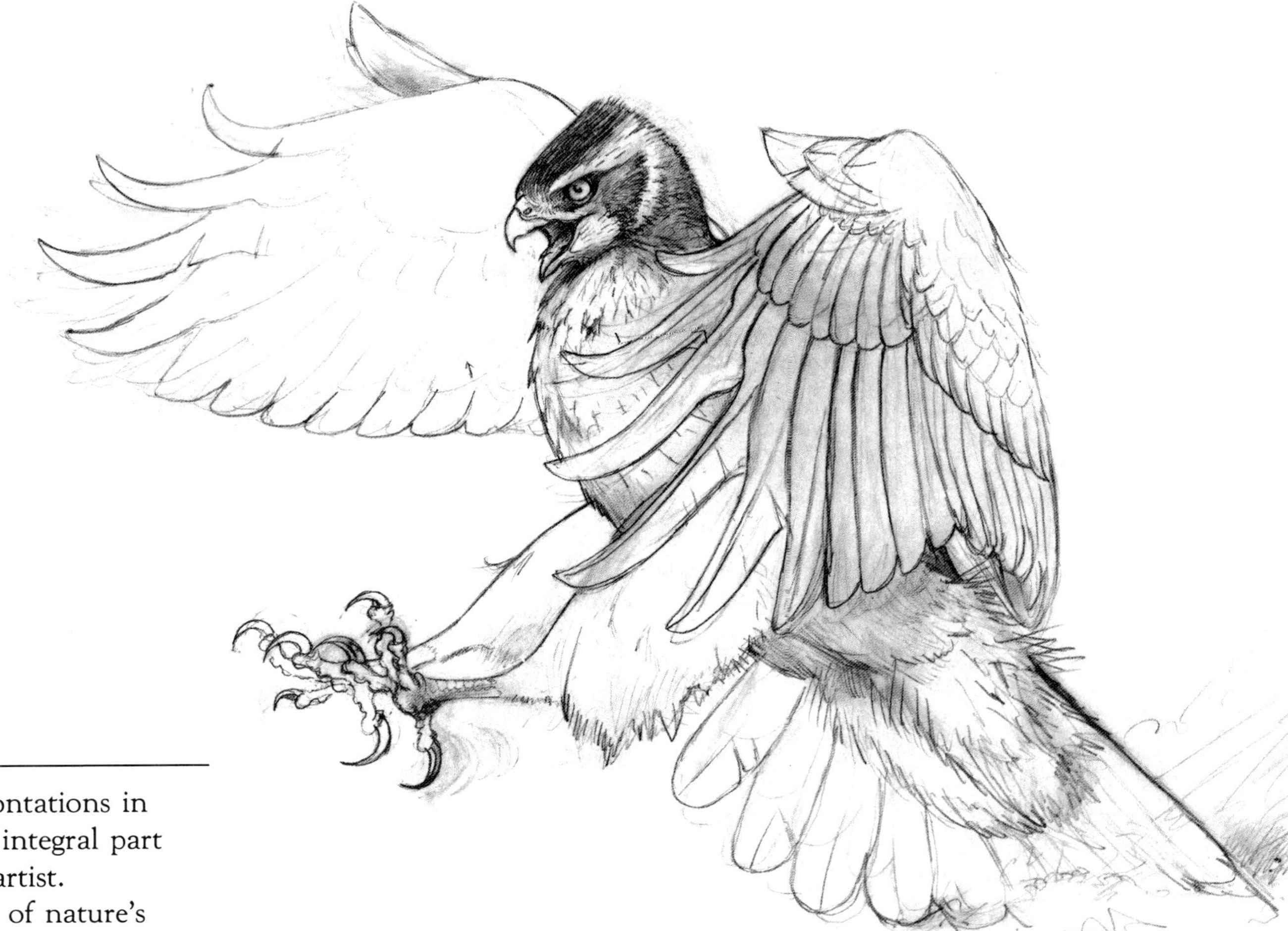

Goshawk Attacking Mink

I have been criticized for presenting too many confrontations in my paintings, but I feel that the confrontation is an integral part of nature, and therefore a legitimate subject for the artist.

This confrontation is a classic one, pitting two of nature's most vicious and efficient predators against one another. The northern goshawk is a bird-killing hawk of the forests, but it will also challenge mammals occasionally. It is incredibly brave, and will go almost anywhere in pursuit of its prey. In fact, a goshawk has actually been known to chase a cat into a farmer's kitchen and snatch it right out from under the stove!

Similarly, the mink is a ferocious killer, ready to stand and fight if necessary. Here, the hawk has spied the mink out in the open and, without hesitation, swoops in for the kill. With a snarl of defiance, the surprised mink makes a desperate dash to gain the safety of the water and avoid the deadly, outstretched talons of the northern goshawk.

Will the outclassed mink survive the onslaught, or will it end up as a meal for the heavier predator? The outcome is left to the imagination of the viewer.

1969, oil, 40″ x 30″

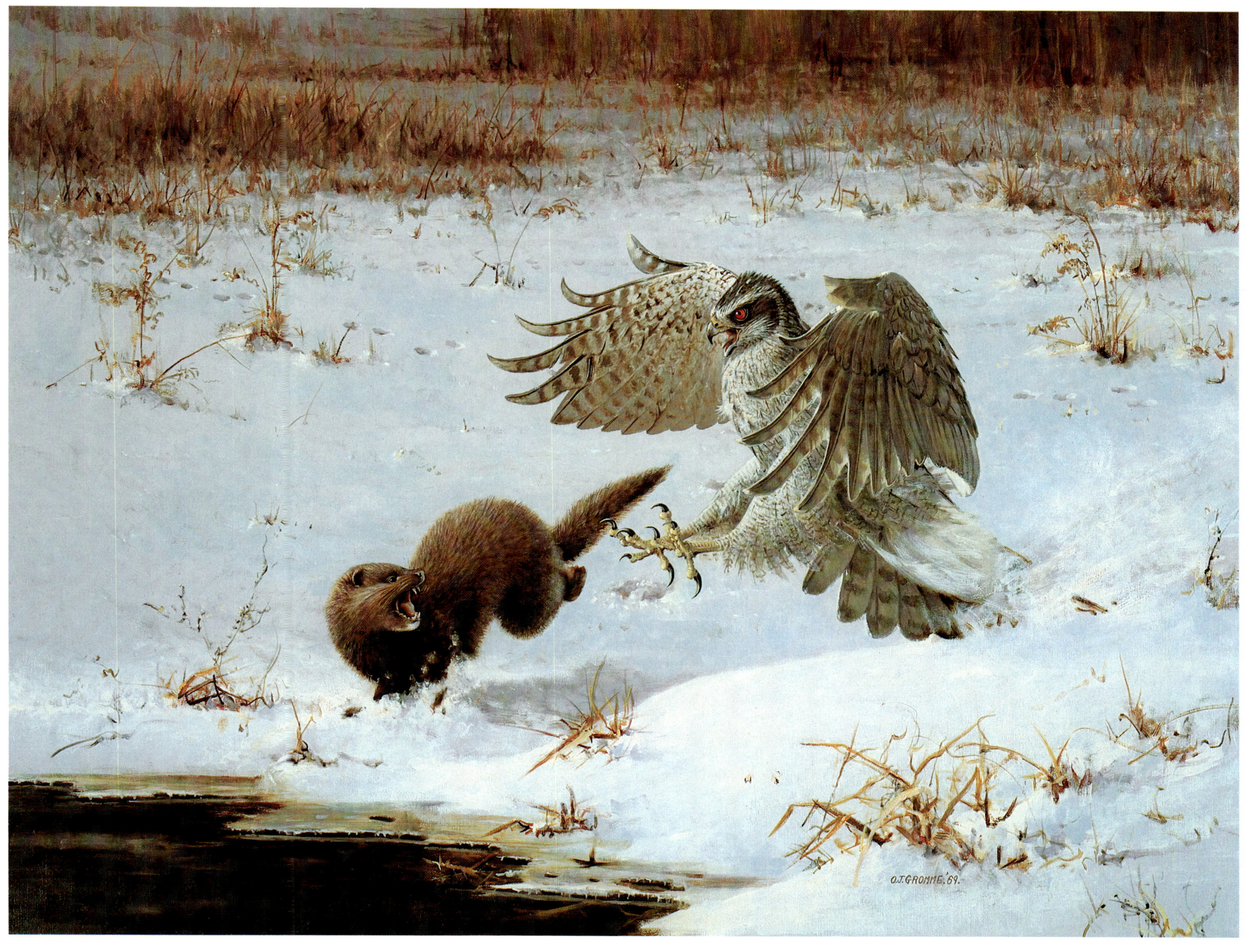
O.J.GROMME '69.

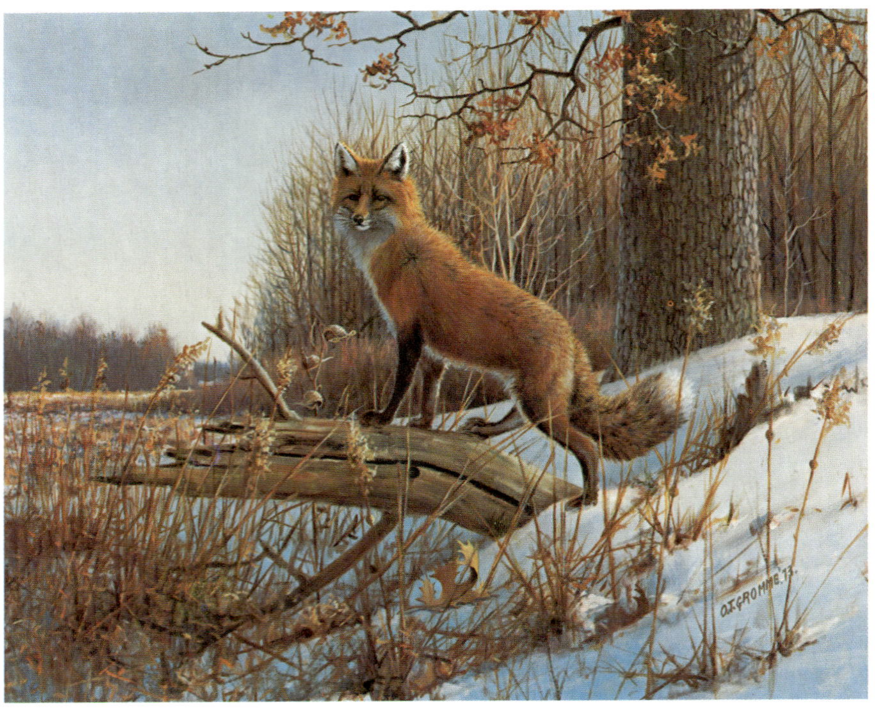

Expectation — Red Fox

Whenever and wherever I can I use the farm as a background for my paintings, but only if it is logically and environmentally correct of course. Why not use an area that I know well, rather than travel far afield? Thus, I get my skies right out of my studio window and many of my settings too! And being familiar with the local vegetation, I can maintain the proper perspective, being careful to show things like the milkweed pod, an old oak stump and the goldenrod with the galls on it, as I have done in this painting. The big oak tree, too, is from our land, holding a few dead leaves as it does in the wintertime.

Here the fox stands, bright and alert, a wary observer of the world. But as red as the fox is, if he stands perfectly still in this fall scene, he can hardly be seen until he moves. I did not draw any fox tracks here, but presumably he came up from the back side of the log and, as a result, didn't leave any tracks.

1973, oil, 30″ x 24″

Reflections — Red Fox

The red fox is at the same time one of the best-loved and most maligned of nature's creatures. We think of him as being quick and clever. We respect him for his intelligence and adaptability. But we also charge him with all kinds of crimes and misdemeanors from stealing chickens to eating grapes. He probably does all of those things, because the fox is a survivor. If he were not so intelligent and so capable of circumventing man, he would probably be long-gone. His fur has been sought for centuries, and he has been considered a criminal all that time. But he still survives, indeed he thrives, on the fringes of civilization.

I painted this fox in a quiet moment as he was crossing the stream on a log, pausing to look into the water. Perhaps the fish that has just dimpled the water has caught his eye. Maybe he wonders what his chances are of catching it. Or perhaps it is his own image that fascinates him. At any rate, the fox is a beautiful animal which very few of us get to see in such a relaxed moment.

1981, oil, 40″ x 30″

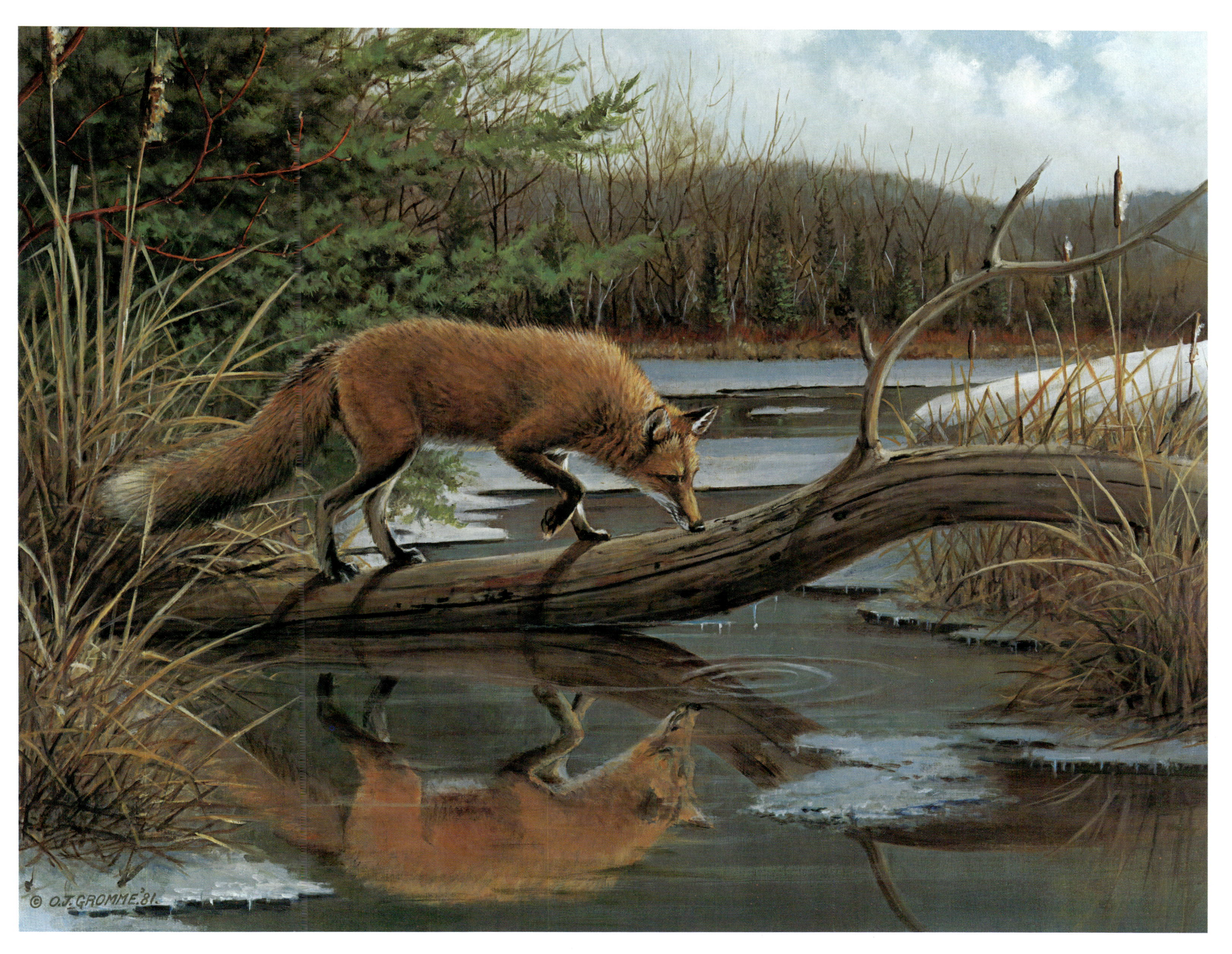
© O.J. GROMME '81

Red Fox — Pheasant Tracks

Nature has many stories to tell if we but take the time to observe. Her tales are revealed in the mud, sand, snow or leaves for those who watch and learn to interpret the signs. *Red Fox — Pheasant Tracks* is one of nature's tales which I was able to observe.

I came upon this scene while out snowshoeing one winter afternoon. The fox didn't notice me watching him from a distance for quite some time. Finally, I made a movement, and he ran away, leaving the story in the snow for me to read. It appears that a pheasant had landed there a short time earlier, its long tail feathers and footprints leaving a trail in the snow. The pheasant eventually wandered off into the stubble of a partially standing corn field.

When the fox came upon the tracks, he stopped and contemplated the possibilities of pursuit. If I had not come along when I did, the fox may have tried it. Or he may have decided that his chances of making a catch in the corn field were not very good. At any rate, he went his way, and the pheasant lived another day.

1967, oil, 36" x 24"

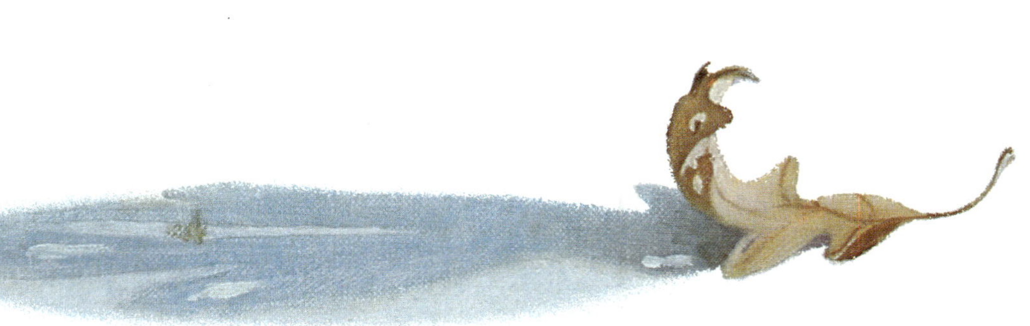

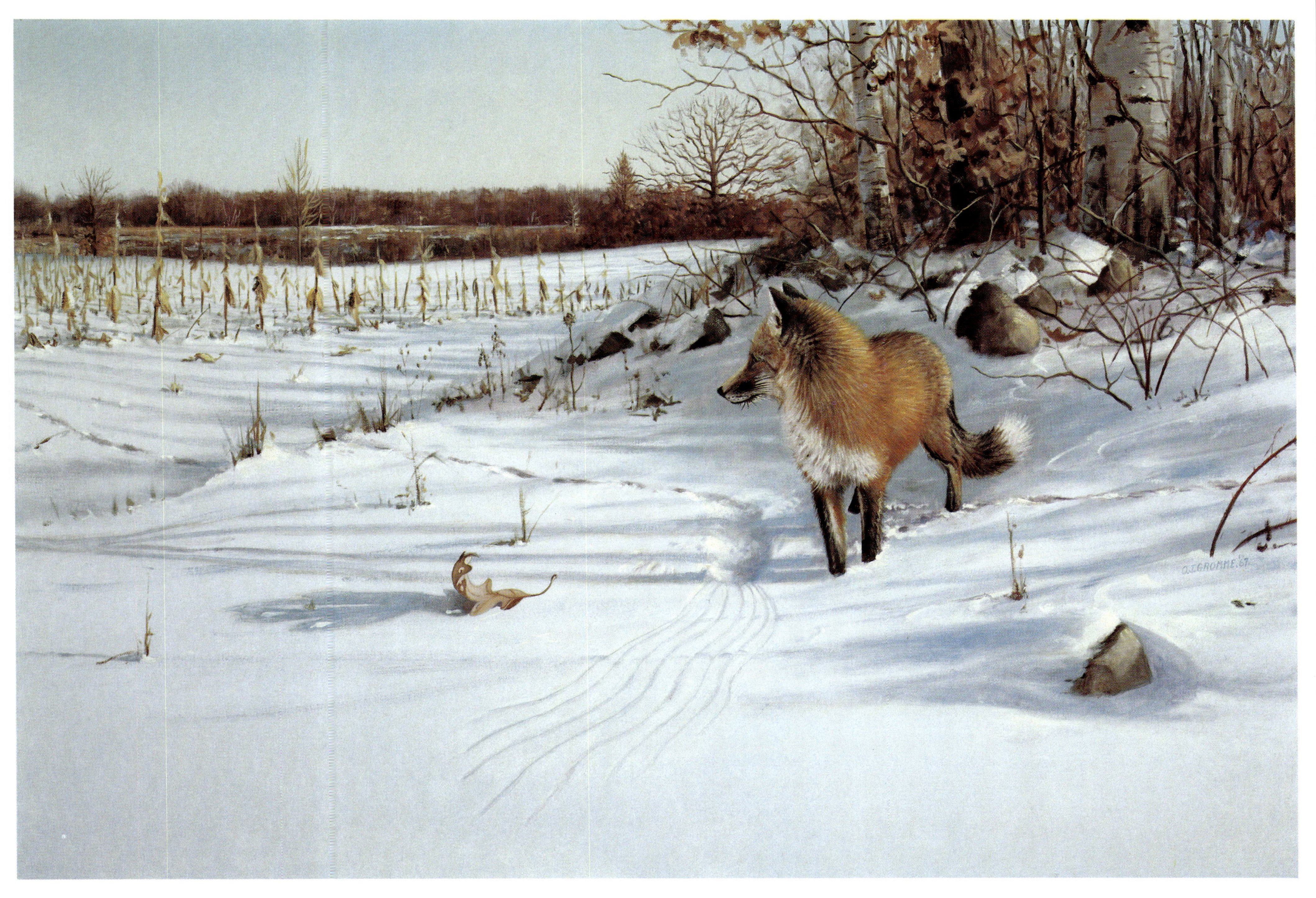
O.J.GROMME '67

Wolf and Swan

Many years ago I read an article in the *Life Histories of North American Wildfowl* by Bent which piqued my imagination. The article told of a swan being observed by a Montana rancher as it swam all alone on a lake, long after its comrades had migrated. Apparently wounded and unable to fly, the swan would keep a small area open in the ice by constantly swimming in a circle. Occasionally it would dive for what little food it could find, but, of course, it always had to come up in the same place. Meanwhile, a coyote, aware of the swan's plight, was constantly circling the area, awaiting the swan's eventual inability to keep the spot of open water from freezing.

Using that story as a point of departure, I painted my own impression of the scene. But I took some liberties — I replaced the coyote with a timberwolf similar to the one that I shot many years ago on the Unuk River in Alaska; and I showed where the wolf had already gone through the ice once, while trying to reach the tundra swan.

Wolf and Swan is a study in futility. We observe both the swan continuously swimming, getting weaker and weaker as the winds blow colder and colder, and the wolf, impatiently awaiting the time when he will inevitably triumph. Or will he?

1967, oil, 36" x 24"

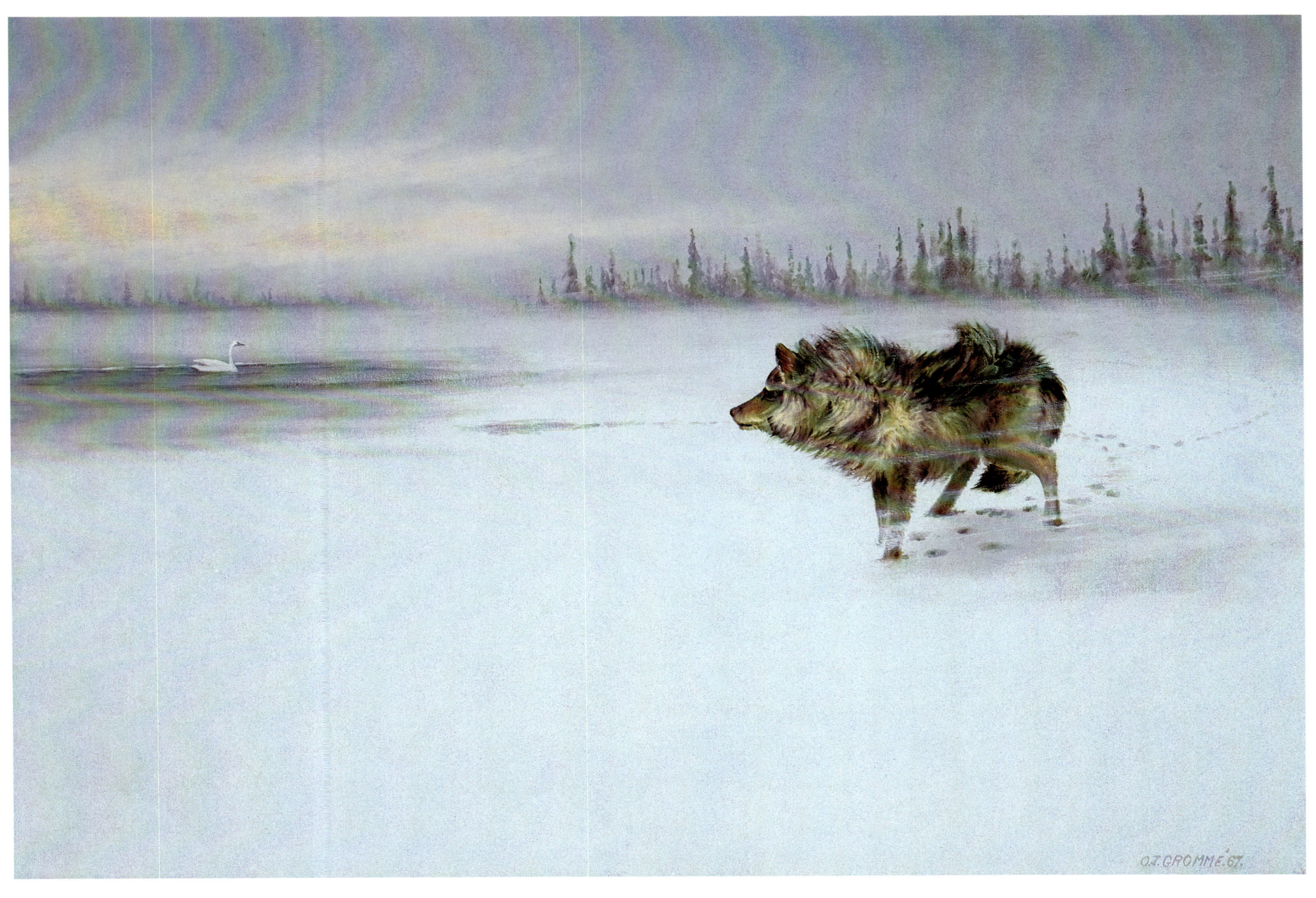
O.J. GROMME. 67.

Polar Bear — Hudson's Bay

I do not know why this is the case, but over the years I have realized that I am oriented to the north. The north wind, the northern lights, the North Star all have a special attraction for me. Having dreamed about it all my life, I find that I also enjoy doing paintings depicting the north. Painting this polar bear picture, for example, brought back all the fond memories of the Milwaukee Public Museum's expedition to the northern Arctic in 1948.

Robert Uihlein, Sr., then vice president of the Schlitz Brewing Company, was the one man who best understood my love of the north, because he shared my feeling. And since he was a student of Arctic and Canadian history, Robert Uihlein and I would spend many a stimulating afternoon in his office at the brewery talking about the north.

For years we at the Milwaukee Public Museum had wanted a good polar bear group. One day I told Mr. Uihlein this and asked if he would be interested in backing an expedition. He was delighted. So we arranged the trip, and Robert Uihlein himself came along to assist with the hunt.

We made a preliminary visit to Churchill, located on Hudson's Bay, in June and returned for our hunt in September. Walter Pelzer, mammal taxidermist at the museum, did all the preparatory work, and he and Robert Uihlein shot all the bears. When we returned, Pelzer mounted the group of three, a female and two young, which is still on display at the Milwaukee Public Museum. Without going into any great detail, I must add that this picture represents for me everything that is the north — the Arctic and all the romance of the great explorers. Of all the expeditions I have been involved with, I felt most at home there in the Arctic.

1954, oil, 30" x 24"

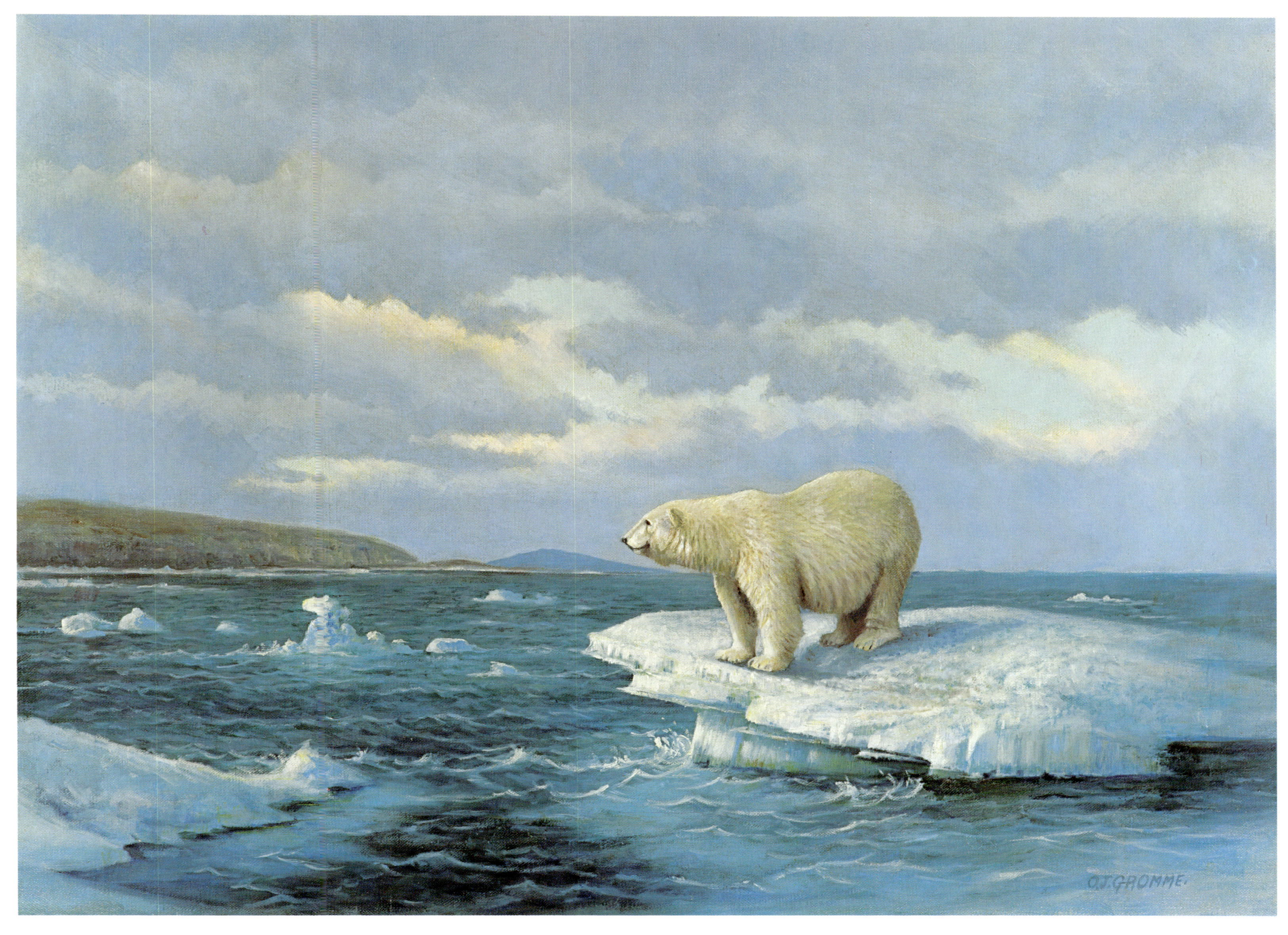
O.J.GROMME.

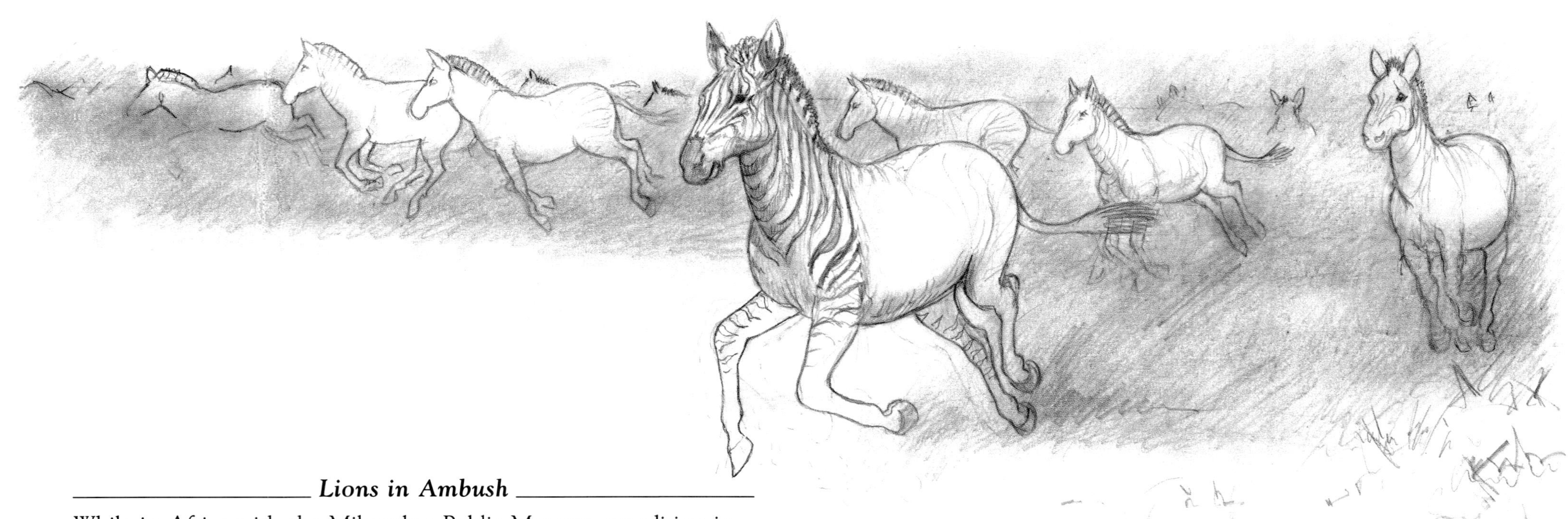

Lions in Ambush

While in Africa with the Milwaukee Public Museum expedition in 1928-29, I became acquainted with Martin and Osa Johnson, well-known wildlife photographers. The Johnsons and we museum people shared many experiences and became very close friends.

Martin Johnson was also hosting three Eagle Scouts, chosen as the top scouts in the United States, whose reward for their accomplishments was a three-month safari in Africa. One day, he decided to give them an opportunity to photograph lions from a truck covered with steel mesh hidden in a thornbush-blind near our camp.

Fresh meat would be needed to attract the lions, so Osa Johnson and I went out on the Serengeti Plain to bring back a zebra for bait. We shot a zebra about six miles from camp and tied it to our bumper, dragging it back so that its scent would attract any lion who crossed the trail.

We were almost back to camp when Osa called my attention to a strange sight. A cloud of golden dust was hanging on the horizon, and back lighting from the setting sun created the appearance of gold-colored smoke. My curiosity was aroused. I was sure it was not a dust storm, so it had to be animals. A stampede? But what had started it? Picking up the binoculars, I stared at tiny black dots barely visible in the dust. They were zebras, in terror, headed right for our truck.

"That's some sight, isn't it?" Osa commented. "You don't usually get very close to them."

Still concentrating on the zebras, I wondered what she meant.

"Well, those lions!" Her words spooked two female lions crouching in ambush on a rock just a few rods from our car. Busy watching the stampede and trying to figure out what had started it, I hadn't even noticed the lions!

Rising slowly, the lionesses walked away with great dignity, feigning lack of interest in the zebras or in us. Then it became apparent to me what had started the stampede — two male lions were chasing the zebras directly past the spot where their mates lay in ambush. Osa and I had foiled their plan! The zebras then ran by, and the lions did not eat that day.

The sight had been thrilling.

"Isn't it too bad," Osa observed, "that the artist doesn't live who could paint that just the way we saw it?"

"Well, Osa," I replied, "maybe he does, and maybe he doesn't. Someday I might try it."

That someday was 49 years later, and *Lions in Ambush* is the result of that striking incident on the Serengeti Plain in 1928.

1977, oil, 48" x 30"

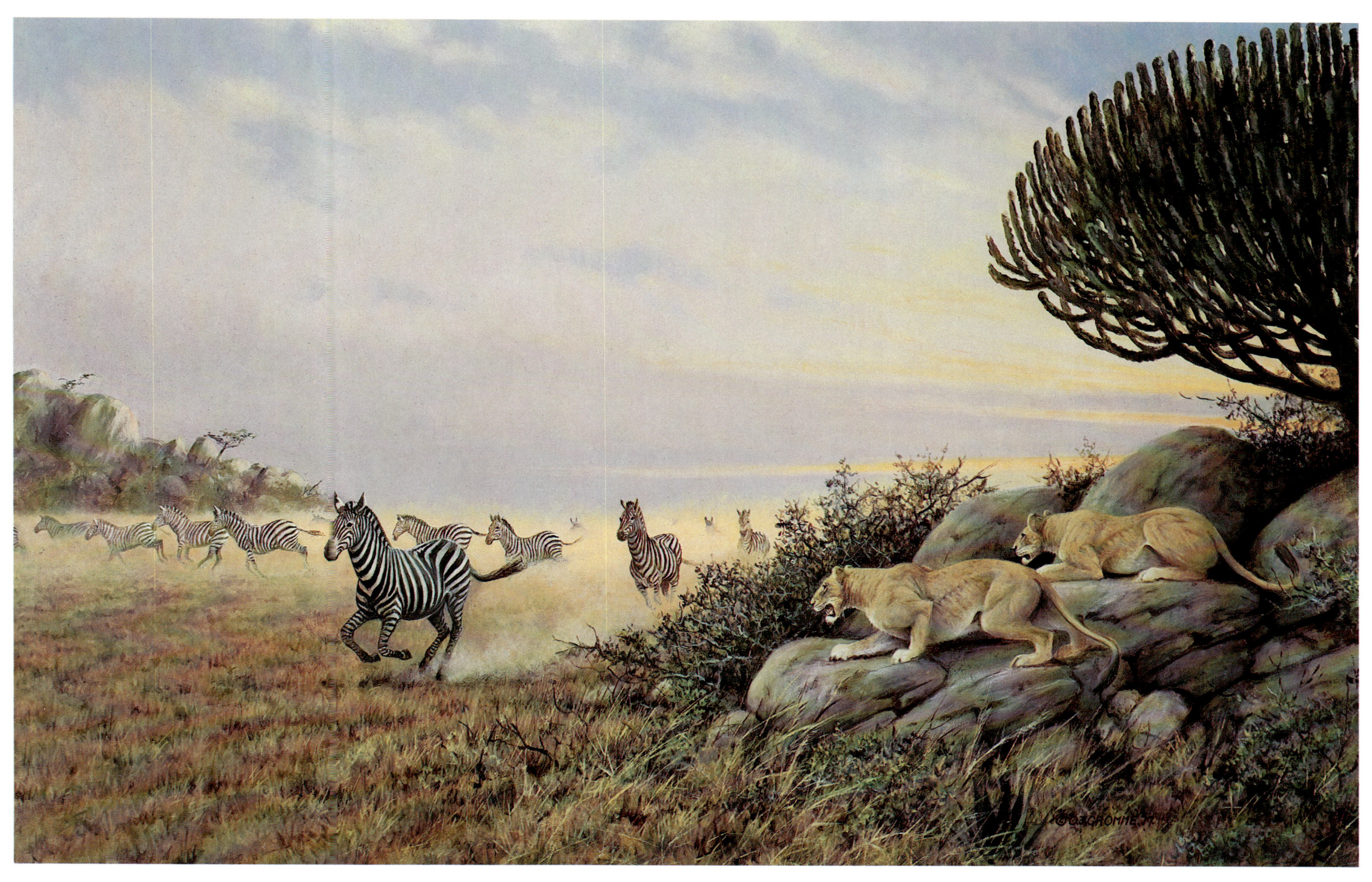

Elephants at Lake Manyara

This painting was commissioned by a man who had been to Africa a few years prior to my second trip there in 1977, and who had described a place near the Ngorongoro crater in Tanzania where he had seen several elephants. He asked me to try to find the place and keep it in mind as a possible background for an elephant painting that he wanted.

Arriving in the African area he had designated, I took careful note of the topography and vegetation, even viewing some elephants in the assigned spot. I have no idea whether they were the same elephants he had seen or not, but they certainly made it much easier for me to recreate this scene.

When I returned home and painted the picture, I was surprised to discover that my patron was absolutely certain that I had found his setting, and, as a result, the picture pleased him very much.

1979, oil, 40" x 28"

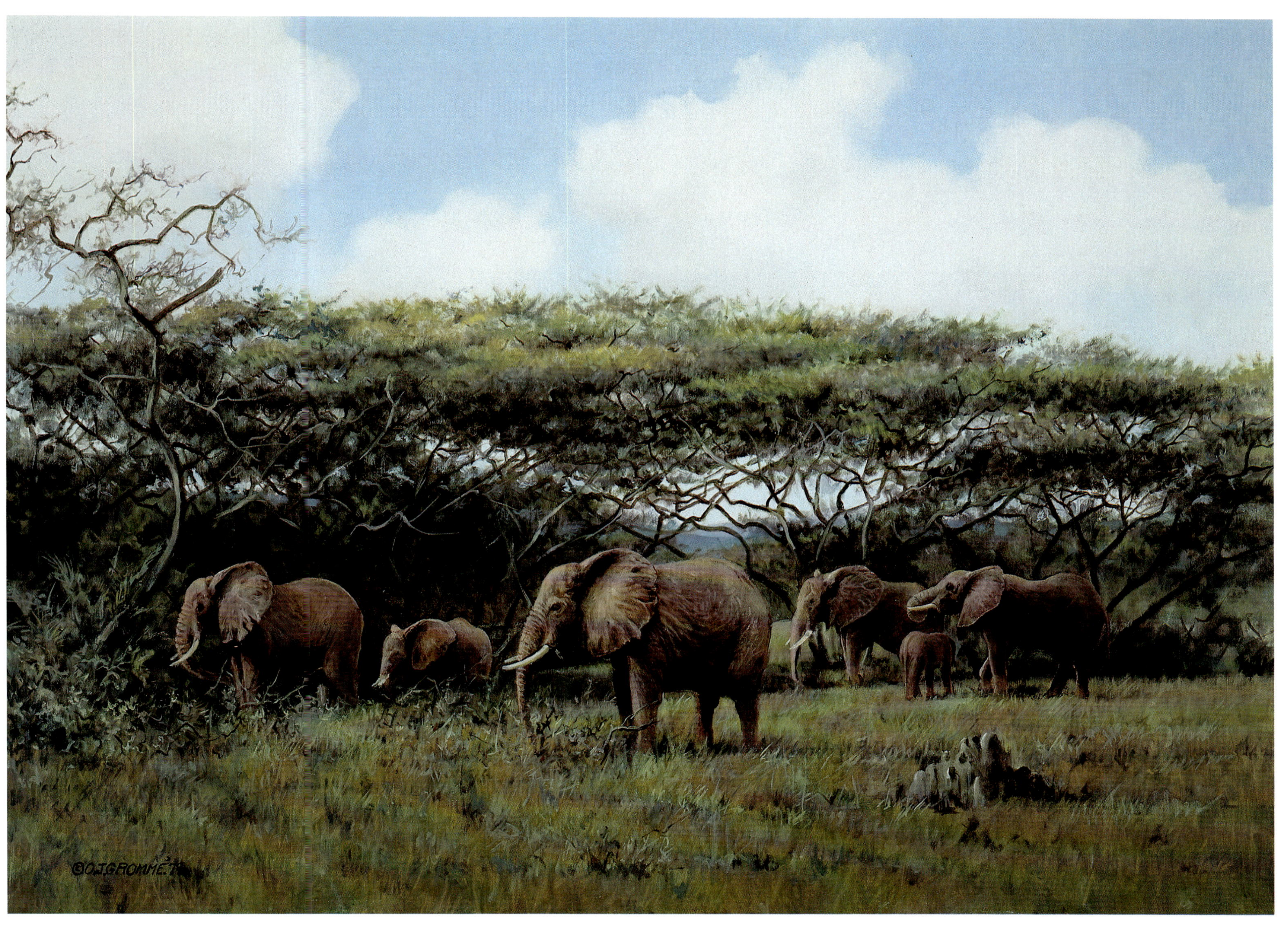
©O.J.GROMME

Stormy Day — Serengeti Buffalo

Sometimes painters are accused of glorifying or exaggerating reality, but this is one case where exactly the opposite is true. I did not paint the actual background for this picture because I was sure no one would believe it. This incident took place in 1977 when Anne and I returned to Africa to refresh my memory from the Milwaukee Public Museum expedition of 49 years earlier.

We were out on the Serengeti Plain before a terrific storm, and we actually saw the funnels of *four* tornadoes off in the distance. They were all emerging from one enormous black cloud. Using that setting for the background of this painting, I decided to put in only one of the funnels, lest I be accused of exaggerating.

The heavy weather also seemed to make the animals nervous, and these African buffalo in particular kept us at a respectable distance. Despite its slow, docile appearance, the cape buffalo is known to be one of the most dangerous animals when wounded or angered, killing lions with their hoofs and horns and creating danger for many a hunter. So we watched them from a distance, and I took mental notes which later provided the basis for this painting. And I reluctantly added only *one* tornado funnel.

1977, oil, 40″ x 28″

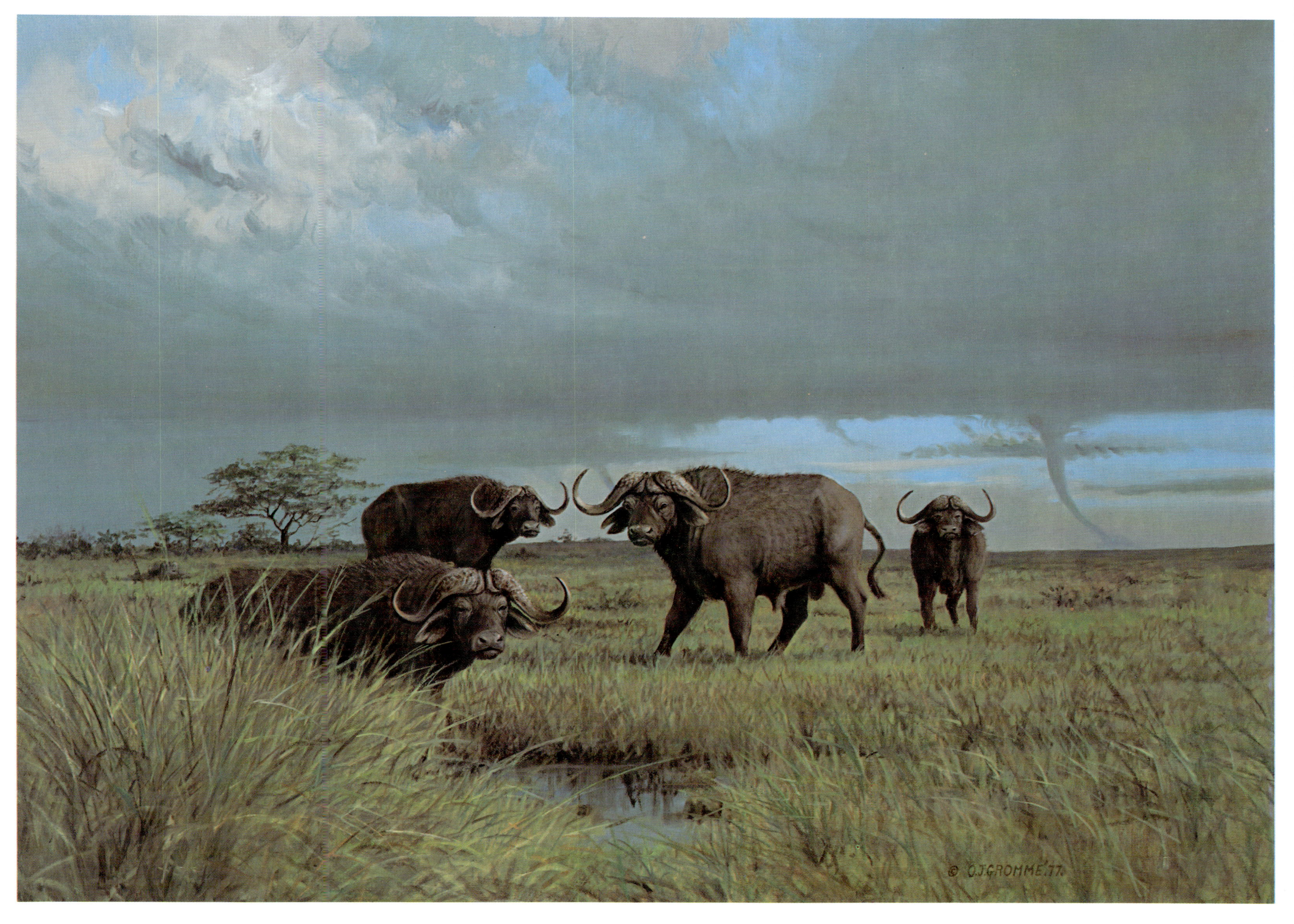
© O.J.GROMME '77

Charging Rhino — Serengeti

On my second trip to Africa, 49 years after the 1928 & 1929 Milwaukee Public Museum expedition, my wife Anne and I retraced many of the trails I had travelled earlier.

While on the Serengeti one day with a very good driver, we encountered a rhinoceros. The little safari wagon we were using was quite maneuverable, so we teased the rhino into charging. The driver got as close as he could without exposing us to real danger, stopping about 125 yards away from the animal. The old rhino just stood there stamping the ground, snorting. Then he started toward us at a slow trot. Our driver accelerated just enough to keep a safe distance ahead of him. Suddenly, the rhino shifted to a regular gallop. It was a good thing the engine didn't stall, or we would have had some second thoughts about what we were doing. But we finally tired the old fellow out, and he gave up the chase.

I painted this picture from memory after we returned home. I was sorry to not have any photographs of the rhino, but we never thought of taking the camera. In fact, the exact spot where the rhino in this painting charged us was within a few miles of the site of our camp of 49 years earlier.

1977, oil, 36" x 24"

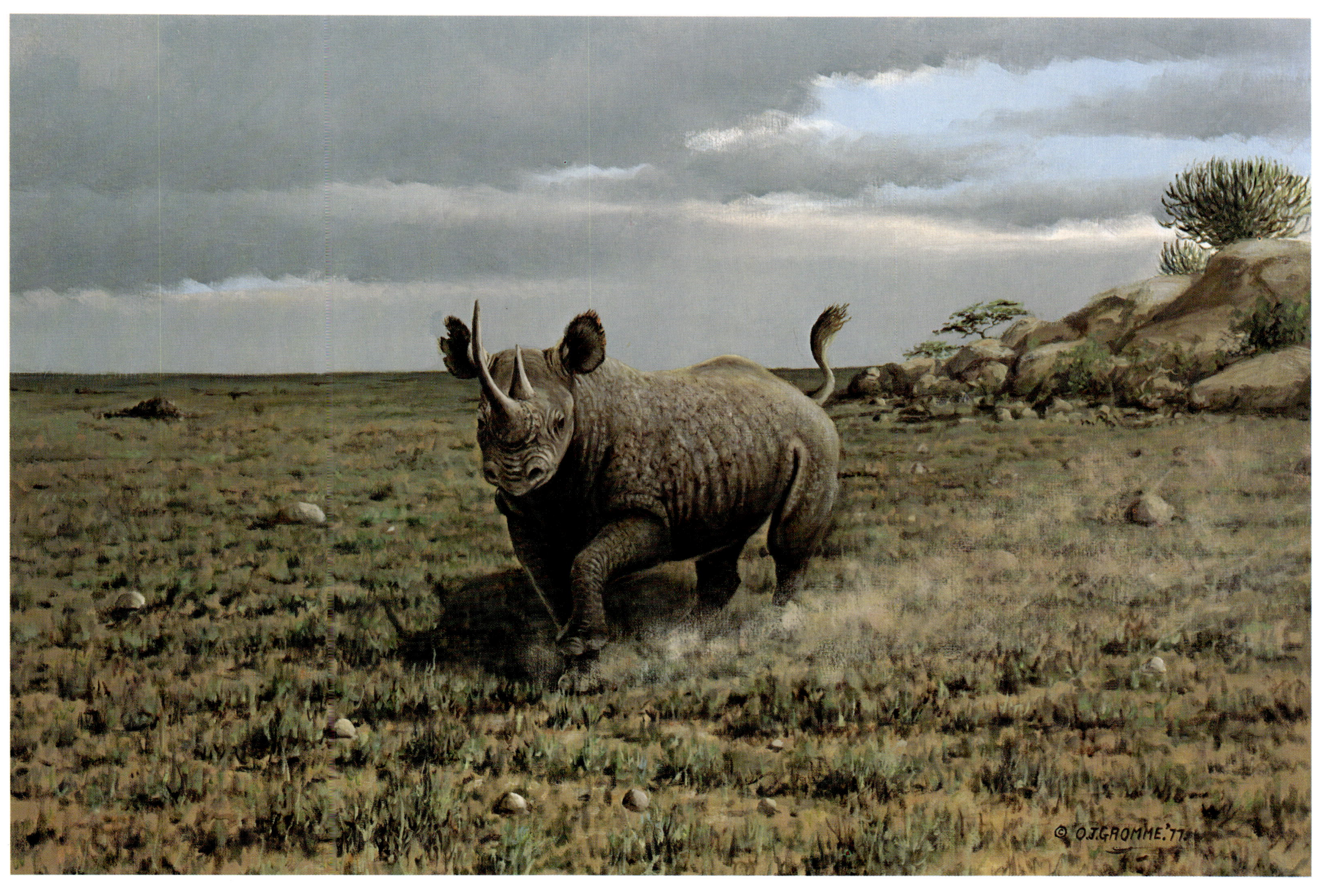
© O.J.GROMME.'77

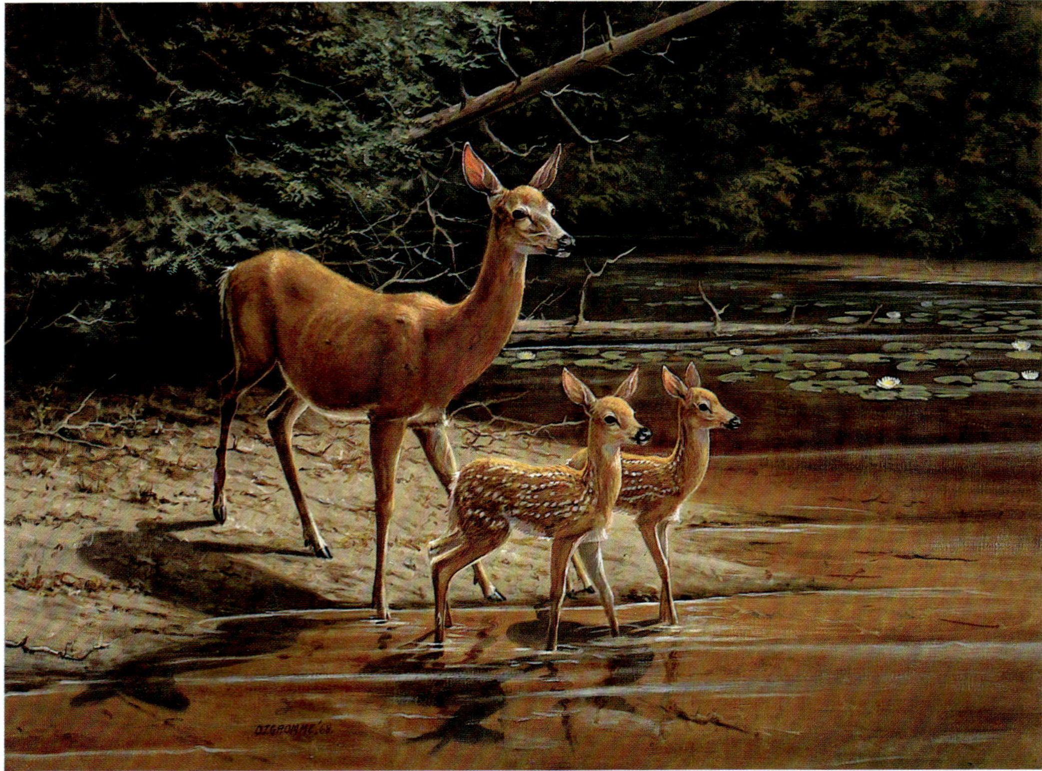

Virginia Deer with Fawns

This picture is the result of frequent contact with these beautiful animals. There is no large mammal which is quite as well-known, or loved, as the white-tailed deer.

One day I very carefully observed this doe and her two fawns as they approached the water for a drink. The sun shone behind the animals, causing the light to filter delicately through their ears, making the ears seem almost translucent.

The mother is a scrawny doe, with her ribs and loins showing; most does are quite lean at this time of year since the nursing fawns keep their mother's weight down. And she has a few scars on her skin where she has been tangled in barbed wire fences. But she makes a beautiful picture with her new fawns.

Finally, the water, coffee-colored due to the tannic acid of the tamarack swamps it flows through, contrasts nicely with the soft green of the summer foliage.

1968, oil, 34″ x 25″

High Country — Mule Deer

This painting was done as a commissioned work for a man from Wisconsin Dells, Wisconsin, who had hunted mule deer in the West many times. He made two requests of me: that I paint the deer which he had collected on one of his hunting trips, and that I use Crested Butte in particular as my background.

My patron brought me the mounted head to observe and paint from, and he also provided me with some fine photographs of the Crested Butte area to use for the background. Although the rack on his mule deer was not outstanding, I made no attempt to embellish it. In my career as a museum man, I had decided to find and display typical, rather than spectacular, specimens.

The mule deer is the western relative of our white-tailed or Virginia deer. Slightly larger than a whitetail, and of stockier build, their habits are much the same. The mule deer runs with a different gait, has a less conspicuous tail, and larger ears from which it gets its name.

1978, oil, 32″ x 24″

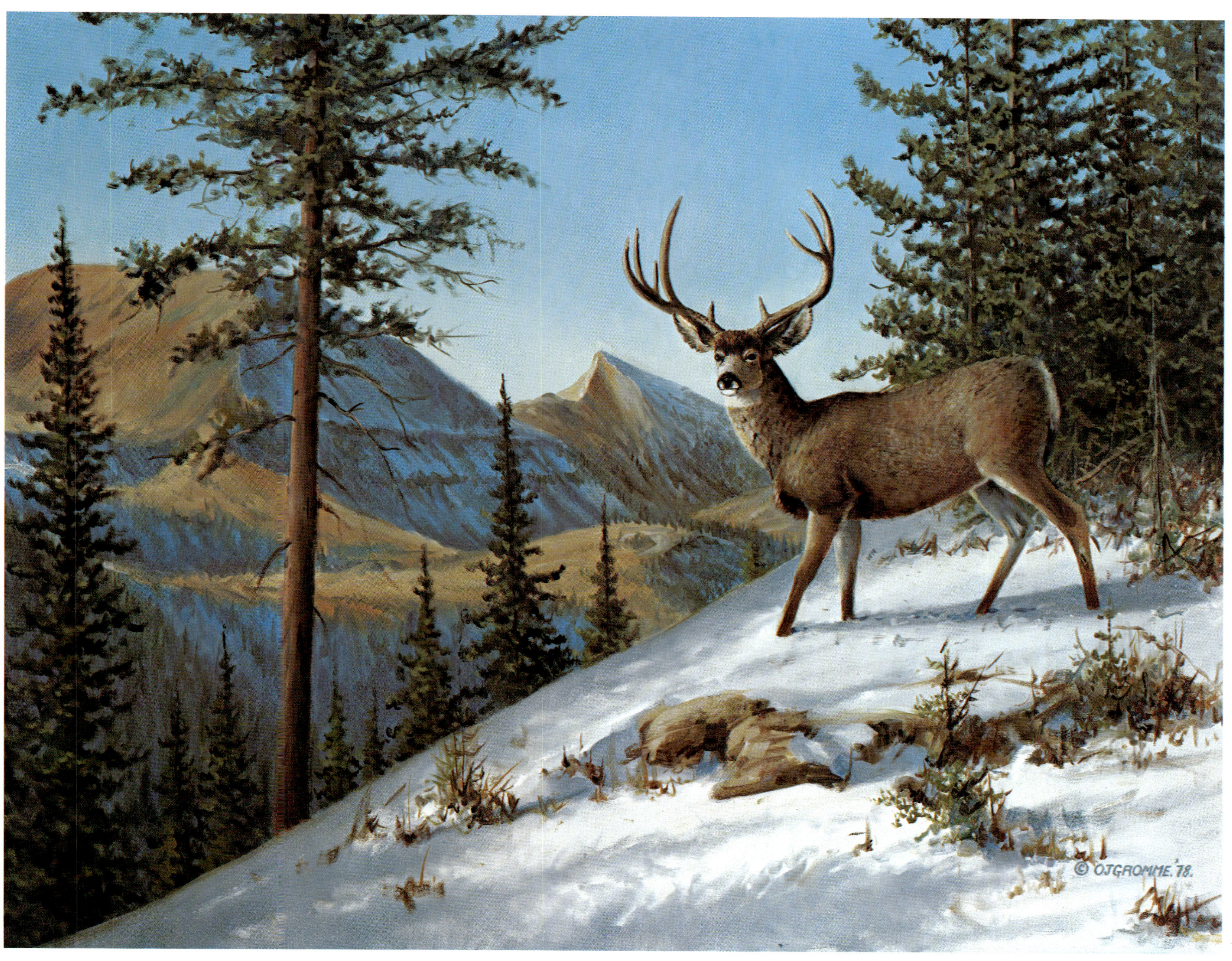
© OJGROMME '78.

Early Snowfall — White-tailed Deer

Most recognized conservation work in the United States is done by the state and federal governments and by large organizations like Ducks Unlimited, the Ruffed Grouse Society, or the Wild Turkey Federation. But individuals can and do make a difference in wildlife's future by setting aside tracts of privately-owned land as wildlife refuges.

The setting for *Early Snowfall — White-tailed Deer* is a private hunting preserve west of Rosendale, Wisconsin. The original tract of land was purchased by Al Steinman of the Steinman Lumber Company of Milwaukee. Since then, others have bought adjoining tracts, and the holdings have been consolidated into a very large hunting preserve and game refuge. Certain areas are designated for hunting, while others are exclusively a refuge.

Good wildlife habitat is becoming more scarce all the time as people clear woodlots, drain marshes, mow fencerows and clear away brush piles. These things are done in the name of economic expedience or "beautification," but such actions will almost certainly come back to haunt us in the future. The more individuals become aware of the plight of our wildlife, the more, it is hoped, they will do to restore its habitat. Fallow farms, brush piles and unmown fields can indeed be beautiful when they provide a place for birds and animals to live. They are "guarantees" for a future for wildlife.

1975, oil, 32" x 24"

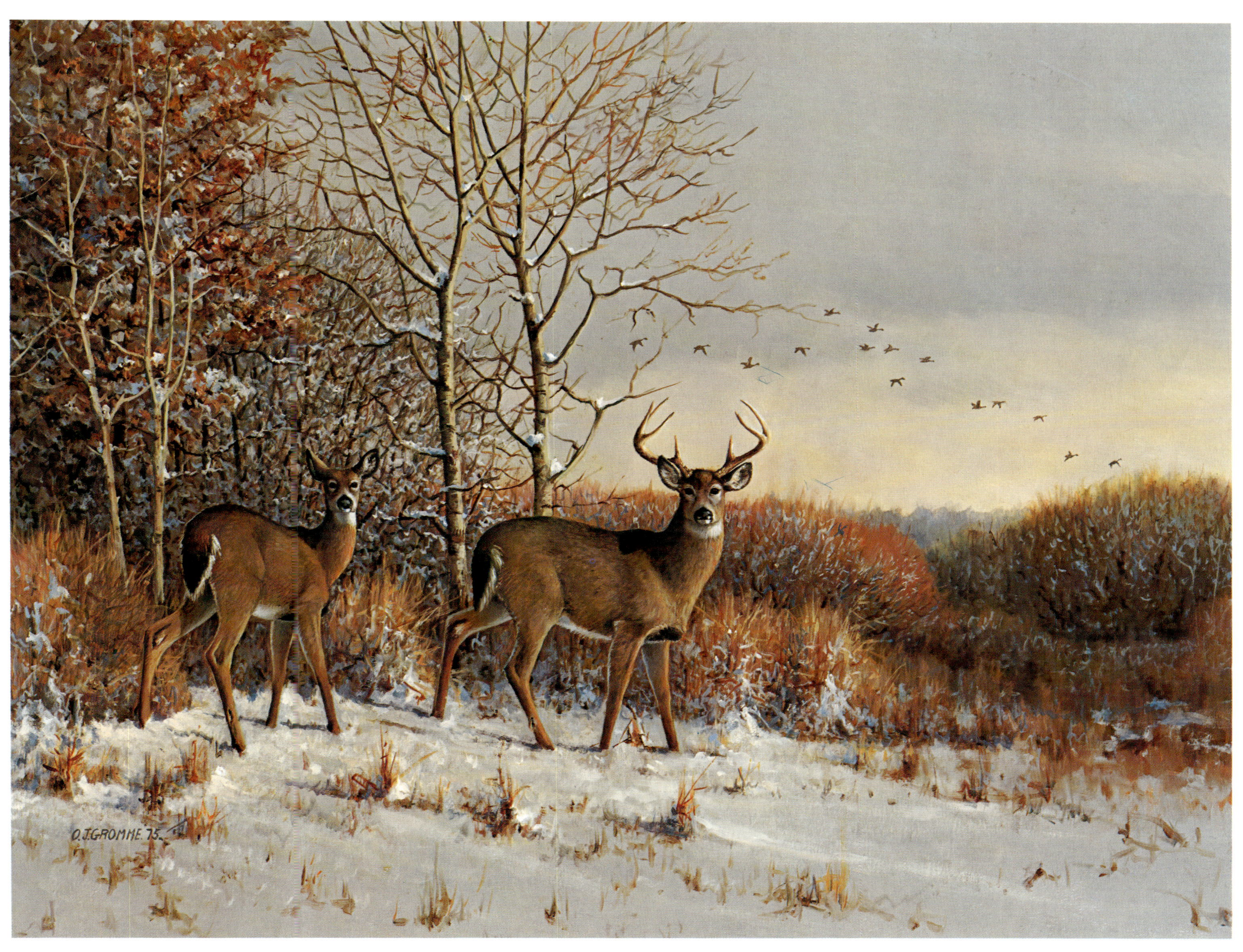
O.J.GROMME 75

Startled Trio — White-tailed Deer

When I paint a picture, one of my primary goals is to create something that people can relate to. Perhaps not everyone can relate to a painting of three deer startled by some unfamiliar sound in the winter woods, but a great many people can. For me, the main purpose of art is to bring pleasure to the viewer by rendering a pleasing scene from nature, one that is true, and accurate, and, if possible, familiar. *Startled Trio — White-tailed Deer* holds true to my artistic philosophy.

I realize that many people do not regard nature as I do. But not everyone has had the opportunities to live as close to it and observe it as I have. So I feel it is my responsibility to use my talents to recreate nature for the public. Thus, for those who spend a lot of time outdoors, my paintings are reminders of familiar sights and good times; for those who do not, my work can serve to broaden their understanding of the natural world. Perhaps my paintings have even inspired a new bird watcher or two.

Many people enjoy this painting because deer are so familiar to them — graceful, gentle and incomparably beautiful. Anyone driving along our Wisconsin countryside could easily come upon this scene and enjoy it, so I have recreated it for those who see it often as well as for those who wish they could see it.

1978, oil, 36" x 24"

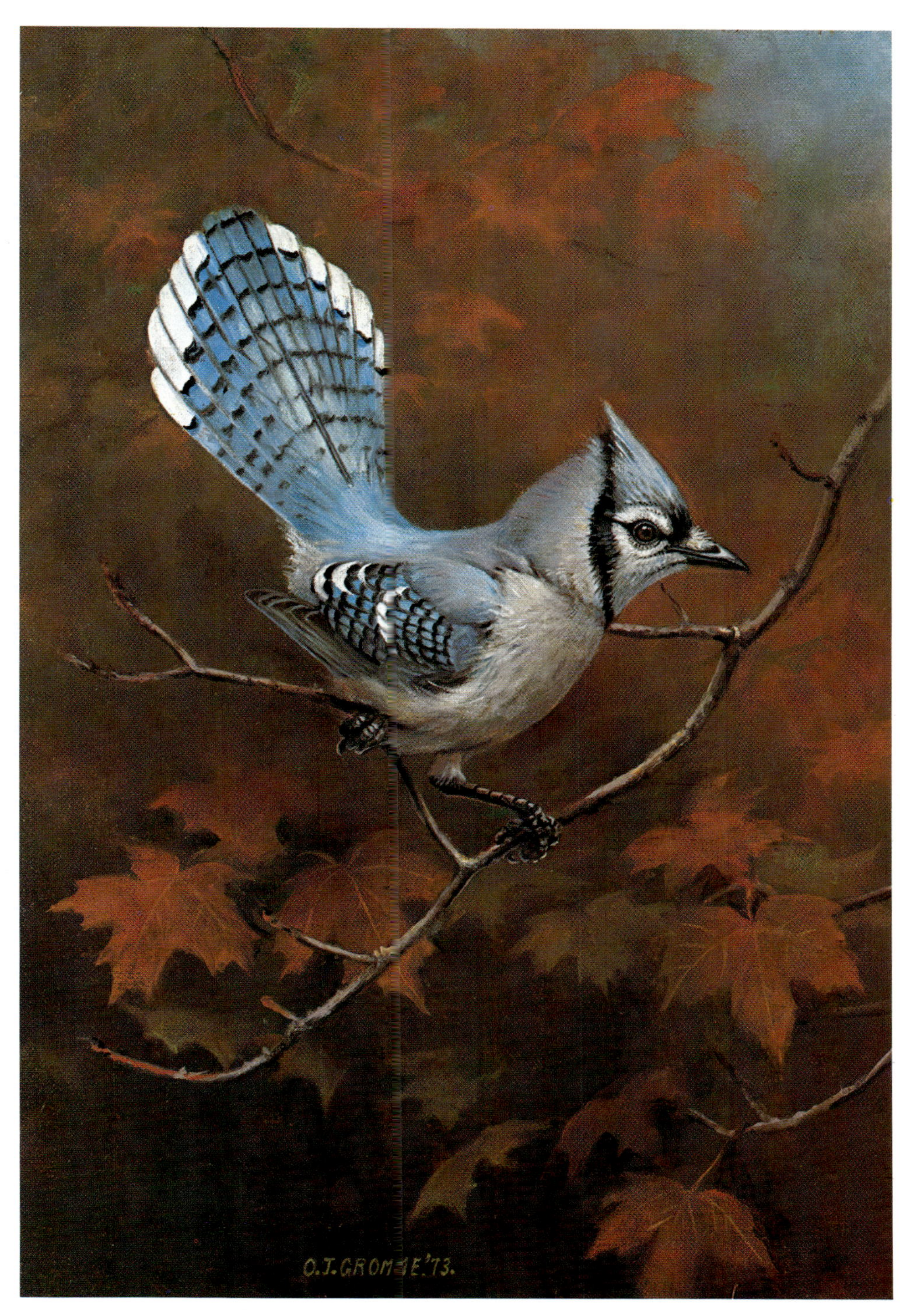
O.J.GROMME'73.

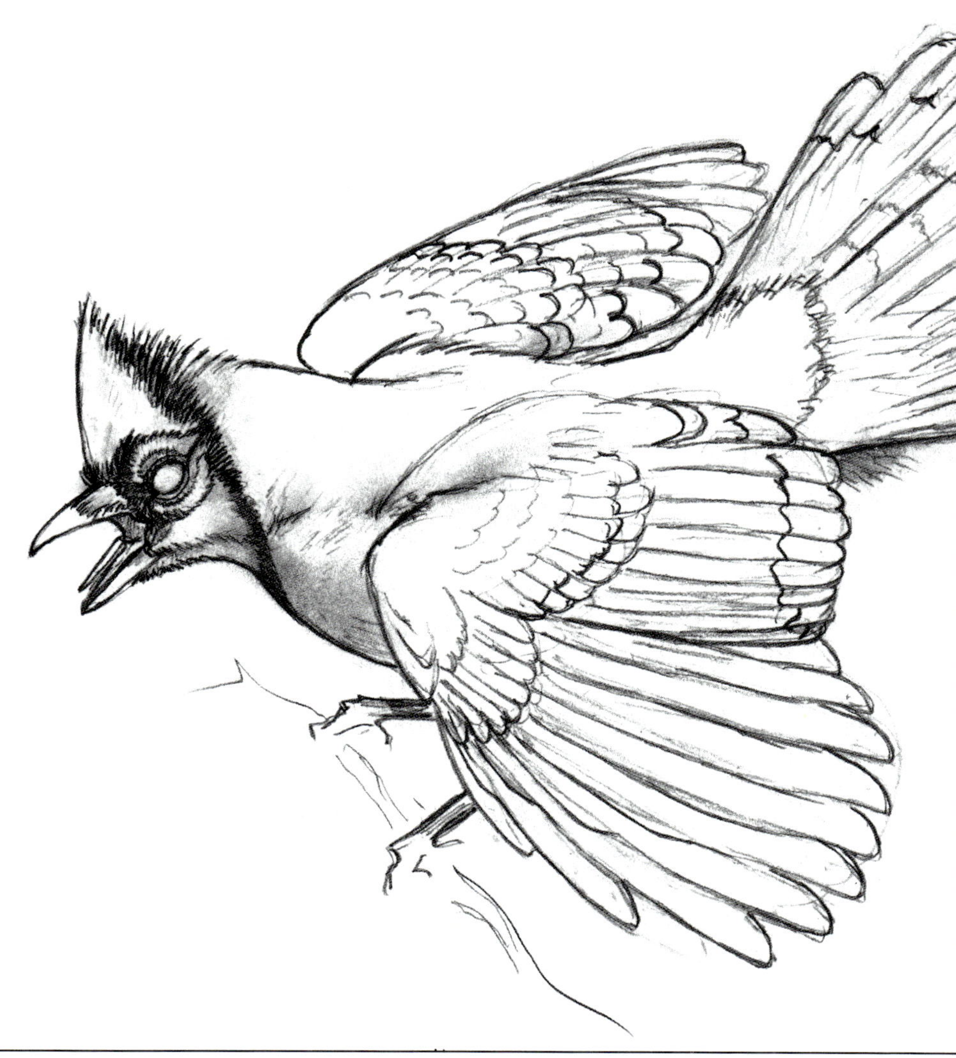

Late Summer — Meadowlark

When painting this eastern meadowlark, I deliberately set the bird in a late summer landscape, because they are usually depicted in the spring. I think that the late August and early September flora, in particular the blazing star, is just as beautiful as any spring flora.

Color is of vital importance to me in my efforts to recreate nature accurately. I have a book of color plates called *Ridgway's Standard Key*, published in 1912, which contains accurate renditions of almost every possible color variation. I have had the book for years (I even took it to Africa with me in 1928), and I would not part with it. The plates are so true to color that I am extra careful not to leave them lying open for fear that they could possibly fade. I often use them in the field when making color notes in order to help me match the colors of beaks, feet, or eyes when I reproduce them.

So the colors, shades and variations I use when painting something like this bird or the flower are no accident. They are derived from careful comparisons and a painstaking mixture of pigments to get just the right shade.

1981, oil, 12" x 16"

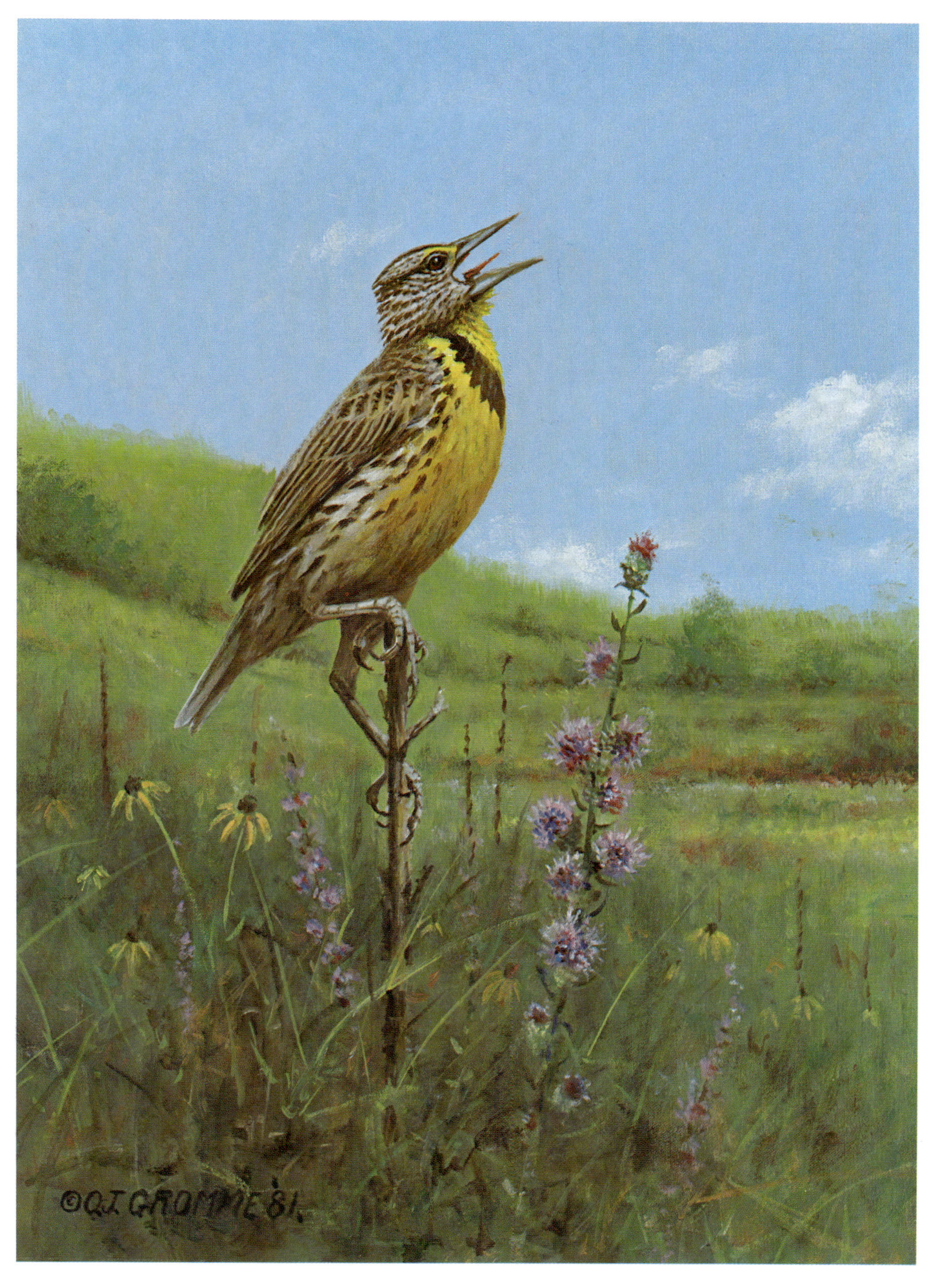
©O.J. GROMME '81.

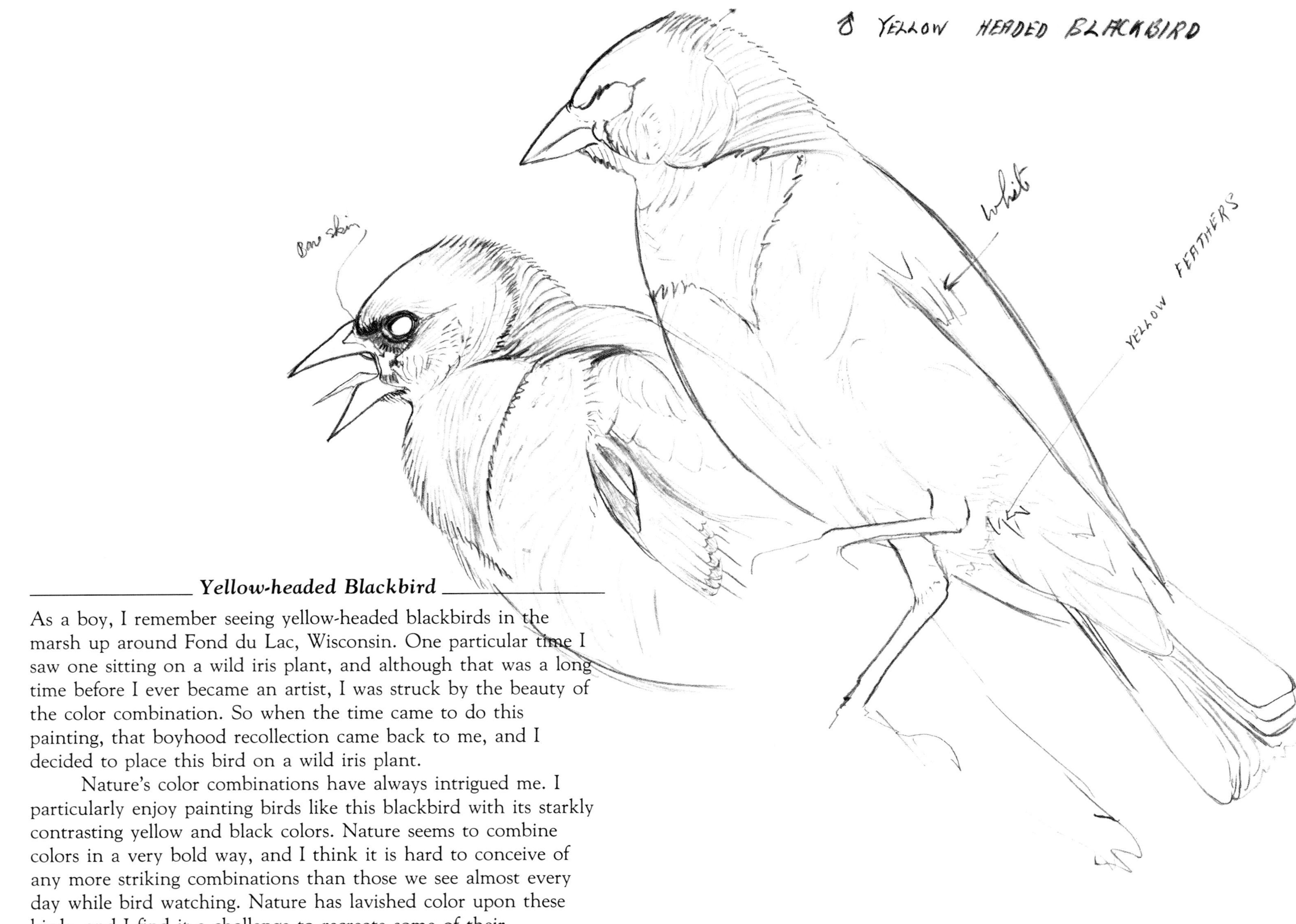

Yellow-headed Blackbird

As a boy, I remember seeing yellow-headed blackbirds in the marsh up around Fond du Lac, Wisconsin. One particular time I saw one sitting on a wild iris plant, and although that was a long time before I ever became an artist, I was struck by the beauty of the color combination. So when the time came to do this painting, that boyhood recollection came back to me, and I decided to place this bird on a wild iris plant.

Nature's color combinations have always intrigued me. I particularly enjoy painting birds like this blackbird with its starkly contrasting yellow and black colors. Nature seems to combine colors in a very bold way, and I think it is hard to conceive of any more striking combinations than those we see almost every day while bird watching. Nature has lavished color upon these birds, and I find it a challenge to recreate some of their extraordinary shades, variations and combinations.

1979, oil, 14" x 18"

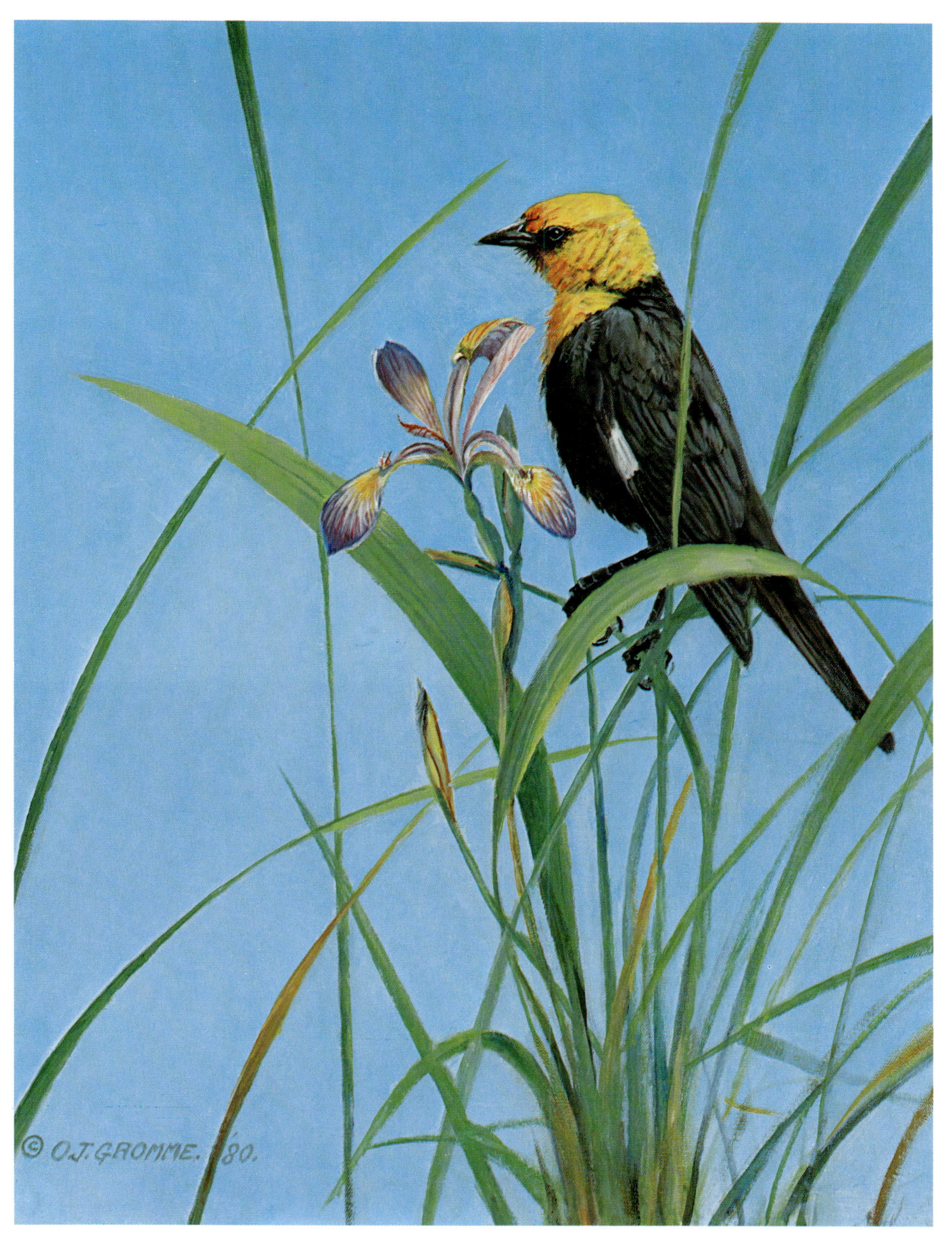
© O.J. GROMME. '80.

Red-winged Blackbird

Even if there are still snow flurries in the air, we know it is spring once we see the first red-winged blackbird return from the south. The males arrive early, often before the last spring storms, and stake out their territory. They like to show off, too, displaying their bright red and yellow shoulder coverts long before the females arrive on the scene. The males preen and puff out their colorful epaulets which so clearly distinguish them as they seem to call to the world, "Look at ME! Look at ME!"

More than any other blackbird, the red-wing personifies the marsh. He nests there, and, perched on the tip of a cattail, he makes it his business to oversee all that goes on. Unfortunately, red-winged blackbirds have become so numerous in some areas that they are a nuisance to farmers and townsfolk alike. The reason there are so many of them now is due, in part, to the diminished number of predators like hawks which had kept the blackbirds in better balance in the past.

1966, oil, 12" x 16"

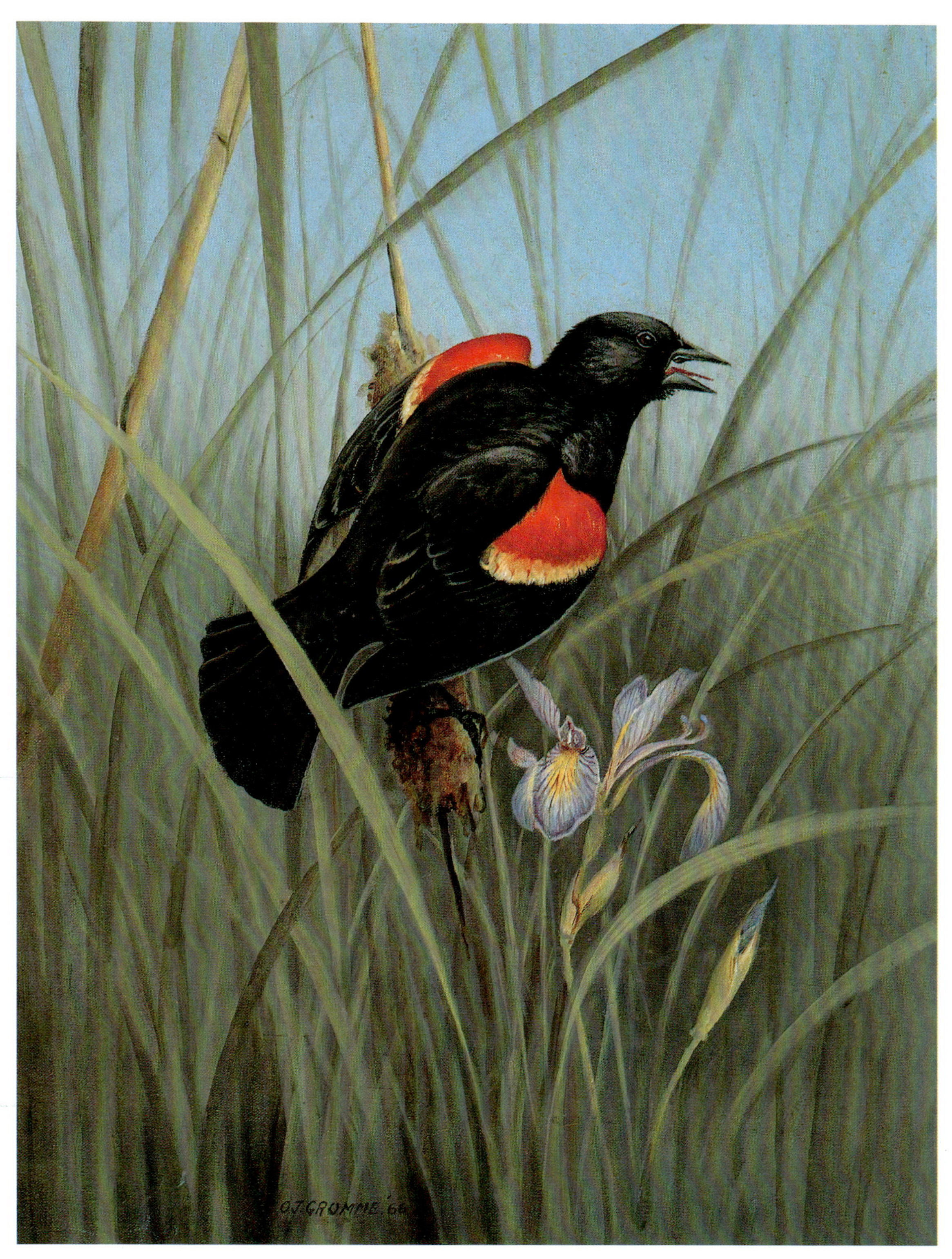
O.J. GROMME '66

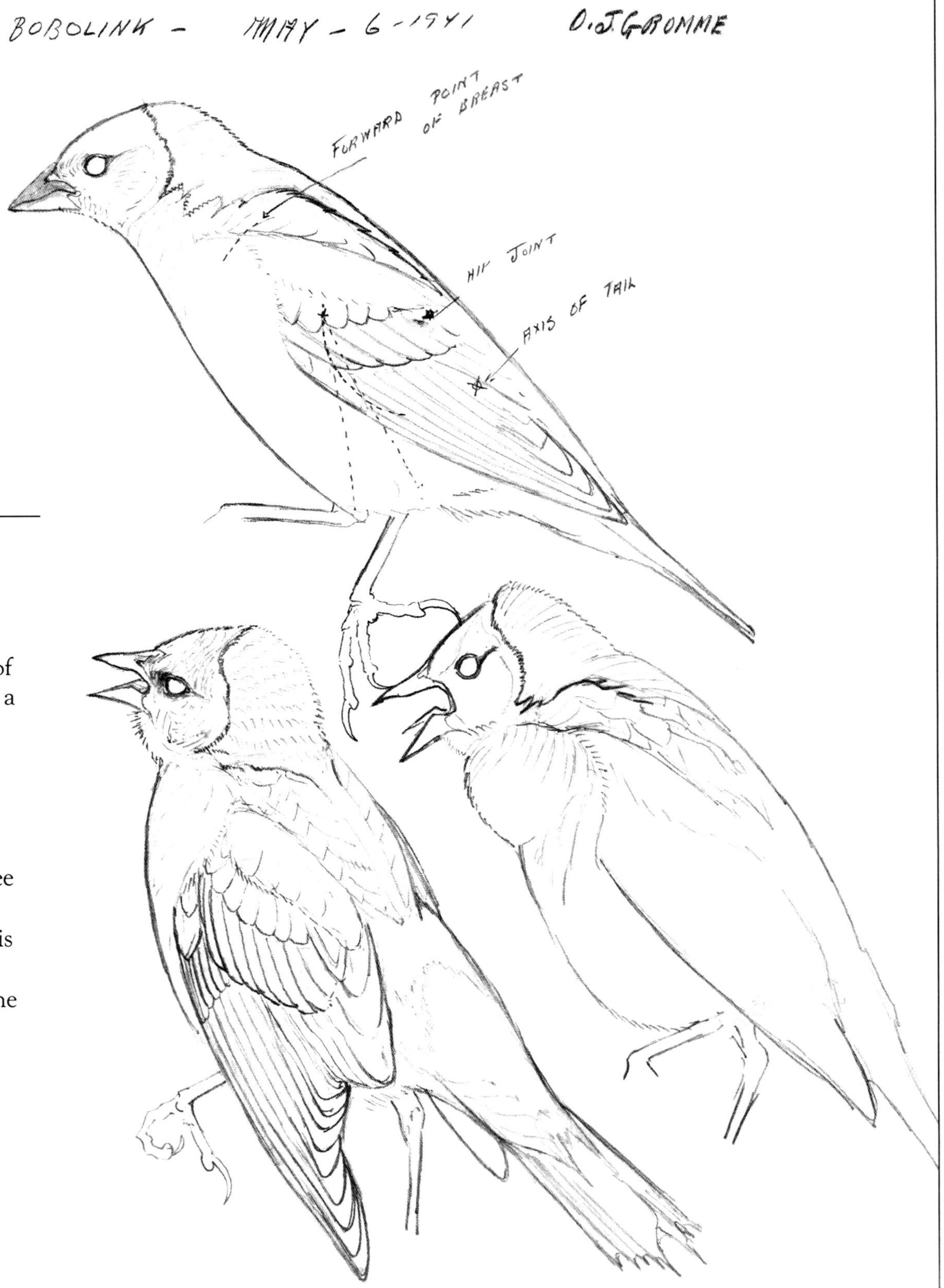

Bobolink

This is a male bobolink in a field of red clover. Bobolinks come north to build their nests early in May and are ready to head south again around mid-July. The males change plumage early in July and are difficult to distinguish from the females.

Some people call the male bobolink a skunk bird because of the similarity of his coloring to that of a skunk — jet black with a beautiful creamy white on the back of his head. During the breeding season, the male bobolinks have a unique flight pattern when in full flight and song — all the wingbeats are below the horizontal.

Unfortunately, bobolinks are subject to the same calamity which befalls ring-necked pheasants and blue-winged teal: all three often build their nests in alfalfa fields. As the first crop of hay matures, with the young still in their nests, the farmer will cut his hay, destroying the nests and killing the baby birds. It is an unfortunate situation, but I am not sure exactly what can be done to change it.

When we first came to Briggsville, Wisconsin, we noticed that there were bobolinks all around. But as it continues to be difficult for them to find safe nesting sites, they are raising fewer young and their numbers are diminishing. I hope that somehow the bobolink can find a way to adapt to this situation, but I am afraid that the outlook is not good.

1966, oil, 10″ x 12″

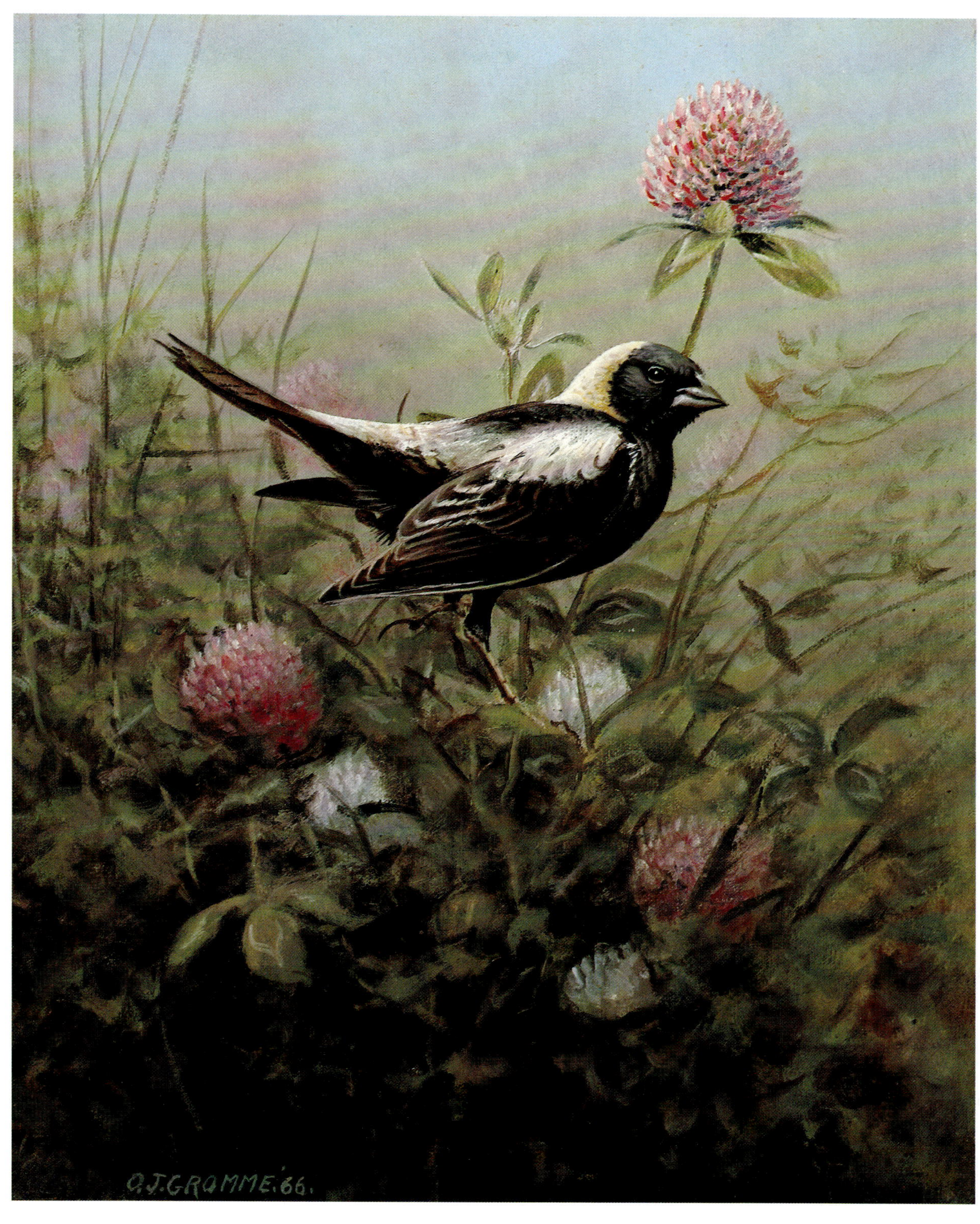
O.J.GROMME.'66.

Goldfinch

My wife Anne and I get a great deal of pleasure out of feeding the birds. We have several feeders around our house and yard, and in an average winter we will use 700 or 800 pounds of sunflower seeds!

One of our most popular backyard birds is the American goldfinch (thistle bird or wild canary as they are interchangeably called). These little fellows, who stay all winter, love the seeds of the Canada thistle, and they line their nests with thistle down. Although the males change their bright-yellow, summer plumage for a duller yellow-green, they are still some of the most colorful winter birds we have here. And a sure sign of spring is the variable green and yellow coloration of the American goldfinch male as he changes back to his summer plumage.

Sometimes there are so many goldfinch about that we can actually feel the vibration of the windows in our house when a car goes by and all the goldfinch fly.

Once in a while one will smash into the window glass and stun itself. But Anne has found a good way to revive them when that happens, as long as they haven't broken their neck or a wing. She picks them up, brings them inside, and puts them in a brown paper bag. Twisting the bag shut, she lays it on the counter where a warm quiet rest will usually bring the bird around. Once the goldfinch is revived, we let it go again. About ninety per-cent of the birds recover this way.

1965, oil, 10" x 12¾"

Hummingbird

The only one of 72 species in North America found in our area, the delightful ruby-throated hummingbird is our tiniest feathered creature. Its nest is a small and intricate work of art; its eggs are no larger than a navy bean.

This little hummer is pictured at a trumpet flower, one of their many favorites. They are especially drawn to red flowers such as cannas and have even been known to be attracted to a person's red nose!

A hummingbird done well in oil reminds me of jewelry in paint. But it is so difficult to portray the blurred movement of their wings, that few artists ever attempt to paint them.

There are many incredible stories about these little jewels. Their aeronautical maneuvers, for example, are something to behold — they can hover, swing like a pendulum, fly forward, backward, or up and down. When they migrate, some hummingbirds fly all the way from the southern tip of Florida across the Gulf of Mexico, a distance of several hundred miles! It was once thought that they migrated on the backs of eagles and hawks, but banding and observation have determined that some of these tiny birds actually do fly across the Gulf of Mexico!

1978, oil, 10" x 14"

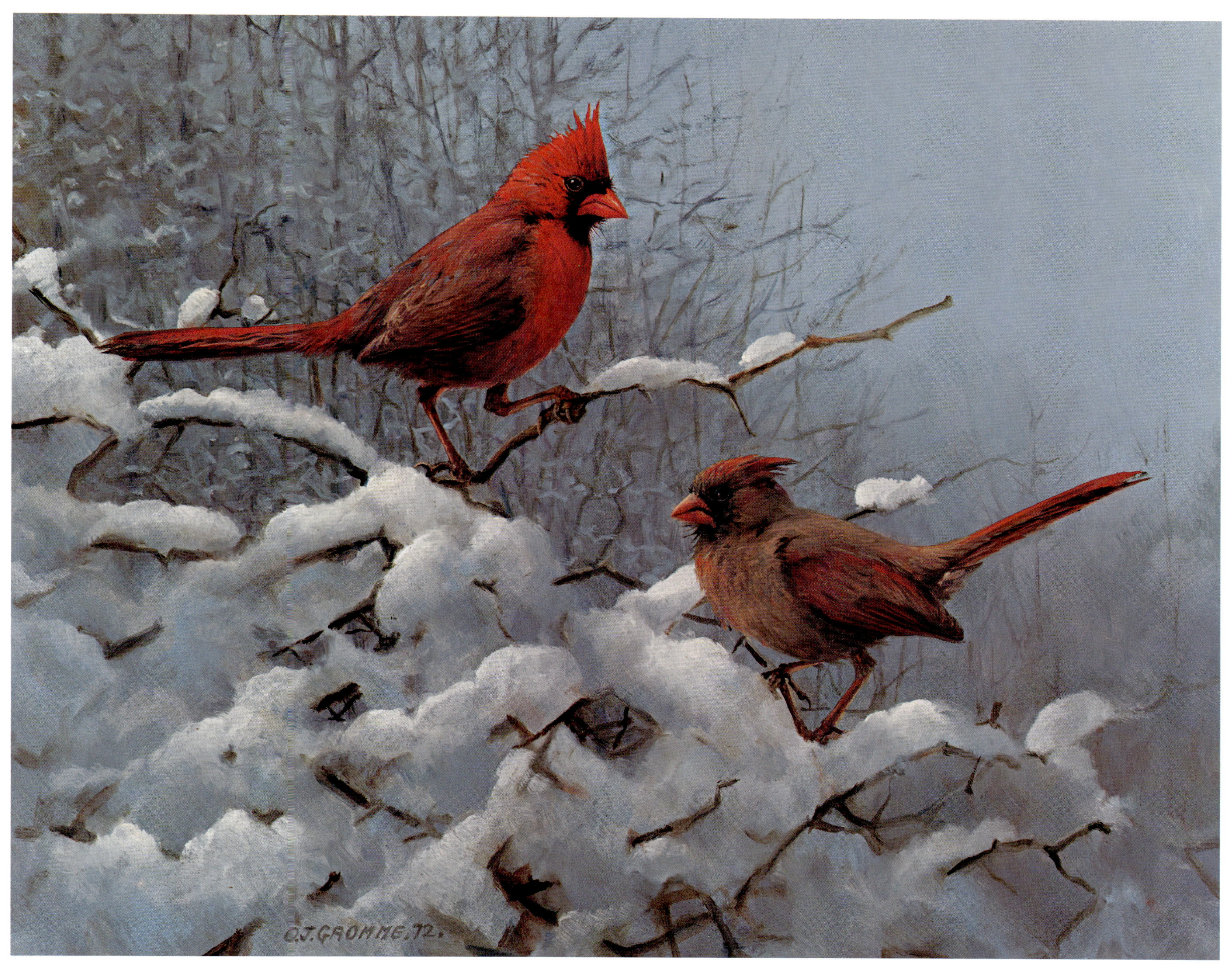
O.J. GROMME. 72.

Spring's Early Arrivals

All last winter that woodpile in our yard wore a heavy cap of snow. When the weather warmed up, the snow melted, forming some interesting icicles. Always observing my immediate environment for intriguing aspects of nature, I decided to include that ice-covered woodpile in a later painting. I left the idea tucked away in my brain, and it wasn't long before I came up with this picture.

Making a rough sketch as I planned this composition, I started off with the woodpile and then added the American robin. In my second sketch, I worked out the refinements and added some detail. Finally, maintaining my original proportions, I transferred the sketch to canvas and began to paint.

Using the frozen woodpile as a point of departure, I established the season by showing a strip of green grass with the robin, newly arrived from the south, looking for a worm in the softening ground. And the crocus helps to make it definite that spring is here. The viewer then is quietly uplifted by the sense that winter is making its exit.

1982, oil, 20" x 16"

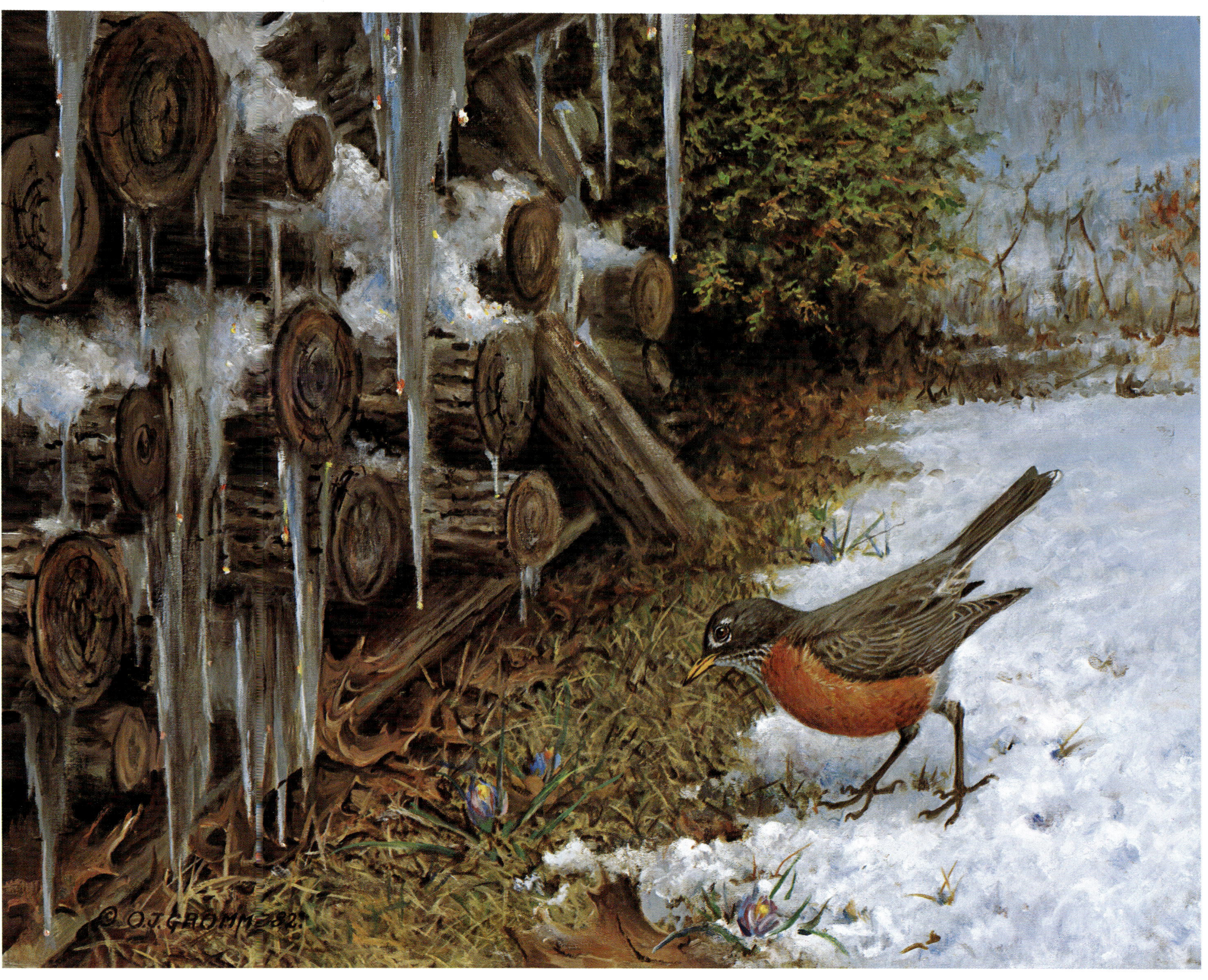
© O.J.GROMME '82

Hen Mallard and Brood

Ideas for paintings come to me from many different sources. Sometimes a patron knows just which bird or animal he or she wants. Or sometimes I will decide to paint something because I find its colors pleasing, or I get an idea for a scene that I have witnessed in my work as a naturalist.

I keep a list of these ideas for future paintings in my head and on paper — there are literally hundreds of them which I believe would make fine paintings. And as I go about my daily life, I regularly come across a landscape, a tree, or a flower which piques my imagination, and I am soon creating a composition in my mind.

Ironically, this painting came about in a somewhat different way. My good friend C.P. "Chappy" Fox asked me to paint it, and he even drew a little diagram of the hen mallard and her ducklings to show me precisely what he had in mind. I then expanded on his idea by adding the red-winged blackbird perched on a cattail scolding the mother duck and her babies. I felt it added interest to the composition.

I like the fact that my ideas and inspiration come from people and nature. I hope that I get the opportunity to paint the many exciting pictures which are catalogued in my brain, just waiting for a chance to be done.

1979, oil, 36" x 24"

Killdeer

When the first killdeer show up, I am satisfied that spring is really on the way. I love killdeer because they are such cheery birds and because they are so beautiful when you get a chance to look at them close-up. Then you can observe the killdeer's most distinctive characteristic — its bright orange eyelid.

Quite a few killdeer will nest around here, and this painting is a composite of perhaps a dozen or more different studies I have made. The two fluffy, newly-hatched chicks and the egg are typical sights for the lucky observer of a killdeer nest.

A shore bird, the killdeer is most comfortable wading through shallow water on its long legs. And even though they will nest in a dry pasture, the killdeer want water readily available.

It seems to me that I don't see as many killdeer as I used to. When I was a boy in Fond du Lac, Wisconsin, I often saw large numbers of them out on the glacial flats near Lake Winnebago. There was plenty of lowland and wet places in the fields for the killdeer.

But today many farmers will drain every little pothole that interferes with their crop yield, thereby diminishing the habitat for killdeer. The process is slow — a little drained here; a little drained there — but eventually the killdeer will be gone.

1976, oil, 16" x 12"

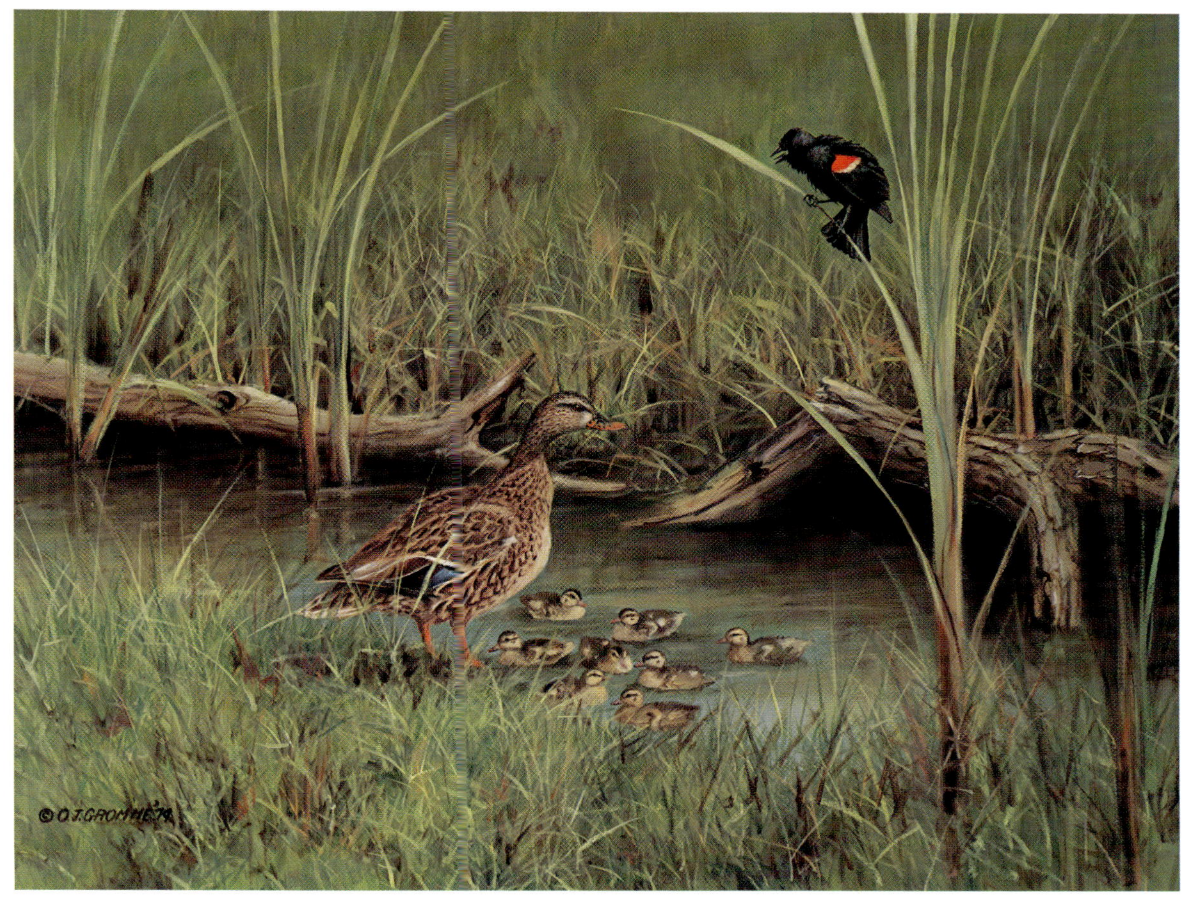

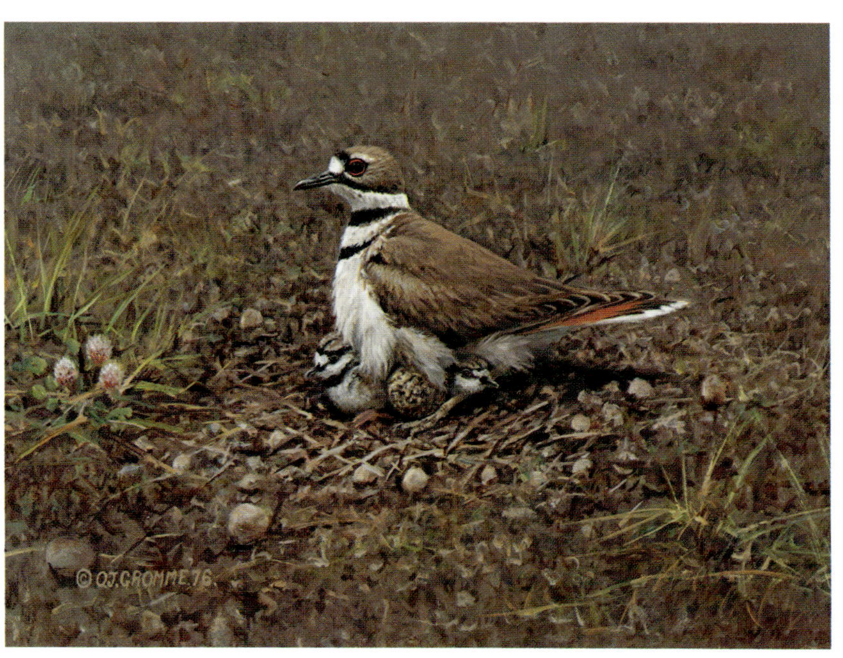

Changing of the Guard — Common Loon

Once while I was in northern Wisconsin trying to get some photographs of a bald eagle's nest for the Milwaukee Public Museum, a young woman told me where I could find a common loon's nest. My eagle expedition was going badly, so I accepted her offer and went to see it. It was a rare opportunity, for the loon let me build a photographic blind within a few feet of the nest. I measured, photographed, sketched and took notes at the set-up. That's where I got the common loon studies which I used for reference when painting this picture.

The loon is a very interesting bird. For example, its family life is unique — both parents share with the incubation of the eggs and the care of the young. Here I show one parent relieving the other of the incubation responsibilities.

Like so many of our waterfowl, loons are being driven north by the pressure of more and more people in their breeding grounds. People chase them with motor boats, and water skiers invade every little bay and inlet in the north. Loons used to nest all over the state, but as agriculture developed and population increased, they have been pushed farther and farther north.

The loon's dilemma is similar to that of so many other birds which formerly bred all over the state — the marshes are drained and their breeding grounds are destroyed. Some species have been pushed to the point where they can no longer nest successfully. Public awareness of the damage being done to our wildlife must bring an end to this invasion of habitat before it is too late.

1981, oil, 36" x 24"

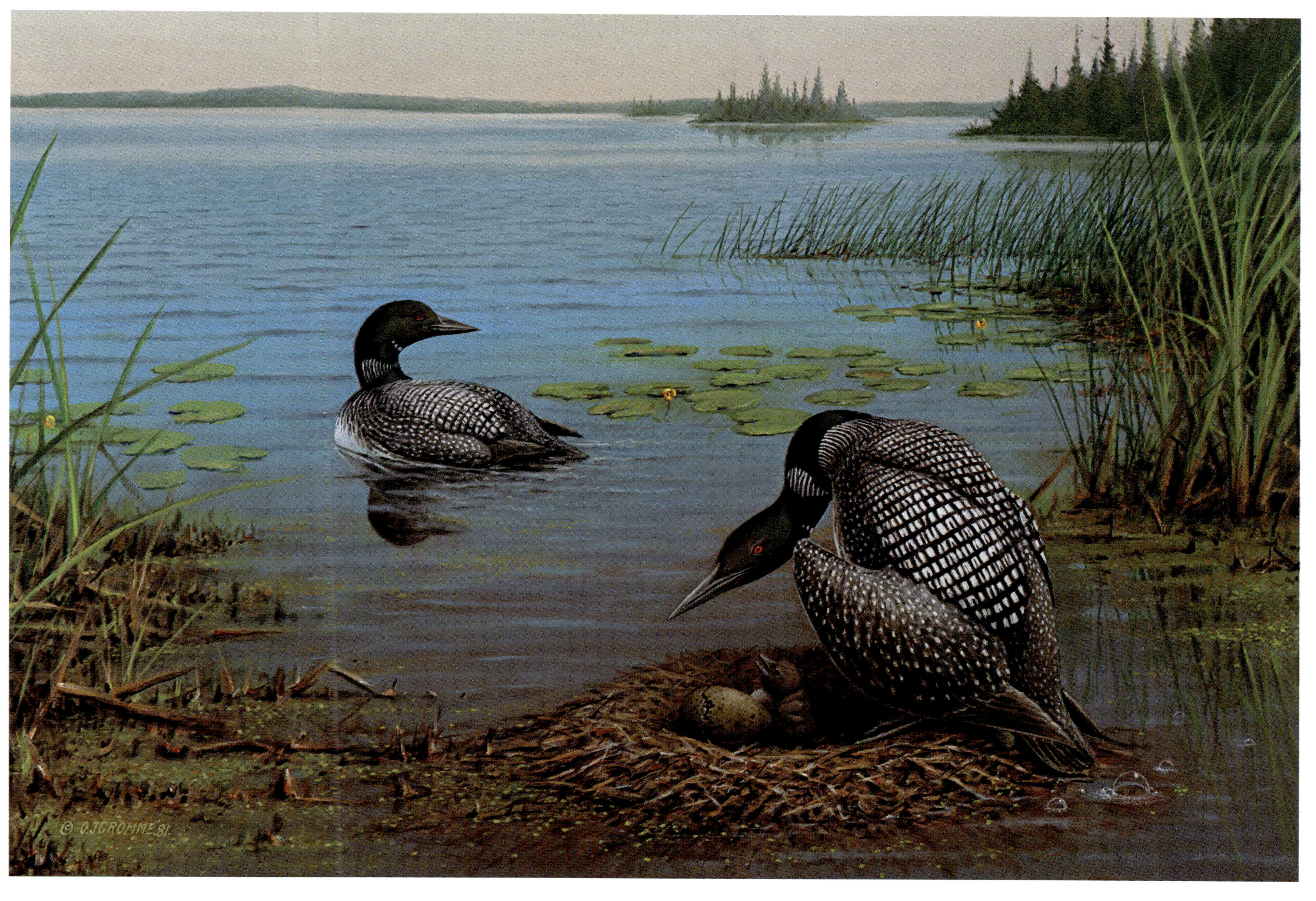
© O.J.GROMME.81.

Common Loon with Young

Having painted so many pictures of lakes, marshes and the accompanying flora, as well as woods, pine trees, islands and rocky shores, I can create a typical place for a common loon from my memory. For example, I know how spruce and pine trees look with their characteristic outlines, and I have painted many a northern Wisconsin island. So, with the exception of the specific details, such as the fine little plants that grow immediately around the loon's nest, I would need very little reference for a common loon painting.

I painted this picture of a female loon and her young, for instance, with no special locale in mind. In fact, it could be one of hundreds of lakes in northern Wisconsin and Minnesota. The adult loon swims peacefully among the spatterdock as her babies look out from the warmth and comfort of her shoulder coverts. Anyone who has ever spent a summer in northern Wisconsin should be familiar with this sight.

1967, oil, 36" x 24"

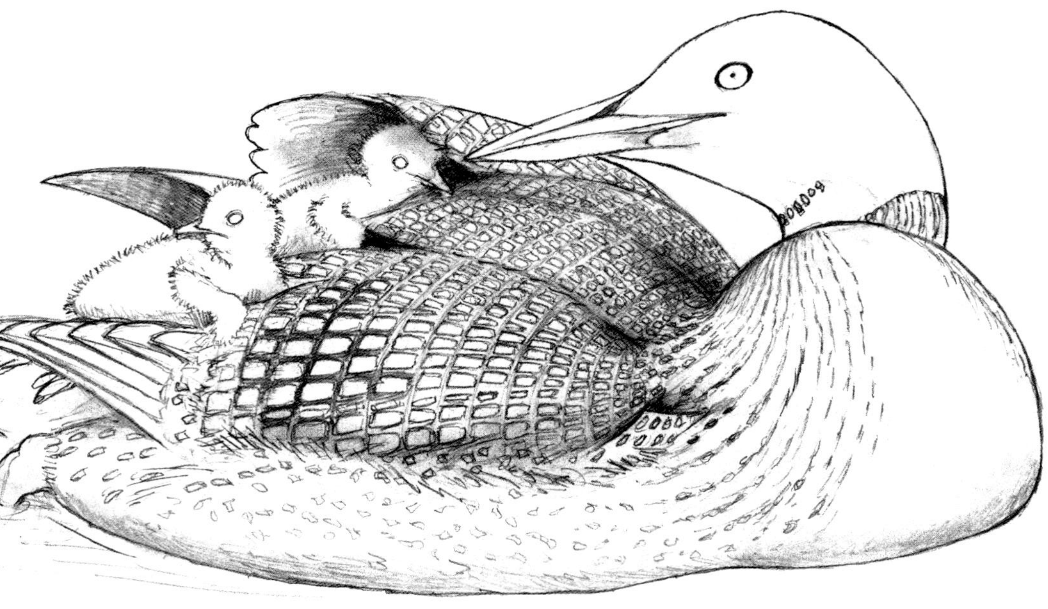

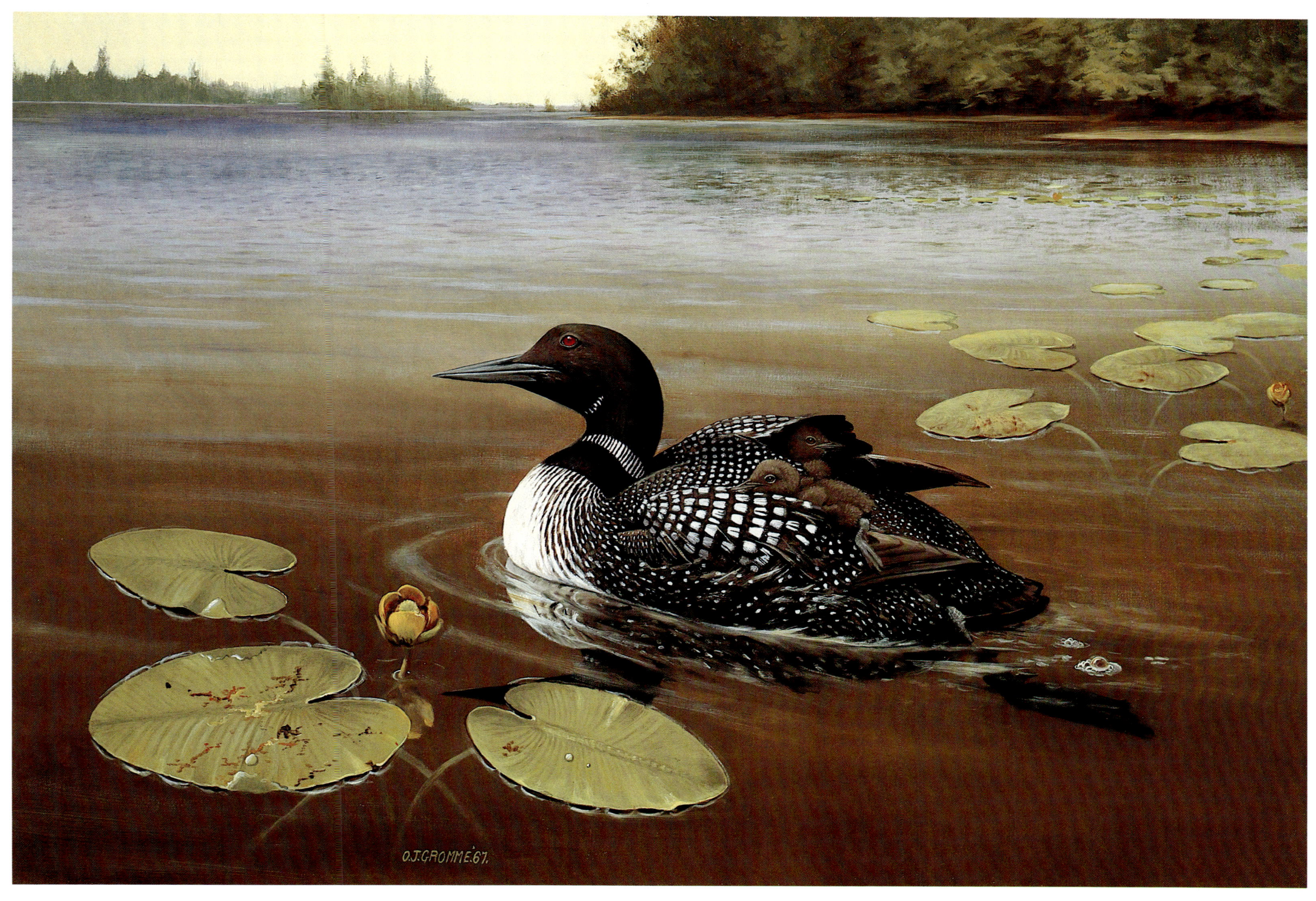
O.J.GROMME.67.

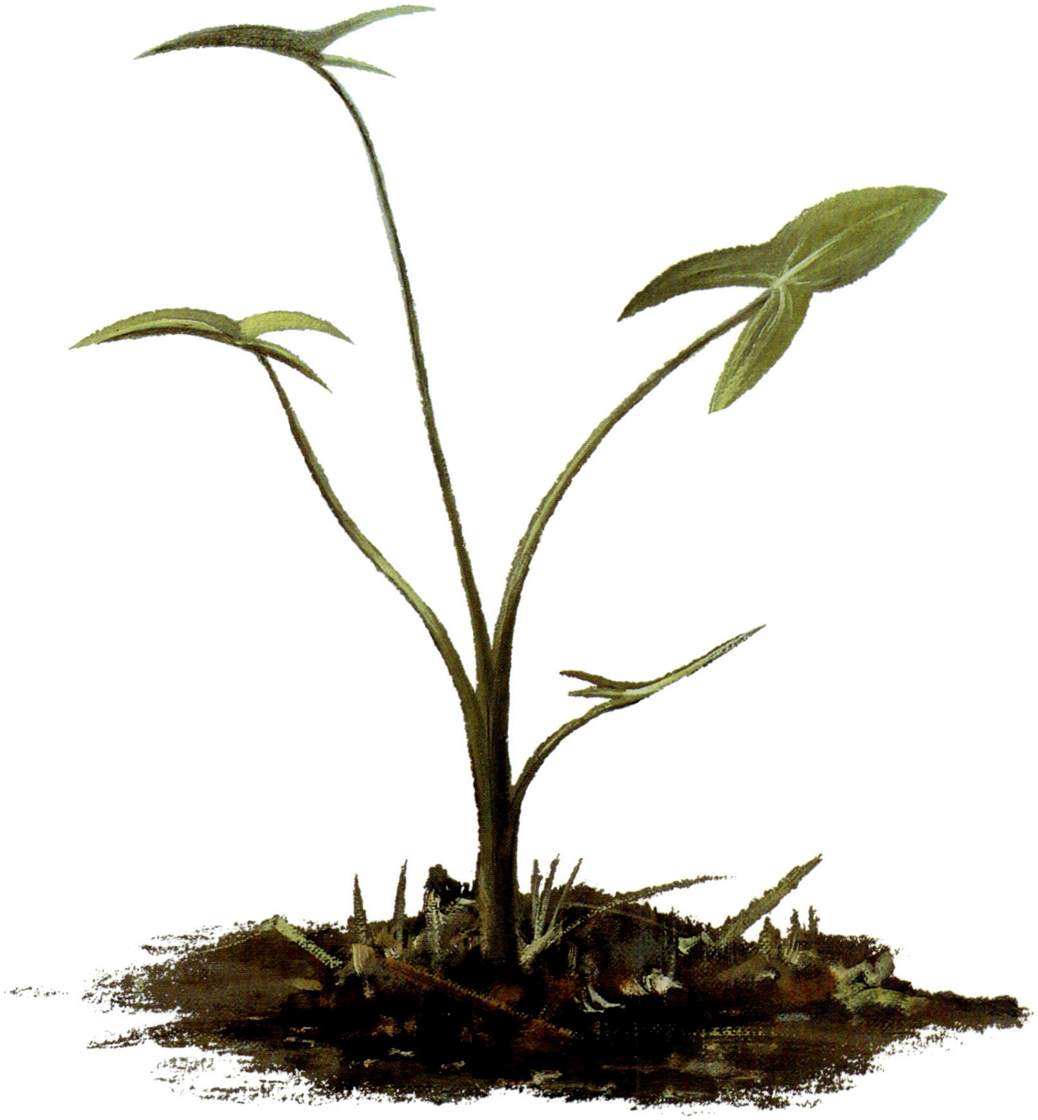

Common Gallinule

The major elements of a wildlife painting are subject, composition, light, color, and detail. These are things which I strive for in each and every painting. I try to make each work that I do better than anything I have ever done before. The completed painting may not be the best that has ever been done, but I want it to be the best that I have ever done.

Take this painting of a common moorhen (gallinule) as an example. In it, I placed the moorhen (or Florida gallinule as they are also known) in a setting which is typical for it. Then I made the plants and land formations lead the viewer's eye to the bird. Without fencing the moorhen in, the plants establish a direction for the eye, always bringing the viewer back to the bird.

As far as light and color are concerned, they are interdependent, for the direction and type of light — morning, midday or evening — largely determine what colors predominate. And the bird itself is portrayed with the kind of *detail* and accuracy that many years of observation bring.

When people ask me how long it takes me to do a painting, I sometimes say that my latest painting took my entire life. By that I mean that all the years of observing and learning about birds and their habits, and all the years of learning how to paint (and I am still learning) go into every painting I do.

1967, oil, 24″ x 18″

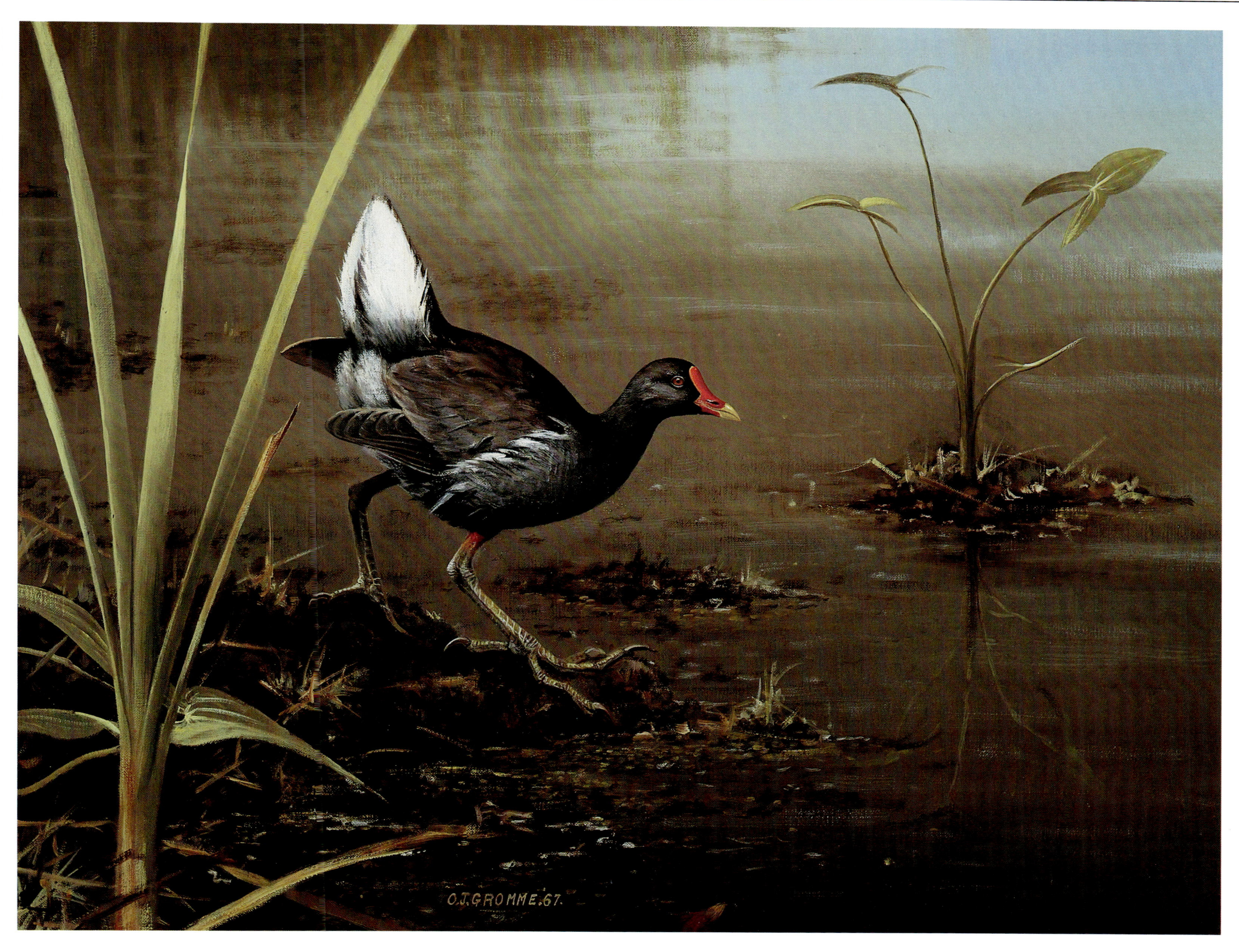
O.J.GROMME.67.

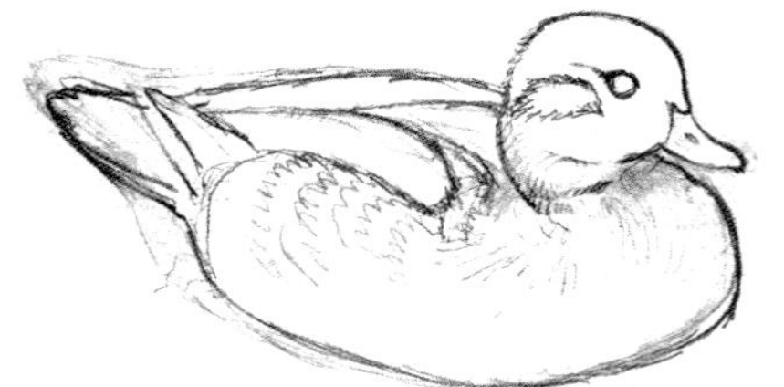

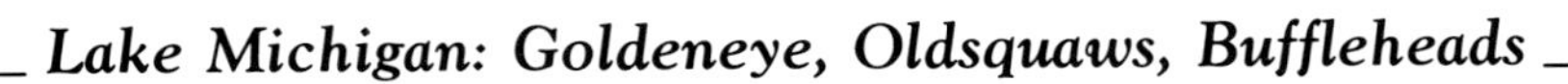

Lake Michigan: Goldeneye, Oldsquaws, Buffleheads

In 1922 and 1923 Herb Stoddard and I collected the ducks that were used in the overhead flying groups in the old Milwaukee Public Museum building. We collected many of them at the Milwaukee lake front, in what is now known as Juneau Park.

Because the Great Lakes remain open all year, they create a favorable wintering area for oldsquaws, scoters, common goldeneyes, buffleheads, red-breasted mergansers, and mallards. Such species can be found in any open water where food is available, and we took advantage of that fact as we tried to complete our groups for the museum.

On this particular day, Herb and I hid among the ice-coated pilings of the old breakwater which we used for a duck blind. It was mid-winter, usually the best time to find the most representative number of birds. The sun shining through the icicles with the ducks in front made a spectacular scene which I recalled many years later as I set out to paint this picture.

1968, oil, 32″ x 26″

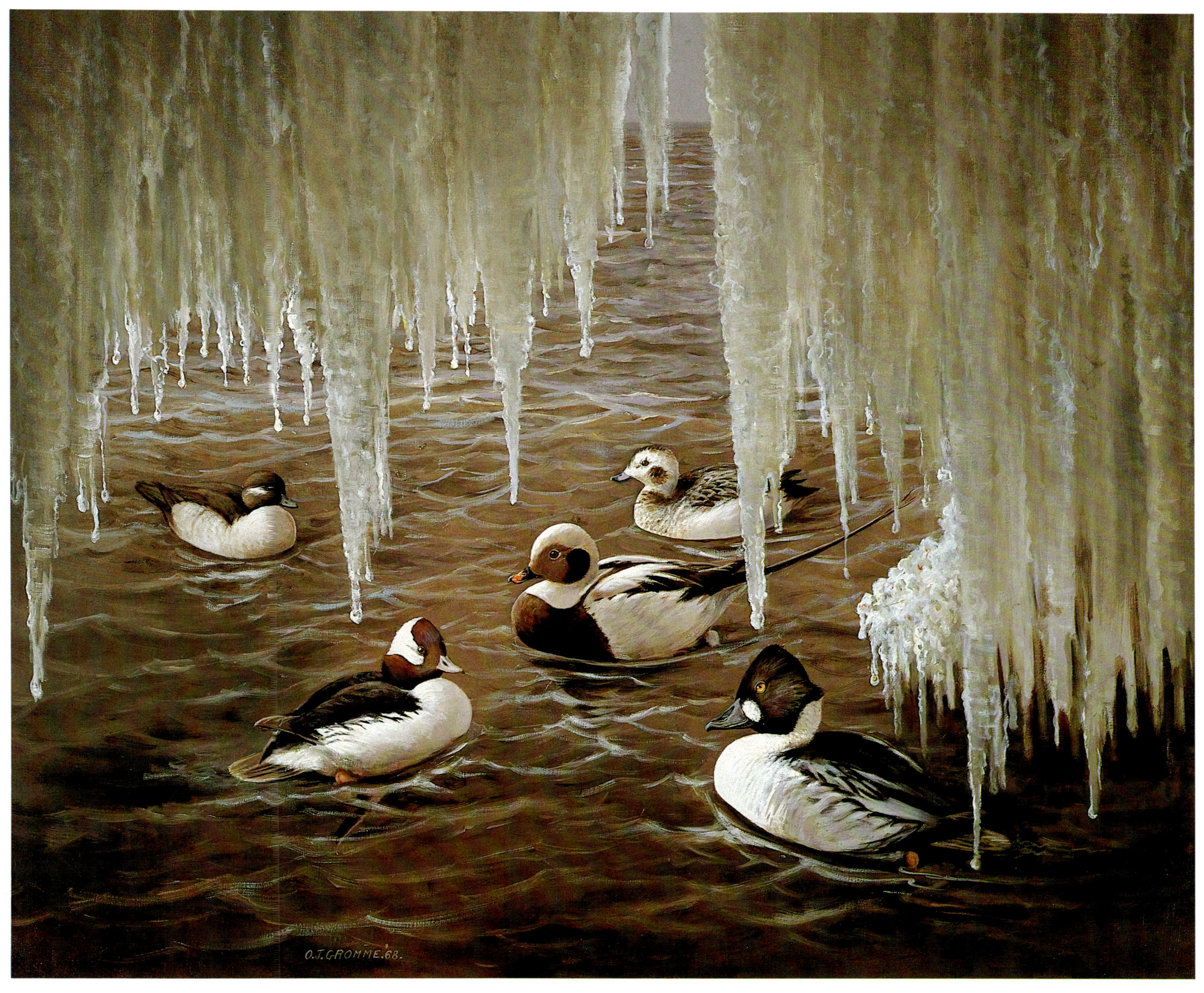
O.J. GROMME. 68.

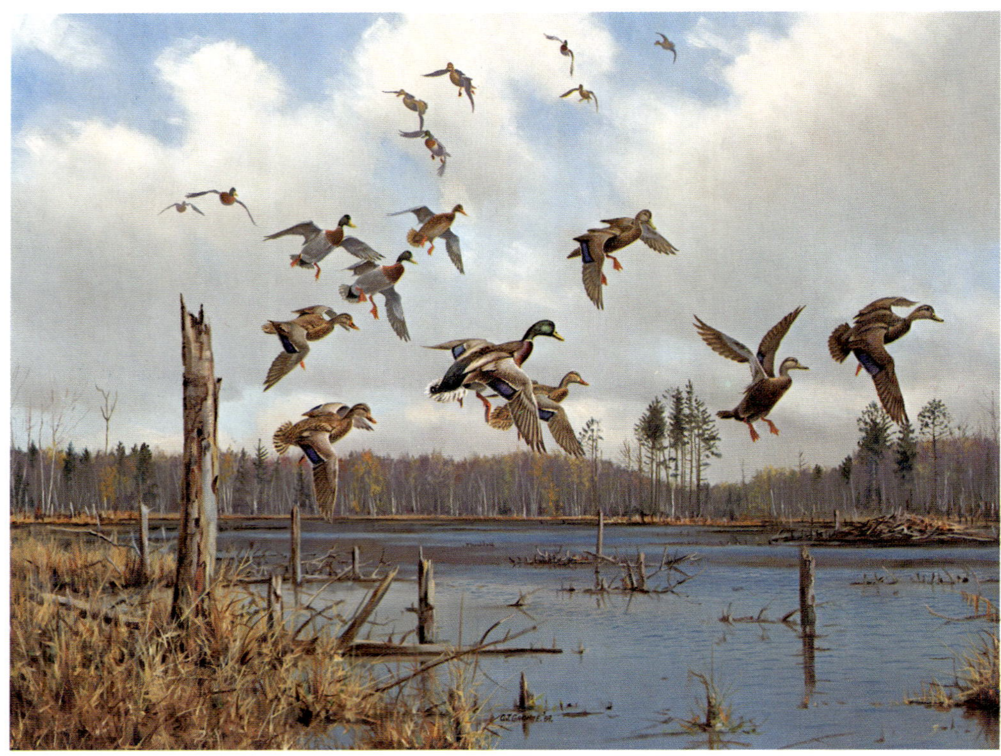

Grandpa's Pond — Mallards and Black Ducks

I plan all of my compositions on paper before transferring them to canvas, starting out with a doodle about a third the size of the final work. Using this painting as an example, I probably began with one bird, like the mallard drake which is just to the left of center here, and I drew him fairly carefully. Then I positioned all the other ducks around that one, properly spacing them and making sure that they contributed to a balanced composition. Next, I determined where the horizon line would be and followed that by painting in trees, bushes, water, rocks and so forth.

I strive for orderliness in my composition, so that nothing in the picture conflicts with anything else. Each part contributes to the whole, and the overall appearance should be pleasingly proportioned.

The pond shown here is on a beaver flowage near Manitowish Waters, Wisconsin, and it is a very typical setting for a painting of waterfowl.

1969, oil, 40″ x 30″

Cedar Creek — Mallards

The background for this painting is Cedar Creek, a spring-fed creek in Washington County, Wisconsin, where my family used to go snowshoeing on winter days. I created this piece as a pleasant reminder of the many times we spent in that area, often seeing mallards in the dead of winter, provided there was open water.

When I plan my compositions, I am careful to leave the bird or animal a way to get out of the picture. These ducks, for example, could conceivably follow the curve of the creek out of the composition, or they could fly straight over the horizon. That suggestion appeals to a viewer's sense of freedom and also contributes to good composition.

I think artists possess a certain instinct for good composition. In my case, never having had an art lesson, I can only believe that this is an inborn ability. That isn't to say that it can't be learned, but it seems to have come naturally to me. Thus, in my work I strive for balance, and a pleasing arrangement of my subjects, keeping my art simple and uncluttered.

Cedar Creek — Mallards is a good case in point. Five ducks in a triangular arrangement are the focal point of the painting, with the "S" curve of the creek leading your eye right to them. I don't really know much about the theory of composition, but I do know what is pleasing to the eye, and I have always let that be my guide.

1955, oil, 30″ x 24″

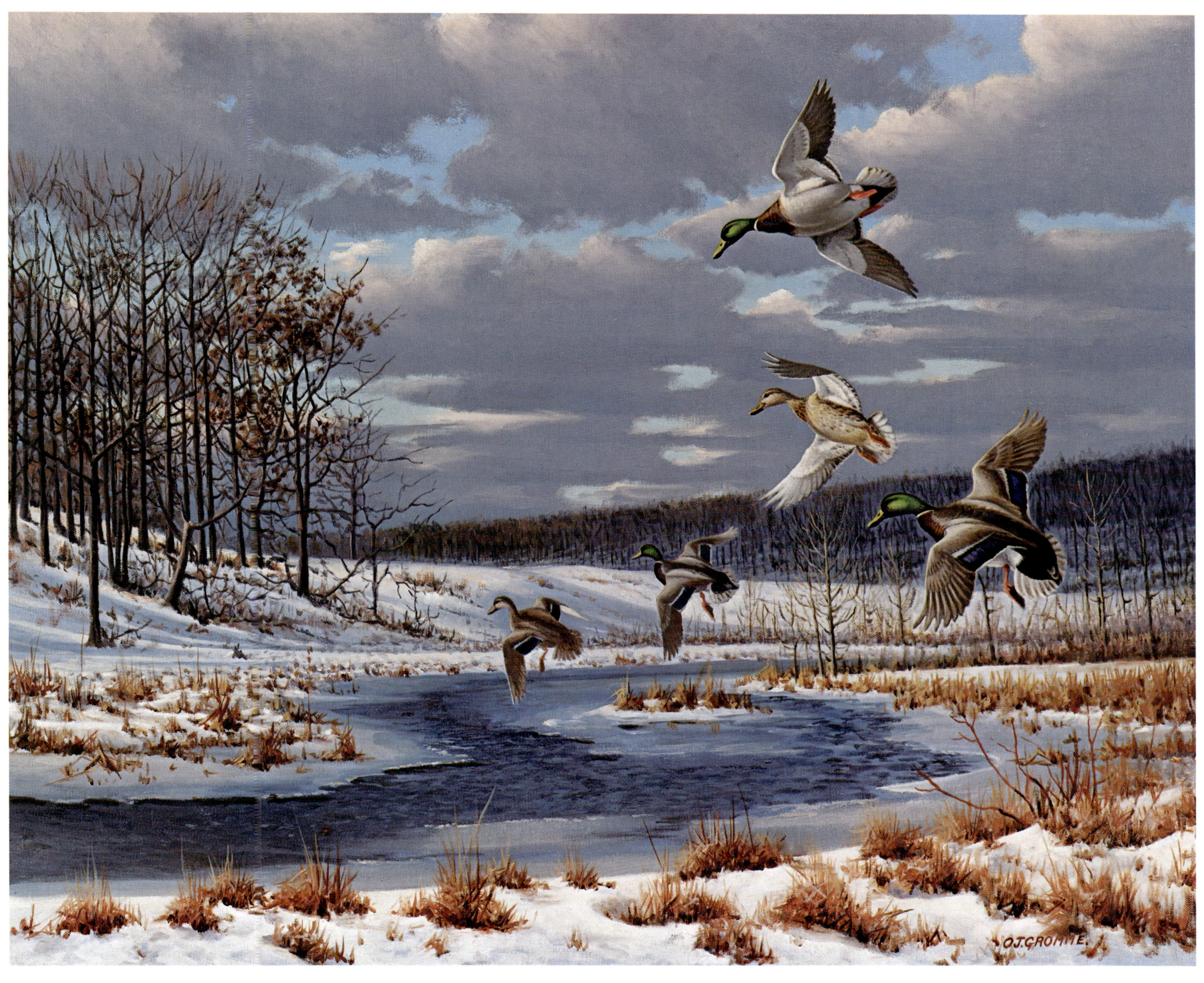
O.J.GROMME.

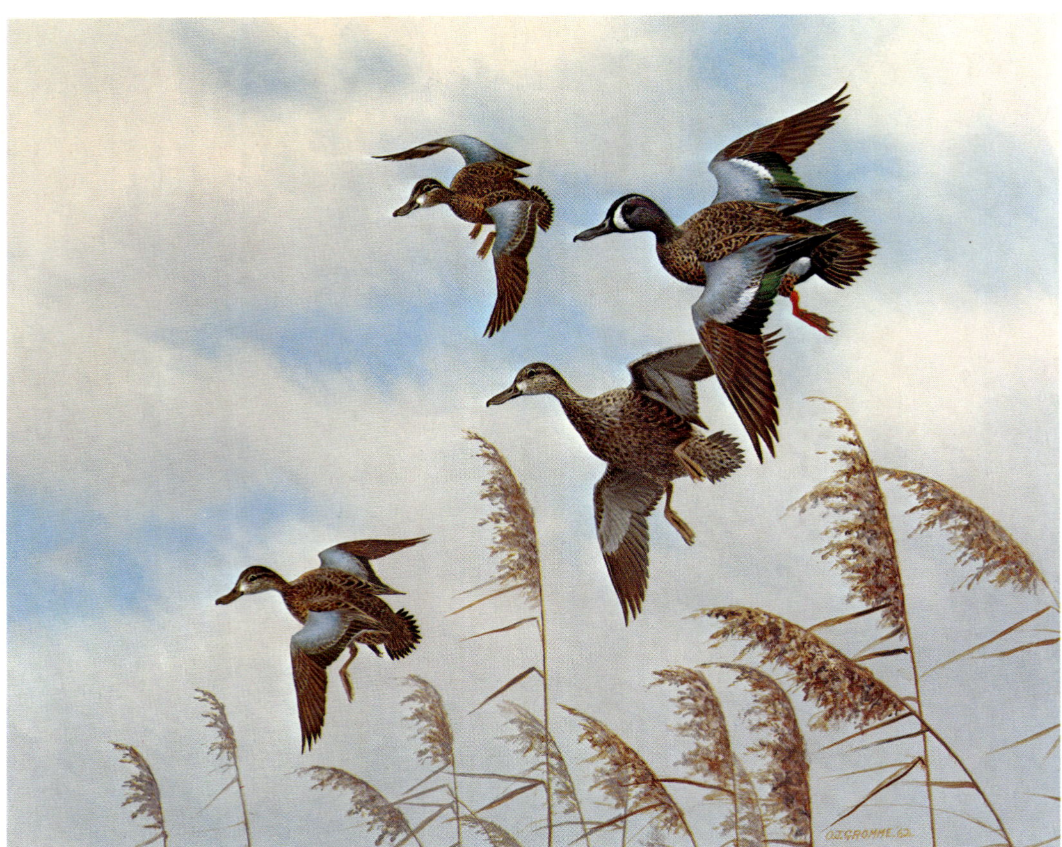

Blue-winged Teal

These small puddle ducks do very well in spite of all the predators, including human, which take a toll on them every year. The blue-winged teal is a familiar sight in small marshes, farm ponds and prairie potholes throughout their range which includes the Upper Midwest and southern Canada. The odds against their survival are great, however, for each year more and more potholes are drained, and the resultant land given over to cultivation.

Ducks Unlimited, Inc., a conservation group based in the U.S. and Canada, has taken on the phenomenal job of trying to keep breeding grounds available because without them all of the puddle ducks — mallards, pintails and the several varieties of teal — would be deprived of a place to nest and raise their young.

1962, oil, 30″ x 24″

Early Blue Wings

One time early in the duck hunting season I was in a blind with several friends trying to get a good photograph of a blue-winged teal. Hunting with a camera is every bit as difficult as hunting with a gun, and even though the birds flew in so close to the blind that they almost knocked our hats off, I did not get a good photograph. So I decided to paint one.

Blue-winged males are such beautiful little fellows in their spring plumage, but we only get to see them like that for a short time just after they return from the south. During the summer molt the males take on the appearance of the females and are difficult to tell apart.

Blue wings nest here in Wisconsin wherever there is water throughout the summer, producing seven to ten eggs. Among the first ducks to migrate, they fly out in late August or early September.

1973-74, oil, 36″ x 24″

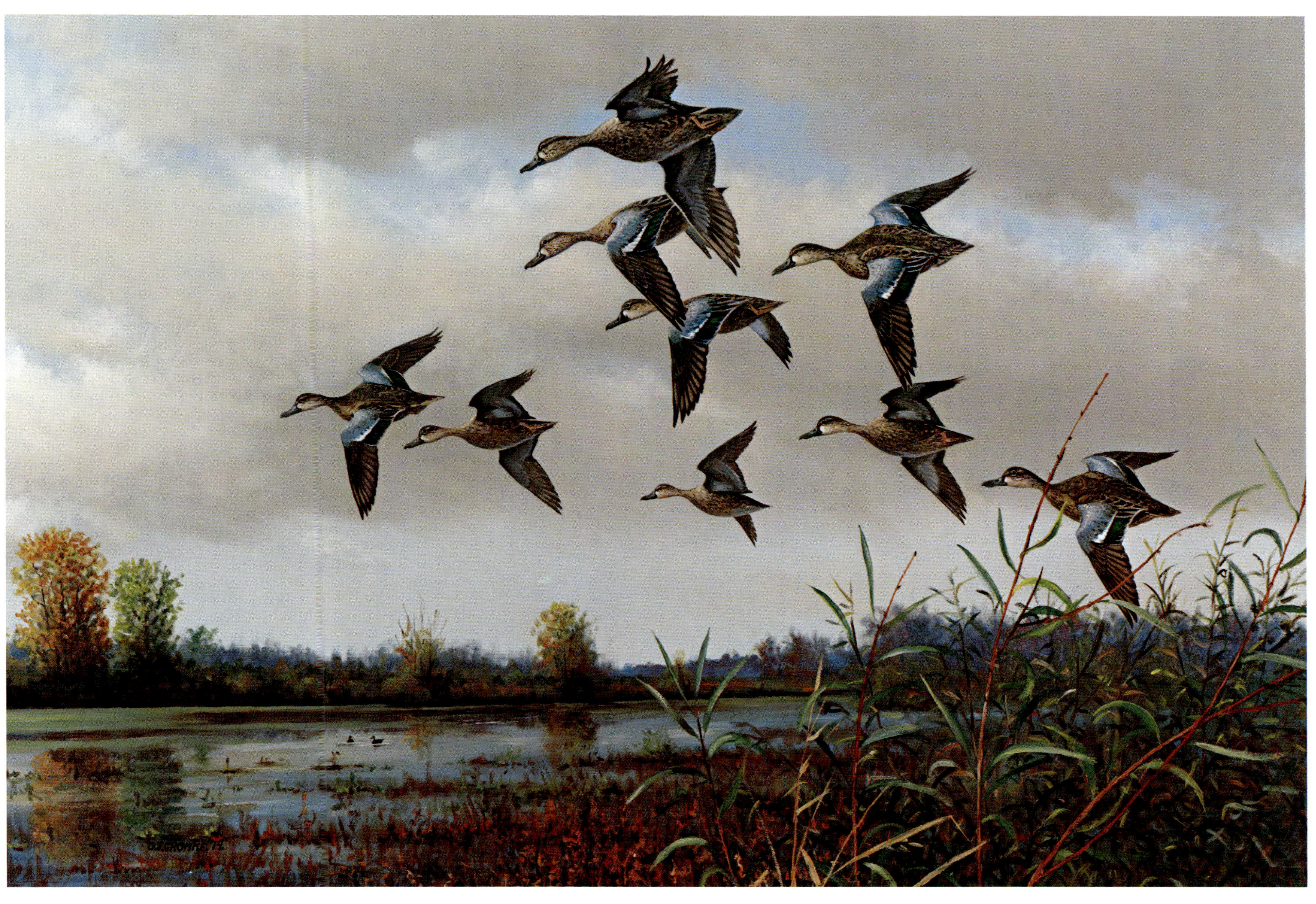

Scurrying Greenwings

The green-winged teal is, with the possible exception of the bufflehead, the smallest of our Wisconsin ducks. Their flight is rapid and remarkably maneuverable. In this picture, I have shown a flock of green-winged teal in a place along the old west marsh near the south end of Lake Winnebago at Fond du Lac. A lot of canebrakes grow along the lakeshore there, and I can remember hunting one day and looking up to see a flock of greenwings swish in behind me. This painting recreates that incident for me.

But there is more to this story. The original of this painting was sold to someone from Menasha, and I knew nothing of it for a long time. Then one day William Webster of Wild Wings, Inc. told me that he had come across the painting but that it was nearly ruined. It had apparently been hung in a smoke-filled room, as it was completely yellowed and quite dirty. Some sort of alcohol had been spilled on it, too, and several holes had been poked in it as well.

Bill Webster bought the picture and took it to an art restorer in Minneapolis. When he brought it back to me afterwards, it looked as fine as the day I had taken it off my easel. In fact, I could not detect where the holes had been. It was such a beautiful job of restoration that Wild Wings and I had it reproduced as a limited edition print. No one can tell that this painting had ever been so badly abused.

1964, oil, 36″ x 24″

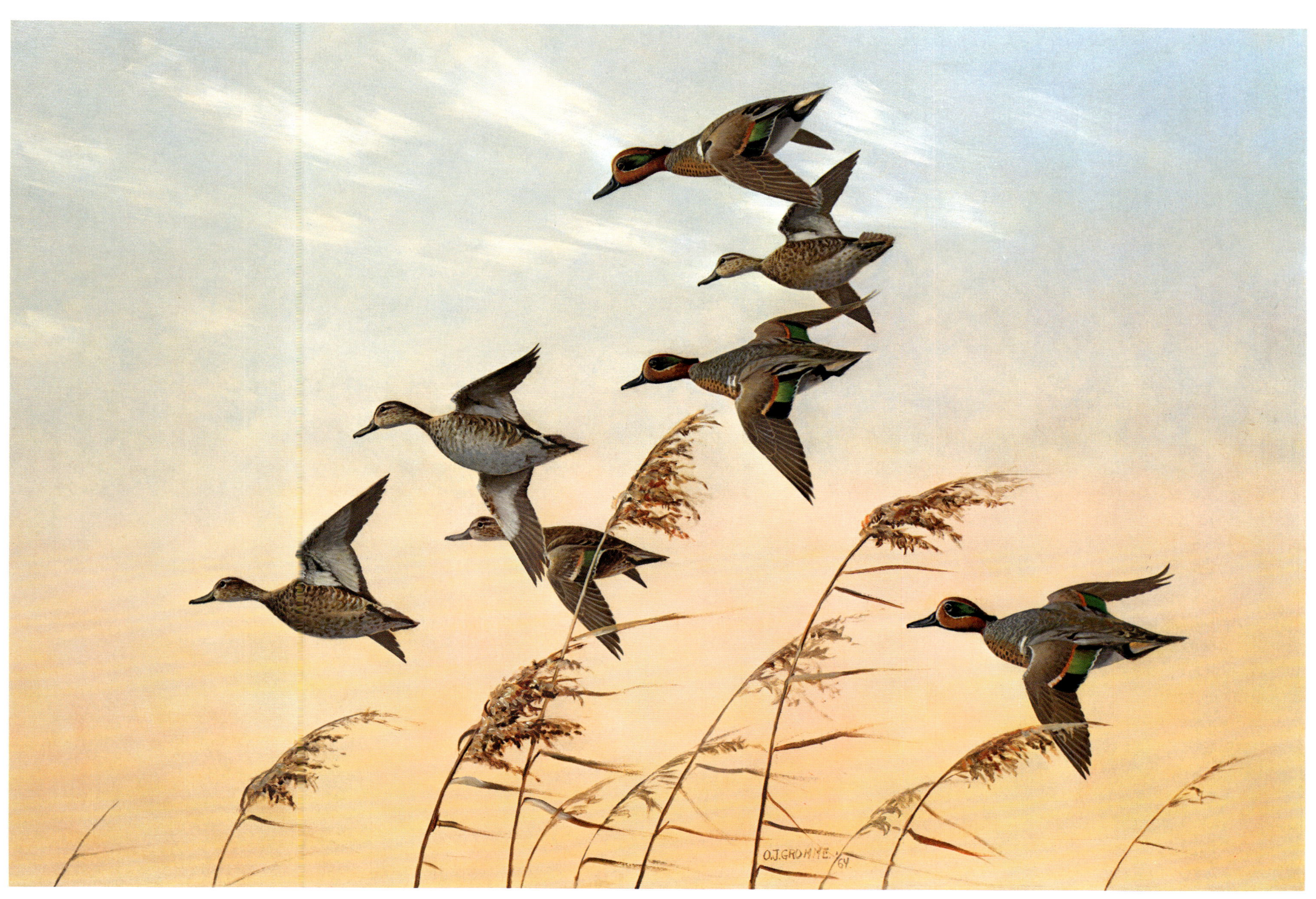

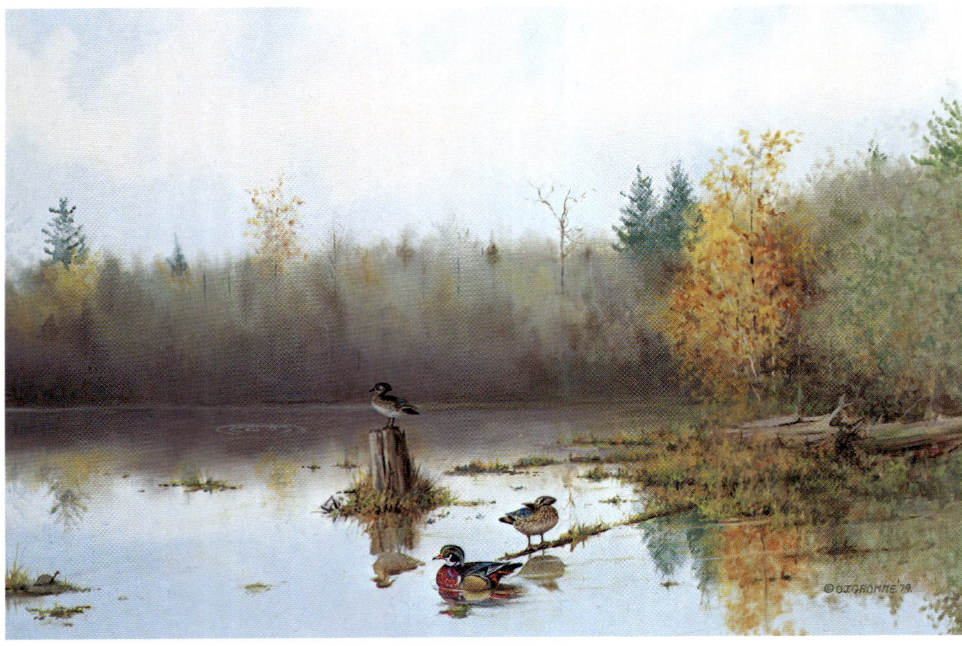

Morning Haze — Wood Ducks

Morning Haze is a fall setting in northern Wisconsin, early in the morning before the mist has lifted. The calm, serene water reflects the birds as they sit quietly in the morning light.

I have been fascinated with wood ducks ever since my early youth. When I was about 14 or 15 years old, just beginning to work as a commercial taxidermist, a wealthy lumberman from Fond du Lac brought me a wood duck to mount. It was a beautiful bird, as all wood ducks are, and I will never forget how I felt as it lay before me on my workbench. I stroked those velvety soft feathers and marvelled at the beautifully blended colors. It was wondrous to me how nature had combined them. I was reluctant to remove the skin for mounting because I hated to disturb all that beauty.

Of course my mounted bird did not in any way compare to the live bird, but I did the best I could as a taxidermist. When the man called for it, he was pleased with the job I had done. He asked me how much he owed me, and I said $1.50. He gave me $3.50 because he was so impressed with the finished mount. It was the first money I ever earned as a taxidermist.

1979, oil, 36″ x 24″

Wood Ducks — Gall's Pond

This is the very first painting I completed for the Milwaukee offices of the Marshall and Ilsley Bank. It reminds me of a Japanese print more than anything else.

One day in early autumn, Anne and I walked up to our neighbor's secluded pond where the wood ducks congregate, approaching the pond from below a rise. It was a bright, windy day with the leaves beginning to turn and the acorns falling. Carefully keeping ourselves concealed, we witnessed an unforgettable sight. There were about a hundred wood ducks around the pond, swimming, sitting in trees, and flying in and out. The sunny day, the brightly-colored ducks, and the autumn leaves combined to create a festival of color. We could even hear the acorns "plop" as they dropped into the water from the oak trees around the pond. We watched for a long time, drinking in the incredible beauty.

I returned the next day to undertake a more careful study of the terrain and the pond before I began to paint. *Wood Ducks — Gall's Pond* is essentially what we saw, except that there were more ducks than I have chosen to show. A small group makes a better composition, so I decided to include only a sample of the actual number.

1966, oil, 40″ x 28″

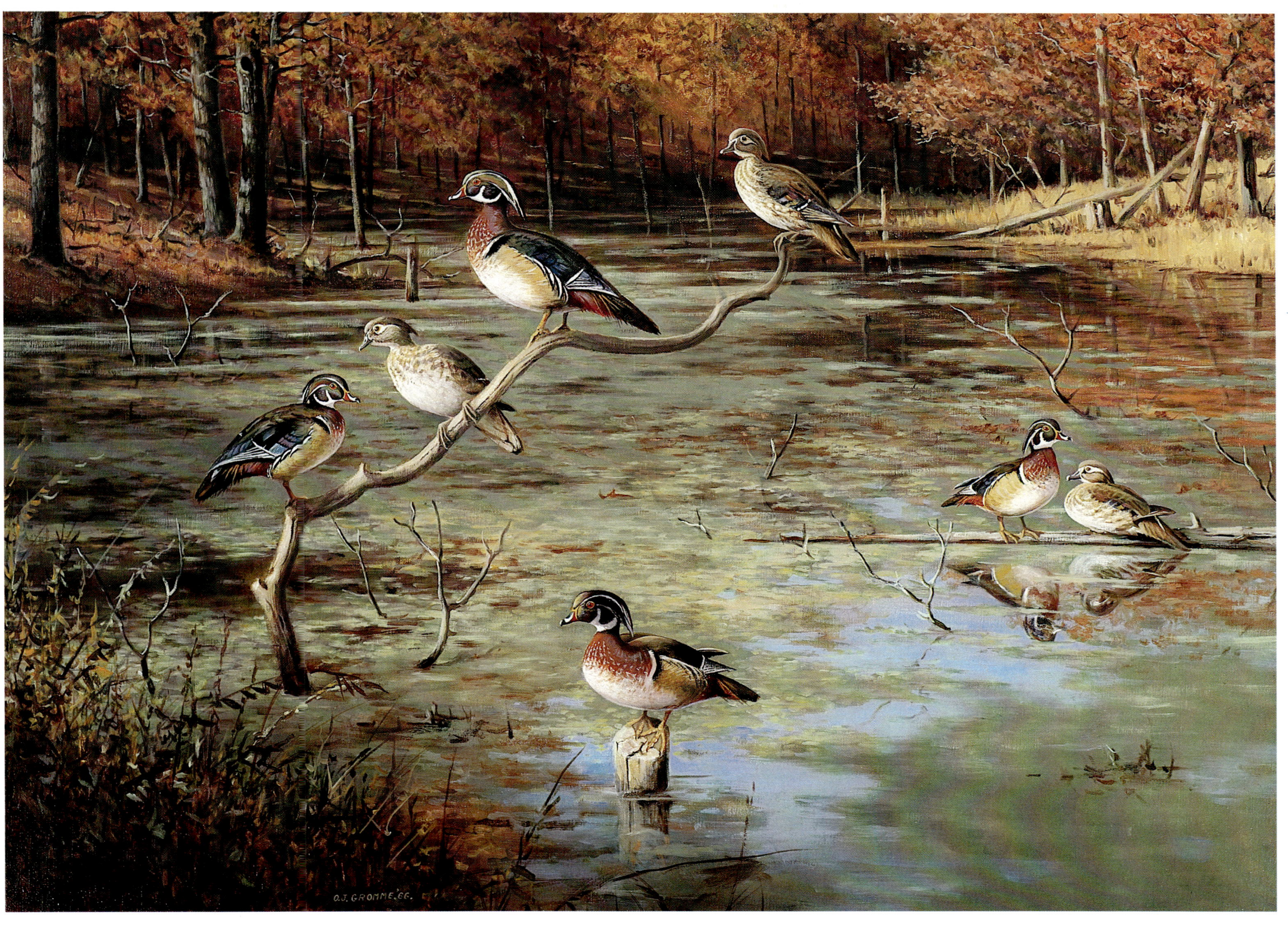
O.J. GROMME.'66.

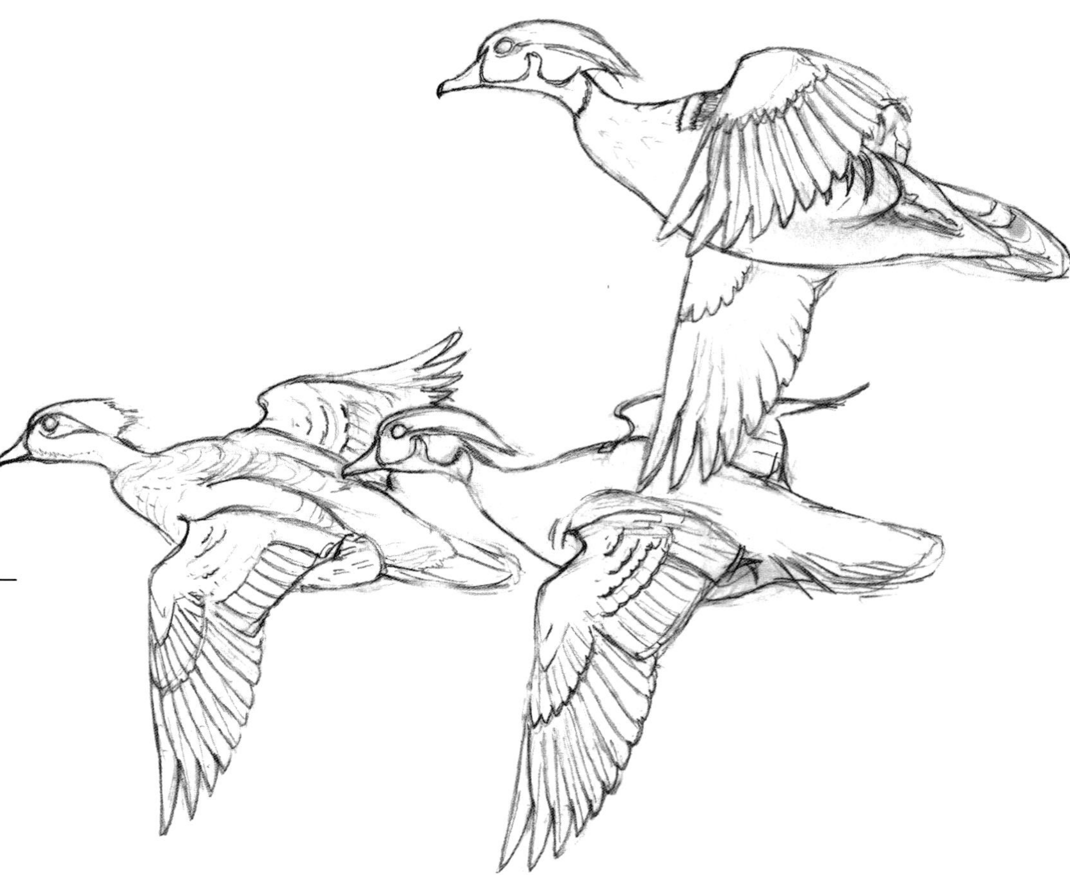

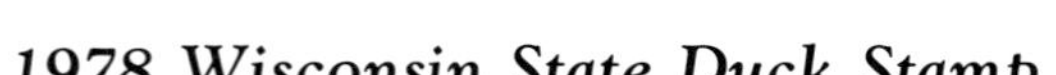

1978 Wisconsin State Duck Stamp

When the Wisconsin Department of Natural Resources (DNR) decided to issue a Duck Stamp, they asked me to design the first one. The Duck Stamp is attached to a regular hunting license, allowing the bearer to hunt ducks in the State of Wisconsin. It adds to the revenues which the state derives from hunting, and a dollar of the cost of each stamp is contributed to Ducks Unlimited, Inc., a conservation group based in the U.S. and Canada, to assist with their activities.

After I had agreed to do the design for the first stamp, the Department requested that I paint wood ducks, because they felt that the wood duck was one of the most popular and most beautiful of our waterfowl.

At present the design of the Wisconsin Duck Stamp is determined by a contest open to all state artists, but I was asked to do the first one, I think, partly because I did the 1945 Federal Duck Stamp, and partly because the DNR considered me to be the best known wildlife artist in Wisconsin at that time (1978).

So, I went down to the pond here on my son's farm and found all the wood ducks I could ever want to paint, along with a brilliantly colored fall background. I have done a lot of paintings of wood ducks, but this one was special, because, being the first Duck Stamp for Wisconsin, it was bound to become a collector's item.

1978, oil, 14" x 10"

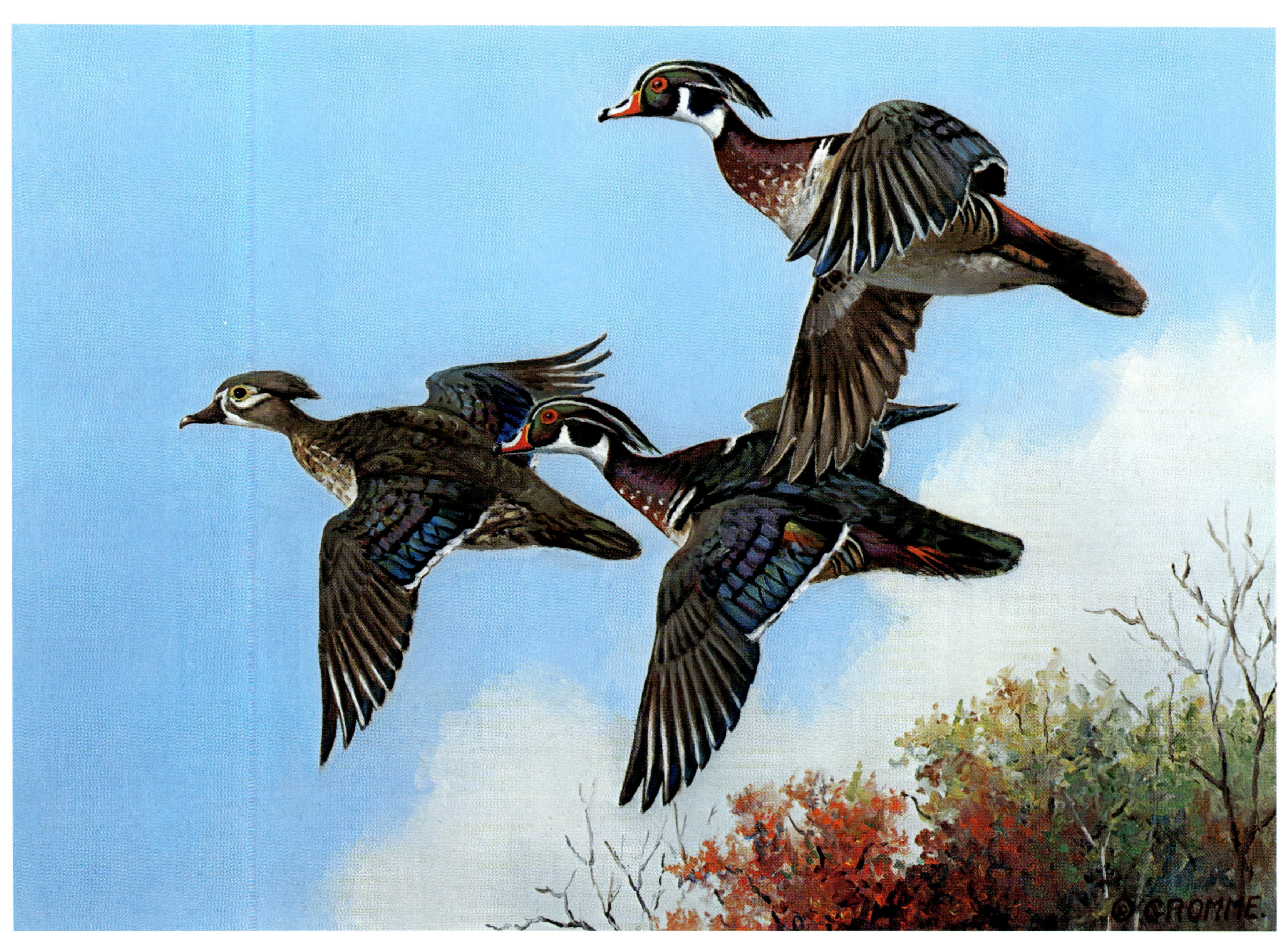
© GROMME.

Fall Kaleidoscope

(Ducks Unlimited Artist of the Year Print) — I was named "Artist of the Year" by Ducks Unlimited, Inc. (DU) in 1978. This organization is deeply involved in maintaining wetland habitat for waterfowl in Canada where most of our ducks and geese have their nesting grounds. When DU informed me of the honor, they asked me to do a painting which they could auction off to raise money for their organization. They also made a print for each of their chapters to auction so that *Fall Kaleidoscope* could be owned and enjoyed by more than just the person who bought the original.

Although I was told by DU that I could paint any kind of duck, they suggested that I paint wood ducks. That suited me well-enough, so I used the pond on my son's farm for my background. Wood ducks like little ponds in the woods where there are lots of oak trees, hence an abundance of acorns, their favorite food.

This is simply a peaceful scene of wood ducks in early autumn. Also noticeable is the spot where a trout has come to the surface to pick off an insect. Yet the strikingly beautiful ducks calmly go about the business of life in the September sun, shortly before migration.

1978, oil, 36″ x 24″

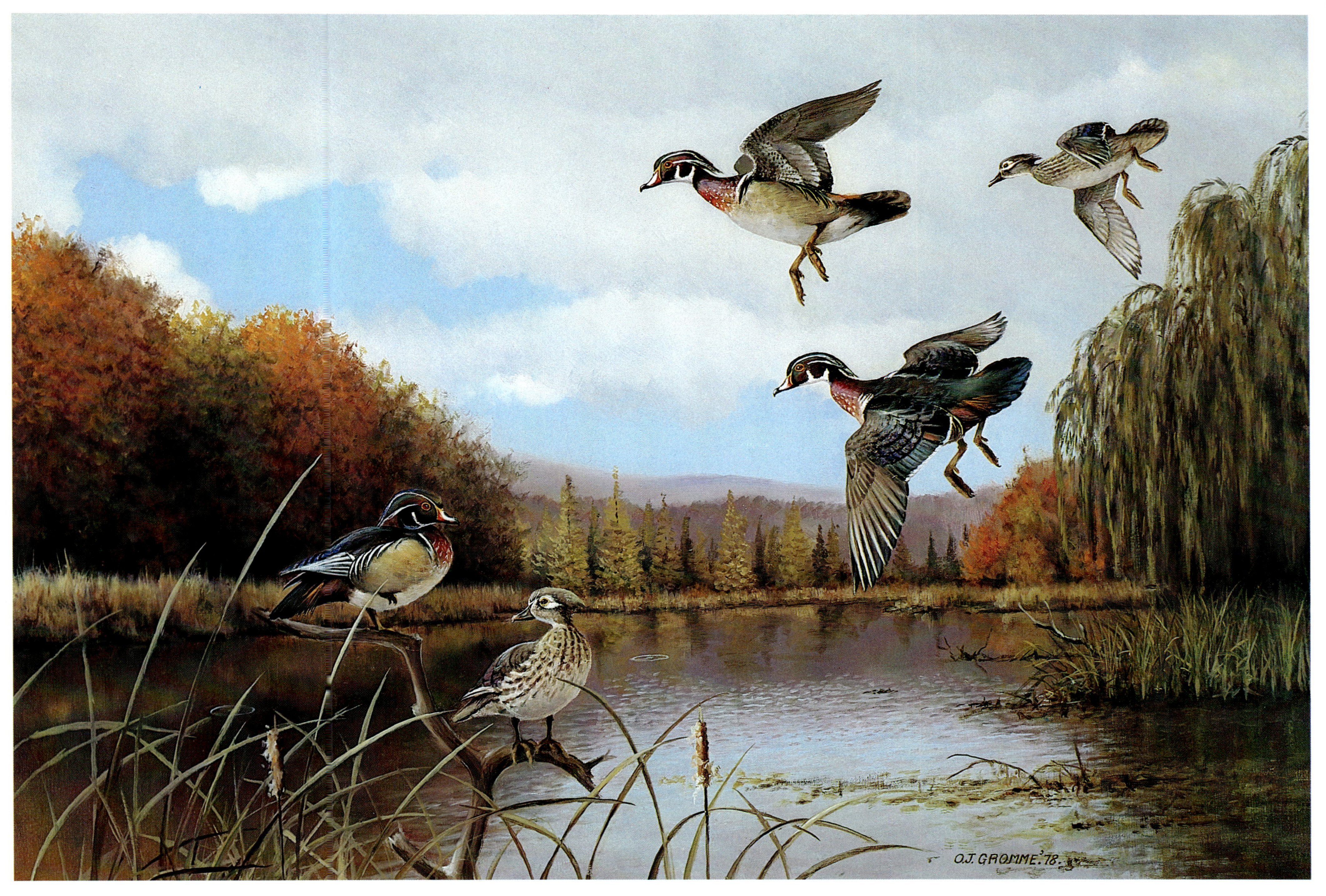
O.J. GROMME. 78.

Icy Weather — Canvasbacks

Here a large flock of canvasback ducks swing in above the western shore of Lake Winnebago in Wisconsin. Canvasback weather comes late in the fall when the shoreline is covered with ice and snow, but the lake is still open. Late migrators, many canvasbacks will stay until absolute freeze-up.

In Wisconsin there is a place on the Mississippi River where practically all of the canvasbacks in this part of the country congregate during their great migration. Several hundred thousand of them appear at one time, sitting out on Lake Pepin or on the Mississippi River, sometimes for weeks without moving on. Then, somehow, when the conditions are right, they rise up and move on, signalling the coming of winter.

The numbers of canvasbacks have been greatly depleted in recent years, mostly due to the drainage of the wetlands the ducks need for breeding grounds. Currently, we are losing our wetlands at the rate of thousands of acres per year. Ducks Unlimited, Inc., a conservation group based in the U.S. and Canada, is working to restore the Canadian breeding grounds, placing particular emphasis on the canvasback and the redhead.

1971, oil, 40″ x 28″

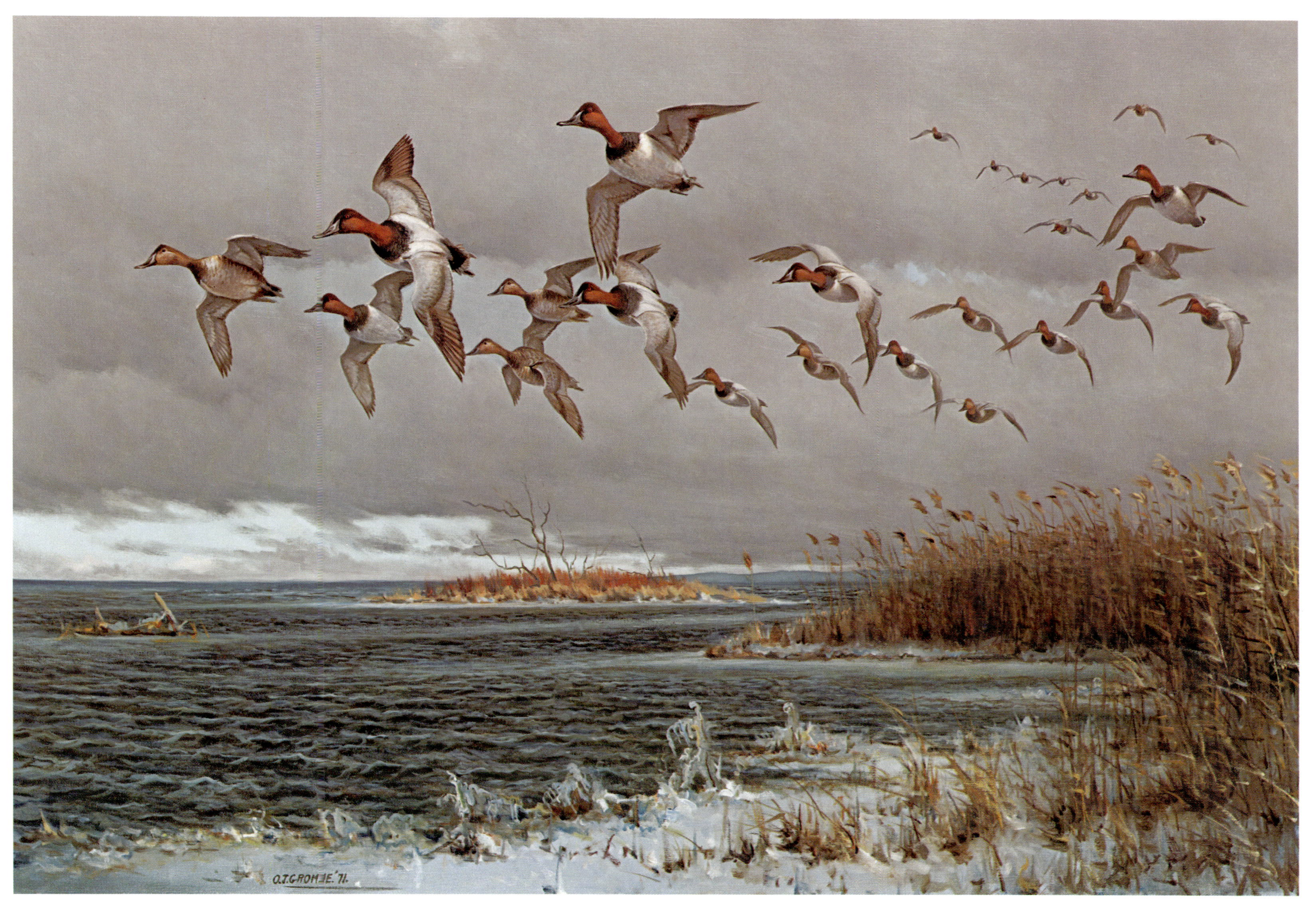
O.J.GROMME.'71.

Bucking the Storm — Canvasbacks

I have a special love for hunting ducks in stormy weather. As a young man, I experienced some of my very best canvasback hunting on stormy, windy days, when retrieving one on the open waves with a duck skiff was tantamount to taking your life in your own hands. But that was all part of what made duck hunting particularly appealing for me.

Canvasbacks fly in a precise, military-like formation, and they come in very fast. A difficult target, they present a real challenge to the hunter. The "cans" remain in Wisconsin until the freeze-up, and some even after that. In fact, I have seen many a duck hunter break the ice to place his decoys, while others have even placed decoys out *on* the ice.

Obviously, canvasbacks are quite hardy — they can live through ice and storms. I guess that's one of the things that makes them a favorite of mine.

1980, oil, 42" x 28"

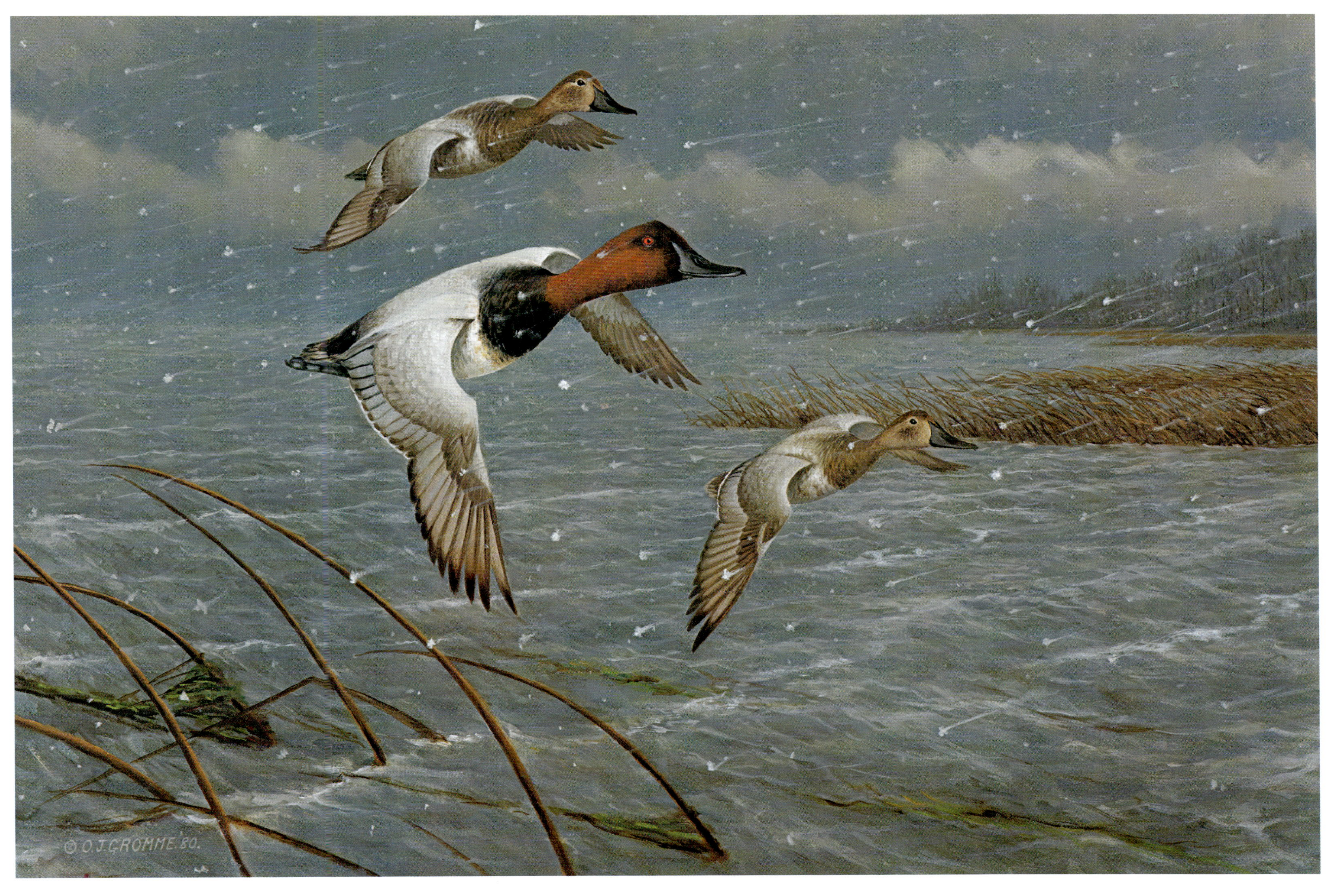
© O.J.GROMME.'80.

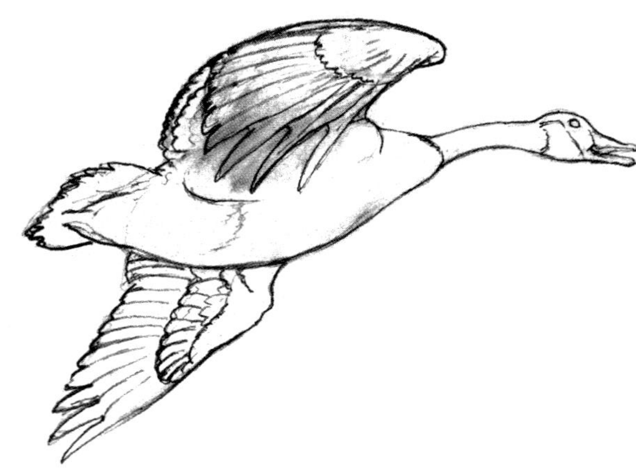

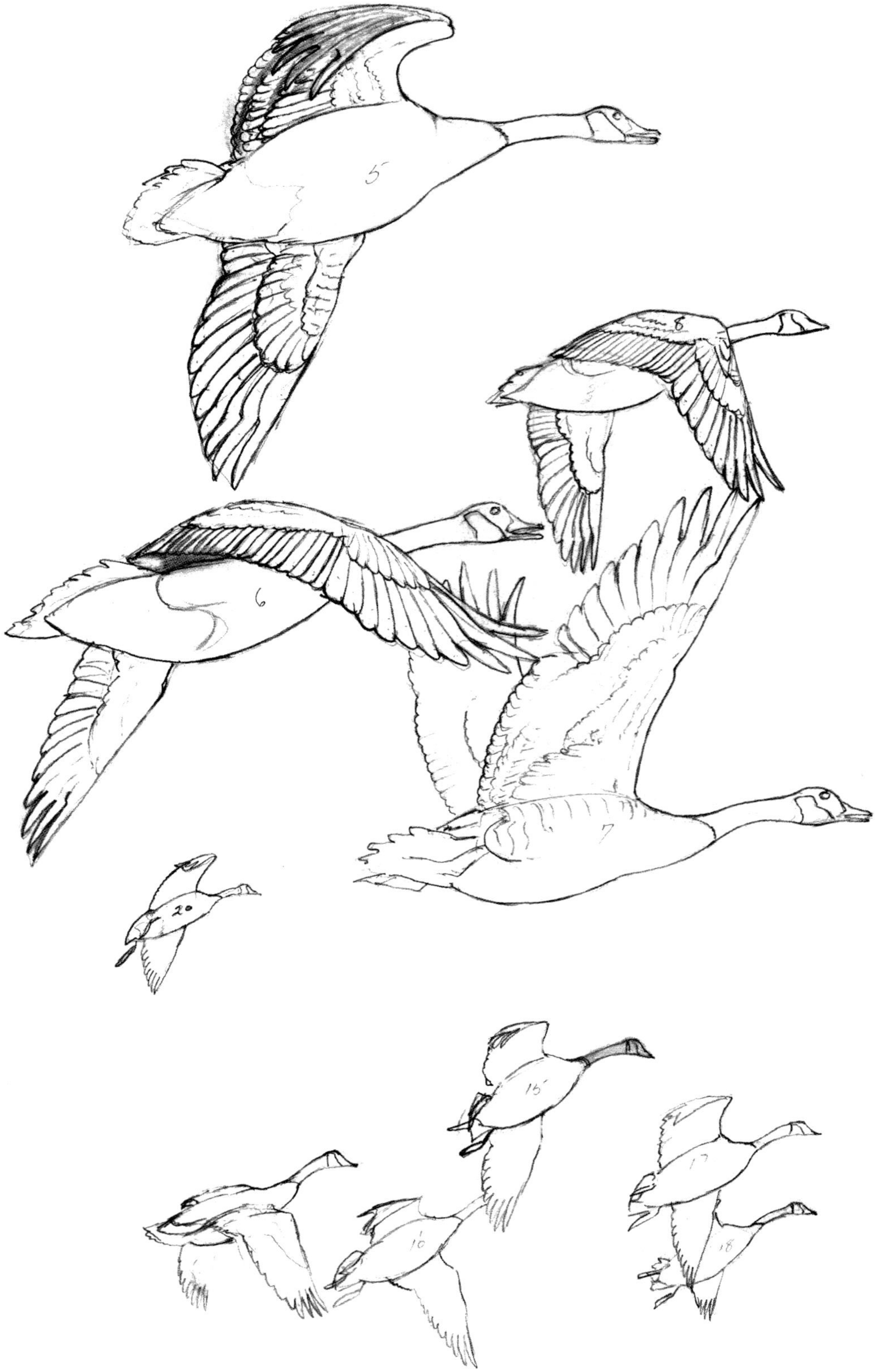

Requiem — Horicon Marsh

Requiem — Horicon Marsh is the only propaganda painting I have ever done. I wanted to make a forceful statement against the re-draining of Horicon Marsh in 1976 and the attempt to drive the geese south to new wintering grounds. Most of Horicon's geese spend the winter around Horseshoe Lake in southern Illinois, but efforts were being made to relocate them along the Gulf coast, where only remnants of the native flock remained.

I painted this picture as a fund raising project for the Citizen's Natural Resources Association (CNRA), an organization established by concerned citizens to act as a watchdog over federal and state agencies and their management policies.

I depicted 13 tired, hungry geese in the painting as they flew in from the north, expecting to find a huge marsh full of shimmering, clean water. Instead, the geese are confronted with a pest hole — a drained, disease-ridden, muck hole created for them by the government in an effort to drive them out to other areas.

The sales from prints of this painting raised enough money to pay lawyers to fight this misguided policy, but we eventually lost in the courts and Horicon Marsh was drained. However, it has been allowed to come back, perhaps as the result of our activity or the activities of others, I am not sure.

Today, we still sell prints of *Requiem* and maintain a treasury for the CNRA that provides funds to continue the fight against similarly destructive bureaucratic policies.

1976, oil, 36" x 24"

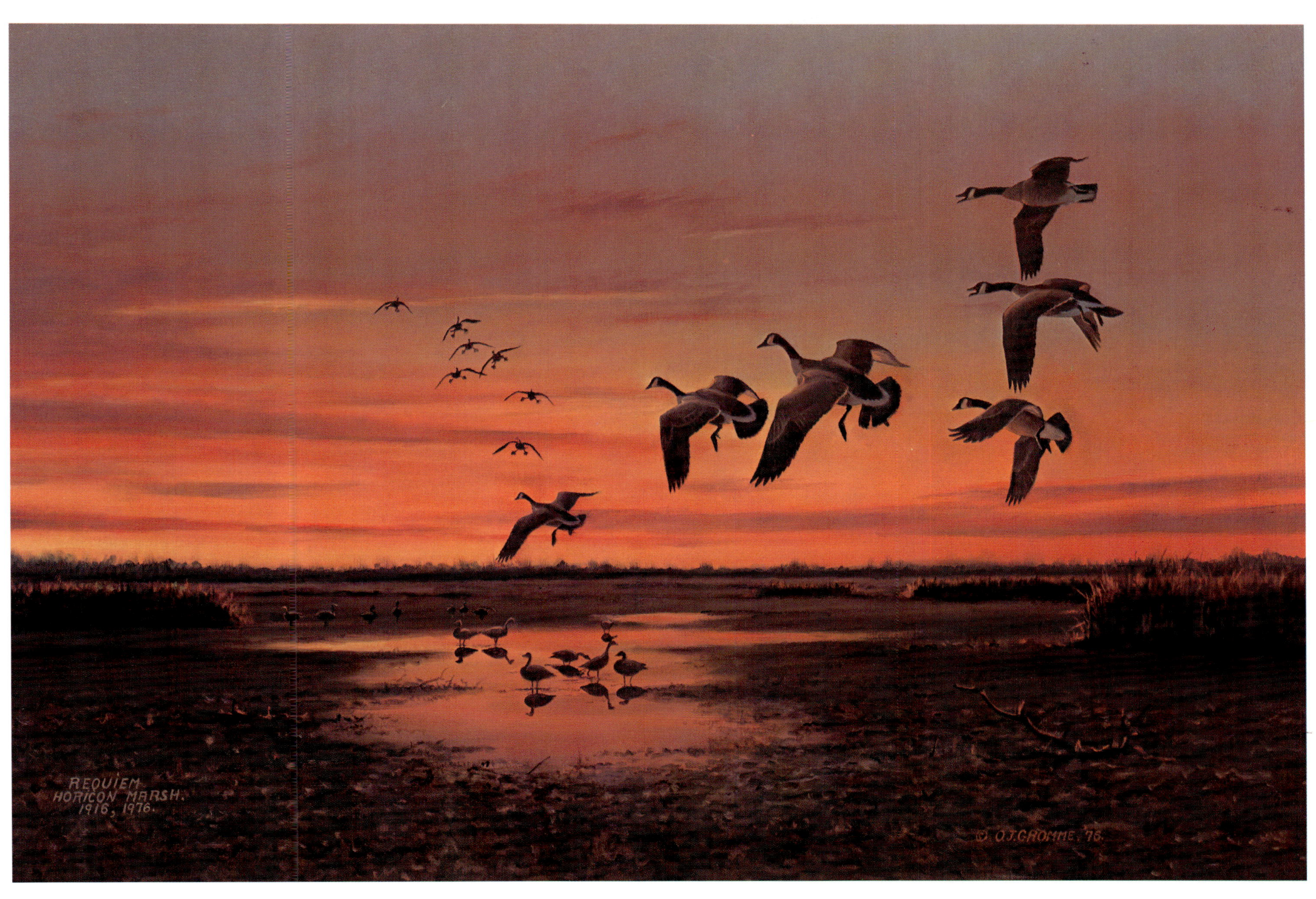
REQUIEM
HORICON MARSH.
1916, 1976.
© O.J.GROMME.'76.

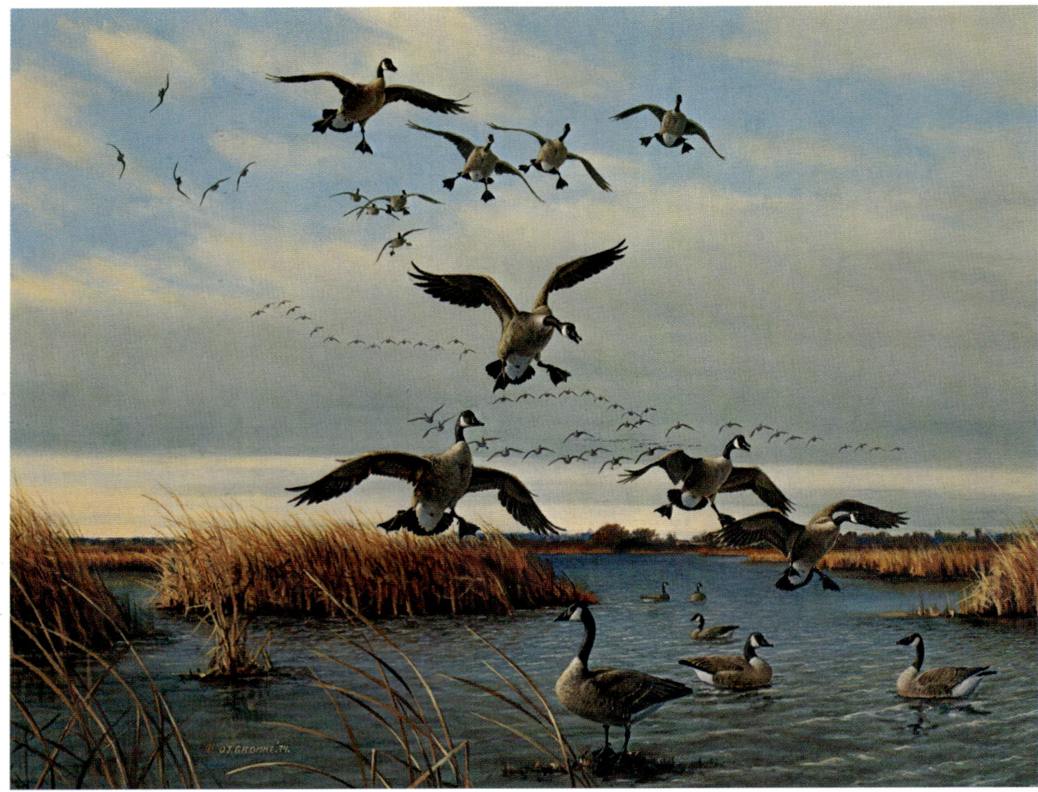

Conner's Ditch — Horicon Marsh

This is a familiar sight to anyone who has ever crossed Horicon Marsh on old Highway 49 in the autumn or spring. Conner's Ditch is a drainage ditch dredged from north to south in Horicon Marsh as a means of draining the marsh. Now it is a well-known landmark. People regularly stop along the highway to look up and down the ditch for geese, ducks or shore birds stopping over at Horicon during their migration.

I was active in establishing the wildlife refuge at Horicon Marsh and in keeping it open when plans to drain it threatened to destroy all that we had worked for. And while Canada geese have certainly made the marsh famous, we did not bring the marsh back for the sole purpose of making a refuge for Canada geese. But it is easy to understand why these strong, intelligent birds are so highly regarded. I guess I am not alone in my intense admiration for them.

1978, oil, 36″ x 26″

A Pair of Canadas

One October day as I was hunting ducks on the Horicon Marsh, this pair of geese landed directly in front of me. There were some storm clouds in the background, but the geese were in the sun, and the light on them was so striking that I decided, years later, to recreate this on canvas.

Intelligent birds, geese mate for life and are living examples of fidelity. If one loses a mate, it will usually go and find another, but as long as the original mate is able to breathe and get around, the goose will stay with it.

Although they are free-spirited, geese adapt surprisingly well to captivity and can become quite tame. I knew of a wounded goose which was taken in by a Wisconsin family and eventually became their pet. It lived in their house, ate with them and literally became one of the family! It was already an adult goose when they got it, and it lived with that family for 40 years! It makes one wonder how old geese can actually live to be.

1949, oil, 20″ x 16″

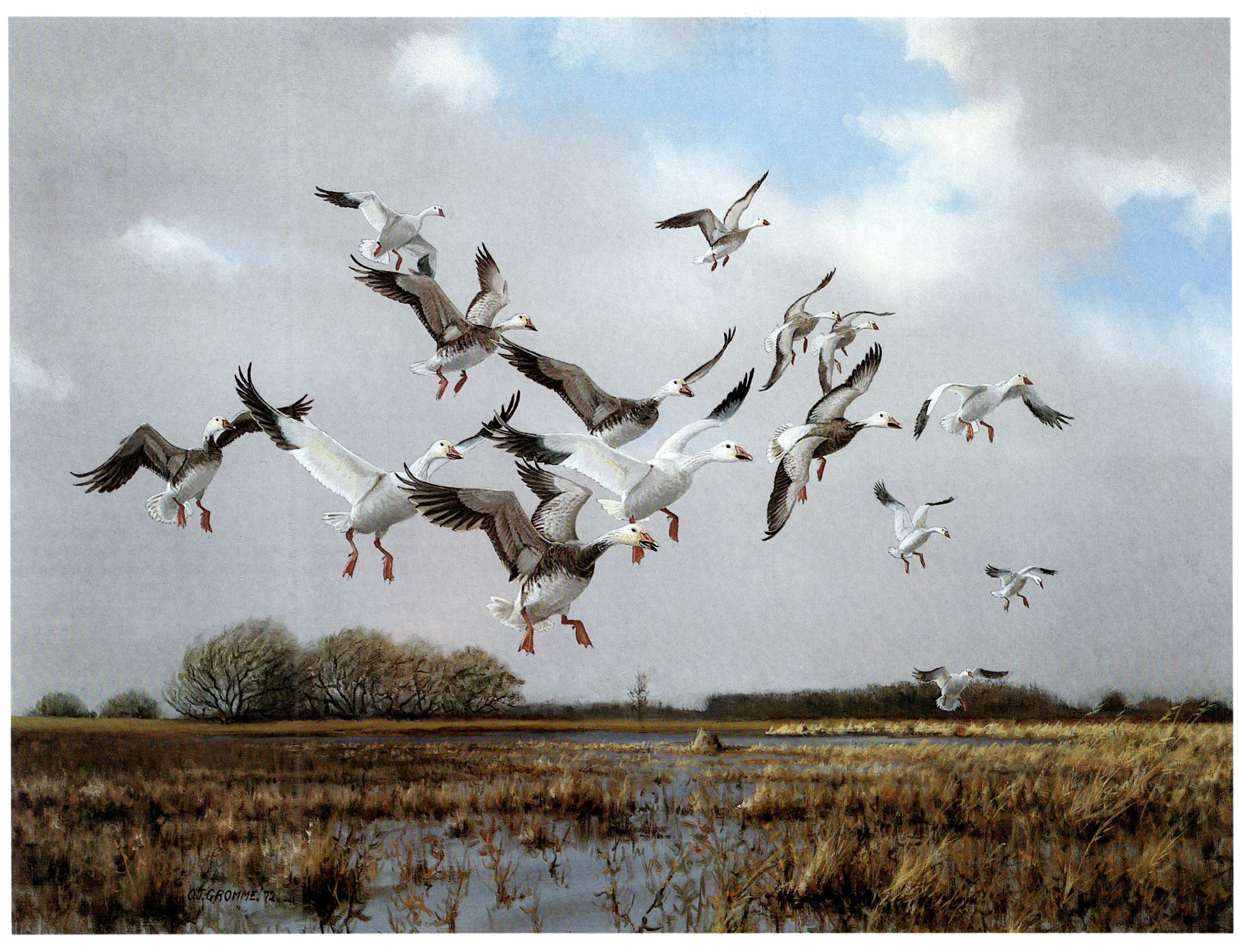
O.J. GROMME. '72.

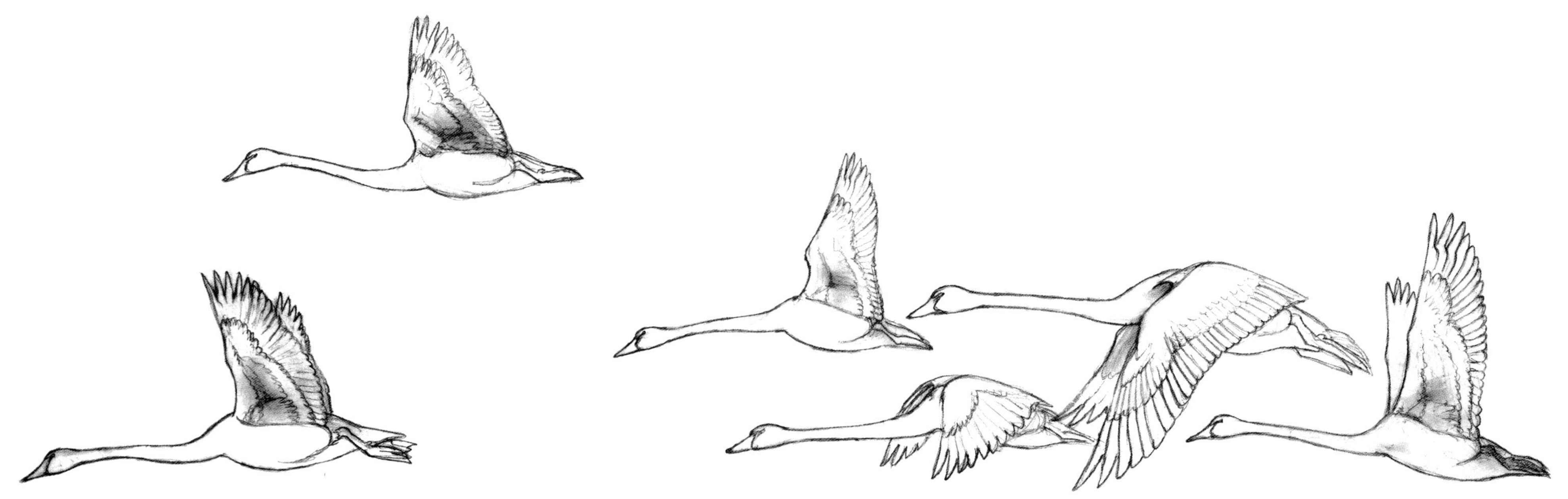

Departure From Lake Katherine

The original of this painting is owned by the Leigh Yawkey Woodson Art Museum of Wausau, Wisconsin, where the Leigh Yawkey Woodson Bird Art Exhibit is held each year during September and October. This is a juried show of the original work of the finest bird artists in the United States — and around the world for that matter!

The painting shows a group of seven tundra swans taking off from Lake Katherine, near Hazelhurst, Wisconsin. Mrs. John Forrester, daughter of Leigh Yawkey Woodson, and her husband own a home on Lake Katherine, and just such a sight could be seen from their window in the spring or fall as the swans pass through on their migratory flight.

Wild Wings, Inc. and I gave the museum a large number of prints from this painting which they in turn sold as a fund raising project. Anyone who purchased one of the prints automatically attained membership in the Friends of the Leigh Yawkey Woodson Art Museum.

Of all the museum shows in the country, the Leigh Yawkey Woodson Bird Art Exhibit has done more than any other to promote critical acceptance of bird art.

1977, oil, 44″ x 32″

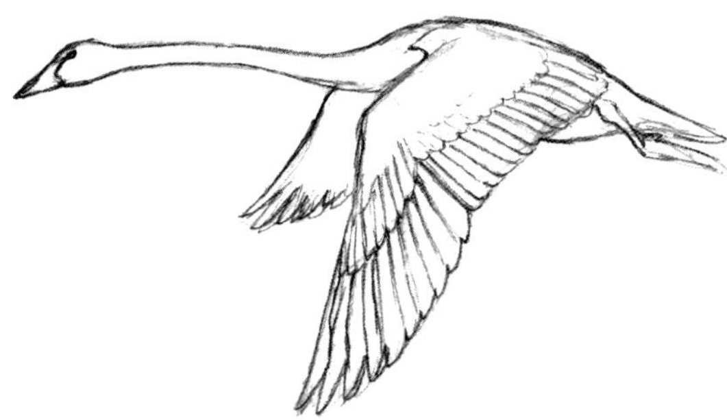

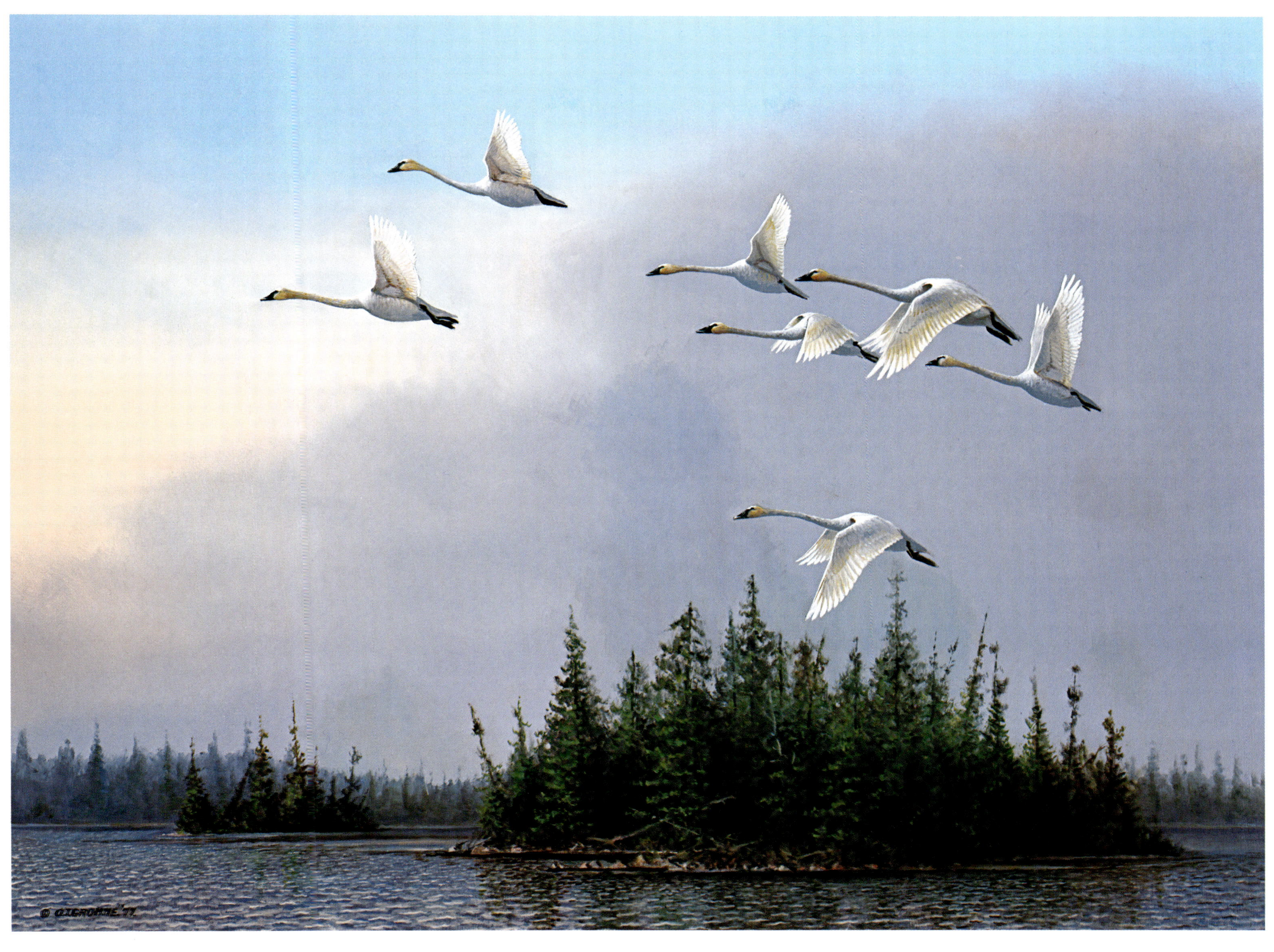

Egrets Below the Bridge

In the southern swamps, hunters used to kill egrets by the thousands for those beautiful, misty plumes that grow on their backs during the nesting season. The plumes are shed soon after nesting, but the plume hunters nearly wiped out the egret because of the lucrative market created by the fashion world (plumes were often worn on women's hats). Then the Audubon Society championed the egrets' cause and insisted that laws be passed to protect them.

The egret has made a marvelous comeback, to the point where many now migrate north to breeding grounds long ago abandoned. One Wisconsin colony that I know of is located on Four Mile Island in the Horicon Marsh. A number of great egrets now nest there every spring.

Egrets commonly make what is called a post-nuptial migration, leaving their nesting grounds and dispersing over a wide area for the remainder of the warm weather. Two years ago about 50 of them spent the summer here along the banks of the Briggsville creek, just below the highway bridge. The great egrets stayed, fishing in the shallow water below the dam for several weeks.

The birds were quite an attraction for the local people because they were visible from cars crossing the bridge. However, the next year the highway department replaced the old bridge, and the birds never did return.

I painted this scene to commemorate that great egret summer, and it has been very popular with the local people because so many of them recall seeing the birds themselves.

1981, oil, 32" x 24"

Color Notes

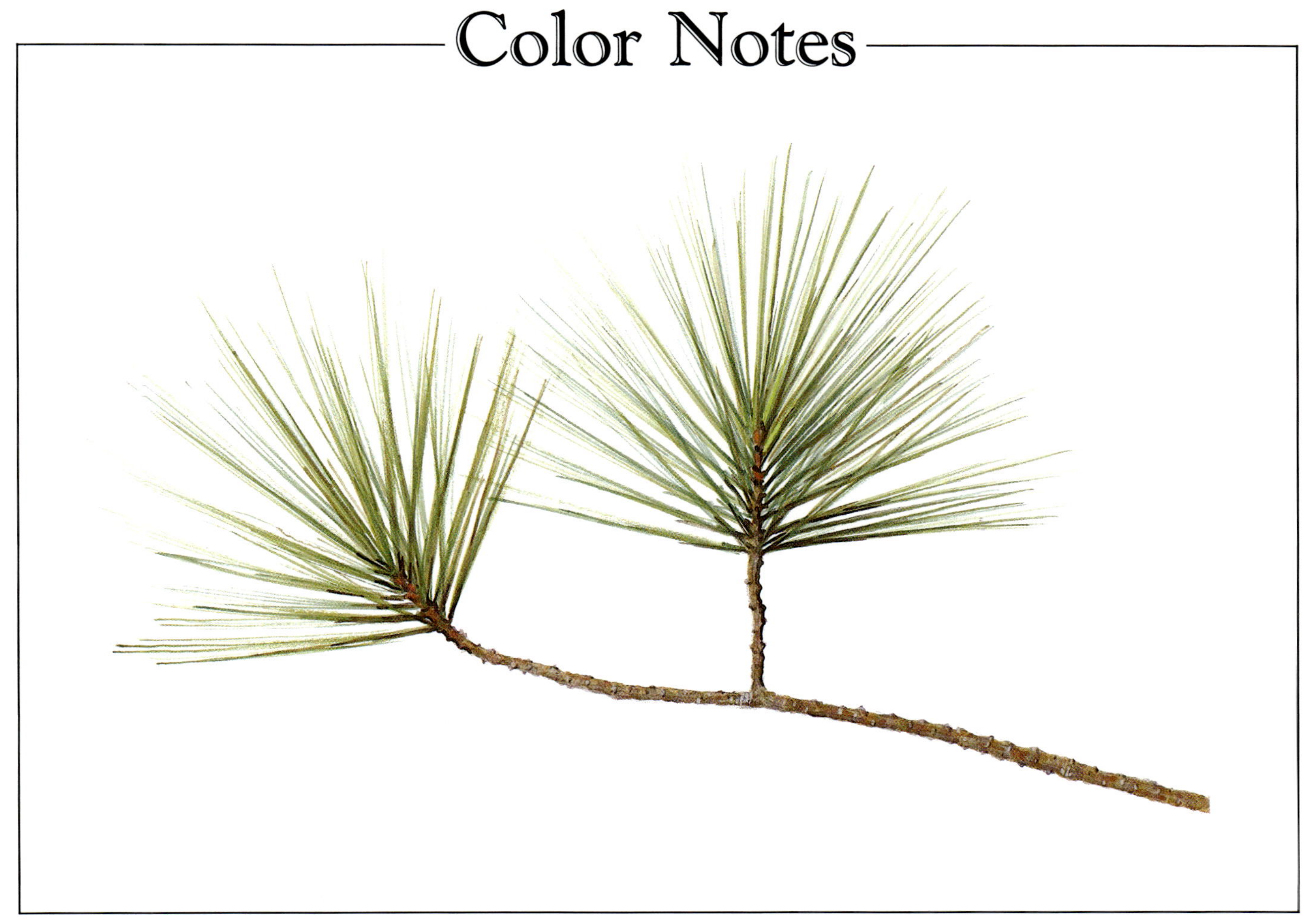

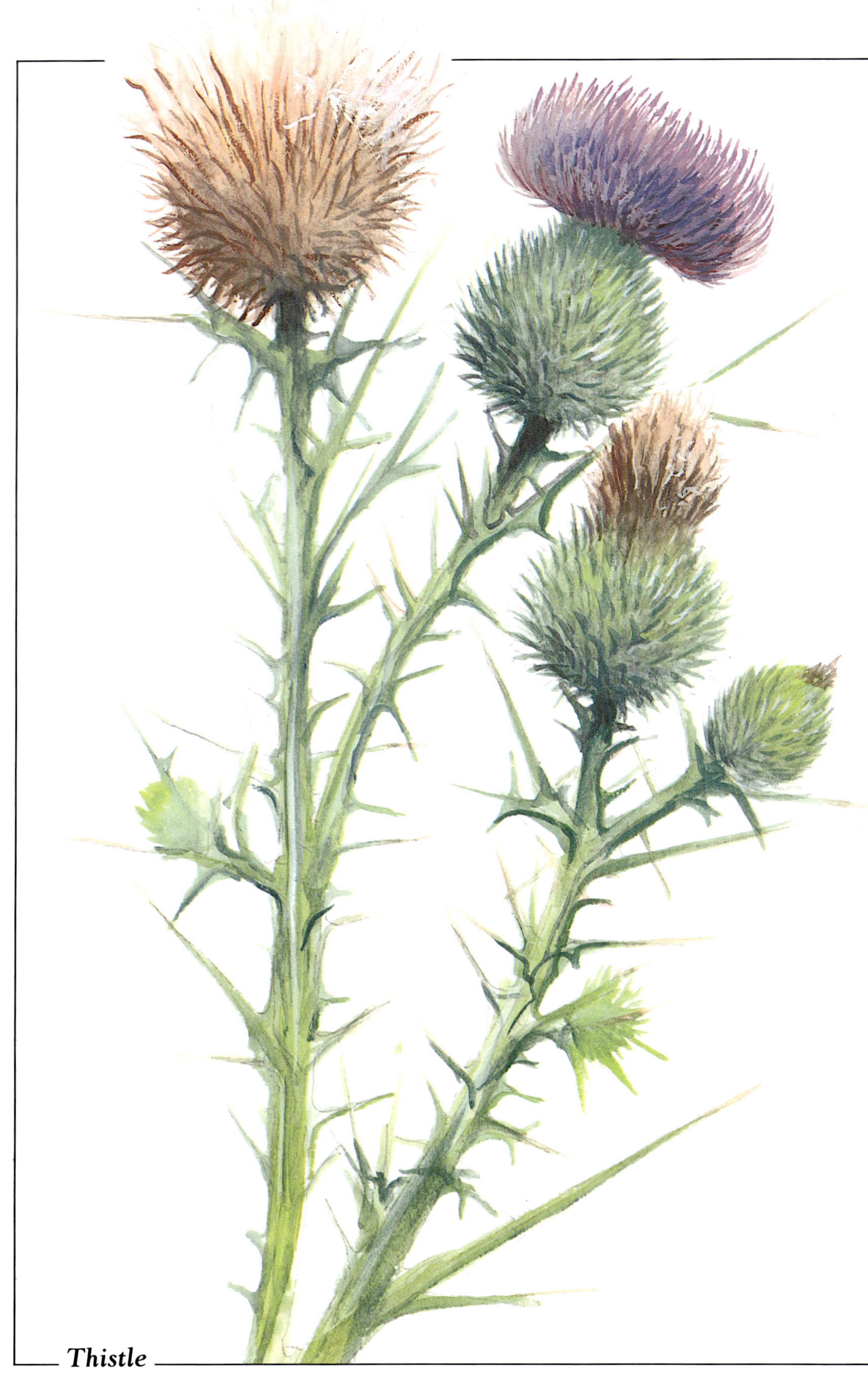

Thistle

One of the first requirements for any museum preparator or scientific field collector is the ability to describe or reproduce their acquisitions in accurate color. Otherwise, the specimen's color will fade with age and the artistic (and scientific) accuracy will be lost forever.

I have applied this construct during my many years of museum work and wildlife painting. In the 1930s and 1940s, when I executed the majority of these color notes, I applied this theory to birds, mammals, and in these particular examples, to flowers since their vivid colors fade so quickly after drying.

Color accuracy can be attained through any of the color mediums — I happened to use watercolor here mainly for covenience — or by written comparison to one of the standard color keys. This "color note" technique is used as a back-up to color photographs that are known to fade after a few years to a point of uselessness. In other words, color notes and color photographs supplement each other. Once a museum preparator or artist has painted a scene for reference, it then becomes much less difficult to reproduce on canvas or on a museum background. As a result, one's powers of recall are enhanced considerably.

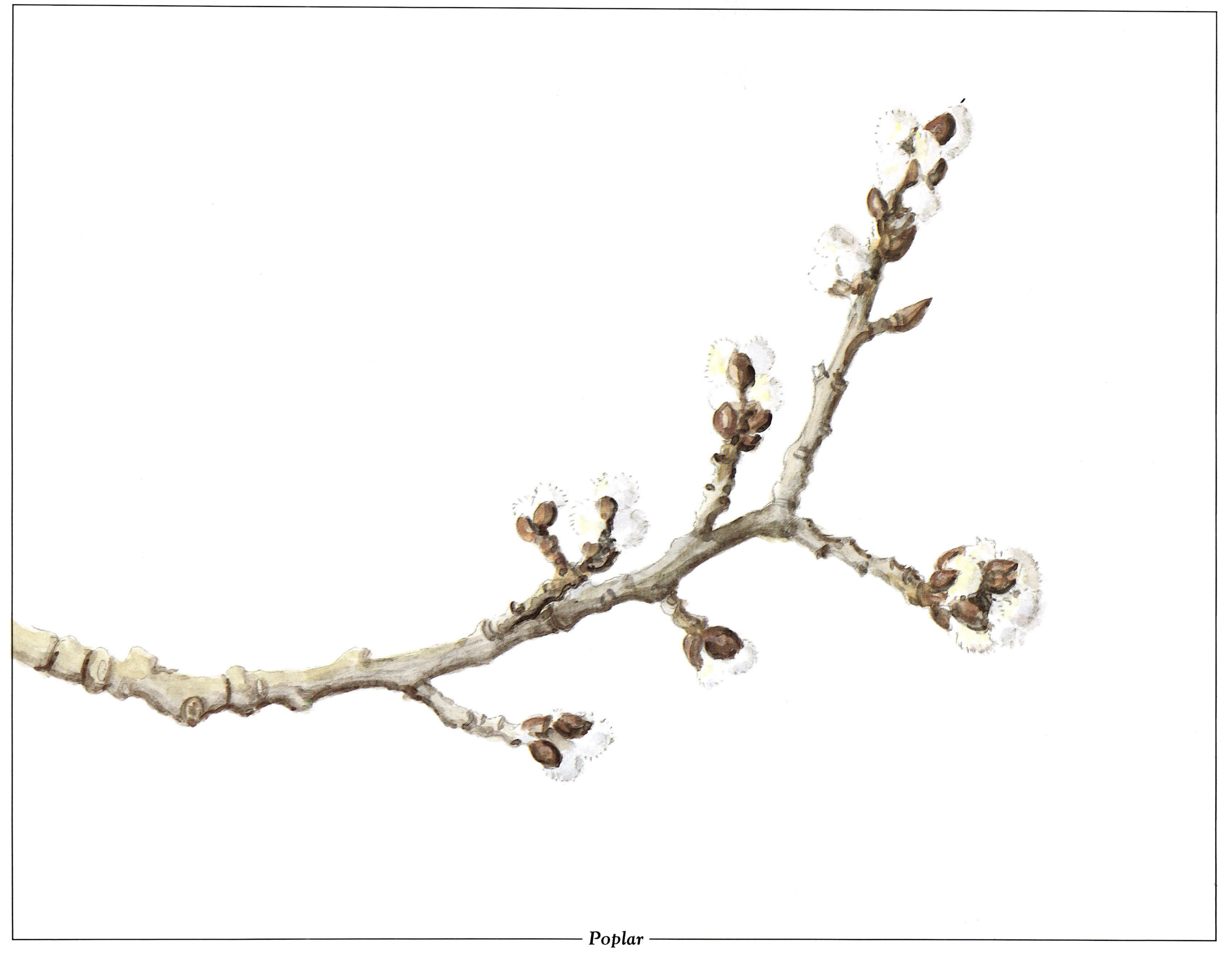

Poplar

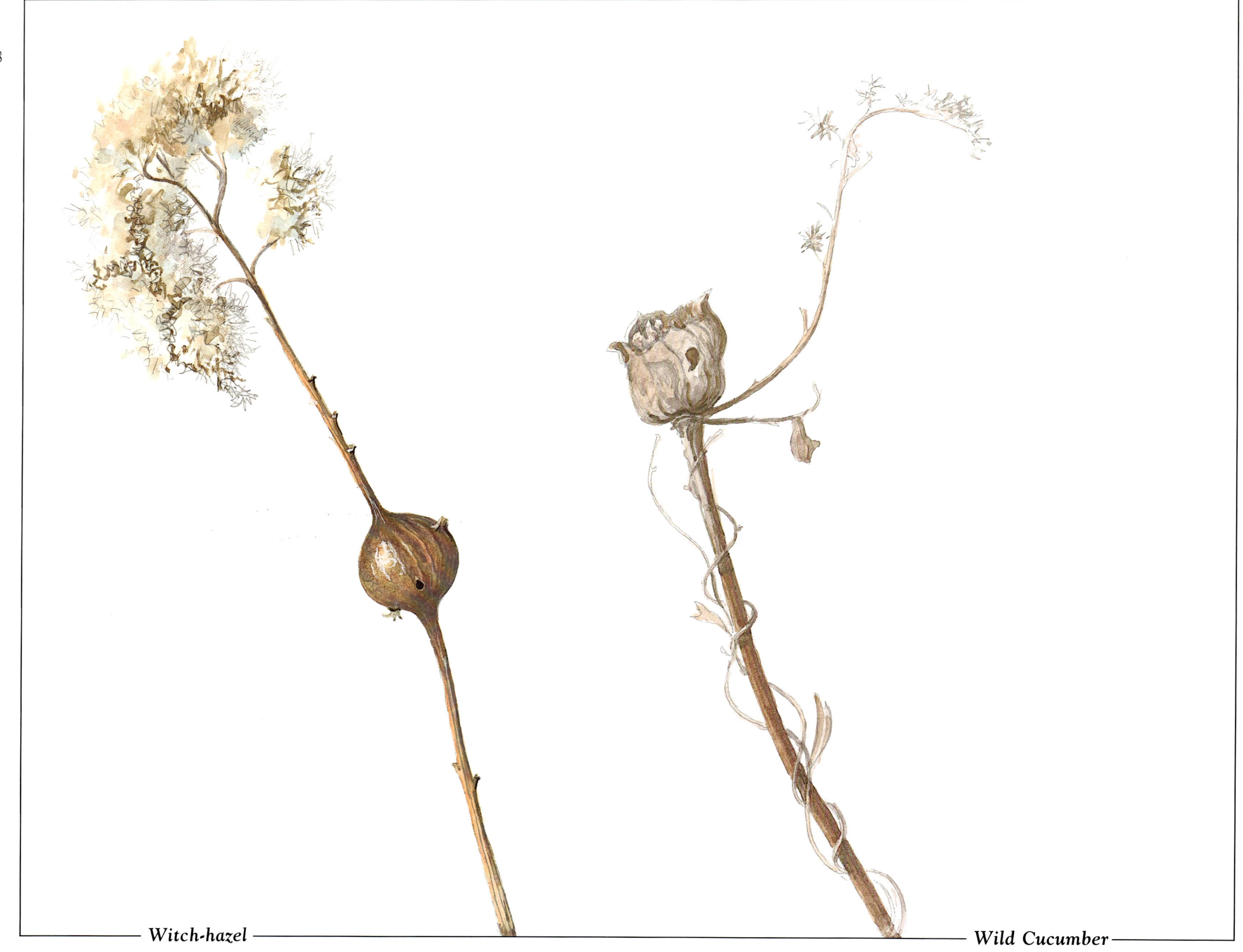

Witch-hazel

Wild Cucumber

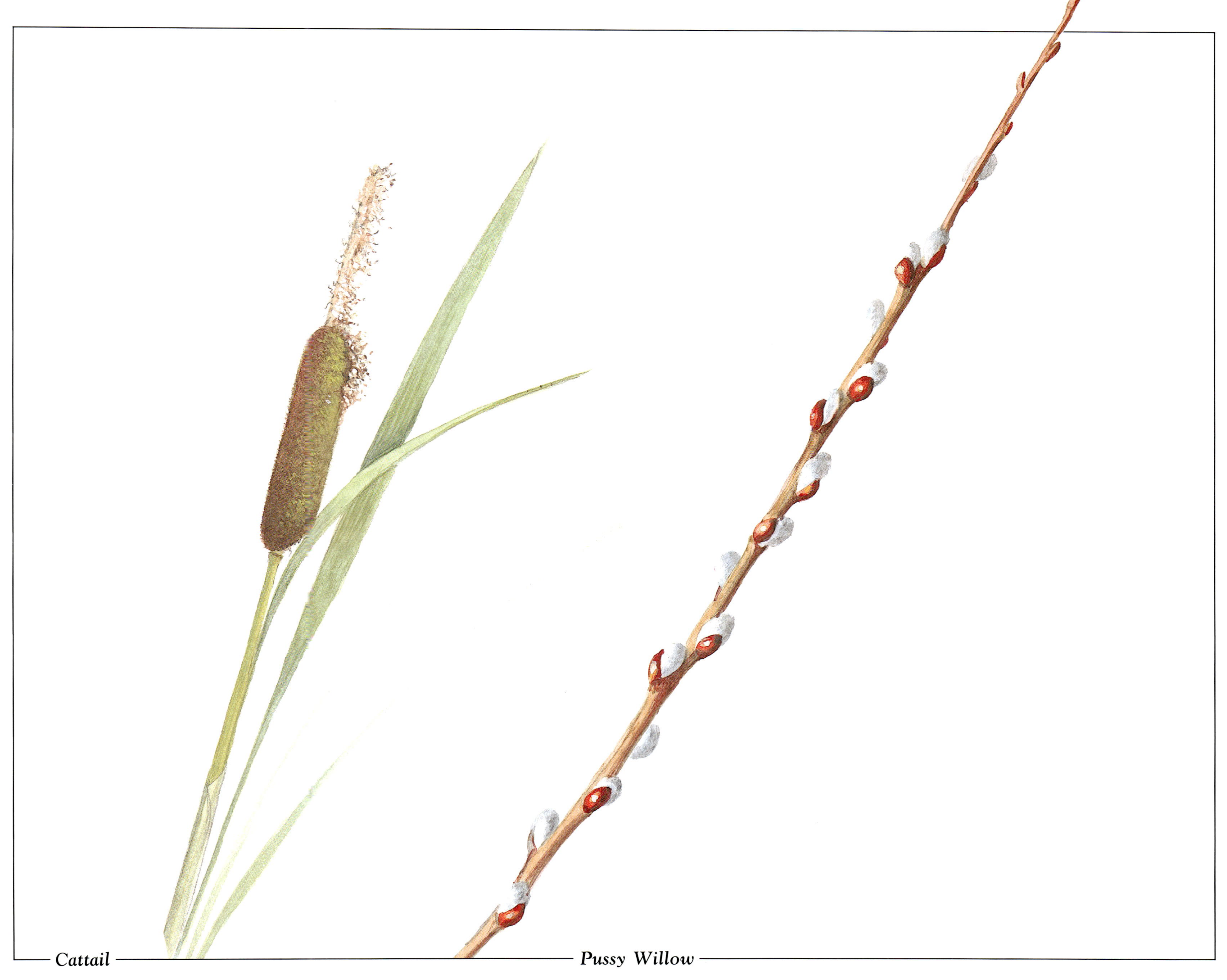

Cattail

Pussy Willow

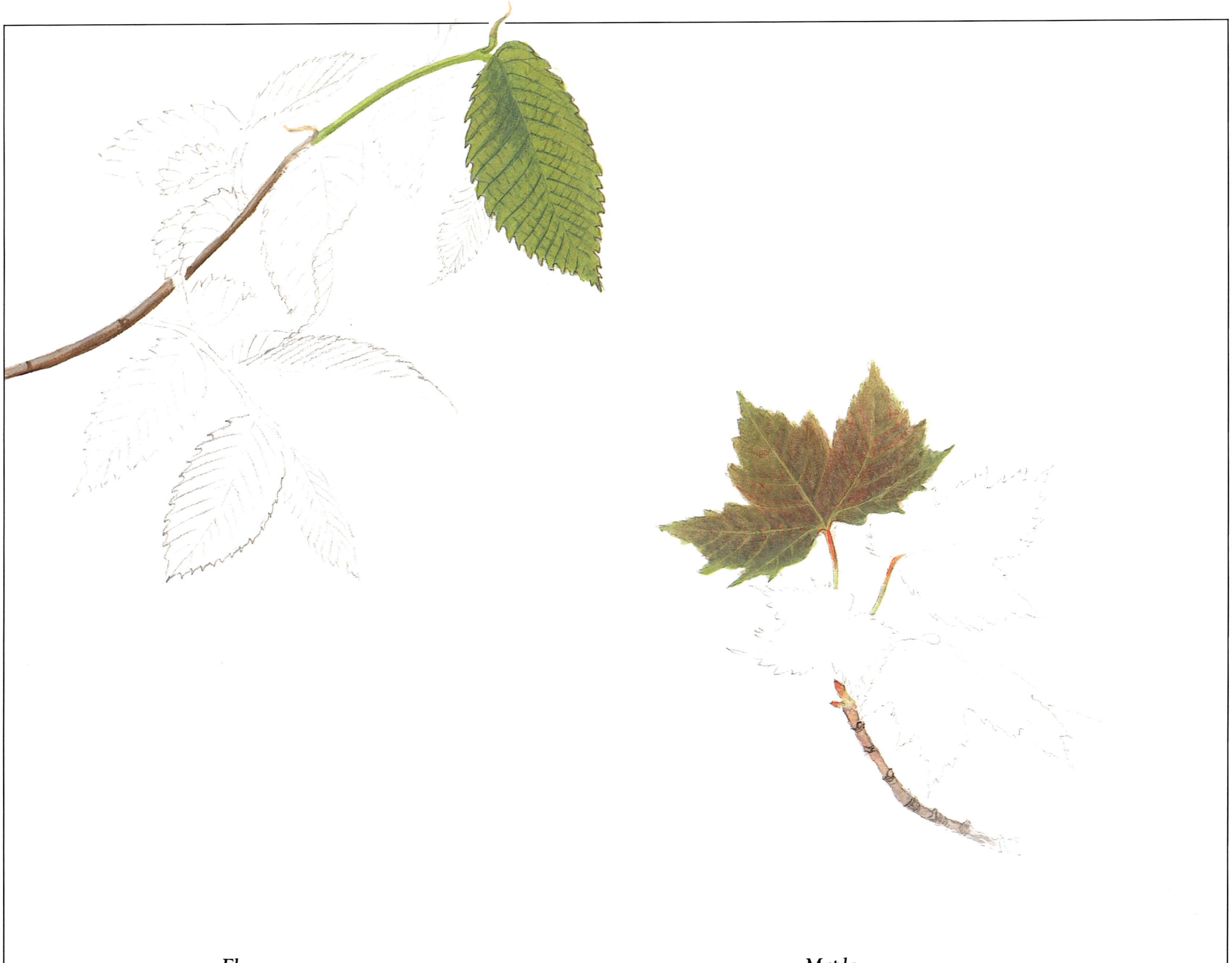

Elm ***Maple***

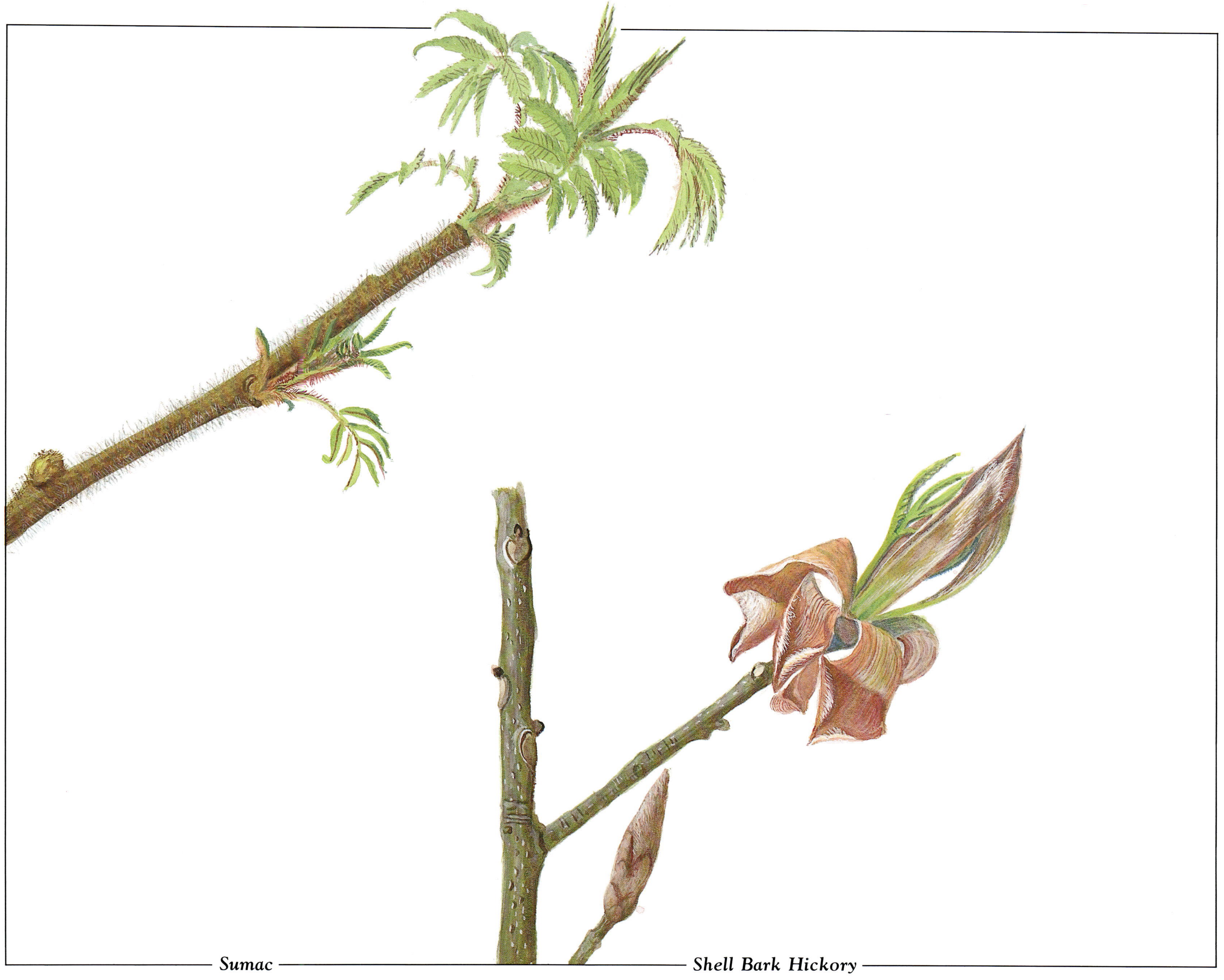

Sumac *Shell Bark Hickory*

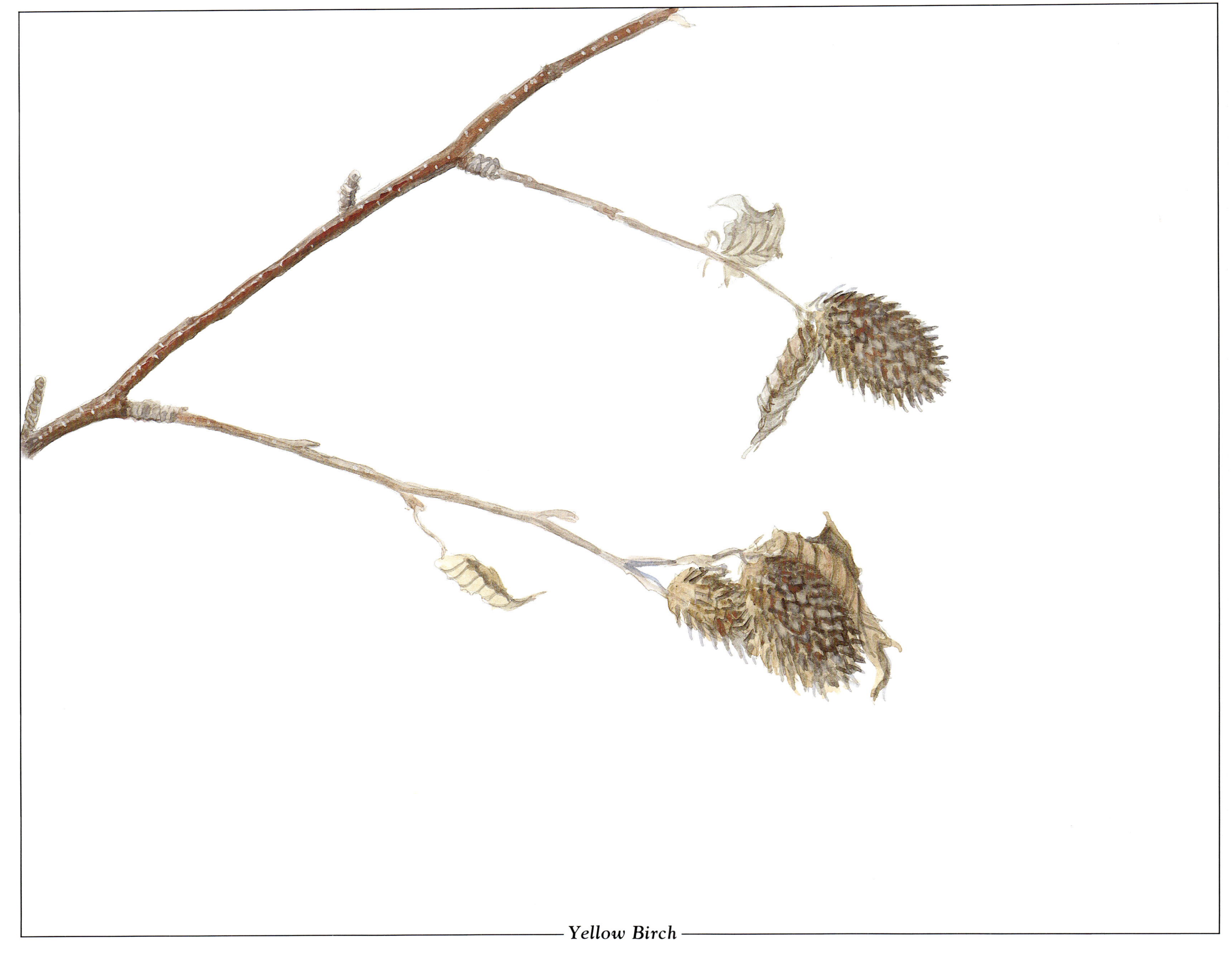

Yellow Birch

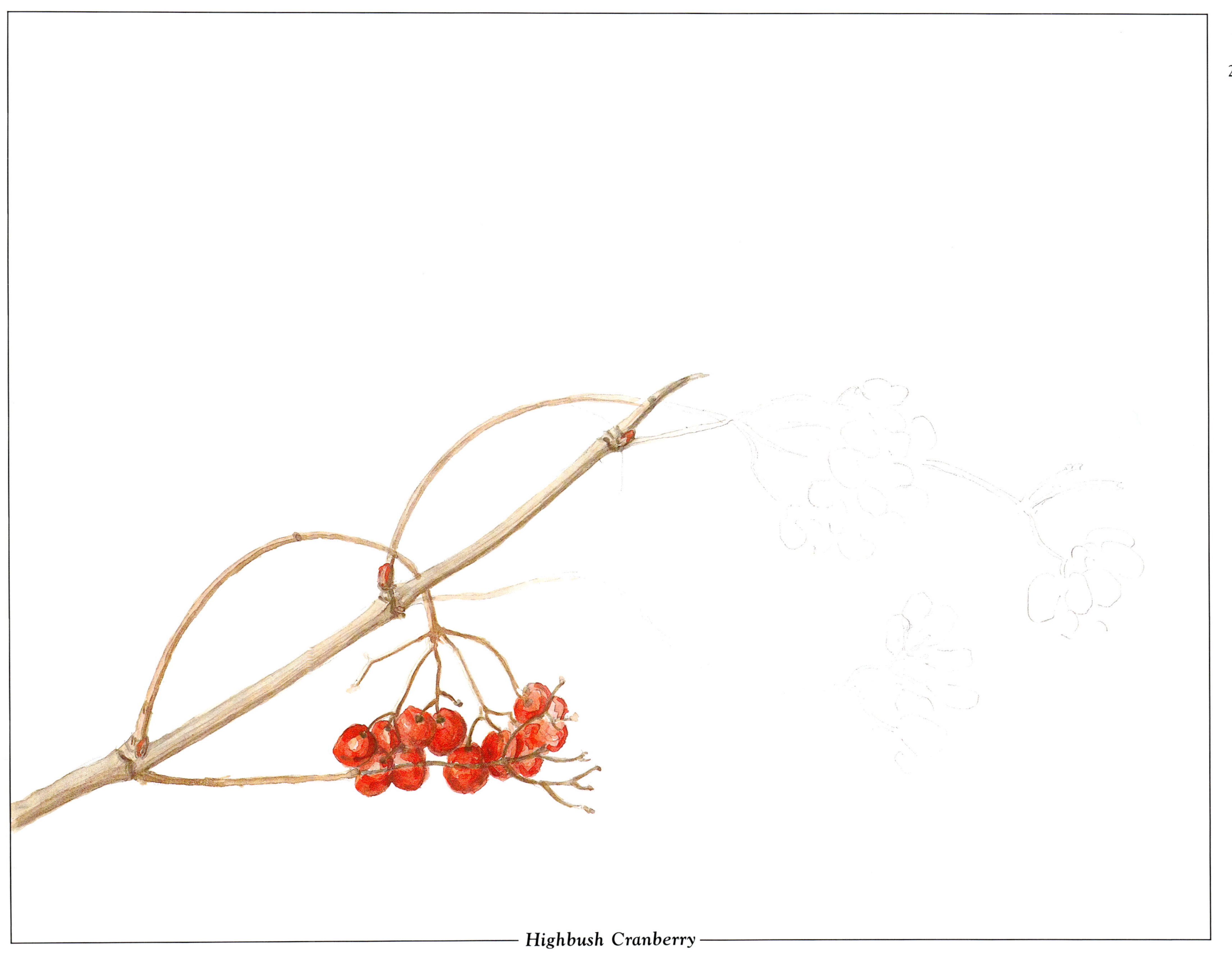

Highbush Cranberry

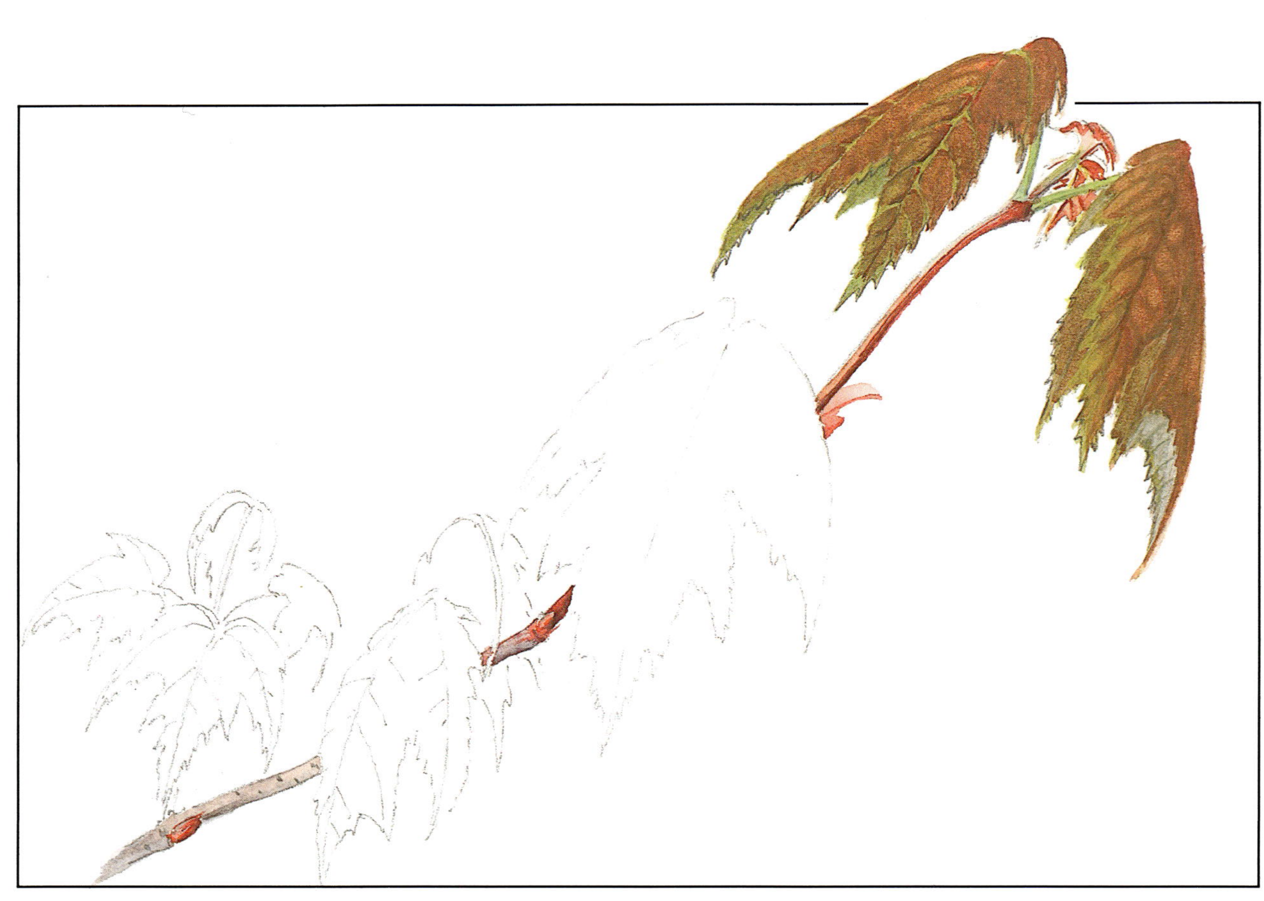

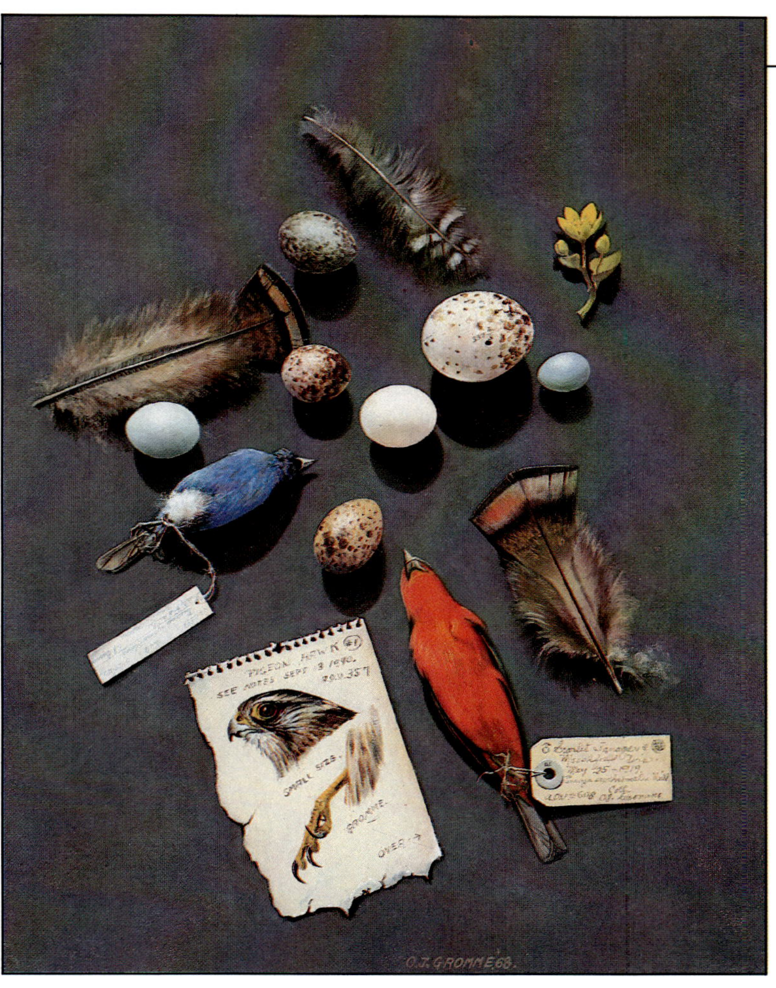

Artist's Studies, 1968, oil, 16" x 20"

Index to the Paintings

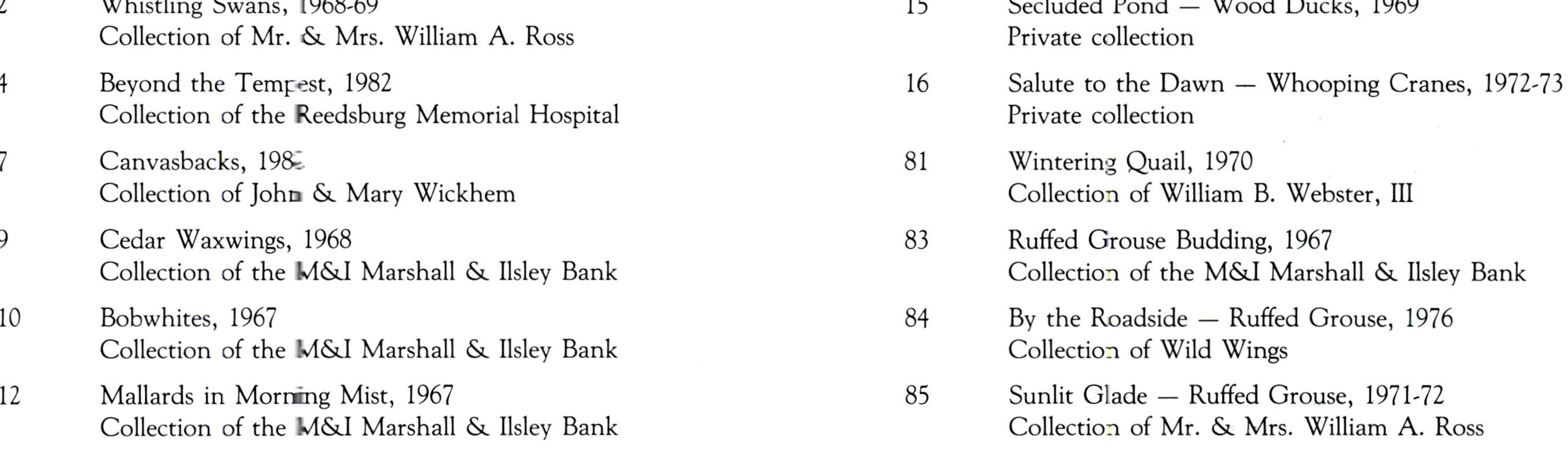

87 Ruffed Grouse, 1963
Private collection

89 Pheasants Alighting, 1966
Collection of John & Mary Wickhem

91 Winter Afternoon — Pheasants, 1962-63
Collection of Wild Wings

92 Hungarian (Gray) Partridge, 1943
Private collection

93 Among the Shocks — Prairie Chicken, 1975
Private collection

95 Prairie Chickens, 1967
Collection of the M&I Marshall & Ilsley Bank

96 Sharp-tailed Grouse, 1975
Collection of Mr. & Mrs. William A. Ross

97 Sharp-tails, Prairie Chickens — Dancing, 1967
Collection of the M&I Marshall & Ilsley Bank

99 Midday Retreat — Bobwhite, 1975
Collection of David A. Maass

101 Bobwhite — Winter Day, 1970
Collection of Lawrence E. Demmer

103 Trio of Bobwhites, 1980
Private collection

105 Dropping In — Mourning Doves, 1974
Private collection

107 Wilson's Snipe, 1967
Collection of the M&I Marshall & Ilsley Bank

109 Southern Pines — Wild Turkeys, 1966
Collection of C. M. Huttig, Jr.

111 Evening Stillness — Barred Owl, 1975
Private collection

112 Snowy Owl, 1980
Private collection

113 Snowy Owl, Bufflehead, Crow — Lake Shore, 1967
Collection of the M&I Marshall & Ilsley Bank

115 Barn Owl, 1971
Collection of Mr. & Mrs. Norman Sauey

117 Early Nester — Great Horned Owl, 1968
Collection of the M&I Marshall & Ilsley Bank

119 Goshawk & Young, 1936
Collection of Mr. & Mrs. William A. Ross

121 Eagles at the Dells, 1979
Collection of the Bank of Wisconsin Dells

123 Marsh Hawks in Spring — Food Transfer, 1968
Collection of the M&I Marshall & Ilsley Bank

125 Goshawk Attacking Mink, 1969
Collection of the M&I Marshall & Ilsley Bank

126 Expectation — Red Fox, 1973
Private collection

127 Reflections — Red Fox, 1981
Collection of the Bank of Wisconsin Dells

129 Red Fox — Pheasant Tracks, 1967
Collection of the M&I Marshall & Ilsley Bank

131 Wolf and Swan, 1967
Collection of the M&I Marshall & Ilsley Bank

133 Polar Bear — Hudson's Bay, 1954
Collection of Mr. & Mrs. William A. Ross

135 Lions in Ambush, 1977
Private collection

137 Elephants at Lake Manyara, 1979
Collection of Gordon Hunter

139 Stormy Day — Serengeti Buffalo, 1977
Collection of Mr. & Mrs. John H. Pfaff

141 Charging Rhino — Serengeti, 1977
Private collection

142 Virginia Deer with Fawns, 1968
Collection of the M&I Marshall & Ilsley Bank

143 High Country — Mule Deer, 1978
Collection of Bud & Joyce Gussel

145 Early Snowfall — White-tailed Deer, 1975
Private collection

147 Startled Trio — White-tailed Deer, 1978
Private collection

148 Edge of the Field — Pointer, 1974
Private collection

149 Brittany on Point — Woodcock, 1970
Collection of William B. Webster, III

151 English Setter, 1973
Collection of Mr. & Mrs. William A. Ross

153 Blue Jay, 1973
Collection of George B. Sletteland

155 Late Summer — Meadowlark, 1981
Collection of Mrs. H I. Radtke

157 Yellow-headed Blackbird, 1979
Collection of Mr. & Mrs. Harold A. Quinton

159 Red-winged Blackbird, 1966
Collection of the M&I Marshall & Ilsley Bank

161 Bobolink, 1966
Collection of the M&I Marshall & Ilsley Bank

163 Goldfinch, 1965
Collection of Mr. & Mrs. William A. Ross

163 Hummingbird, 1978
Private collection

165 Purple Martins, 1980
Collection of the Tommy Bartlett Foundation

165 Kingfisher, 1980
Collection of Mr. & Mrs. Dion Henderson

167 Red-headed Woodpeckers, 1980
Private collection

167 Pileated Woodpeckers, 1967
Collection of the M&I Marshall & Ilsley Bank

169 Cedar Waxwings in Summer, 1963
Private collection

171 Evening Grosbeaks, 1968
Collection of the M&I Marshall & Ilsley Bank

173 Cardinals in the Snow, 1972
Private collection

175 Spring's Early Arrivals, 1982
Private collection

177 Hen Mallard and Brood, 1979
Collection of C. P. Fox

177 Killdeer, 1976
Collection of Robert & Frances Tracy

179 Changing of the Guard — Common Loon, 1981
Collection of the American Museum of Wildlife Art

181 Common Loon with Young, 1967
Collection of the M&I Marshall & Ilsley Bank

183 Common Gallinule, 1967
Collection of the M&I Marshall & Ilsley Bank

185 Lake Michigan: Goldeneye, Oldsquaws, Buffleheads, 1968
Collection of the M&I Marshall & Ilsley Bank

186 Grandpa's Pond — Mallards and Black Ducks, 1969
Private collection

187 Cedar Creek — Mallards, 1955
Private collection

188 Blue-winged Teal, 1962
Collection of Marian Mueller Dolan

189 Early Blue Wings, 1973-74
Private collection

191 Scurrying Greenwings, 1964
Collection of Wild Wings

192 Morning Haze — Wood Ducks, 1979
Collection of John & Mary Wickhem

193 Wood Ducks — Gall's Pond, 1966
Collection of the M&I Marshall & Ilsley Bank

195 1978 Wisconsin State Duck Stamp, 1978
Collection of Mr. & Mrs. William A. Ross

197 Fall Kaleidoscope, 1978
Private collection

199 Icy Weather — Canvasbacks, 1971
Collection of William Schuett

201 Bucking the Storm — Canvasbacks, 1980
Private collection

203 Requiem — Horicon Marsh, 1976
Private collection

204 Conner's Ditch — Horicon Marsh, 1978
Private collection

205 A Pair of Canadas, 1949
Private collection

206 Easing In — Canada Geese, 1976
Collection of Wild Wings

207 Snows and Blues, 1972
Private collection

209 Departure from Lake Katherine, 1977
Collection of the Leigh Yawkey Woodson Art Museum

211 Egrets Below the Bridge, 1981
Private collection

213 Great Blue Herons, 1935
Collection of John & Mary Wickhem

215 Sandhill Cranes with Young, 1968
Collection of the M&I Marshall & Ilsley Bank

217 Marshland Elegy — Aldo Leopold, 1978
Collection of the Madison Kipp Corporation

219 Tancho, 1981
Collection of Mr. & Mrs. Samuel C. Johnson

221 Sacred Cranes Over Hokkaido, 1973
Collection of the Tommy Bartlett Foundation

223 The Last Toki, 1983
Collection of the World Working Group

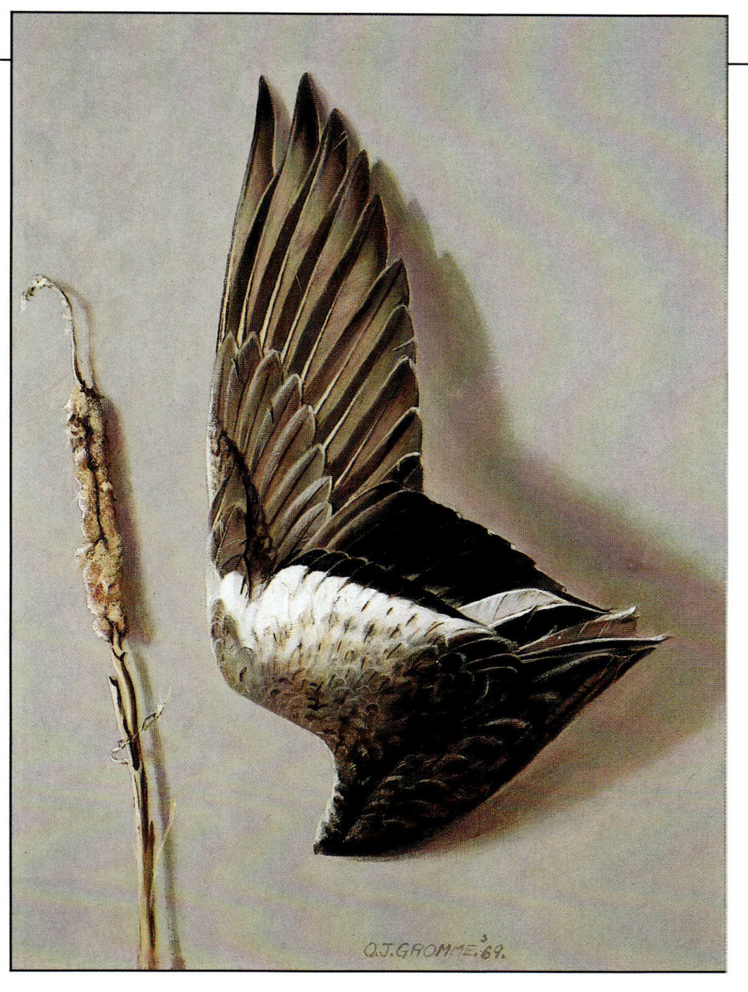

American Widgeon Wing and Cattail, 1969, oil, 12" x 16"

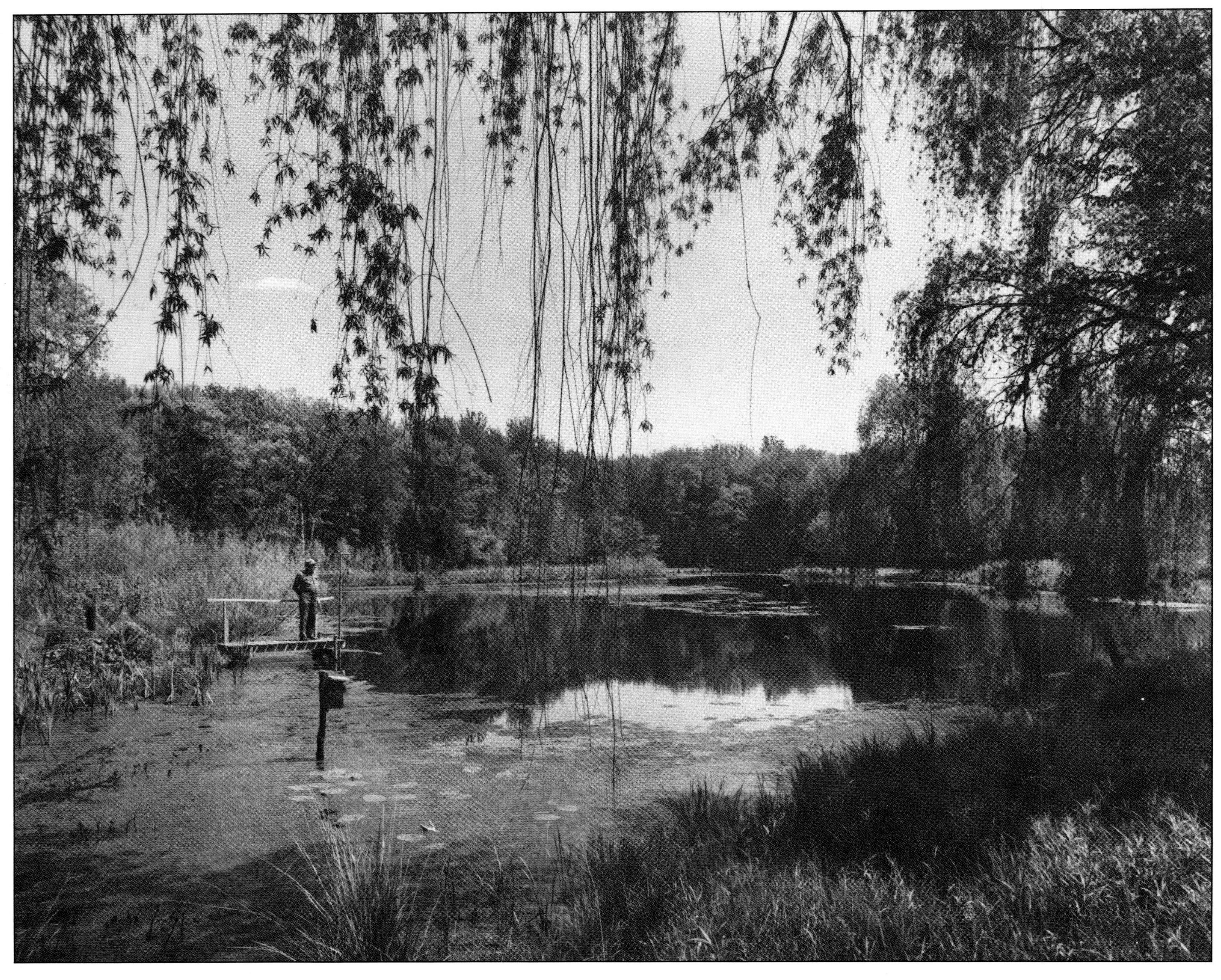